RE-IMAGINING CURRICULUM
spaces for disruption

EDITOR
LYNN QUINN

Re-imagining Curriculum: Spaces for disruption

Published by AFRICAN SUN MeDIA under the SUN PReSS imprint

All rights reserved

Copyright © 2019 AFRICAN SUN MeDIA and the authors

This publication was subjected to an independent double-blind peer evaluation by the publisher.

The authors and the publisher have made every effort to obtain permission for and acknowledge the use of copyrighted material. Refer all enquiries to the publisher.

No part of this book may be reproduced or transmitted in any form or by any electronic, photographic or mechanical means, including photocopying and recording on record, tape or laser disk, on microfilm, via the Internet, by e-mail, or by any other information storage and retrieval system, without prior written permission by the publisher.

Views reflected in this publication are not necessarily those of the publisher.

First edition 2019

ISBN 978-1-928480-38-9
ISBN 978-1-928480-39-6 (e-book)
https://doi.org/10.18820/9781928480396

Set in Caecilia LT Std 9/14

Cover design, typesetting and production by AFRICAN SUN MeDIA

SUN PReSS is an imprint of AFRICAN SUN MeDIA. Scholarly, professional and reference works are published under this imprint in print and electronic formats.

This publication can be ordered from:
orders@africansunmedia.co.za
Takealot: bit.ly/2monsfl
Google Books: bit.ly/2k1Uilm
africansunmedia.store.it.si *(e-books)*
Amazon Kindle: amzn.to/2ktL.pkL

Visit africansunmedia.co.za for more information.

CONTENTS

Acknowledgements ix

Acronyms and abbreviations xi

Foreword xiii

1   Why the focus on curriculum? Why now?
    The role of academic development 1
    Lynn Quinn & Jo-Anne Vorster

2   Decolonising the curriculum: Recontextualisation, identity and
    self-critique in a post-apartheid university 23
    Kathy Luckett, Shannon Morreira & Mohini Baijnath

3   Decolonising university curricula: Reflections on an institutional
    curriculum review process 45
    Sally Matthews

4   Disrupting single stories through participatory learning
    and action 65
    Kasturi Behari-Leak

5   Re-imagining knowledge in the curriculum: Creating critical
    spaces for alternative possibilities in curriculum design 87
    Sherran Clarence

| 6 | Transforming curriculum development through co-creation with students | 107 |

Alison Cook-Sather, Kelly E Matthews & Amani Bell

| 7 | Integrating academic literacies into the curriculum in Occupational Therapy: Currents of disruption and congruence in a collaborative process | 127 |

Arona Dison & Lucia Hess-April

| 8 | Uncovering the complicit: The decoding interview as a decolonising practice | 149 |

Lee Easton, Roberta Lexier, Gabrielle Lindstrom & Michelle Yeo

| 9 | Reconfiguring academic development through feminist new materialist and posthuman philosophies | 171 |

Vivienne Bozalek

| 10 | Academic developers as disruptors: Reshaping the instructional design process | 193 |

Keisha Valdez & Dianne Thurab-Nkhosi

11 "I've got a deep complicated relationship with technology":
   Towards an understanding of the interplay of barriers and
   agency in academics' educational technology practices 217
   Nompilo Tshuma

12 Re-imagining curriculum development and the role of
   academic developers in a university of technology
   in the post-colonial setting 235
   'Mabokang Monnapula-Mapesela, Ntsoaki Malebo & Isaac Ntshoe

13 Constructing curriculum in a time of transformation:
   A department's experience in South Africa 259
   Theresa Gordon & Gilberte Lincoln

14 Defending the diploma: Academic developers as curriculum
   collaborators in technical contexts 283
   Christine Winberg

15 Disrupting academic reading: Unrolling the scroll
   for academic staff 307
   Sandra Abegglen, Tom Burns & Sandra Sinfield with Dave Middlebrook

16 Advancing democratic values in higher education through
    open curriculum co-creation: Towards an epistemology
    of uncertainty 325
        Asanda Ngoasheng, Xena Cupido, Oluwaseun Oyekola,
        Daniela Gachago, Ashton Mpofu & Yolisa Mbekela

17 "I just felt like I was trying to swim through molasses":
    Curriculum renewal at a research-intensive university 345
        Cecilia Jacobs

18 Academic development insights into decolonising
    the Engineering curriculum 363
        Karin Wolff

19 Creating spaces for the emergence of new realities in science
    curriculum thinking 387
        Ann Cameron & Kershree Padayachee

20 Cognitive justice and the higher education curriculum 403
        Brenda Leibowitz

Index 419

Notes on contributors 425

Acknowledgements

First and foremost, I would like to thank the forty-one authors who contributed to the chapters in this volume and for reviewing first drafts of one another's chapters. I feel privileged to have worked with such an interesting range of higher education practitioners. The diversity of the chapters in terms of focus, context, theoretical framing and ways of writing make for rich and interesting reading. Hopefully, the book will make a significant contribution to the theoretical underpinnings and practices of those working in the area of curriculum development and/or review.

I would also like to acknowledge the contribution of: the anonymous external reviewers for their insightful feedback and guidelines for revising the chapters; Chrissie Boughey for writing the foreword for the book; my colleagues in the Centre for Higher Education Research, Teaching and Learning at Rhodes University, particularly Jo-Anne Vorster and Sioux McKenna, for their advice and moral support every step of the way; the Rhodes University Research Office for financial support; and the staff at African Sun Media for the crucial role they played in the production of the book.

LYNN QUINN
Rhodes University
South Africa

Acronyms and abbreviations

5D-CTM	Fifth Dimension Curriculum Transformation Model
ADDIE	Analysis, Design, Development, Implementation and Evaluation design model
ADU	Academic Development Unit
AMOEBA	Adaptive, Meaningful, Environmental-based Architecture for online course design model
CCWG	Curriculum Change Working Group
CHE	Council on Higher Education
CHEC	Cape Higher Education Consortium
CHED	Centre for Higher Education Development
CPUT	Cape Peninsula University of Technology
DCS	Decolonisation Conversation Series
DHET	Department of Higher Education and Training
DIT	Durban Institute of Technology
DUT	Durban University of Technology
EiC	Engineering-in-Context project
ER	Epistemic relations
FMF	#FeesMustFall protest movement
HEQSF	Higher Education Qualifications Sub-Framework
LCT	Legitimation Code Theory
LMU	London Metropolitan University

MALTHE	Master's in Learning and Teaching in Higher Education
NATED	National Education Department
NQF	National Qualifications Framework
NRF	National Research Foundation
OBE	Outcomes-based education
PGCert	Postgraduate Certificate
PGDip	Postgraduate Diploma
RSA	Republic of South Africa
RMF	#RhodesMustFall protest movement
SACPLAN	South African Council for Planners
SaLT	Students and Learners and Teachers
SAQA	South African Qualifications Authority
SERTEC	Certification Council for Technikon Education
SGBs	Standards generating bodies
SoTL	Scholarship of Teaching and Learning
SR	Social relations
STEM	Science, Technology, Engineering and Mathematics
UCT	University of Cape Town
UWC	University of the Western Cape
Wits	University of the Witwatersrand

Foreword

Across the world, dominant higher education discourses privilege the need for what is termed "widening participation" in the United Kingdom or, more overtly, "social inclusion" in South Africa. In Australia and New Zealand, the concern is for indigenous peoples. In the United States it is for marginalised social groups such as Latinos and black people who neither participate in nor have as much success in higher education as others, typically the children of middle class, educated parents.

Much of the focus on providing more access and success to diverse groups of students has fallen on "practical" measures such as funding. However, there is a much wider consideration that needs attention - that of the curriculum.

For many, the curriculum is simply a list of topics that will be taught. However, anyone with any knowledge of educational theory would say that curriculum encompasses not only the "what" of content but also the "how" of teaching and assessing and the "who" of who teaches and who is taught. Although this is a more comprehensive understanding of something that is core to the university and the work of all academics who are responsible for it, dominant discourses continue to construct the curriculum as neutral with the result that there is an enormous reluctance to grasp the role of curriculum as a mechanism for distributing access to knowledge and knowing.

The very idea that the curriculum is political, social and cultural continues to evade institutional managers, and others responsible for curriculum change and review, in spite of the fact that the people they most want to include in "widening participation" discourses are the socially, culturally and politically marginalised. Instead, where work on the curriculum does take place it tends to be dominated by, for example, the move to use learning outcomes as an organising principle following the introduction of national qualifications frameworks towards the end of the last century. Pedagogical approaches can also inform curriculum reform, problem-based learning or inquiry-based learning being but two concepts that have been current in recent years.

Possibly because of my experience of working in a country where social inclusion continues to dominate all areas of thinking twenty-five years after an enormous political shift intended to bring about equality (South Africa), my own sense is that all this misses the mark and that it is only when and if we begin to appreciate the complexity of curriculum work and its fundamental nature as political, social and cultural that we will begin to address the biggest issue confronting higher education systems today – the need for more equality where a qualification can mean the difference between work and no work, a good job and a job paying the minimum wage.

This book draws on the work of academics located at a range of universities who share such understandings of the complexity of curriculum. The chapters they have contributed provide rich examples of how dominant ways of knowing and forms of knowledge can be questioned as well as the way prevailing approaches to solving "problems" such as the difficulties students experience with reading and writing in the university that we can provide students with what South African scholar, Wally Morrow[1] called the "epistemological access" needed for them to succeed. Morrow's central point was that we can provide "formal access" to the university by increasing funding, developing alternative admissions mechanisms and so on, but it is only providing them with access to the ways of knowing, and the values and attitudes that underpin them, that sustain the university.

More latterly, and there is evidence of this across the world, the need to trouble dominant epistemologies and forms of knowledge has come to the fore. Many of the contributors to the book show how they have engaged with this "troubling" in substantive ways.

My hope is that this book will be widely read in any country which has drawn on dominant discourses constructing higher education as a means to economic empowerment and which has developed its higher education system with this end in mind (and here I refer to the majority of countries that

---

1 Morrow, W. 2008. *Bounds of Democracy Epistemological Access in Higher Education*. Pretoria: HSRC Press. [http://repository.hsrc.ac.za/handle/20.500.11910/4739]

I have encountered in my own academic work). It needs to be widely read if we are ever to make any sort of dent in the common-sense assumptions about the curriculum as neutral and thus "fair".

The contributors have a great deal to offer us in a world where higher education promises so much but, for some, delivers so little.

CHRISSIE BOUGHEY
Rhodes University
South Africa

CHAPTER 1

Why the focus on "curriculum"? Why now?

The role of academic development

Lynn Quinn & Jo-Anne Vorster

Introduction

As a result of the changing higher education context, institution-wide curriculum renewal or review projects are common and, in some institutions, there are dedicated curriculum units with dedicated academic (or curriculum) developers[1] tasked with assisting academics to (re)design curricula. Few academics come into higher education with any qualifications or "training" for

---

1   In South Africa, the term "academic development" is generally used to mean "all aspects of support for higher education learning and teaching, including professional learning and student learning" (CHE, 2013). In this book the term "academic developers" refers to academic staff developers, curriculum developers and educational developers. See Quinn (2012:2-4) for a brief discussion on contested terms and concepts in the field of academic development.

their teaching role[2] and find the processes of curriculum design particularly challenging. Ironically, the academic developers tasked with assisting them have themselves had to learn how to work with curricula in their institutional contexts through trial and error and from the findings of scholarship, that is, both their own research activities and reading research undertaken by others. The purpose of this book is to share theoretical perspectives and practical ideas for ways in which academic developers (and academic leaders) can work in partnership with lecturers and students to respond to the urgent calls for curriculum transformation and decolonisation. The book is intended to make a scholarly contribution to the theory and practice of curriculum development.

The purpose of this chapter is to "set the scene" for this book. The chapter begins with a brief overview of some of the contextual factors that impact on, and account for why we believe a much greater emphasis on curriculum in contemporary higher education globally, and specifically in South Africa, is necessary. Although South African academics or academic developers wrote many of the chapters, we believe that international readers will find aspects of interest for their contexts. We then go on to discuss the roles of academics, academic leaders, and particularly those of academic developers in curriculum development processes. The chapter concludes with giving readers some idea of what to expect from the other chapters in this book.

"Context is everything"

Globalisation

Higher education is part of the global environment and is thus affected by its immediate contexts as well as global changes. Philip Altbach (2004:5) defines globalisation, in the context of higher education, as

> ... the broad economic, technological, and scientific trends that directly affect higher education and are largely inevitable. Politics and culture are also part of the new global realities. Academic systems and institutions may accommodate these developments in different ways, but they cannot ignore them. These phenomena include information technology in its various manifestations, the use of a common language for scientific communication, and the imperatives of both mass demand for higher education (massification) and societal needs for highly educated personnel.

---

2   Luckett (2011:147) points out that in South Africa, and probably in many countries internationally, academics are not required to obtain an educational qualification of any kind "and so do not necessarily think of curriculum development as a practice requiring specialisation or expertise".

Historically universities have had to balance tensions between national realities and international trends. Higher education has become increasingly important, within countries and internationally, for educating people for the new knowledge economy of the 21st century. In contemporary higher education globally there thus is, and needs to be, a strong focus on curricula that prepare students for this knowledge economy and "high-skills" occupations. Globalisation and the internationalisation of higher education have resulted in universities needing to ensure that students have the knowledge and capabilities to live and work, not only in their local contexts but also in global contexts. As Nyna Amin (2016:163) points out, it is no easy task to design curricula that prepare students to leave university

> ... with competencies that are relevant, with attitudes that are appropriate, with sensitivities that are responsible and responsive to work and society's needs, and ... people who can embrace uncertainty in a world that is glocal, polyvalent, unpredictable and undecidable.

However, globalisation does not benefit everyone equally. In some contexts, globalisation opens access and enables scholars to study and work anywhere in the world; in other contexts, the effects of globalisation reinforce existing inequalities and create new barriers to effective higher education. The challenge for higher education is to recognise this and do all in its power to ameliorate the inequalities of the global academic environment. "These tasks, in the context of marketisation and the pressures of mass higher education, are not easy ones. Yet, it is important to ensure that globalisation does not turn into the neo-colonialism of the 21st century" (Altbach, 2004:24).

Growth of the higher education system

In most countries globally, higher education has changed from being an elite system to a mass system. There are two main reasons for the increased numbers of students entering higher education. The first, as already alluded to, is linked to the knowledge economy that has led to countries needing far more skilled "knowledge workers". The second has been a global call for the democratisation of education, where higher education, through providing access to more students, is regarded as having a crucial role to play in resolving social and economic inequalities present in societies through providing access to more students (Hornsby & Osman, 2014) (more on this later). In South Africa increased access to higher education for black students has thus been seen as key to overcoming apartheid inequalities and producing the high-level skills believed to be needed to drive economic growth. As early as 1994, Wally

Morrow, talking about the post-apartheid South African context, pointed out that providing students with "formal" access to university, was different to ensuring that previously excluded students were given "epistemological" access which he describes as "access to the knowledge which universities distribute" (Morrow, 2007:17). The same point is made in 2019 by Naledi Pandor, that formal access without evidence of success does not eradicate inequality or make up for the injustices of the past. In Pandor's words: "Universities are designed for those who were schooled in privilege and not for those who were schooled in squalor" (Pandor, 2019:134). The implication of this is that universities have themselves not transformed sufficiently to meet the needs of the students they admit.

The massive increase in enrolments and concomitant increased diversity of the student population have meant that academics need to think carefully about their curriculum choices, including pedagogies and assessment methods. The days of academics selecting the content they are most interested in and then "casting their pearls" before their students are no longer tenable. Increasing the numbers of students, formally admitted to universities, may have addressed issues of equity of access, but as Goolam Mohamedbhai points out, particularly in the African context, "the equally important issue of ensuring equity in success for the enrolled students has received limited attention" (2014:59). Stephanie Allais outlines the challenges of ensuring that "higher" learning can take place in the context of large classes: "Students who have little experience in engaging in complex ideas, reading and critiquing texts, and mastering concepts, are likely to be the most disadvantaged by finding themselves in a large class, as they are the most likely to not follow the exposition of concepts" (2014:730).

In addition, expanding student numbers has, in many contexts, not been accompanied by more academic staff or better infrastructure, leading to academics working in overcrowded lecture halls without even the basic resources they need to teach their students. Many academics are overworked with little time and intellectual energy for in-depth curriculum planning. Globally many institutions have turned to the affordances of information and communication technologies to solve the challenges presented by large classes (for example, Hornsby & Osman, 2014; Snowball, 2014). However, many higher education practitioners are aware of the limitations of what information and communication technologies can achieve and are unconvinced that "technology will save us" (Allais, 2014; Shrivastava & Shrivastava, 2014).

The reality is that large class sizes and continued increases in enrolments are here to stay. It is thus a crucial contextual reality both academics and academic developers have to face up to, and in which they need to collaboratively find ways of designing curricula, pedagogies and assessment methods that ensure that the majority of the diverse students acquire epistemological access to the disciplines (Morrow, 1994).

Managerialism

Another imperative for academics, academic developers and those who occupy academic leadership positions in institutions is to pay particular attention to curriculum development and to ensure that control of the academic project is not slipping out of the hands of academics. Since the mid-1980s, in response to a globalised world where profits and market-driven policies have eclipsed politics and ideology (Nixon, Scullion & Hearn, 2016), there have been far-reaching changes in universities with the introduction of managerialism resulting in "an audit and evaluation culture"; "coercive and authoritarian governmentality" (Shore & Wright, 1999:557); an emphasis on "particular forms of accountability, the development of a market-orientation" and increased concern with efficiency and economy (Anderson, 2008). Elizabeth Nixon et al. (2016:4) provide searing commentary on the potentially devastating consequences of the market logic for the core values, purposes, and ideals of the academic project:

> Marketisation enshrines the satisfaction of the sovereign student as a legitimate and central imperative of higher education institution. It increases the pressure to be seen to be responsive to student desires, wants and 'needs', despite the ancient insight that seeking the learner's satisfaction extinguishes more enduring intellectual development engendered through challenge, struggle and problem-solving ... Rather than the pursuit of knowledge and learning through a 'three-cornered conversation' between students, tutors and the object of enquiry (Nixon, 1996:11), the so-called quality logics propel student satisfaction measurement mania in which scores are endlessly sought, captured, codified and used to assist staff performance management.

Universities are becoming corporations or what could be called administrative universities "without truly understanding how such initiatives chip away at the very purpose of higher education: the academic project" (McKenna, 2018:n.p.). Some would argue that there is now a global struggle for the "academic soul" of universities. It is therefore essential that academics do not make curriculum decisions based on customer service models, and that these decisions do not lie with administrative staff or staff in executive positions. Academics, academic developers and academic leaders have to resist processes that result in the scenario described by Johnson (1994:379):

> It no longer really matters how well an academic teaches and whether or not he or she, sometimes, [inspire] their pupils; it is far more important that they have produced plans for their courses, bibliographies, outlines of this, that and the other, in short, all the paraphernalia of futile bureaucratization required for assessors who come from on high like emissaries from Kafka's castle. (In Shore & Wright, 1999:567)

All role players of the academic project need "to participate in processes aimed at keeping the academic project as their university's central driving logic" (McKenna, 2018:n.p.) rather than only working at complying with national and institutional policy imperatives. Nowhere is this more important than in spaces where curriculum decisions are being made.

Social justice

As already mentioned, another reason for the present focus on curriculum globally, but particularly in South Africa, is the need for universities to contribute to the social justice agenda by ensuring that previously marginalised groups can access higher education. However, formal access is insufficient if students are not succeeding in their studies. Social justice requires paying attention to how curricula and pedagogy can facilitate students' access to disciplinary knowledge and knowledge practices.

Given South Africa's racialised colonial and apartheid past, it is unsurprising that the post-apartheid government, in keeping with the country's new constitution, devised policies and processes for restructuring the higher education system and for ensuring that deserving black students, formerly denied access, were now admitted to institutions of higher learning. As part of restructuring higher education, a National Qualifications Framework (NQF) was introduced to facilitate the development of programmes of study in line with the so-called knowledge economy and to ensure equivalence and portability of credits and qualifications across institutions. The NQF, underpinned by outcomes-based education, was devised as a key mechanism for transforming the racially divided and unequal education system in South Africa. However, the hoped-for "magic bullet" of the NQF and outcomes-based education have failed to live up to their expectations.[3] Jansen (2009:197) makes the astute observation that it is "easier to deal with regulatory and technical

---

3   See Allais (2007) for an extended discussion on the reasons for this failure.

requirements than with the more troublesome matters that demand personal and emotional changes in understanding and commitment".

Another transformation initiative that has taken place, in this case for facilitating greater demographic and epistemological access for students, is extended degree programmes (also called foundation programmes or access programmes in other contexts) designed for students who do not meet the entrance requirements of universities or who may need additional support to succeed. Although the curricula of these programmes differ across institutions, their purpose in all cases is to bridge the articulation gap between school and university and to prepare students for successful engagement in university studies. Although there are educational gains for students participating in such programmes, there are political and social critiques associated with them. Students can either feel marginalised or forced to assimilate into traditional ways of knowing, being and doing in the university. In addition, it could mean that traditional curricula, pedagogies and assessment methods are not questioned and remain unchanged, resulting in social justice aims not being addressed (Vorster & Quinn, 2017). All curricula should be designed to suit the learning needs of the majority of students. If higher education continues to predominantly serve the interests of the "haves" and not the "have-nots", there is little chance of curricula promoting social justice. Higher education needs to be reclaimed as a "public good", and curricula should be designed in ways that "offer all students a fair chance of flourishing and achieving both public and personal 'goods'" (Luckett & Shay, 2017:1).

As things are now, the majority of South African students are not flourishing. Since 1994, student enrolments in South African higher education have more than doubled, 79 per cent of students are black, and there have been improvements in staff demographics. Despite the improved student access, other changes in the higher education system and the rhetoric around the need for curriculum transformation, it is clear that little real transformation has occurred (Case, 2015) and the hoped-for student success has not materialised. According to recent statistics, only about 25 per cent of students graduate in the prescribed time; 35 per cent graduate in five years and approximately 55 per cent of a given intake never graduate. Also, success and completion rates remain racially skewed with far more black students than white students dropping out or failing (CHE, 2013).

Students' frustration with the lack of real change in the system boiled over in the form of student protests in 2015 and 2016. The underlying issues and manifestations of the protests were different in different contexts and at different times. Many students expressed extreme anger at the slow pace of change, particularly in relation to institutional cultures and curricula. They argued that curriculum content continues to draw mainly from the global North and that teaching, and assessment are not responsive to the more diverse student body. It would seem then that the discourse of transformation that was intended to radically change higher education in South Africa has now run its course (Vorster & Quinn, 2017).

Calls for the decolonisation of curricula

It took the student protests of 2015 and 2016 for institutions and academics to understand how alienated many students feel from institutional cultures and curricula (Pather, 2016).[4] Thus, perhaps the major impetus for the increased focus on curriculum in the last few years, in South Africa particularly, has been the growing awareness of the urgent need for academics to acknowledge the effects that apartheid and coloniality have on their curriculum decisions. Jansen, talking about former Afrikaans institutions, says: "[J]ust below the external changes of the institutional curriculum to conform with new regulatory demands lies an as yet undisturbed set of assumptions about race, knowledge, and identity" (2009:183). We would argue that this is the case in many universities in South Africa and possibly beyond. Many of the chapters in this book explore why it has become imperative to re-imagine curricula at this point in the history of higher education.

It is no longer appropriate for curriculum decisions to be based only on a list of topics or texts to be studied. It is also not sufficient for lecturers to simply transmit the knowledge enshrined in the canons of their disciplines to students – with little thought to who their students are, where they come from and what their legitimate learning needs are. There is growing impatience amongst students who are no longer prepared to accept that existing university cultures are "right" and comfortable spaces of learning (Behari-Leak, 2015). Even though the idea that universities are not prepared for the students they admit has been part of the discourse of higher education in South Africa since the 1990s, the student protests were dramatic reminders that not enough has been done to design curricula and pedagogical processes to facilitate epistemological access for the majority of students. As Aslam Fataar argues: "Universities' unchanged institutional cultures are a reflection

---

4   Although we focus mostly on the South African context, many believe that the struggle for the decolonisation of higher education is a global one.

of the failure of universities to transform their functional environments to adapt to the socio-cultural and educational requirements of first-generation black students" (2018b:2).

The student protests placed the need for the decolonisation of institutions and the curriculum firmly on the agenda – especially so at historically white universities. They have prompted many academics, academic developers and academic leaders[5] to critically evaluate how they understand the curriculum in their contexts and how both curriculum content and pedagogical processes serve to exclude a large majority of the student body. Thus, any curriculum planning must include decisions about what to teach and consider who the students are; it must take account of both epistemology and ontology.

Epistemological concerns

> ... knowledge is the very basis of education as a social field of practice; it is the production, recontextualization, teaching and learning of knowledge that makes education a distinct field. (Maton & Moore, 2010:2)

Doing curriculum work requires both a theory of curriculum as well as a theory of knowledge (Young, drawing on Bernstein, 2011:197). A theory of curriculum includes philosophical orientations to the curriculum; the purposes of the curriculum, that is, what students need to learn to become particular kinds of knowers; the relationship between curriculum content, pedagogy and assessment. In this volume, several authors share a range of curriculum theories and frameworks that have informed their curriculum practices.

As the main aims of universities are the generation, dissemination and application of knowledge, academics engaging in curriculum practice need a theory of knowledge that enables them to:

- Articulate to themselves what constitutes knowledge in their disciplines, and (where appropriate) in their fields of practice;
- Understand the knowledge structure/s of their disciplines; and
- The nature of knowledge creation processes in their disciplines.

We discuss each of these ideas briefly below.

Drawing on social realist tenets, Basil Bernstein (2000) distinguishes between everyday knowledge and the kind of specialised knowledge taught in schools

---

5   See Grant, Quinn and Vorster (2018) for a case study of how heads of department at a historically white institution in South Africa responded to the student protests.

and universities. "Everyday knowledge" is learned in contexts of application, through direct experience and enables people to act in particular ways in specific contexts; it is not necessarily useful beyond those contexts. On the other hand, "specialised knowledge", such as the knowledge linked to specific disciplines, is systematic knowledge through which different aspects of the world are treated as objects that relate to other objects in the world in very distinctive ways. Disciplines explore the methods and procedures through which it is possible to understand and discover more about the world (Allais, 2014, drawing on Charlot, 2009). Such disciplinary knowledge has the power to transcend specific contexts and enables the holder of that knowledge to explain how things are in the world, to understand why things are the way they are and then to act in appropriate ways. This is often termed "powerful knowledge". Young (2014:74) argues that knowledge is powerful "if it predicts, if it explains, if it enables you to envisage alternatives". He goes on to describe three features of powerful knowledge, namely, it is not common-sense knowledge, it is systematic, and it is specialised. It is the kind of knowledge that is produced by disciplinary specialists, and that is taught in educational institutions. Tony Harland and Navé Wald (2018:615) argue that the "'power' in powerful knowledge is realised in what is done with that knowledge, that its purpose is social since it allows the holder to make a better contribution to society". Giving students access to powerful knowledge is a social justice imperative (Wheelehan, 2010). Therefore, academics and academic leaders need to identify powerful knowledge in their disciplines to select curriculum content.

An understanding of how knowledge is structured as well as of the history of ideas in the discipline is necessary to ensure that students are introduced to knowledge in the appropriate order, at the most appropriate time and the right level of difficulty. In hierarchically structured disciplines, such as in the natural sciences, knowledge builds incrementally, systematically and cumulatively. If students are to learn the essential facts, concepts, principles, methods and procedures of the discipline, it is important that the curriculum reflects that pattern and that knowledge is introduced to them systematically and cumulatively. In horizontally structured disciplines, such as the human and social sciences, curriculum designers have greater freedom of choice in terms of the selection and sequencing of knowledge. However, in all disciplines, principled decisions, underpinned by an understanding of disciplinary knowledge structures, need to be made about what knowledge is selected, how it will be sequenced, what time needs to be spent on each aspect (pacing), and how students will be assessed (Bernstein, 2000).

Not only is university teaching about enabling students to gain access to the powerful knowledge of the disciplines, it is also about learning how that knowledge came to be so that students themselves can become producers of knowledge. Integrated into curricula should be a focus on how knowledge is created in the disciplines – the research methods and procedures through which disciplinary knowledge is generated.

The argument made thus far in this section, is that having a theory of knowledge is central to the curriculum. This, however, does not imply that academics and students should not be critical of disciplinary canons, of the knowledge that is selected for inclusion in a curriculum. The calls for the decolonisation of the curriculum have challenged academics to consider powerful knowledge that traditional disciplinary canons have to date excluded.

As pointed out by decolonial theorists, curriculum knowledge in most disciplines draws on Western knowledge produced by white researchers (see, for example, Maldonado-Torres, 2011; Mignolo, 2009). This challenges the notion of what can be considered "powerful knowledge" and who can be legitimate knowers of this knowledge. Particularly during the recent student protests in South Africa and elsewhere, it was brought to academics' attention that many students feel alienated from this knowledge as they do not believe that it has relevance to their lives and the lives of black people generally. "Students have made a call for an 'all-inclusive' approach to knowledge to inform our curriculum initiatives. Africa-centredness, they suggested, ought to be at the heart of university knowledge" (Fataar, 2018a:n.p.). Thus, although we earlier argued for the importance of powerful disciplinary knowledge, we also realise the importance of interrogating knowledge that "served the purpose of promoting an imperialist view of the world that justifies colonisation premised on European epistemological supremacy" (Tuck & Gaztambide-Fernández, 2013:75).

Fataar (2018a) offers an argument for the decolonisation of knowledge in the curriculum, based on both a theory of knowledge and a theory of curriculum. He argues that it is possible to bridge the gap between the modernist view that values objective, scientifically generated knowledge and the decolonial view that there is a plurality of knowledges that recognises the contributions from Africa, Asia and South America to the pure and applied sciences as well as to the humanities and social sciences. He demonstrates how hitherto subjugated knowledges can be incorporated into the curriculum by calling on social realist curriculum theory that recognises the structured nature of different knowledge fields (as discussed above). Curriculum designers can use different curriculum logics to decide which knowledges to draw from for their curricula. For example, the logic of horizontal or vertical knowledge structures, or the logic based on the relationship between concepts of the discipline/field and how they relate to real-world contexts (Muller, 2009). Fataar shows how horizontal knowledge fields can include African and other southern epistemologies by critiquing the canon or adding to the canon, and how the natural sciences, could include the study of the origins of their fields in the global South. In these ways, Fataar asserts that the decolonisation of the curriculum can address the coloniality of power, of knowledge and of being.

Ontological concerns

Education is both an epistemological and an ontological project; it is about both knowing and being. To undertake curriculum work, academics need to be concerned about more than only the selection of appropriate knowledge, but also for what Fataar (2018b) calls the "epistemic becoming" of students. This entails academics understanding who their students are and what kinds of knowers they wish to shape.

The student protests of 2015 and 2016, particularly at historically white universities in South Africa, made it abundantly evident that we have not paid sufficient attention to who our students are, to their lived realities. Many students feel alienated as if they do not belong in our universities – many modelled on European institutions. For the majority of students, the curricula they study and the pedagogic processes they experience result in a sense of "a hierarchy of superior and inferior knowledge and, thus, of superior and inferior people" (Grosfoguel, 2007:214). The calls for the decolonisation of education and curricula are responses to the misrecognition of students (Fraser, 2009), of their histories and of the communities they come from, their experiences of coloniality, and of their ways of thinking and being in the world.

When making curriculum and pedagogic choices, academics need to be sensitive to where their students come from, their previous learning experiences, their current legitimate learning needs, and their aspirations for the future. They also need to be able to articulate clearly what kinds of learners, professionals and citizens they want their students to become. Epistemic becoming necessitates curriculum decisions and pedagogies centred on the development of student identities in terms of knowing, acting and being (Barnett, Parry & Coate, 2001). What students come to know, who they become through acquiring disciplinary knowledge, and what practices they engage in are dependent on the identities they develop through teaching and learning processes (Dall'Alba & Barnacle, 2007). For Dall'Alba and Barnacle, this means designing curricula and teaching in ways that promote self-awareness and reflective practice and that encourage students to engage with "being-in-the-world differently" (2007:688).

Summary of this section

Nowhere is the expression "context is everything" more important than in education. In this section, we have briefly summarised some of the main contextual realities that we believe account for the present need to focus on curriculum in contemporary higher education. It is crucial for academics, academic developers and academic leaders to be aware of and to critique the construction of the university in global discourses. We argue that these role players need to understand the effects of globalisation, massification, managerialism, and democratisation in their specific contexts. To undertake meaningful curriculum work we need to interrogate our own understandings of the purposes of higher education so that we do not inadvertently get caught up in marketised constructions of the purposes of higher education at the expense of designing curricula that contribute to social justice and that are able to ensure both epistemological and ontological access to the "goods" of higher education for our students

In the following sections, we discuss the roles of academics, academic leaders (briefly) and academic developers in curriculum practices and processes.

The role of academics[6]

Curriculum, as used in this volume, includes what is taught, how it is taught and assessed, as well as who the teachers are, and who the students are. Curriculum lies at the heart of the academic project. Conceptualising, planning and enacting curricula are central to what academics do as part of their teaching role.

Curriculum practices are influenced by the contextual conditions outlined in the previous section, as well as other factors such as institutional histories, types and cultures. Public universities in South Africa are divided into three types: traditional universities that offer theoretically-oriented university degrees; universities of technology, that offer vocationally-oriented diplomas and degrees; and comprehensive universities, that offer a combination of

---

6   We use academics, lecturers and teachers interchangeably.

both types of qualification.[7] The South African higher education system is still trying to recover from historical inequities and deficits amongst institutions in terms of racial segregation, funding, geographical location, the language of instruction, and so on. As is noted in several chapters in this volume, institutional contexts (including histories) and different institutional cultures impact on the way curriculum work is undertaken, particularly between historically white and historically black institutions in South Africa. A challenge faced by universities of technology is that the former technikons had what was called a "convener system", which entailed a few people from each field/discipline designing curricula for implementation across the technikon sector. This means that many universities of technology lecturers have no experience of curriculum design. Also, at universities of technology and in professional programmes at other universities, many professional staff members are brought in for contract teaching. This and the increase in the casualisation of academic staff (in all types of institutions in South Africa and internationally) means that there are fewer academics in departments who are committed to ensuring that qualifications/programmes are coherently designed and taught.

Curriculum practices are different in different disciplines and in qualifications preparing students for particular vocations and professions. Curriculum choices are thus made based on what disciplines and vocations/professions value and what academic departments and individual academics find interesting and believe to be useful for students to learn and know. In some cases, professional bodies stipulate curriculum content, and teaching and assessment methods that academics must comply with for their students to register as professionals in those fields.

Like all aspects of education, curriculum is underpinned by values, beliefs and ideologies. Curriculum is value-based, and teachers' beliefs about the discipline, the nature of knowledge, the nature of teaching and learning, and their understandings of the purposes of assessment will all play a part in curriculum decision-making. The kind of learning teachers want students to engage in will frame many of the curriculum choices they make.

Academics need to be aware of and take into account the "clamour of contending purposes" of higher education, including debates about the

---

[7] This is similar to different types of universities in the UK (UKuni, 2019) and in the USA (TopUniversities, 2015).

university as both public and private good – what this means to them and for their curriculum decisions.

> Higher education institutions are attempting to respond simultaneously to the entrepreneurial demands of the knowledge economy and the broader 'social good' aspirations of the knowledge society ... The debate on higher education and the public good is a reflection of competing expectations from contemporary higher education, [reposing] questions about the ideological and practical implications of the changing 'social compact' between higher education and society. (Singh, 2014:99)

Drawing on a range of theorists, Singh summarises the central purposes of higher education as needing to:

> ... afford transformatory intellectual and cultural experiences for students as well as opportunities for personal development ... ensure that there are spaces for the pursuit of knowledge which is not narrowly instrumental ... promote public discourse ... contribute to the building of critical and civic capabilities for democratic citizenship ... and provide a far-seeing intellectually imaginative leadership ... (Singh, 2014:105)

For academics to undertake meaningful curriculum work they need not only to consider the different purposes of higher education, but, as noted above, they also need a theory of knowledge, curriculum theories and tools, and an understanding of the implications of the calls for decolonisation for curriculum. As many of the chapters in this volume demonstrate and as is further discussed below, academic developers, working collaboratively with academics and academic leaders in the disciplines, have the potential to share their knowledge of the field of higher education to inform curriculum practices.

The role of academic leaders in curriculum processes

Academic leaders (such as heads of departments and deans) need to provide the kind of leadership that encourages academics to work on curricula in teams to ensure qualification and programme alignment (both horizontally and vertically). Through their leadership, they need to create the kinds of spaces that require curriculum teams to explore what Bernstein (2000) calls the regulative, the instructional and the pedagogic discourses of curricula. The regulative discourse entails identifying the moral values, attitudes and beliefs that underpin the curriculum and that shape the kinds of knowers the curriculum wishes to shape. Embedded in the regulative discourse is the instructional discourse that is content knowledge, theories and concepts introduced to the students (called "powerful knowledge" earlier). Finally, the pedagogic discourse is how teachers will undertake the teaching. If a team of curriculum developers can articulate the nature of these discourses in their contexts, they will be able to work together towards a common goal of enabling epistemological access for students. Working in such teams, sometimes with the assistance of an academic developer, is also a way of inducting/mentoring new academics into their teaching roles. The case studies in this volume will assist those in academic leadership positions to consider how they can move beyond merely managing curriculum processes to how they can exercise meaningful curriculum leadership in their departments and/or faculties.

The role of academic developers in curriculum processes

For academic developers to work with academics, they themselves need to have engaged with curriculum theories, and they need to have developed the appropriate dispositions required for working collaboratively with academics from a range of fields and disciplines. Many of the chapters in this book describe the curriculum theories and tools used by academic developers and the ways that they have worked with these in their institutional contexts. A main focus of the book is thus on how academic developers and academics conceptualise and enact their roles in relation to curriculum development.

What is clear from the chapters in the book is that for all the contributors "[c]urriculum development is an ongoing faculty project, an intellectual undertaking, not an organisational restructuring or bureaucratic manipulation" (Pinar, 2016:143). And the role of academic developers has to go beyond simply dealing with the "technical" aspects of the curriculum and helping academics to comply with institutional policies and national frameworks (such as the Higher Education Quality Sub-Framework in South Africa). It is the role of academic developers to make sure that academics are aware of the neoliberal, capitalist forces that are at play, and that may influence curriculum decisions. Academic developers need to support academics in not relinquishing their responsibility for maintaining the integrity of the academic project in the face of new managerialist demands and practices.

Many of the chapters highlight the role of academic developers working in collaboration with colleagues across disciplines. What emerges strongly in these chapters is the importance for academic developers, if they want to move beyond only technicist approaches to curriculum work, to have deep knowledge of theoretical tools to contribute to curriculum discussions and decisions. Academic developers need to be able to draw on and engage with a range of strong (although sometimes contesting) curriculum theories and tools to earn legitimacy to work with colleagues across a range of disciplines and fields and in different institutional types. The latter need to be introduced in ways that make sense to and are useful for different disciplinary colleagues.

Chapter authors draw on a range of theories, concepts and ideas to describe their work and in so doing offer tools for use by academic developers and academic staff for undertaking curriculum work. Theories and concepts such as feminist new materialist philosophies, Bernstein's pedagogic device, decoding the disciplines, epistemological access, new literacy studies, Legitimation Code Theory, decolonial theory including concepts of cognitive and epistemic justice and social inclusion and exclusion, the nature and structure of different kinds of knowledge (and ways of knowing), are used both to critique current curriculum practices and to suggest toolkits or frameworks for ways in which academic developers, academic leaders, lecturers, community and industry partners, and students can work collaboratively in dialogic spaces to design curricula appropriate for students at this time and in specific contexts.

Academic developers need to find ways of engaging in productive conversations with their colleagues about knowledge in their disciplines or fields – about how they select curriculum knowledge and how this knowledge is "recontextualised" (Bernstein, 2000) as curriculum knowledge. Barnett, Parry and Coate (2001:436) point out that "curricula will be shaped in significant degrees by the values and practices of the different knowledge fields". They go on to explain that behind knowledge fields are:

> ... a hinterland of contending interests of shifting epistemologies, academic communities, institutions, professions, the corporate world, students and state agencies. A curriculum, in other words, is a dynamic set of forces: the actual form that curricula take in particular settings represents the balance of the interplay of the separate interests. (Barnett, Parry & Coate, 2001:438)

It is, therefore, important for academic developers, as far as possible, to be aware of these dynamics and to understand the nature of the fields and disciplines in which they work. They need to be able to bring together curriculum theory and a deep understanding of specific fields and disciplines (Young, 2011).

In addition, academic developers need to cultivate appropriate dispositions and ways of engaging in meaningful and productive conversations, that will encourage collaboration amongst colleagues and with academic developers. This means being respectful of colleagues' disciplinary knowledge and identities. Sutherland (2018), drawing on Clegg (2003:46), argues that we should not ask "academics to leave aspects of their identity at the door" when engaging them in professional development activities. However, academic developers also need to be prepared to challenge and disrupt common-sense approaches to curriculum. They need to encourage scholarly approaches that will contribute to academics' designing curricula that give students access to powerful knowledge and that pay attention to who students are and their legitimate learning needs (Vorster & Quinn, 2017).

Some chapters describe curriculum processes in different institutional contexts, such as curriculum renewal at a research-intensive university, and the changing role of academics and academic developers concerning curriculum when technikons became universities of technology. Another focuses on one particular faculty to better understand what the implications of students' demand for decolonising the curriculum might mean for curriculum development in that faculty. Several chapters focus on curriculum processes in particular disciplinary fields, for example, Occupational Therapy, Physics, Engineering (as part of STEM), and Town and Regional Planning. One chapter focuses on how faculty-based academics and academic developers might collaborate in the development of appropriate curricula for diploma-level qualifications in technical fields.

Many of the chapters (not all) are written by South African academic developers and academics, some of whom are grappling with how to respond appropriately to the calls made by protesting students to decolonise curricula. Many of the issues they raise are relevant to an international audience. Decolonisation of university curricula has been a topic of debate elsewhere in Africa since the 1960s, and has also been highlighted in more recent critiques of the "whiteness" of university curricula at Western universities. One of the chapters in this book explores the ways in which academic developers can work with lecturers in Canada to uncover complicit knowledge that silently reproduces a settler-colonial society and its practices, and strengthens epistemologies based on Western worldviews. Another chapter is written by colleagues in the United Kingdom who work in what is referred to as a "widening participation" university that recruits "non-traditional" students, shares a pedagogic strategy aimed at re-imagining reading as part of a more inclusive curriculum.

A number of the chapters describe close-up research in which authors set out to interrogate current practices in their specific contexts. Some chapters describe research on particular academic development initiatives, such as curriculum development short courses offered to academics; regular dialogue sessions for academic developers on decolonising curricula; collaborative work amongst academic developers and disciplinary colleagues related to academic literacy, online and blended learning, innovative pedagogical strategies, knowledge in the curriculum, involving students much more in curriculum processes and so on.

The chapters of the book vary in all ways: in terms of their foci, the contexts from which they are written, the topics covered and ways of writing. However, to give the book coherence chapters were arranged with the following logic in mind (although of course there are overlaps). Chapters 2 to 4 deal with the different ways in which people and institutions have responded to the students' calls for decolonisation. Chapters 5 to 11 offer readers insights into a range of theoretical frameworks and practical tools for undertaking different types of curriculum work. The following six chapters (12 to 17) document a variety of curriculum processes and practices in different types of universities – the first five in what could be called "non-traditional universities" in South Africa and the UK and the last one documents curriculum renewal processes at a traditional or research-intensive institution. Chapters 18 to 19 focus on different ways in which academic developers have worked with academics in STEM education and at a Science faculty in a traditional university. The final chapter of the book, re-published with permission from the *Journal of Education*, is included in memory of one of the most influential academic developers in the history of academic development in South Africa, Professor Brenda Leibowitz.

The book argues that academics, academic developers and academic leaders need to undertake curriculum work in their institutions that has the potential to disrupt common-sense notions about curriculum and create spaces for engagement with scholarly concepts and theories, to re-imagine curricula for the changing times. Now, more than ever, in the history of higher education, curriculum practices and processes need to be shared; the findings of research undertaken on curriculum need to be disseminated to inform curriculum work. We hope the book will enable readers to look beyond their contextual difficulties and constraints, to find spaces where they can dream, and begin to implement, innovative and creative solutions to what may seem like intractable challenges or difficulties.

References

ALLAIS, S. 2014. A critical perspective on large class teaching: the political economy of massification and the sociology of knowledge. *Higher Education*, 67:721-734. [https://doi.org/10.1007/s10734-013-9672-2]

ALLAIS, S. 2007. Why the South African NQF Failed: Lessons for Countries Wanting to Introduce National Qualifications Frameworks. *European Journal of Education*, 42:523-547. [https://doi.org/10.1111/j.1465-3435.2007.00320.x]

ALTBACH, P. 2004. Globalisation and the University: Myths and Realities in an Unequal World. *Tertiary Education and Management*, 10(1):3-25. [https://doi.org/10.1023/B:TEAM.0000012239.55136.4b]

AMIN, N. 2016. Curriculum without Borders? In: M.A. Samuel, R. Dunpath & N. Amin (eds). *Disrupting Higher Education Curriculum. Undoing Cognitive Damage*. Rotterdam: Sense Publishers, 291-304. [https://doi.org/10.1007/978-94-6300-896-9_17]

ANDERSON, G. 2008. Mapping Academic Resistance in the Managerial University. *Organization*, 15:251-270. [https://doi.org/10.1177/1350508407086583]

BARNETT, R.; PARRY, G. & COATE, K. 2001. Conceptualising Curriculum Change. *Teaching in Higher Education*, 6:435-449. [https://doi.org/10.1080/13562510120078009]

BERNSTEIN, B. 2000. *Pedagogy, symbolic control and identity: Theory, research and critique*. Lanham, MD: Rowman and Littlefield.

BEHARI-LEAK, K. 2015. After Protests, It Can't Be Business as Usual at South Africa's Universities. *The Conversation*, 18 November. [https://bit.ly/2koiIFK]

CASE, J. 2015. Reimagining the Curriculum in a Postcolonial Space: Engaging the Public Good Purposes of Higher Education in South Africa. Keynote address. HELTASA, North-West University, Potchefstroom, 17-20 November. [https://bit.ly/2m2wSgs]

CHE (COUNCIL ON HIGHER EDUCATION). 2013. *A proposal for undergraduate curriculum reform in South Africa: The case for a flexible curriculum structure*. Pretoria: CHE. [https://www.che.ac.za/sites/default/files/publications/Full_Report.pdf]

DALL'ALBA, G. & BARNACLE, R. 2007. An ontological turn for higher education. *Studies in Higher Education*, 32(6):679-691. [https://doi.org/10.1080/03075070701685130]

FATAAR, A. 2018a. (How) can decoloniality inform "educational (curriculum) knowledge" selection? LitNet University Seminar in November. [https://bit.ly/2mppA6v]

FATAAR, A. 2018b. From the shadows to the university's epistemic centre: Engaging the (mis)recognition struggles of students at the post-apartheid university. Thinkpiece for the 9th Higher Education Close-Up Conference, Cape Town, 15-19 November. [http://www.hecu9.co.za/images/Aslam_Fataar_ThinkPiece.pdf]

FRASER, N. 2009. *Scales of justice: reimagining political space in a globalizing world*. New York: Columbia University Press.

GRANT, C.; QUINN, L. & VORSTER, J. 2018. An exploratory study of Heads of Departments' responses to student calls for decolonised higher education. *Journal of Education*, 72. [https://doi.org/10.17159/2520-9868/i72a05]

GROSFOGUEL, R. 2007. The Epistemic Decolonial Turn: Beyond Political-Economy Paradigms. *Cultural Studies*, 21(2-3):211-223. [https://doi.org/10.1080/09502380601162514]

HARLAND, T. & WALD, N. 2018. Curriculum, teaching and powerful knowledge. *Higher Education*, 76:615-628. [https://doi.org/10.1007/s10734-017-0228-8]

HORNSBY, D.J. & OSMAN, R. 2014. Massification in higher education: large classes and student learning. *Higher Education*, 67:711-719. [https://doi.org/10.1007/s10734-014-9733-1]

JANSEN, J. 2009. *Knowledge in the Blood. Confronting Race and the Apartheid Past*. Stanford, California: Stanford University Press.

LEIBOWITZ, B.; BOZALEK, V.; GARRAWAY, J.; HERMAN, N.; JAWITZ, J.; MUHURO, P.; NDEBELE, C.; QUINN, L.; VAN SCHALKWYK, S.; VORSTER, J. & WINBERG, C. 2017. Learning to Teach in Higher Education in South Africa. An investigation into the influences of institutional context on the professional learning of academics in their roles as teachers. *Higher Education Monitor*, 14. Pretoria: CHE. [https://bit.ly/2kVdi5h]

LUCKETT, K. & SHAY, S. 2017. Reframing the curriculum: a transformative approach. *Critical Studies in Education*, 1-16. [https://doi.org/10.1080/17508487.2017.1356341]

LUCKETT, K. 2011. Inquiring into the Higher Education Curriculum. A critical Realist Approach. In: E. Bitzer & N. Botha (eds). *Curriculum Inquiry in South African Higher Education. Some scholarly affirmations and challenges*. Stellenbosch: African Sun Media, 135-155. [https://doi.org/10.18820/9781920338671/06]

MCKENNA, S. 2018. Here are five signs that universities are turning into corporations. *The Conversation*, 13 March 2018. [https://bit.ly/2kTfBG8]

MALDONADO-TORRES, N. 2011. Thinking through the Decolonial Turn: Post-Continental Interventions in Theory, Philosophy, and Critique – An Introduction. *Transmodernity: Journal of Peripheral Cultural Production of the Luso-Hispanic World*, 1(2):1-14.

MIGNOLO, W.D. 2009. Epistemic Disobedience, Independent Thought and De-Colonial Freedom. *Theory, Culture and Society*, 26(7-8):1-23. [https://doi.org/10.1177/0263276409349275]

MOHAMEDBHAI, G. 2014. Massification in Higher Education Institutions in Africa: Causes, Consequences and Responses. *International Journal of African Higher Education*, 1:59-83. [https://doi.org/10.6017/ijahe.v1i1.5644]

MORROW, W. 2007. *Learning to Teach in South Africa*. HSRC Press: Cape Town.

MORROW, W. 1994. Entitlement and achievement in education. *Studies in Philosophy and Education*, 13:33-47. [https://doi.org/10.1007/BF01074084]

MULLER, J. 2009. Forms of knowledge and curriculum coherence. *Journal of Education and Work*, 22(3):205-226. [https://doi.org/10.1080/13639080902957905]

NIXON, E.; SCULLION, R. & HEARN, R. 2016. Her majesty the student: marketised higher education and the narcissistic (dis)satisfactions of the student-consumer. *Studies in Higher Education*, 43(6):927-943. [https://doi.org/10.1080/03075079.2016.1196353]

PANDOR, N. 2019. Contested meanings of transformation in Higher Education in Post-Apartheid South Africa. Unpublished PhD thesis. The University of Pretoria.

PATHER, R. 2016. Students in New York rise up in solidarity with #FeesMustFall. *Mail & Guardian*, 18 October. [https://mg.co.za/article/2016-10-18-students-in-new-york-rise-up-in-solidarity-with-feesmustfall]

PINAR, W. 2016. What knowledge is of most use? The question of undergraduate curriculum reform. In: M.A. Samuel, R. Dunpath & N. Amin (eds). *Disrupting Higher Education Curriculum. Undoing Cognitive Damage*. Rotterdam: Sense Publishers, 133-152. [https://doi.org/10.1007/978-94-6300-896-9_9]

QUINN, L. 2012. Introduction. In: L. Quinn (ed). *Re-imagining academic staff development: Spaces for disruption*. Stellenbosch: African Sun Media. [https://doi.org/10.18820/9781920338879]

RSA (REPUBLIC OF SOUTH AFRICA). 1997. *Higher Education Act 101 of 1997*. Pretoria: Government Printing Works.

SHORE, C. & WRIGHT, S. 1999. Audit Culture and Anthropology: Neo-Liberalism in British Higher Education. *Journal of the Royal Anthropological Institute*, 5(4):557-575. [https://doi.org/10.2307/2661148]

SHRIVASTAVA, M. & SHRIVASTAVA, S. 2014. Political economy of higher education: comparing South Africa to trends in the world. *Higher Education*, 67:809-822. [https://doi.org/10.1007/s10734-013-9709-6]

SNOWBALL, J.D. 2014. Using interactive content and online activities to accommodate diversity in a large first-year class. *Higher Education*, 67:823-838. [https://doi.org/10.1007/s10734-013-9708-7]

SINGH, M. 2014. Higher Education and the Public Good: Precarious Potential? In: R. Munck, L. McIlrath, B. Hall & R. Tandon (eds). *Higher Education and Community-Based Research: Creating a Global Vision*. New York: Palgrave Macmillan US, 199-216. [https://doi.org/10.1057/9781137385284_14]

SUTHERLAND, K.A. 2018. Holistic academic development: Is it time to think more broadly about the Academic development project? *International Journal for Academic Development*, 23:261-273. [https://doi.org/10.1080/1360144X.2018.1524571]

TopUniversities. 2015. Guide to Types of University in the US. TopUniversities.com [https://bit.ly/2mqJazi]

UKuni. 2019. Types of UK universities. UKuni.com [https://www.ukuni.net/articles/types-uk-universities]

Vorster, J. & Quinn, L. 2017. The 'decolonial turn': What does it mean for academic staff development. *Education as Change*, 21(1):31-49. [https://doi.org/10.17159/1947-9417/2017/853]

Wheelahan, L 2010. *Why Knowledge Matters in Curriculum. A Social Realist Argument*. London: Routledge.

Young, M. 2014. Powerful knowledge as a curriculum principle. In: M. Young, D. Lambert, C. Roberts & M. Roberts (eds). *Knowledge and the future school: curriculum and social justice*. London: Bloomsbury Academic, 65-88.

Young, M. 2011. Curriculum theory: What it is and why it's important. *Cadernos de Pesquisa*, 44(151):191-201. [https://doi.org/10.1590/198053142851]

CHAPTER 2

Decolonising the curriculum

Recontextualisation, identity and self-critique in a post-apartheid university

Kathy Luckett, Shannon Morreira
& Mohini Baijnath

> To see is not the same as to look. You can look without seeing. And it is not clear that what one sees is in fact what is. But looking and seeing have in common the fact that they solicit judgment, enclosing what is seen or the person who is not seen in inextricable networks of meaning – the beams of history ... the colonial gaze also serves as the very veil that hides this truth. Power in the colony therefore consists fundamentally in the power to see or not to see, to remain indifferent, to render invisible what one wishes not to see ...
> (Mbembe, 2017:111)

Introduction

This chapter is written from the context of South African higher education post the student protests of 2015–2017. The student movement critiqued our university for the racism of its institutional culture and for the Eurocentrism of its curricula – which students demanded should be "decolonised". This chapter responds to this criticism and also more generally to the "decolonial turn" in the literature on higher education, that has been taken up in South African universities (Heleta, 2016; Mbembe, 2016; Le Grange, 2016). The authors are two white female academics and a black female student whose master's thesis in sociology (reported on here) was supervised by the two academics (2015–2017). The data referred to in this chapter was collected from academics in the Faculty of Humanities (which comprises Arts and Social Sciences) at the University of Cape Town (UCT), the historically white university where the #RhodesMustFall protests first irrupted in 2015. The chapter also draws on our own experience as academic developers working on curriculum development in the Faculty from our location in the Humanities Education Development Unit at UCT. Our deliberations, therefore, focus particularly on what the implications of the students' demand for decolonising the curriculum might mean for curriculum development in the Humanities in a South African university.

The chapter begins with a brief analysis of the policy context of South African higher education since 1994. We then highlight in more detail the student demands as they related to curriculum reform and some examples of academics' responses derived from the findings from our small case study in the Humanities Faculty at UCT. In the third section, we present what we consider to be the key concepts for our purposes here, from the corpus of decolonial theory. In the fourth and main section on curriculum theory and practice, we work with Bernstein's (2000) "regulative discourse" as a concept that might shed light on where to locate and unpack the traces of "coloniality" that black students experience. We track the theme of coloniality through Bernstein's three fields of the pedagogic device: knowledge-as-research, knowledge-as-curriculum, knowledge-as-student-understanding(2000). We then take a more in-depth look at the regulative discourse in relation to students' accusations of "whiteness" to show how this could be working to undermine institutional conditions for learning. We conclude with a call to self-critique and the implications of critique for practice. In this regard, in the Appendix, we provide a set of questions as points of departure for undertaking a self-critique of curriculum practice – both as designed and as enacted in the classroom.

Policy context

Ever since the White Paper on the Transformation of Higher Education (RSA DoE, 1997), South African institutions of higher education have been under pressure from the state to transform. However, as Lange (2017) argues, the neoliberal framing of new higher education policies led to a focus on the production of high skills for employability and economic growth in the global market and a failure to deal adequately with the social and cultural legacies of the apartheid regime. Over the past two decades state policy interventions have focused on improving access and the efficiency and outcomes of the system, using planning, funding and quality assurance as mechanisms to steer the system (Luckett, 2010). Education Development policy, as enacted through the Foundation Grant, has continued to focus on providing access to first-generation black students (who formed the majority of the student protestors) and to improve their retention and success rates mostly through pedagogic interventions located in separate state-funded extended degree structures. Despite the state's rejection of a proposal for a more flexible undergraduate degree structure (CHE, 2013a), some progress towards transformation has been made with respect to access, enrolments, student composition and financial aid (CHE, 2013b; Luckett & Shay, 2017). But the mainstream curriculum – what gets taught and how – has remained mostly untouched, ring-fenced as the domain of disciplinary expertise and often defended by the liberal ideology of academic freedom (Baijnath, 2017). Inherited institutional cultures, including approaches to curriculum development, the language of learning and teaching and academic development programmes remain based on assimilationist models and hegemonic norms. These models reproduce "colonial difference" in that they misrecognise (Fraser, 2009) black students' social and cultural capital; positioning them as "disadvantaged", "underprepared" and in need of development (Luckett & Naicker, 2016). These models place the onus on black students to "catch up" and overcome their structurally induced educational and cultural "deficits". Such institutional norms have not gone unnoticed by students (Sebidi & Morreira, 2017), and particularly in the historically white universities, this is the situation against which students were protesting. According to Badat (2017:8-9):

> The presence of black students and black staff has not translated into genuine respect for difference, into significant appreciation of diversity, into meaningful linguistic, social, cultural and academic inclusion.

The data presented in this chapter suggests that there is serious theoretical, political and empirical work to be done to provide "points of departure" and set up dialogical spaces where radical curriculum and pedagogic decolonisation work can be undertaken. In a recent address, Badat (2017:19) notes:

> While transformation efforts have to be informed by research and robust scholarly and intellectual debates, they have to ultimately realize concrete and perceptible changes in the curricula of disciplines and fields.

This chapter seeks to address the gap between abstract decolonial and curriculum theories and work on the ground with academics and students that institutionalises concrete changes at programme, course and classroom levels.

A curriculum development context close-up

In 2015, soon after its formation, #RhodesMustFall (RMF) defined itself as:

> ... a collective movement of students and staff mobilising for direct action against the reality of institutional racism at the University of Cape Town ... The fall of Rhodes is symbolic for the inevitable fall of white supremacy and privilege at our campus.
>
> (RMF, 2015)

When RMF students first began to protest against the institutional culture at the university, they released a list of long-term goals (RMF, 2015) that was circulated amongst University management, staff, students and beyond, via social and formal media. The list began with calls for shifts in the material and institutional culture of the University before moving to the curriculum. The fourth goal on the list was to implement a curriculum which critically centres Africa and the subaltern. By this, they meant treating African discourses as the point of departure *through addressing not only content, but languages and methodologies of education and learning* – and only examining Western traditions in so far as they are relevant to our own experience (RMF, 2015) (emphasis not in original).

RMF also called for the university to "Introduce a curriculum and research scholarship linked to social justice and the experiences of black people" (Goal 10) and to "Improve academic support programs" (Goal 11). This comprehensive list of 28 long-term goals was thus fairly explicit concerning the sort of work the institution needed to do. Over time, however, the shorthand of "decolonised, free education" began to be used by the student protests nationally to refer to the above, quite diverse, set of issues; and to refer to a complex body of decolonial theory imported from other subaltern parts of the world (discussed further below). University management, too, took on the shorthand of "decolonised education". In 2017, the Humanities Faculty at UCT, for example, sent out a call to all departments asking that they submit documentation to show how they were, or were not, engaged in the process of "decolonising curricula and pedagogy". It quickly became apparent, from our position as members of Faculty and as members of an academic development unit, that academics across the University were not clear on what exactly was meant by such a call. Some departments explicitly called out the Faculty for not providing some framework to guide curriculum issues in a highly politicised space. From the Humanities Education Development Unit, we established in 2015 a National Research Foundation funded project and Working Group called "Decolonising Pedagogy in the Humanities", which comprised course conveners, teaching assistants, tutors and student representatives to think through how to respond to the student protests.

As part of this project on decolonising the Humanities and Social Science curriculum, the authors conducted fifteen interviews with academic staff at the university, to explore the effects of the student movement on academics' teaching practices (including curriculum and pedagogy). Respondents were chosen on the basis that they taught in the Humanities Faculty and were permanent members of academic staff who could be expected to enact longer-term curriculum change. The interviews were conducted with academics from a wide range of disciplines and with diverse demographic characteristics. The sample was small, as the aim was to collect detailed data to enable qualitative depth around how issues of decolonisation were understood and what, if any, changes were being enacted. We thus do not draw conclusions about the general population of lecturers broadly, but instead, use the experiences and opinions of those interviewed as a means of engaging with broader issues facing curriculum reform. This research, in turn, was used as a platform to engage with departments going forward and to provide us with points of departure for further discussions around curriculum change.

The key findings from this set of interviews, and more extensive participatory research carried out as part of the Working Group's research showed that there was little to no consensus on what decolonisation might mean. Some academics struggled to reconcile ideas of academic freedom with external demands for change through student protests. During the protest period politics came to the fore for staff as well as students, and in some cases, acted as an inhibitory mechanism for change. Few academics had a sufficient grasp of either curriculum theory or decolonial theory with which to attempt radical curriculum reform.

One of the interview questions asked lecturers to explain what they understood by the concept of "decolonising the curriculum", and what decolonised knowledge would look like to them. Nine of the fourteen participants spoke about the inherent complexities of "decolonising". When asked about what decolonisation meant to them, answers varied. One white, middle-aged, male lecturer acknowledged the complexity of the idea but said that he "was not yet sure that it was a coherent one", while a second white male lecturer was afraid of the sorts of intellectual policing it might lead to, such that some texts were viewed as "good" and others as "bad". He saw the need for curriculum reform as being one of uncovering the histories of debates in the discipline, such that "we expose ourselves to debates that have happened in other parts of the world, our part of the world, and let's see how people have thought about it. And that to me, I don't know if it's decolonising, but it's showing the workings of how a curriculum came to be what it is."

Overall, the responses of the lecturers showed very different conceptions of what decolonising the curriculum might entail. There was thus little consensus amongst lecturers on how one might apply decolonial principles, or even what those principles were. Lecturers found themselves entangled in a plethora of expectations, with a vague, contested view of what progressive, decolonised knowledge might be. Lecturers were also unsure of the efficacy of calls to shift the curriculum. A black non-South African male commented on what he saw happening as a result of calls to decolonise thus: "You remember how in feminism they would say 'add a little gender and stir', and you have your gender perspective? You could also say 'add a little blackness and stir', and then you have your new curriculum. So, most efforts now are laughable because it's more like a knee-jerk reaction."

Nonetheless, RMF (see Mangcu, Kasibe & Hendricks, 2015) played an essential role in igniting conversations in the public sphere and within the university space about decolonisation. Some lecturers saw this impact as positive, and some as negative. A white female lecturer perceived the movement as positive in that it affected "the way we teach, what we're assessing, how we're assessing, the kinds of conversations we're having with students". She was not, however, able to give concrete details of pedagogical shifts. Another positive reaction came from a black female lecturer who had used the moment to explicitly incorporate decolonial theories into her curriculum as a means of reflecting on the history of her discipline. For some academics, however, RMF did not necessarily introduce anything new but instead gave public impetus to changes that were already occurring. For example, one respondent, a black male lecturer, said that RMF had had little impact on his curriculum, because "I think that the kinds of issues that they raised were things that I already taught". For some, then, decolonisation was already happening (see also Morreira, 2017), and for others the debates raised by RMF had a negative impact. One white female lecturer argued that student protests had brought identity politics to the fore, such that academics felt that what they were teaching, or how they were teaching it, was not as important as the identity students had ascribed to them in their classes. A white male argued that academic freedom was under threat, in that the calls to decolonise took agency away from academics and demanded that they speak and teach from a particular political position.

Respondents also highlighted the tensions and contradictions of attempting to decolonise knowledge at the University within the framework of institutional norms, that dictated multiple constraints upon lecturers. A white female lecturer, for example, stated that the time constraints she was forced to deal with daily meant that trying to keep up with what was going on in the daily administration of her department while simultaneously re-developing her curriculum was almost impossible. A black female lecturer explained that a significant challenge was to tailor lectures to the assigned forty-five minutes. Time constraints also meant that she did not have time to think about creative curriculum development. A black male lecturer made the point that in developing a new course, one needed weeks of preparation. Yet in a research-intensive institution, if one were to succeed, any time not devoted to teaching needed to be spent on research and not on curriculum development work.

Our work with lecturers and across the faculty more broadly showed an unusual absence in the debates around decolonisation related to the forms of pedagogy that might be used to operationalise decolonial ideas. In their discussions, lecturers emphasised the content of curricula, with little understanding of how different sorts of pedagogical approaches and methods might be employed such that classroom practices – as well as course content – might shift.

Overall, our research suggests that apart from a small minority who claimed to have already decolonised their curricula, the majority of academics interviewed expressed a desire to respond to the decolonising call. But they found themselves caught in an ambivalent space where they lacked institutional support and adequate knowledge of both decolonial and curriculum theory to act decisively in changing their curriculum practice.

It has to be acknowledged that the "ambivalent space" experienced by most of the white academics in the UCT study (and probably by many white academic development staff as well) about becoming agents of decolonisation is unlikely to be resolved quickly. For, as we will see, decolonial theory gives epistemic privilege to the lived experience of subordinated groups, meaning that academics from privileged strata, by definition, are not seen as authentic agents of decolonisation (UCT, 2018). In a recent insightful paper on the implications of the decolonial turn for academic staff development,

Vorster and Quinn (2017) suggest that academics' sense of uncertainty and ambivalence (referred to above) may lie in the contradictory situational logics in which people find themselves. For example, pressure on academics to function in a global publication market and at the same time teach in ways that are responsive to local contexts or where long-held ideas about academic freedom are inconsistent with political pressure to "decolonise". Writing from a place of ambivalence, we recognise that, initially at least, white academics must accept our status as outsiders with limited agency in the decolonising project. As such, one might hope to be invited to listen in and learn from others' conversations about how to decolonise the University. In the meantime, we argue in this chapter that a constructive first step for white academics might be to heighten our capacities for self-critique and reflexivity about the production of our subjectivities, our theoretical frameworks and their assumed worldviews and attendant educational practices. But first, we summarise some key concepts from decolonial and curriculum theory.

A decolonial perspective on curriculum

Our data above shows there is little consensus on the part of academics attempting to operationalise decolonisation. The "decolonial turn" in South African universities has drawn on an extensive literature on decoloniality, but not all academic staff are well versed in it. In what follows, we discuss the ways in which reading of more recent decolonial theory can assist in understanding what operationalising the call to "decolonise the curriculum" might entail.

Decolonisation has presented several manifestations between the twentieth and the twenty-first centuries. The wave of decolonial theory that arose in the 1980s out of reflection on Latin American political and cultural realities focused on the politics of knowledge production rather than on the attainment of political sovereignty. It is this Latin American thread of decolonial thinking that we find most useful for thinking through the implications of curriculum reform in the present moment. Recent decolonial thinkers such as Nelson Maldonado-Torres (2005, 2011) and Walter Mignolo (2006, 2011) argue that, while colonialism – the temporal period of political oppression that ended with the coming about of majority rule in former colonies – has ended, coloniality, a concomitant set of epistemological and ideological positions, has remained in the present. Thus, we must make an important distinction between decolonisation – a mostly political and territorial project – and decoloniality – a primarily ideological and epistemological one.

To decolonial thinkers coloniality and modernity are deeply entangled: decolonial thinkers argue that modernity is predicated upon coloniality, and that one product of modernity has been the creation and maintenance of a "colonial matrix of power" (Mignolo, 2012:ix) consisting of interrelated forms of control such as patriarchy, racism, knowledge, authority, and the economy, which underlie Western civilisation. In decolonial theory and crucially important for the South African context, the ideology of race and the violent, destructive practices of racism are viewed as constitutive of modernity. Given the enduring legacy of coloniality, a key concept in decolonial theory is that of "modernity/coloniality" – meaning that because colonialism was constitutive of modernity (its "darker side") – the two concepts must be held together to describe a single power system that historically has served the demands of capitalist accumulation and the interests of whites/Europeans (Quijano, 2007; Escobar, 2010). Modernity/coloniality continues to be manifest through an entangled set of hierarchies that work intersectionally through global class formations of the core/periphery world system; through racial-gender social hierarchies that privilege Western, heterosexual, patriarchy and in Westernised universities through the domination of knowledge production by the West.

Decolonial theorists apply the concept of modernity/coloniality to the politics of knowledge production, and they see the same patterns of power working to determine who produces knowledge, who owns it and who legitimates it. Gordon (2014) is critical of how, historically, knowledge has been colonised and centralised by Europe in ways that validated only one form of knowledge, not only delegitimating the knowledges of others; but undermining the very conditions for epistemic life (Gordon, 2014:85). He critiques modern epistemology for colonising reason, for attempting to confine thought within its rational system when reality always exceeds the bounds of any epistemology. He thus rejects the "self-justificatory standards" of the West against which all others are to be measured (2014:89). Thus, a key decolonial critique is that knowledge produced in the West has been universalised as the only legitimate form of knowledge. Grosfoguel (2013) argues that the modern episteme has been institutionalised and universalised through the modern university system, the modern disciplines and the five hegemonic (ex-colonial) European languages (2013:74). The work of decoloniality then is to disrupt these forms of global power that place European thought as universal and therefore as the only legitimate form of knowledge.

Student protests have drawn on this high-level decolonial theory in their critiques. These decolonial perspectives do important work in theorising the relationship between knowledge and power in "modernity/coloniality", including asserting the possibility and legitimacy of Southern knowledges produced by subalternised subjects. However, data from our small-scale research project suggests that for many academics, "decolonising the curriculum" is not seen as a project of undoing the matrices of modernity, and of attempting to re-think the neoliberal, supposedly post-colonial, university structure in deeper ways. Instead, some academics saw the decolonial turn as political pressure from above and below, which threatened their autonomy, while others saw it as the addition of "blackness" to curriculum content. Overwhelmingly, what our research shows is that academics are currently conceiving of curriculum reform as a reform of what is being taught. The broader structures of power are not being interrogated. We argue that a decolonial reading of the failure of South African historically white universities to transform since 1994 is because the transformation policy discourse and practice is framed by a modernising developmentalist episteme that fails to hold modernity and coloniality together as a mutually constitutive concept. Universities have been encouraged to respond to the demands of global capitalism within a neo-liberal frame that occludes the need to properly attend to the legacy of colonialism and apartheid. This has allowed the old apartheid deficit model of curriculum to continue, whereby first-generation black students are positioned as "problems" – "disadvantaged" and "underprepared" for university study. Instead of institutional adaptation, the advantaged middle-class white student has remained the norm, the curriculum's "imaginary student". Student protests have attempted to interrupt this episteme, but our case study research suggests that most academics do not have adequate curriculum theory, decolonial theory or, indeed, time at their disposal to enact the radical curriculum reform entailed in the RMF long-term goals. We now turn to curriculum theory, selectively, to see which concepts may be helpful in thinking through how to operationalise the decolonial critique that modernity and coloniality are mutually constitutive.

Interrogating the recontextualisation of curriculum knowledge

We are interested in theorisations of curriculum that shed light on unpacking the concept modernity/coloniality for curriculum practice to respond to students' demand for "a curriculum [...] linked to social justice and the experiences of black people" (RMF, 2015). While it is evident that the curriculum of the modern university delivers access to forms of modernity, what is less obvious, especially in a post-colonial university, is where and how this curriculum also carries traces of "coloniality" (modernity's "darker side"). Given that the curriculum is one of the most formative aspects of the student experience, why do many black students at our university perceive the curriculum to be socially unjust and unrelated to the black experience? What are students learning from our curriculum and what are its unintended outcomes?

Following world systems neo-Marxist theory, the decolonial theorists assume a conflict theory of society on a global scale (North v. South, West v. East, coloniser v. colonised, and so on). They then apply this grand narrative about the inequality and injustice of the global political economy to the production and control of knowledge by the West. Thus, if the decolonial theorists were to theorise education systems, they would likely follow the well-trodden path of social reproduction theories but apply these on a global scale. These theories of education, initially developed as internal critiques of class-based societies in the metropoles where systems are seen to work to serve the interests of dominant classes, reproducing the social hierarchies and inequalities of society from one generation to the next. Reproduction theories tend to be stronger on critique than on mapping out how human agency might interrupt reproductive cycles and work for change. But the decolonial theorists suggest taking the experience of subaltern groups as the starting point for analysis in the social sciences (Gordon, 2014). This means taking what black students say about their experience of the curriculum very seriously and using this as a point of departure for our analysis.

In the quest to understand how modernity/coloniality works through modern higher education systems in post-colonial contexts, we decided to critically appropriate some of Bernstein's (2000) concepts from his theory of the "pedagogic device". He too, as a neo-Marxist working from the 1960s to the late 1990s, used a class-based analysis to critique the UK schooling system; but he also theorised the internal "social biases" of the curriculum to find out how to interrupt the "education as social reproduction" cycle described above.

> Education is central to the knowledge base of society, groups and individuals. Yet education also ... is a public institution, central to the production and reproduction of distributive injustices. Biases in the form, content, access and opportunities of education have consequences not only for the economy; these biases can reach down to drain the very springs of affirmation, motivation and imagination. In this way, such biases can become, and often are, an economic and cultural threat to democracy. Education can have a crucial role to play in creating tomorrow's optimism in the context of today's pessimism. But if it is to do this, then we must have an analysis of the social biases in education. These biases lie deep within the very structure of the educational system's processes of transmission and acquisition and their social assumptions.
>
> (Bernstein, 2000:xix)

Bernstein looks at how education institutions transform knowledge through three stages or levels, knowledge-as-research; knowledge-as-curriculum; and knowledge-as-student-understanding (Ashwin, 2009). Regarding the first, knowledge-as-research, we have already noted that epistemology and knowledge production are the focus of the decolonial theorists who are critical of how knowledge production is complicit in reinforcing and prolonging the power relations of coloniality based on notions of European supremacy and "colonial difference". The decolonial theorists would undoubtedly critique Bernstein as a modernist, for he understood the school to offer pupils a (modern) identity and role independent of that provided by their local traditions, community and family socialisation (Gamble & Hoadley, 2011) through offering them access to abstract, decontextualised forms of school knowledge which he privileged over contextualised local knowledge. However, it is aspects of his conceptualisation of knowledge-as-curriculum that we wish to bring into conversation with decolonial theory and re-work.

Regarding knowledge-as-curriculum, Bernstein (2000) shows how the powerful have the resources (economic, political, and cultural) to set the rules for what counts as legitimate curriculum knowledge. As well as being shaped by knowledge-as-research – disciplinary expertise and power – curriculum knowledge is constituted by a range of contingent forces and contexts (called "recontextualising rules") such as national policy, professional bodies, institutional norms and rules, and the worldviews, beliefs and assumptions of individual teachers or academics. These "recontextualising rules" all influence how curricula in the modern university are constructed and ultimately how student performance is evaluated and assessed. This means understanding curriculum as a highly ideological hybrid discourse, "a space where ideology can play" (Bernstein, 2000:32), which is far removed from the discourses of knowledge-as-research.

Bernstein (2000) makes an analytic distinction between the "instructional discourse" of a curriculum (the cognitive order, the overt content and skills taught) and its "regulative discourse" (the social and moral order[1] and ways of being) that underpin it. This analytic distinction between the instructional (explicit) and regulative (mostly implicit) discourses of the curriculum is useful for our purposes. Our case study data suggests that academics tend

---

1   Again, the decolonialists would critique Bernstein for the modernising content he gave to his theory of the regulative, namely, following Durkheim, he saw the culture and rituals of the schools as a means of inculcating in pupils respect for impersonal authority and the law, that would be internalised as the self-discipline required for dutiful and responsible citizenship (Gamble & Hoadley, 2011).

to focus on and foreground the instructional discourse, the content of their curricula, while the regulative discourse (its norms and cultural and ontological assumptions) remains largely taken-for-granted and therefore opaque to them. Whereas for subaltern (black) students it is the other way round – they clearly see the regulative discourse (its norms and linguistic, cultural and ontological assumptions – which they experience as excluding and alienating), while the instructional discourse often remains opaque to them, inaccessible and hard to grasp due to wrong assumptions by academics about their levels of English language proficiency and prior learning.

For the rest of the chapter, we work with the concept of the regulative discourse which we suggest is the space where the "coloniality" of the curriculum, as experienced by black students, is most likely to be located. Despite its importance for decolonising the curriculum, we do not deal here with the instructional discourse because this is where to date most discussion and debate has focused, whereas the regulative tends to remain hidden, especially from those in positions of power.

Interrogating the pedagogisation of curriculum knowledge

We now move from knowledge-as-curriculum to knowledge-as-student-understanding linked to pedagogic practice, the third level of the pedagogic device. As implied above, academics are the key agents of recontextualising knowledge (curriculum design) and also of pedagogising knowledge (teaching), which is intended to lead to learning (knowledge-as-student-understanding). But as noted above, given their identity as disciplinary experts, academics tend to focus on the instructional discourse (curriculum content) and often fail to understand how the regulative discourse of their curriculum and teaching practice enables or disables learning. Bernstein tells us that pedagogic practice is constituted by "evaluative rules" – what matters and in what ways – which form the criteria against which we judge students. Important for our argument is the point that when we assess students we are assessing both the instructional and the regulative discourses of our curricula (in practice, it is one discourse).

This suggests that when we assess students, we are not only marking the cognitive content of their answers, but are also judging them based on all that is culturally arbitrary and contingent in the curriculum, for example, the degree to which their work meets the grammatical standards of native speakers of English. In post-colonial contexts, the continued dominance of colonial languages and cultures in the modern university and the delegitimisation of those of previously colonised peoples, continues to work as a severe social bias that "lie[s] deep within the very structure of the educational system's processes" of teaching and learning (Bernstein, 2000:xix). The enduring and much-lamented discrepancy between student performance when disaggregated by race in the South African higher education system (CHE, 2015) suggests that it may be this bias, the "coloniality" of the curriculum, that serves to reproduce rather than interrupt the social inequalities of society.

If we regard "curriculum" as including "knowledge-as-student-understanding", then we need to understand better how students learn. So, what do we know about learning? For our purposes we highlight here understandings of learning as a fundamentally relational, participatory, social practice. We are all embodied social beings: in a post-colonial context usually embedded in multiple systems of signification on which we depend for languages and ways of being. Learning depends on particular social contexts to generate semiotic and linguistic interaction leading to shared meaning-making and hence to the cognitive and personal development of the individuals concerned (Packer & Goicoechea, 2000).

Regarding learning, it is noteworthy that the evaluative rules constitute not only the criteria for the formal assessment of learning but also criteria for how teachers informally signal their approval or disapproval, recognition or misrecognition of who students are and how they behave and interact in the classroom (this is the regulative discourse in operation). Thus, the question to be asked is to what extent do the regulative discourses of our institutions, curricula and classrooms create hospitable shared contexts where all students feel affirmed, recognised and a sense of belonging that permits them to contribute, participate and learn? How far do we share language, culture, intersubjectivities, interpretive horizons and frames of reference with our students? To what extent is the inter-subjective mediation of our semiotic and linguistic interactions around curriculum knowledge accessible, open and explicit to all students? These are crucial questions because without social affirmation and sufficient intersubjectivity between teacher and learner, the conditions for learning will not obtain – students will not access curriculum knowledge, find a voice to participate in meaning-making and become epistemic agents (Thayer-Bacon, 1997). All persons need to develop a sense of self and a voice through our relationships with others; until this occurs, we cannot become social actors or knowers (Archer, 2003). If students and academics are not enabled to develop a "sense of self" in a learning environment, they will feel excluded and alienated; leading to demotivation, demoralisation and loss of the "will to learn". When this happens, we suggest that it is here – in these (failed or absent) interpersonal relationships, where there is a lack of inter-subjectivity between lecturers and students – that the micro-practices of misrecognition and exclusion occur, that is, traces of coloniality. Where this situation pertains across an institution, it could be a significant contributing factor to poor academic performance by black students and to their sense of outrage. In post-settler societies such as ours, this situation can easily be worded in terms of race and "whiteness" – fuelling anxiety, mistrust and fear.

Self-critique as a point of departure

In a post-colonial university such as ours, it is unlikely that anyone still subscribes to the much-vilified 18th century notions of biological "racial purity" that evolved from social Darwinism. It is a well-known fact that this ideology of race was used during the colonial and imperial eras to produce a colonial identity based on the production of otherness as racial difference; while the suppression, degradation and demonisation of the other was used to legitimate European superiority and normative violence against colonised peoples (Monahan, 2011). However, in contemporary societies, Charles Mills defines "whiteness" as an "epistemology of ignorance, a cognitive dysfunction … that prevents white people from understanding the world they themselves have made" (Mills, 2007:14). Along similar lines, Alcoff (2006) writes about the need for those socially positioned as white to acknowledge that their very perceptions of reality are already affected by being constituted as "white".

In South Africa, identities are still highly "raced" in the collective social imagination meaning that whether we like it or not, a racialised social reality conditions our subjectivities; we cannot avoid the attribution of raced identities (Monahan, 2011). In this context, we want to suggest that the assertion of "blackness" on historically white campuses by black students and staff may be a consequence of their misrecognition and silencing by "whiteness". If this is the case, then we could view the return of identity politics to South African campuses as a healthy form of insurrection, a project of affirmation and recognition and a means of reclaiming agency by subordinated groups to correct ongoing social and epistemic injustices. In South Africa, we have yet to learn to work together to understand when it is appropriate to form solidarity groups within difference and when it is appropriate to work across difference.

For academic staff, these theorisations of "whiteness" reinforce our assertion about the opacity of the regulative discourses that underpin our curricula.

All of this suggests that self-critique, based on listening to others, especially black students and staff, maybe a good point of departure for "decolonising the curriculum". For it is subalterns who are well placed to see and critique the norms and assumptions made by those in power in the university. Those situated within a dominant position need the perspectives of "others" to help see their own cultures and the production of our subjectivities. Without romanticising the views of black students, white academics and academic developers must nonetheless carefully attend to students' grievances and their opinions on how the curriculum undermines their sense of self.

Going deeper, we could look at the historical production of white subjectivities and identities; at how these affect the perceptions, of the normative frames and the interpretive horizons from which white academics interact with students. As academics, we could ask ourselves how we see and interpret others and how they see and interpret us – and how this impacts our teaching practice. We could also think about our rationales for our legitimacy and authority as lecturers, as academic developers, and as disciplinary experts.

Implications for teaching practice

Finally, what might all of this imply for teaching practice? Clearly, it means the creation of safe, caring and respectful classroom spaces that can generate learning. However, we want to stress that the onus is on academics' "hegemonic ear" to listen and respond to black students' evaluations and moral reasoning about the regulative discourse of the curriculum and how it affects their sense of agency and becoming. Secondly, we think it is essential to put out for discussion with students the norms and assumptions of our regulative discourses. For example, we could declare up-front our social positioning and discuss its effects in the classroom. We could acknowledge how we all speak from particular historicised perspectives; we are always someone else's "other". In doing so, we could begin to take responsibility for how "coloniality" and other relations of power have played out historically in constituting our subjectivities (Monahan, 2011).

Ironically, as noted by some of our respondents, modernity's objectification and calculations of time, space and human performance militate against making time and space in the curriculum for this kind of interpersonal work. Modernity's imposition of market, auditing and individualistic values on the modern university have encroached the space for dealing with coloniality (Mbembe, 2016).

Conclusion: Curriculum as critical social practice

The curriculum is a highly ideological hybrid discourse that includes implicit ways of knowing, ways of doing and ways of being, as well as content. In this chapter, we have suggested that academics typically frame their responses to calls for curriculum reform in terms of only curriculum content, that is, the instructional discourse. We have further argued, however, that a key location where "coloniality" might reside in the curriculum is not merely in content, but in the regulative discourse – in the sets of (often implicit or tacit) rules and practices that accompany what we teach, that are themselves underpinned by a particular normative and social positionings, subjectivities and interpretive horizons. In South Africa, because of a history of settler colonialism, this normative and social positioning has been racialised in a very particular way; and is thus sometimes referred to in student critiques through the shorthand term of "whiteness". It is not useful, therefore, for white academics to argue that their practices are not intentionally or explicitly racial. Instead, we could begin by recognising that what is perceived as "whiteness" might be located in the regulative discourses of our curricula and teaching practices, and that we need to think carefully and reflexively through ways to interrupt regulative practices that are seen by our students as limiting and damaging. Learning is a fundamentally interactive social practice: where there is no shared intersubjectivity between the student and the taught curriculum, the student will fail to learn. We have thus presented a series of questions in the Appendix to encourage academics and academic developers to unearth some dimensions of the regulative discourses that may be entangled in curricula, such that the "how" as well as the "what" can be thought through self-critically as a first practical step towards "decolonising" our curricula.

References

ALCOFF, L.M. 2006. *Visible Identities: Race, Gender, and the Self*. Oxford: Oxford University Press. [https://doi.org/10.1093/0195137345.001.0001]

ARCHER, M.S. 2003. *Structure, Agency and the Internal Conversation*. Cambridge: Cambridge University Press. [https://doi.org/10.1017/CBO9781139087315]

ASHWIN, P. 2009. *Analysing Teaching-Learning Interactions in Higher Education: Accounting for Structure and Agency*. New York: Continuum.

BADAT, S. 2017. Trepidation, longing, and belonging: Liberating the curriculum at universities in South Africa. Public Lecture Series: Curriculum Transformation Matters: The Decolonial Turn, 10 April. Pretoria: University of Pretoria. [https://doi.org/10.13140/RG.2.2.31255.57765]

BAIJNATH, M. 2017. Engaging with Transformation of the Humanities Curriculum at an English-medium Research-intensive South African University: Decolonisation and Academic Agency in an Era of Uncertainty. M SocSci thesis, University of Cape Town.

Bernstein, B. 2000. *Pedagogy, Symbolic control and Identity: Theory, research, critique*. Revised Edition. Oxford: Rowman & Littlefield.

CHE (Council on Higher Education). 2013a. A proposal for undergraduate curriculum reform in South Africa: The case for a flexible curriculum structure. Task Team Report: Undergraduate Curriculum Structure, August 2013. Pretoria: CHE. [https://bit.ly/2kGUQO1]

CHE (Council on Higher Education). 2013b. *VitalStats for Public Higher Education 2013*. Pretoria: CHE. [https://bit.ly/2kEgHFL]

Escobar, A. 2010. 'Worlds and Knowledges Otherwise': The Latin American modernity/coloniality Research Program. In: W. Mignolo & A. Escobar (eds). *Globalization and the Decolonial Option*. Abingdon: Routledge, 33-64.

Fraser, N. 2009. *Scales of Justice: Reimagining Political Space in a Globalising World*. New York: Columbia University Press.

Gamble, J. & Hoadley, U. 2011. Positioning the Regulative Order. In: B.D. Ivinson & J. Fitz. *Knowledge and Identity: Concepts and Applications in Bernstein's Sociology*. London: Routledge.

Gordon, L.R. 2014. Disciplinary Decadence and the Decolonisation of Knowledge. *Africa Development*, 39(1):81-92. [https://bit.ly/2kFNJW5]

Grosfoguel, R. 2013. The Structure of Knowledge in Westernized Universities: Epistemic Racism/Sexism and the Four Genocides of the Long 16th Century. *Human Architecture: Journal of the Sociology of Self-Knowledge*, 11(1):73-90. [https://bit.ly/2kTZacG]

Heleta, S. 2016. Decolonisation of Higher Education: Dismantling epistemic violence and Eurocentrism in South Africa. *Transformation in Higher Education*, 1(1):1-8. [https://doi.org/10.4102/the.v1i1.9]

Lange, L. 2017. Twenty Years of Higher Education Curriculum Policy in South Africa. *Journal of Education*, 68:31-57. [https://doi.org/10.17159/10.17159/2520-9868/i68a01]

Le Grange, L. 2016. Decolonising the University Curriculum. *South African Journal of Higher Education*, 30(2):1-12. [https://doi.org/10.20853/30-2-709]

Luckett, K. & Naicker, V. 2019. Responding to misrecognition from a (post)/colonial university. *Critical Studies in Education*, 60(2)1-18. [https://doi.org/10.1080/17508487.2016.1234495]

Luckett, K. & Shay, S. 2017. Reframing the curriculum: a transformative approach. *Critical Studies in Education*, 26 July. [https://doi.org/10.1080/17508487.2017.1356341]

Luckett, K. 2010. A 'Quality Revolution' Constrained? A Critical Reflection on Quality Assurance Methodology from the South African Higher Education Context. *Quality in Higher Education*, 16(1):71-75. [https://doi.org/10.1080/13538321003679556]

Maldonado-Torres, N. 2005. Frantz Fanon and CLR James on Intellectualism and Enlightened Rationality. *Caribbean Studies*, 33(2):149-194. [https://bit.ly/2m29QWF]

Maldonado-Torres, N. 2011. "Thinking Through the Decolonial Turn: Post-continental Interventions, in Theory, Philosophy, and Critique – An Introduction." *Transmodernity: Journal of Peripheral Cultural Production of the Luso-Hispanic World*, 1(2):1-14. [https://escholarship.org/uc/item/59w8j02x]

Mangcu, T.; Kasibe, W. & Hendricks, A. 2015. *UCT: Rhodes must fall*. Facebook page. [https://www.facebook.com/RhodesMustFall/]

Mbembe, A. 2017. *Critique of Black Reason*. Translated by Laurent Dubois. Durham: Duke University Press. [https://doi.org/10.1215/9780822373230]

Mbembe, A. 2016. Decolonising the University: New Directions. *Arts & Humanities in Higher Education*, 15(1):29-45. [https://doi.org/10.1177/1474022215618513]

Mignolo, W. 2012. *Local histories/global designs: Coloniality, subaltern knowledges, and border thinking*. Princeton, New Jersey, USA: Princeton University Press. [https://doi.org/10.1515/9781400845064]

Mignolo, W. 2006. De-linking: Don Quixote, Globalization and the Colonies. *Macalester International*, 17(1):8-17. [https://core.ac.uk/download/pdf/46721797.pdf]

Mills, C. 2007. White Ignorance. In: S. Sullivan & N. Tuana (eds). *Race and Epistemologies of Ignorance*. New York: State University of New York Press, 13-38.

Monahan, M. 2011. *The Creolizing Subject: Race, Reason and the Politics of Purity (Just Ideas)*. New York: Fordham University Press. [https://doi.org/10.5422/fordham/9780823234493.003.0004]

Morreira, S. 2017. Steps Towards Decolonial Higher Education in Southern Africa? Epistemic Disobedience in the Humanities. *Journal of Asian and African Studies*, 52(3):287-301. [https://doi.org/10.1177/0021909615577499]

Packer, M, J. & Goicoechea, J. 2000. Sociocultural and constructivist theories of learning: Ontology, not just Epistemology. *Educational Psychologist*, 35(4):227-241. [https://doi.org/10.1207/S15326985EP3504_02]

Quijano, A. 2007. Coloniality and Modernity/Rationality. *Cultural Studies*, 21(2-3):168-178. [https://doi.org/10.1080/09502380601164353]

RMF (#RhodesMustFall). 2015. UCT Rhodes Must Fall Mission Statement. *The Salon*, 9(6-8). [https://bit.ly/2kEh9DX]

RSA DoE (Republic of South Africa. Department of Education). 1997. Education White Paper 3: A Programme for the Transformation of Higher Education. *Government Gazette*, Notice 1196 of 1997, 24 July.

Sebidi, K. & Morreira, S. 2017. Accessing Powerful Knowledge: A Comparative Study of Two First Year Sociology Courses in a South African University. *Critical Studies in Teaching and Learning* (CriSTaL), 5(2):33-50. [https://bit.ly/2kvuVss]

Thayer-Bacon, B.J. 1997. The Nurturing of a Relational Epistemology. *Educational Theory*, 47(2):239-260. [https://doi.org/10.1111/j.1741-5446.1997.00239.x]

UCT (University of Cape Town). 2018. *Curriculum Change Framework*. Cape Town: UCT.

Vorster, J. & Quinn, L. 2017. The 'Decolonial Turn': What does it mean for Academic Staff Development? *Education as Change*, 21(1):31-49. [https://doi.org/10.17159/1947-9417/2017/853]

Appendix

These questions were developed for use by course teams, including academic development staff, working on new or revised courses in the Humanities Faculty. They are based on discussions that occurred during 2017 in a Working Group called "Decolonising Pedagogy in the Humanities", which comprised course conveners, teaching assistants, tutors and student representatives established by the Humanities Education Development Unit, an academic development unit at UCT, to think through how to respond to the student protests.

i. Knowledge
- How do you view "knowledge"? To what extent is it a product separate from society?
- How self-reflexive is your discipline about its historical development, its dominant paradigms and methodologies, and what epistemological and ontological assumptions are these based on?
- What are the epistemic dialectics and debates that you and your colleagues engage in, who do you read and talk to, who comprises your communities of practice? Who are the peers whom you look to who validate your research? What conferences do you attend, and where do you publish?
- To what extent does your discipline regard the global South and Africa as sites of theoretical production as opposed to application and sites for data-gathering?
- What are the absences and silences in your research field, what issues could it address, but does not and why? To what extent does your field undertake research that addresses the problems and complexities of Southern issues?
- Which researchers in your department engage with the lived experiences of subordinated groups?

ii. Curriculum
- What principles, norms, values and worldviews inform your selection of knowledge for your curriculum? Think about absences as well as presences, centres as well as margins.
- Does your curriculum articulate clearly for students your own intellectual and social position and that of the authors you prescribe?
- For whom do you design your curriculum? Who is the ideal/imagined student that you hold in mind and what assumptions do you make about their backgrounds, culture, languages and schooling?
- How do these assumptions play out in the criteria that you use to assess students?
- How does the current South Africa socio-political context affect your curriculum design choices? How does your curriculum reflect its location in Africa and the global South? To what extent does it draw on subjugated histories, voices, cultures, languages and/or address the meaning of their absences?

- How does your curriculum draw on the critical Humanities to historicise, relativise and deconstruct inherited curricula and dominant worldviews?
- How does your curriculum promote epistemic and social justice?
- How does your curriculum level the playing fields by requiring traditional/ white students to acquire the intellectual and cultural resources to function effectively in a plural society?

iii. Pedagogy

- Do you articulate clearly for your students your own social and intellectual position – from where you speak when lecturing?
- To what extent does your pedagogy avoid compelling all students to become assimilated into dominant practices, dispositions and Western culture? What can you do in your classroom to facilitate inclusion without assuming assimilation?
- What proportion of your class comes from subordinated groups? How does your pedagogy recognise and affirm the agency of black and first-generation students? How does your pedagogy legitimate and respect them, their experiences and cultures and use their languages in the classroom – and for what purposes?
- What delivery methods can you use to move from monological to dialogical teaching methods that might encourage students to learn actively from each other and to produce their own forms of knowledge?
- What can you do to make your assessment practices more fair and valid for all students, without inducing high levels of anxiety and trauma? What assessment methods would play to students' strengths, promoting their agency and creativity?
- What proportion of academics in your department can speak indigenous/ regional languages and relate to the cultures and lived experiences of subordinated groups?

CHAPTER 3

Decolonising university curricula

Reflections on an institutional curriculum review process

Sally Matthews

Introduction

Recent calls by student movements for the decolonisation of university curricula have intensified the pressure on South African universities to transform, and have brought the question of curriculum transformation (or decolonisation) into sharp focus. This chapter describes and reflects upon a curriculum review process introduced at my institution, Rhodes University, to explore what happens when an institution decides to review its curricula. My interest in this topic stems partly from my involvement in heading up the curriculum review process within my department which was undertaken as part of the broader institutional curriculum review. As I watched the curriculum process unfold at my institution, it was striking to me how the original call by student activists for the decolonisation of university curricula was interpreted and acted upon in so many different ways by various actors within the institution.

The reflections to follow grapple with this curriculum review process with the goal of better understanding of how we might approach curriculum review in the context of debates about the decolonisation of university curricula.

The chapter begins with an outline of the context in which calls for curriculum decolonisation took place, followed by a discussion of how to theorise curriculum reform in which I draw on decolonial theory to explore what curriculum decolonisation may entail. I then turn to the question of what happens *on the ground* when academics are pressured into reviewing their curricula. By tracing the curriculum reform process in one faculty at one South African higher education institution, the chapter reveals some of the challenges that arise when academics interpret and respond to calls for curriculum decolonisation. I conclude by reflecting on ways in which academic developers might best facilitate and encourage curriculum review processes. The chapter uses the experiences of one Humanities Faculty at one South African university as an illustration and, as such, my reflections are particularly relevant to those working in the Humanities in South Africa. However, much of the discussion also has relevance for all those interested, more generally, in curriculum transformation.

Context: Calls for decolonised curricula

The years 2015 and 2016 were years of heightened protest at South African higher education institutions. While protest is certainly not an uncommon phenomenon at some South African higher education institutions (particularly historically black institutions), the 2015 and 2016 protests were exceptional in that they included almost all South African higher education institutions and attracted considerable media attention (Badat, 2016; Behari-Leak, 2016; Evans, 2016; Mkhize, 2015; Poho, 2016). During these protests, calls were made for education to be both "free" and "decolonised". The focus of this chapter is on the latter call – the call for education to be "decolonised". While talk about decolonising universities was particularly prominent in 2015–2016 in South Africa, such calls are not new nor are they specific to South Africa. The decolonisation of university curricula was a topic of much debate elsewhere in Africa in the 1960s and 1970s (see, for example, Ngugi, 1995), and has also been highlighted in more recent commentary about the "whiteness" of university curricula at Western universities (see, for example, Hussain, 2015; Peters, 2015). While the question of curriculum decolonisation is thus most obviously pressing in South Africa, it is also of relevance to higher education institutions elsewhere.

In this section of the chapter, I explore what those who called for the decolonisation of university curricula seemed to be asking for – what did they mean when they insisted that the education that they receive, and the institutions that provide it, must be "decolonised"? What were they asking for in terms of changes to the curriculum?

The first thing to note is that there were diverse views about what decolonised education would entail. Although it is possible to pick up certain common themes, it must be acknowledged that various protesting groups used the term in different ways. For example, Langa (2017:10) points out that while students at historically white institutions were principally concerned about their curricula being colonial and alienating to black students, students at the University of Limpopo's concerns about curricula were focused upon a sense that the curricula they receive are not of the same good quality as that offered at the historically white institutions. Thus, calls for the decolonisation of university curricula at the University of Limpopo meant something quite different to what they meant at the University of the Witwatersrand. However, with that proviso, it is possible to identify some of the most common ways in which students articulated and explained their call for education to be decolonised.

One feature that comes through very strongly in student activists' calls for the decolonisation of university education is that the students understood decolonisation as being related to race and racism. When articulating their calls for universities to be decolonised, student activists made it clear that they understood the decolonisation of higher education to mean less dependence on the authority and expertise of white people and more on the authority and expertise of black people. Consider the following claims, all made by student protestors in the context of calling for the decolonisation of South African higher education institutions:

> We study all these dead white men who presided over our oppression, and we are made to use their thinking as a standard and as a point of departure.
> (Athabile Nonxuba, quoted in Evans, 2016)

> ...the task of decolonisation cannot be left to the coloniser. We refuse to let white men take the lead in deciding the fate of black lives. (RMF, 2015)

> We're sick of being taught Eurocentric ideology when there's plenty of perfectly good Afrocentric scholarship on the continent. We don't want a European university in Africa. We want a world-class African university in Africa.
> (Lwazi Samoya, quoted in Foster, 2015)

> ... we are calling for FREE DECOLONISED INTERSECTIONALITY EDUCATION. This is uncontaminated education which speaks to blacks.
> (Anonymous student, quoted in Maringira & Gukurume, 2017:38)

> When we speak about decolonisation, we speak about the curriculum speaking to us, not to white people. (Anonymous student, quoted in Maringira & Gukurume, 2017:39)

> These are white lecturers, teaching us through a white curriculum ... how does this equip a black student who is supposed to be an integral part of the 'Rainbow Nation'?
> (Anonymous student, quoted in Maringira & Gukurume, 2017:39)

> The curriculum being used is old fashion[ed] and has nothing to do with black people.
> (Anonymous student, quoted in Malabela, 2017:114)

Student activists clearly viewed curriculum decolonisation to be closely related to questions of race and racism and linked calls for curriculum decolonisation with calls for the appointment of more black academic staff. This is evident, for example, in the #TransformWits manifesto which lists the "Africanisation of all University Curricula" and the "Africanisation of Academic Staff Contingency" alongside each other when listing the "pillars" of demands (cited in Zidepa, 2015). Similarly, the University of Cape Town #RhodesMustFall Mission Statement accompanies their call for a "curriculum which critically centres Africa and the subaltern" with a call for increased representation of black lecturers (RMF, 2015b). Thus, we cannot interpret the call for decolonisation of the curriculum as simply, or even principally, being about a change in content. Instead, the students making this call clearly interpret it as being related to a change in who is teaching and whose scholarly writing is included in the curriculum and, in so doing, are clear in their demand that greater prominence and authority be given to black scholars.

This brief overview of the context which informs the discussion that follows shows that in this context, attempts to re-imagine the curriculum need to pay careful attention to race and need to avoid focusing principally on content when thinking about curriculum transformation. Instead, we need to ensure that sufficient attention is given to the marginalisation of black scholars in university curricula. It should also be noted that while this chapter relates particularly to the South African context, these concerns around race and the marginalisation of black scholars are certainly not unique to South Africa. As noted above, such concerns have also been raised by student protestors at other African universities and at Western universities (see Ngugi, 1995; Hussain, 2015; Peters, 2015).

Theorising curriculum reform, transformation and decolonisation

When faced with calls to decolonise the curriculum, an obvious starting point is to explore existing theorisation about curriculum reform to see how such theorisation can assist us in responding to these calls. Curriculum theory lays out different approaches to what the curriculum is and to how we should go about developing our curricula. In terms of what is meant by the term "curriculum", there is a range of different ways in which the word is defined. According to Wilson (n.d.), "curriculum" has Latin origins and originally meant "to run a course". In the university context, the word can be used in several different ways. Perhaps, as a starting point, we can define it very widely – Wilson (n.d.), for example, describes it as "anything and everything that teaches a lesson planned or otherwise". If we understand curriculum in such a broad way, then curriculum theory is simply "the interdisciplinary study of educational experience" (Pinar, 2012:2).

This interdisciplinary area of study needs to grapple with the demands made by recent student protestors. As Vorster and Quinn (2017) point out, the "decolonial turn" presents a profound challenge to current approaches to thinking about higher education. They argue that the "discourse of transformation", which has dominated debates about higher education in South Africa has run its course requiring a radical rethinking of our practices. Similarly, Ramrathan (2016) argues that discussions on curriculum transformation in South Africa have focused on "counting numbers", whereas greater attention needs to be given to the "curriculum intellectualism" – we need to move the discussion on curriculum transformation beyond a focus on increasing access and throughput of students. A relevant challenge here is that much writing on curriculum gives insufficient attention to the idea that there might be entire systems of knowledge which have been marginalised in much higher education globally. Paraskeva (2011:152) talks about how there has been a lack of attention given to "cognitive pluralism" and "epistemological diversity". The decolonial turn in higher education studies forces us to go beyond what Paraskeva (2011:152) calls "the Western epistemological platform" to think more about what we teach rather than focusing primarily on how we teach it.

Once we introduce a concern with decolonisation of the curriculum into the discussion, the whole way we approach curriculum reform is likely to shift substantially. This is evident when we look at a key South African document on curriculum reform issued in 2013, the Council on Higher Education's proposal for undergraduate curriculum reform (CHE, 2013). Like current calls for decolonisation, this document shows concern for the well-being and success of students, and issues of equity and redress. Indeed, it begins by quoting an assertion made in Education White Paper 3 (RSA, 1997) on the importance of "equity of access and fair chances of success to all who are seeking to realise their potential through higher education, while eradicating all forms of unfair discrimination and advancing redress for past inequalities" (Education White Paper 3, cited in CHE, 2013).

However, the approach it adopts is very different from the approach of student activists in that it is focused on thinking about how to improve graduate throughput rates – basically on how to get more students to succeed *in accessing the knowledge currently on offer*. Equity is understood in this document in terms of trying to ensure that more students succeed in acquiring the knowledge presently on offer in South African universities, with little critical attention to the nature of that knowledge. In a scathing critique of this proposal, Pinar (2016:145) accuses it of risking being "another reiteration of [the] colonising project" because of its failure to interrogate broader questions about knowledge and its value.

The student protests have unsettled this narrow approach to curriculum reform and have introduced a whole other vocabulary to debates on curriculum. Whereas the focus in South African discussions on curriculum reform had been on providing students with epistemological access, which focuses on assisting them to meaningfully access the knowledge on offer at universities (see Morrow, 1993, 2007). The student protests have pushed us to consider that perhaps our focus should not be on facilitating access to the current curriculum, but on reshaping the curriculum. As Vorster and Quinn (2017:38) point out, while there has been a lot of emphasis on increasing black students' physical and epistemological access to higher education institutions, there has been insufficient critique of the epistemologies to which we are granting students access. The protests have brought to the fore concerns on the part of students that accessing the knowledge on offer at South Africa universities, requires them to become alienated from a part of who they are. Calls for decolonisation imply that students are no longer willing to experience cultural alienation to access knowledge. Rather, they want institutions to offer them access to knowledge that they believe accords with and affirms who they are. Some may argue that their demands were impractical, unclear or unreasonable. That may be so. However, it seems fair to at least engage with their demands and to consider them seriously, rather than to dismiss them.

To engage seriously with these concerns, we can draw on the growing body of literature on decoloniality which directly addresses concerns about the destruction and marginalisation of forms of knowledge coming from outside the West. This literature's key feature is the way in which it opposes coloniality defined as "long-standing patterns of power that emerged as a result of colonialism, but that transcended colonialism to be constituted in culture, labour, intersubjective relations, and knowledge production" (Ndlovu-Gatsheni, 2013:30).

While it is not within the scope of this chapter to comprehensively review literature on decoloniality, I briefly summarise below some of the most relevant aspects of this literature in terms of thinking about the decolonisation of the curriculum. The first relevant aspect of literature on decoloniality is its strong emphasis on the idea that knowledge is always situated (Mignolo, 2009:16). Like post-colonial scholars such as Edward Said (2003) and feminist scholars such as Donna Haraway (1988), Mignolo (2009:160) and his fellow decolonial thinkers reject the idea that those who produce knowledge can be "transparent, disincorporated from the known and untouched by the geo-political configuration of the world in which people are racially ranked and regions are racially configured". Instead, they argue that knowledge must be understood as situated somewhere – that is to say that when we make knowledge claims, we speak from a particular place and the knowledge we produce is marked by our location. This approach to knowledge is compatible with calls for the decolonisation of university curricula in that it insists that we recognise that while currently dominant knowledge has often been presented as neutral and universal, it takes shape in a particular geopolitical context and thus bears the marks of the place from which it originates.

A second relevant point emerging from literature on decoloniality relates to how this literature insists that full decolonisation entails the decolonisation of knowledge. Literature on decoloniality avoids treating colonisation as only a political or economic project and views the production of knowledge as an integral part of the broader colonial project. Consequently, Mignolo (2009:171) argues that "we know that we have to decolonise being, and to do so we have to start by decolonising knowledge". Similarly, Ndlovu-Gatsheni (2013:5) argues that knowledge plays a role in the perpetuation of coloniality. This means that dismantling higher education apartheid in South Africa requires more than just opening up access to black students. Rather than focusing only on "opening the doors of learning", we must critically interrogate the learning on offer beyond those doors.

Like students' calls for the decolonisation of the curricula, a decolonial approach insists that decolonising knowledge is more than just spending more time focusing on Africa and other parts of the Global South. As Grosfoguel (2007:211) puts it, decolonising knowledge is not so much about producing knowledge *about* the subaltern, but about producing knowledge *from* the subaltern. Drawing on the work of Frantz Fanon (1967) to explain this idea, Mignolo (2009:176) argues that it is not enough to study the black experience "using the arsenal of neuroscience, social sciences, and the like", preferably in a decolonial approach "it is the Negro body that engages in knowledge-making to decolonise the knowledge that was responsible for the coloniality of his being". If we adopt this approach, South African universities cannot only respond to calls for decolonisation by introducing more courses *about* Africa or other previously marginalised parts of the world. Instead, it is necessary for universities to include knowledge *from* Africa and the rest of the Global South in the curriculum as well as to facilitate the further production of such knowledge.

A final relevant feature of writing on decoloniality is its rejection of what Grosfoguel (2007:211) calls "third world fundamentalisms". By this, he refers to approaches that suggest that "there is only one sole epistemic tradition from which to achieve Truth and Universality" (Grosfoguel, 2007:212). Thus, a decolonial approach rejects the view that any particular location (be it Europe, Africa or elsewhere) is the only place from which scholars can produce legitimate knowledge. This means that the decolonial position would not support the idea that African universities should rely *only* on knowledge produced in Africa or should favour only an Afrocentric approach. Relatedly, the decolonial approach rejects closing off parts of the world in a parochial manner where each part of the world produces knowledge relevant only to that part. Instead, decolonial thinkers favour a "concrete" (rather than "disembodied") universalism that emerges through horizontal dialogue between different parts of the world (Grosfoguel, 2012:96).

This last point less obviously resonates with students' calls for the decolonisation of university curricula as at least some calls for curriculum decolonisation seemed to favour the adoption of an exclusively Afrocentric approach or the complete rejection of knowledge coming from the West. For example, when student activists insist on having "uncontaminated education which speaks to blacks" (Anonymous student, cited in Maringira & Gukurume, 20176), it is implied that only knowledge from Africa is regarded as legitimate, which fits Grosfoguel's (2007:211-212) description of "third world fundamentalisms". It may be that some students do not share decolonial theorists' rejection of such fundamentalisms. However, to call for the decolonisation of knowledge does not necessarily mean that one favours a kind of third world fundamentalism which rejects knowledge from anywhere other than Africa. There is at least potential compatibility between curriculum decolonisation and the forms of universalism which are favoured by decolonial thinkers and which allow for dialogue between different parts of the world (Grosfoguel, 2012:96).

In this section, I have argued that to seriously consider what students' calls for curriculum decolonisation entail, it is useful to draw on literature on decoloniality as such literature helps us think through the meaning of calls for the decolonisation of university curricula.

Rhodes University's response to calls for the decolonisation of university curricula

Thus far, this chapter has discussed the context of protest and contestation that led to pressure being placed on South African higher education institutions to decolonise their curricula and has touched on some possible ways in which we might think through what decolonising the curriculum would entail. This section of the chapter turns to the question of what institutions did in response to calls for curriculum decolonisation. I take my institution, Rhodes University, as an example, using it to explore how calls for curriculum decolonisation might be interpreted by university communities.

It should be borne in mind that the 2015–2016 protests placed higher education institutions under pressure in relation to a whole range of issues, most notably the question of fees. This meant that complex issues like curricula did not always make it very high on the agenda. Nevertheless, Rhodes University did not entirely ignore calls for decolonisation as will be shown in the discussion of the University's response.

The rest of this chapter examines Rhodes University's attempt to roll out a process of Curriculum Review, paying particular attention to how the Faculty of Humanities heeded this call. The Rhodes University Curriculum Review process was not the only way in which various actors within the University reacted to calls for the decolonisation of the curriculum,[1] but it was the only institution-wide response involving the whole University in a coordinated fashion.

---

1   Another example of a response to the call was the series of talks called "Curriculum Conversations" that were organised by the Centre for Higher Education Teaching and Learning (CHERTL) at Rhodes University. These are discussed in Vorster (2016:4-5).

This process began in 2016 when the University introduced a university-wide curriculum review process. In the proposal which introduced this process, it is clear that the process was initiated in response to students' calls for the decolonisation of the curricula, rather than as a result of an independent decision to institute a curriculum review. This is also evident in a 2018 report on progress on the curriculum review process which states that the review "emanated from calls by students for the 'decolonisation' of the curriculum" (Rhodes University, 2018). However, the documentation also notes that even without such calls, a university-wide review was needed, given that the last such review had taken place in 2004.

The proposal for curriculum review suggests that the review process be driven by faculties which should each establish a curriculum review committee or working group. This body should oversee a process whereby each department is asked to nominate at least one course used as a starting point for the review. The course in question should be reviewed through a three-step process:

- Firstly, student performance data and feedback in relation to the particular course should be analysed.
- Secondly, attempt to account for any patterns observed.
- Thirdly, changes should be proposed and shared with the Faculty.

The proposal emphasised that the focus on a single course was intended to kick start the process and that other courses would most likely need to be reviewed at a later stage. The plan was that each department would complete its review (focusing on a single course). They would then report to their respective faculties and the faculties, in turn, would report to Senate.

It is striking that although this curriculum review process arose in response to students' calls for the decolonisation of the curriculum, the University's proposal does not mention decolonisation except in an Appendix, where the idea of decolonisation is provided as one example of a possible framework that could be used during the curriculum review. In other words, focusing on decolonising the curriculum is presented not as necessary, but rather as one possible option when thinking about how to review the curriculum. However, it is the only example of a possible framework to use provided in the document, so this seems to imply that a focus on decolonisation is an important consideration.

It is also striking how race enters the conversation very differently in the Rhodes University documentation than it does in the students' calls for curriculum decolonisation. The students frequently refer to race when talking about curriculum decolonisation. As discussed earlier, students relate the decolonisation of the curriculum to concerns that the current curriculum is too white or is alienating to black students and to demands for more inclusion of black academics and the scholarly work of black people in the curriculum. In contrast, race enters the discussion in the Rhodes University documentation only concerning student performance. When revising the chosen course, departments are encouraged to compare student performance along the lines of race, gender, socio-economic status and year of study. This is to determine how "different groups of students fare" with a view to considering ways to address any differences in performance. In other words, we are being asked to explore whether or not black students perform at the same level as white students and then to attempt to explain and account for such differences. In no other way is race attended to in the University's discussion of the review process.

Thus, although the University's proposed process came in response to the students' calls, it adopts a markedly different tone to that of the students. While there is a call to review curricula, there is nothing in the University's approach to suggest that current curricula are Eurocentric or "white" or alienating to black students. Instead, the principal concern seems to be with the academic success of students as the proposed review sets out to determine how specific demographic groups of students perform academically. This approach could be criticised for being inattentive to one of the features of the students' discourse on decolonisation, namely the concern they express that current university curricula facilitate the assimilation of black students into a white or Eurocentric worldview. Take, for example, the following comments from students:

> [Rhodes University] is home for those who are white and middle class or those who are prepared to *assimilate* into whiteness and the middle class. (Alasow, 2015)

> You have to die for you to live; you have to lose everything about yourself and learn to socialise yourself again into the culture here. Most of us who have come out tops here, we have lost ourselves as a black child because we are trying to be something we are not; we all trying to be white. We are all trying to learn another culture that is alien to us, because of the system. (Anonymous Wits student, cited in Malabela, 2017)

> By transformation I do not mean the cop-out version where white minds in white skins are allowed to be replaced by white minds in black skins – the version of transformation that is widely supported by the elite public sphere in South Africa. By using the term 'transformation' I am rather referring to the radical process of including methods, people and ideas where they have been systematically excluded. (Alasow, 2016)

These kinds of comments suggest that existing university curricula may be damaging to black students even if such students manage to achieve academic success, because this success comes at the price of losing a part of themselves through assimilation. However, the way the Rhodes University curriculum review is conceptualised, a department could conceivably restructure its curriculum with a view to improving the academic performance of black students (or any group of students deemed to be "underperforming") without considering broader issues such as Eurocentrism, alienation and assimilation.

At this point, it is also worth noting that the University's proposal is very similar in structure to the proposal on curriculum reform made by the Council on Higher Education in 2013 and discussed above (CHE, 2013). This proposal suggests a very similar three-part process:

- Firstly, an assessment of performance;
- Secondly, the identification of obstacles to student success; and
- Thirdly, corrective action to improve student success.

The focus of the proposal is on restructuring the undergraduate curriculum, but there is little consideration of concerns related to decolonisation of the curriculum. Like Rhodes University's proposal for curriculum reform, the CHE's proposal is concerned about improving "throughput" of students but does not seem to consider broader critiques about the colonial and Eurocentric nature of university curricula. The similarities between the approach adopted by the CHE and that adopted at Rhodes University suggest that the Rhodes University proposal is embedded in a broader, national discourse on curriculum reform which may be shared amongst decision-makers at higher education institutions but which is at odds with how students understand curriculum reform. It also suggests that Rhodes University may have approached the curriculum review process in a way that drew principally on existing, familiar discourses on transformation, rather than principally on the new approaches being articulated in discussions on decolonisation.

The curriculum review in practice

In the previous section, I described a process initiated by Rhodes University in response to calls for the decolonisation of the curriculum. In so doing, I described and commented on the documentation that was put forward to guide this process of curriculum review. However, as I indicated above, the proposal was that each faculty drive their process. Furthermore, it was emphasised in the proposal that a variety of different approaches could be used and that there was no one single format that needed to be followed for each department or faculty's review. This very open-ended proposal was perhaps intended to win reluctant academics over to the process and to ensure that academics did not feel that their academic freedom or autonomy was being undermined.

It is important to move beyond the original proposal to look at how this very non-prescriptive proposal was taken up by various actors within the institution, to understand how the University responded to the call for the decolonisation of the curricula. When I commenced this project, the faculty which had responded most comprehensively to the review was the Faculty of Humanities which had received reviews from all except one department. Other faculties' reviews were either outstanding or incomplete. Also, the leadership of the Faculty of Humanities was not very prescriptive about how the review should be done, resulting in a variety of very different review processes emerging which helps to give a sense of the variety of ways that a curriculum review can be done. For these reasons, the review will focus on the Faculty of Humanities.

As the intention of this chapter is to offer guidance to academic development practitioners on how best to support processes of curriculum review, I will not identify departments by name or provide a critique of the review processes conducted by individual departments. The aim is not to assess different departments' submissions. Instead, I would like to identify the key features of the ways in which the review was attended to overall. The goal in so doing is to get a sense of what happens when an institution is asked to review its curriculum. What is examined? What is left unexplored? What is unearthed? What is changed? What remains the same?

The first thing that is evident when looking over the curriculum reviews submitted to the Faculty of Humanities is that individual departments responded to the call to review their curricula in very different ways. At the time of writing, reviews had been submitted by all but one department in the faculty.[2] The length of these reviews differed greatly, from very short reviews of fewer than five pages to reviews that stretched beyond 50 pages.

---

2   Some departments in the Faculty of Humanities are organised into schools and submitted their reviews as a school rather than as individual departments within the school. For the sake of simplicity, I will refer throughout to "departments", but some of the reviews submitted were reviews submitted by schools rather than departments.

It is also clear from the various curriculum reviews that Humanities departments interpreted the University's call for a review of the curriculum in entirely different ways. This is partly due to a lack of a centralised process within the Faculty of Humanities. By contrast, the Faculty of Commerce submitted a single document in which each department had followed the same process in reviewing their curriculum (although some parts were incomplete at the time the report was made available to me). The Faculty of Humanities gave no clear guidelines other than those provided by the University management when calling for the review and departments were encouraged by the Faculty to follow whatever process they felt would best facilitate the review. Some departments chose to follow the guidelines provided by the University's proposal for curriculum review. These guidelines (discussed above) suggested the choice of one particular course, an analysis of student performance data and student feedback in relation to this course, and a discussion and analysis of this data in terms of what changes to the curriculum might be proposed based on the data. Other departments also followed these guidelines but only in a cursory fashion – for example, one department compiled student performance data along demographic lines, but did not analyse the data (at least not in the document they submitted) and did not use it to propose any changes to their curriculum. Other departments included some analysis of student performance data (sometimes concerning a single course, other times concerning several courses) and supplemented this with broader reflection on the curriculum or with discussion and analysis of student feedback. And some departments did not include any analysis of student performance data at all. Thus, the University guidelines were attended to in vastly different ways and, in some cases, did not seem to influence the review process at all.

One reason for the lack of analysis of performance data might be that Humanities departments were not well equipped to analyse this kind of data – only one department did a statistical analysis of the performance data, while others approached the data in a range of different ways. These reviews were being conducted by staff members in Humanities departments who are not typically well versed in statistical analysis, and so they chose various ways of handling and interpreting the data, some that might be considered questionable. For example, some departments only provided some basic information on the marks of students of various demographic groups and then made comments along the lines of "the differences observed were not very great".

It was clear from the reviews that the review process was not only driven by the institution's proposal and guidelines, but was also influenced by broader debates on curriculum decolonisation. While two of the reviews submitted do not mention decolonisation, all the other reviews touch on the theme of decolonisation at least briefly with some spending quite some time reflecting on what the decolonisation of the curriculum might mean. Consider the following extracts from the reviews which suggest consideration of (and critical engagement with) debates about the decolonisation of the curriculum:

> Although there is no one definition of the process of decolonisation, there can be no doubt colonial legacy of many South African tertiary institutions is something with which all in the academy must grapple. The [name removed] department is committed, in principle and practice, to an ever-evolving process of curriculum review so as to ensure that we continue to facilitate knowledge, and so that the content and means of teaching are relevant, challenging, educational, entertaining and valuable for and to our students. Yet, our intention is not merely to affirm the subject positions and thought processes of our students, but also to challenge these so as to produce ... scholars of the highest quality. For this reason, the department considers decolonisation of the curriculum an open process of identification *and* estrangement.

> Transformation and decolonisation of the curriculum is not viewed simply as a matter of changing Eurocentric content with South African and African content; it looks at destabilising the authorial voice of control, debriefing teacher-centred education, creating dialogues and conversations about the curriculum, locating discursive and creative spaces for student learning, opening up tertiary education in [name removed] studies, and creating spaces for discussion, negotiation, communication and interaction.

> ... decolonising the curriculum entails both looking at the existing curricula differently (rather than simply discarding them) and also opening up space for other kinds of knowledge to be attended to at our universities.

It is clear from these comments that these departments have given some thought to the idea of decolonising the curriculum but are also not in favour of an approach to decolonisation which involves a complete rejection of current curriculum content.

Other departments mentioned decolonisation, but did not define it, showing an awareness that the University conducted this review in a climate where the decolonisation of university curricula was at issue, but not engaging at length with what this might mean. For example, one department stated the following, but did not go on to explain their understanding of what decolonising the curriculum might mean:

> ... we are all well aware of the demands for the transformation and decolonisation of ... We have attempted to be pro-active rather than make 'knee-jerk' responses to such demands. Indeed, we are constantly engaged in revising the curriculum.

It was also evident in the tone of some of the reviews that there is a general perception that curricula are viewed critically and that academics may need to account for their curricula and to explain the relevance and appropriateness of what they teach. Consequently, some departments used the review to explain and defend existing curriculum choices. Nevertheless, there was also some self-criticism in the reviews with some departments admitting that their curricula needed changing and committing to making some necessary changes. Consider the following comments:

> There is evidence of efforts to ensure that topics covered are relevant to our South African context, this could be done more consistently across modules, and there are modules that could include more knowledge about and from Africa.

> The authors of our prescribed readings are mostly white, male and based in the West. As such, our department reflects rather than adequately challenges the global dominance of white, male, Western authors in academia.

However, in general, departments did not suggest that their curriculum needed to be substantially changed. No department laid out any firm plans to radically alter their programme, with most proposed changes being along the lines of shifts in emphasis, minor changes in assessment practices or addressing particular issues that were not working. The call for curriculum review does not, therefore, seem to have stimulated any dramatic changes to any department's curriculum. Consequently, it is unlikely that the changes would satisfy the student protestors whose call for curriculum decolonisation led to the curriculum review process in the first place.

It is possible that the curriculum review process provoked thought which that may lead to more substantial change later on. Anecdotally, I have heard academics make comments along these lines – for example, one department subsequently made substantial changes to their assessment practices, noting that the curriculum review process had stimulated debate which had later led to the introduction of these changes. Similarly, in my department, we are still reflecting and debating on aspects raised in the curriculum review and changes may be introduced which were not a direct outcome of the review, but which were at least partly a result of the process of reflection and debate stimulated by the review. It may, therefore, be the case that the results of such a review process will only be evident a few years on.

Conclusion: Supporting curriculum review

In this chapter, I have outlined a process of curriculum review followed by one faculty at one South African university. No doubt, there have been many other responses to the calls for the decolonisation of the curriculum, many of which might look quite different from the process(es) described above. However, the preceding description brings to light a few key issues that are of importance to consider when thinking more generally about how to re-imagine curricula. In this conclusion, I will lay out some of these issues with the aim of contributing to discussions about how best academic developers can support curriculum review processes.

Before continuing, it is necessary to acknowledge that academic developers play different roles in different institutions and are not always positioned in ways that allow them to assert much influence on curricula. They can only play a significant role in pushing for curriculum review if they are given support by University management and if academics in the various disciplines respect them. While academic developers in some South African universities may have such support and respect, it is by no means clear that academic developers are always well positioned to be able to effect significant curriculum changes.[3] Nevertheless, even without adequate support, there are some possible ways in which academic developers (and others committed to curriculum reform) may be able to play a role in decolonising South African university curricula.

The first point to highlight is that there is a need for greater theorisation of what it means to review or reform curricula in the context of concerns about university curricula being Eurocentric or "white". As Vorster and Quinn (2017) argue, academic developers have not yet fully explored the implication of the "decolonial turn" for higher education. Academic developers could contribute to greater theorisation of curriculum review processes, allowing for the implications of this "decolonial turn" to be explored in greater depth.

Secondly, there seem to be quite marked differences in the way in which university activists spoke about the need for curriculum reform and how University management and individual departments interpreted this call. The activists closely related concerns around the decolonisation of the curriculum to concerns about race, racism and lack of representation on

---

3 I thank Arona Dison for this insight into the role of academic developers.

campus. They also insisted that institutions revise curricula in ways that would make them less white and Eurocentric. The above discussion shows that while various actors at the University did attend to the general call for the curriculum to be reformed, the interpretation of that call downplayed the activists' concerns around race, representation and Eurocentrism. While it is understandable that universities did not uncritically concede to all the demands made by activists, the lack of engagement with these demands is worrying. Given that activists had expressed concerns that curricula were "un-African", racist and alienating to black students, focusing on improving the pass rates of "underperforming" groups and making slight alterations to course content cannot be considered an adequate response to these concerns. Going forward, those working in the area of academic development and curriculum reform need to more thoroughly engage with the concerns placed on the table by student activists.

Thirdly, the open, fairly non-prescriptive process followed by Rhodes University has both advantages and disadvantages. Because the process was non-prescriptive, departments were perhaps more willing to engage with it than they would have been had it been very prescriptive and top-down. Furthermore, the openness of the process (at least as the Faculty of Humanities interpreted it) meant that departments could tailor the call for curriculum reform to their discipline and could use it as an opportunity to reflect broadly on what they teach and how they teach it. It is clear from the reviews submitted that some departments (or at least some individuals within departments) used the review process as an opportunity to do some "soul searching" and to think of ways to improve their teaching. On the more negative side, an open, non-prescriptive process meant that departments could also choose not to engage or to engage very minimally with the process. Engagement across faculty was very uneven, and departments were not pushed to take the review in any particular direction. means that while under some pressure to produce some review, departments were free to review what they wanted to review and to change what they wanted to change. University management does not seem to be taking any action against departments who did not submit reviews or whose reviews were very cursory. While this kind of approach can be commended for being respectful of academic freedom and autonomy, it does mean that if a department has a curriculum that is indeed alienating to black students or deeply problematic in some other way, this kind of process is unlikely to result in change unless there are individuals within the department who push for such change. The tension between protecting academic freedom while ensuring adequate and meaningful curriculum review is not easy to resolve, but academic developers could play a more influential role in persuading academics of the importance of curriculum review, to encourage academics to willingly and meaningfully engage in curriculum review processes. This is a challenging role to play as academics are not likely to engage meaningfully if they are "forced" to participate. Therefore, academic developers need to find a way to encourage meaningful involvement, while not infringing on academic freedom or causing academics to resent the process due to feeling forced to engage. Of course, academic developers can best play this kind of role if given adequate institutional support from their institutions. However, even without such support, academic developers can contribute to the creation of academic spaces that encourage careful and rigorous curriculum review.

References

ALASOW, J. 2015. What about Rhodes (University) Must Fall? *Daily Maverick*, 23 March. [https://www.dailymaverick.co.za/opinionista/2015-03-23-what-about-rhodes-university-must-fall/]

ALASOW, J. 2015. Rhodes: A Perfect Name for a Perfect Fit. *Oppidan Press*, 21 March. [https://oppidanpress.atavist.com/decolonisation]

BADAT, S. 2016. 'Deciphering the Meanings and Explaining the South African Higher Education Protests of 2015-16'. *Pax Academica African Journal of Academic Freedom*, 1:71-106. [https://bit.ly/2m0EAaU]

BEHARI-LEAK, K. 2016. After protests, it can't be business as usual at South Africa's universities. *The Conversation*, 16 August. [https://bit.ly/2kHhTrY]

CHE (COUNCIL ON HIGHER EDUCATION). 2013. A proposal for undergraduate curriculum reform in South Africa: The case for a flexible curriculum structure. Task Team Report: Undergraduate Curriculum Structure. Pretoria: CHE. [https://bit.ly/2kGUQO1]

EVANS, JENNI. 2016. What is Decolonised Education? *News24*, 25 September 2016. [http://www.news24.com/SouthAfrica/News/what-is-decolonised-education-20160925]

MANGCU, T.; KASIBE, W. & HENDRICKS, A. 2015. RMF April 13 Press Statement. *UCT: Rhodes Must Fall*. Facebook Page. [https://bit.ly/2kRZSam]

FANON, F. 1952. *Black Skin, White Masks*, translated by C.L. Markmann. New York: Grove Press.

FOSTER, DOUGLAS. 2015. After Rhodes Fell: The New Movement to Africanize South Africa. *The Atlantic*, 25 April. [https://bit.ly/2kEt44F]

GROSFOGUEL, R. 2007. The Epistemic Decolonial Turn: Beyond Political-Economy Paradigms. *Cultural Studies*, 21(2-3):211-223. [https://doi.org/10.1080/09502380601162514]

GROSFOGUEL, R. 2012. Decolonizing Western Uni-versalisms: Decolonial Pluri-versalism from Aimé Césaire to the Zapatistas. *Transmodernity: Journal of Peripheral Cultural Production of the Luso-Hispanic World*, 1(3):88-104. [https://escholarship.org/uc/item/01w7163v]

HARAWAY, D. 1988. Situated Knowledges: The Science Question in Feminism and the Privilege of Partial Perspective. *Feminist Studies*, 14(3):575-599. [https://doi.org/10.2307/3178066]

HUSSAIN, M. 2015. Why is My Curriculum White? *National Union of Students*, Wednesday, 11 March. [https://www.nus.org.uk/en/news/why-is-my-curriculum-white/]

LANGA, M. 2017. Researching the #FeesMustFall Movement. In: M. Langa (ed). *#Hashtag: An analysis of the #FeesMustFall Movement at South African universities*, 6-12. Johannesburg: Centre for the Study of Violence and Reconciliation (CSVR). [https://bit.ly/2mk36Uk]

MALABELA, M. 2017. We are already enjoying free education: Protests at the University of Limpopo (Turfloop). In: M. Langa (ed). *#Hashtag: An analysis of the #FeesMustFall Movement at South African universities*. Johannesburg: CSVR, 108-120.

Maringira, G. & Gukurume, S. 2017. Being Black in #FeesMustFall and #FreeDecolonisedEducation: Student Protests at the University of the Western Cape. In: M. Langa (ed). *#Hashtag: An analysis of the #FeesMustFall Movement at South African universities*. Johannesburg: CSVR, 33-48.

Mignolo, Walter. 2009. Epistemic Disobedience, Independent Thought and Decolonial Freedom. *Theory, Culture and Society*, 26:159-181. [https://doi.org/10.1177/0263276409349275]

Mkhize, N. 2015. Protests are Shaping the Political Landscape. *Business Day*, 3 November. [https://bit.ly/2mlH6bH]

Morrow, W. 1993. Epistemological access in the university. *Academic Development Issues*, 1:3-4. [https://bit.ly/2lTBxkB]

Morrow, W. 2007. *Learning to Teach in South Africa*. Cape Town: HSRC Press. [http://www.hsrcpress.ac.za/product.php?productid=2196]

Ndlovu-Gatsheni, Sabelo J. 2013. *Empire, Global Coloniality and African Subjectivity*. New York: Berghan Books.

Ngugi, J.T. 1995. On the Abolition of the English Department. In: B. Ashcroft, G. Griffiths & H. Tiffin. *The Post-colonial Studies Reader*. London: Routledge. [https://bit.ly/2kS0kp4]

Paraskeva, J.M. 2011. *Conflicts in Curriculum Theory: Challenging Hegemonic Epistemologies*. New York: Palgrave Macmillan.

Peters, M.A. 2015. Why is My Curriculum White? *Educational Philosophy and Theory*, 47(7):641-646. [https://doi.org/10.1080/00131857.2015.1037227]

Pinar, W. 2016. What Knowledge is of Most Worth? The Question of Undergraduate Curriculum. In: M.A. Samuel, R. Dhunpath & N. Amin (eds). *Disrupting Higher Education Curriculum: Undoing Cognitive Damage*. Rotterdam: Sense Publishers, 133-151. [https://doi.org/10.1007/978-94-6300-896-9_9]

Pinar, W.F. 2012. *What is curriculum theory?* New York: Routledge. [https://doi.org/10.4324/9780203836033]

Poho, K. 2016. Free Quality Decolonised Education. *Wits Vuvuzela*, 1 October. [http://witsvuvuzela.com/2016/10/01/free-quality-decolonised-education/]

Ramrathan, L. 2016. Beyond counting the numbers: Shifting higher education transformation into curriculum spaces. *Transformation in Higher Education*, 1(1):1-8. [https://doi.org/10.4102/the.v1i1.6]

RMF (#RhodesMustFall). 2015. UCT Rhodes Must Fall Mission Statement. *The Salon*, 9(6-8). [https://bit.ly/2kEh9DX].

Rhodes University. 2018. The 2017 Curriculum Review Process. Composite Report to the Senate Committee on Teaching & Learning, March 2018.

RSA DoE (Republic of South Africa. Department of Education). 1997. Education White Paper 3: A Programme for the Transformation of Higher Education. *Government Gazette*, Notice 1196 of 1997, 24 July.

Said, E.W. 2003. *Orientalism*. London: Penguin Books.

Vorster, J. & Quinn, L. 2017. The 'Decolonial Turn': What Does it Mean for Academic Staff Development. *Education as Change*, 21(1):31-49. [https://doi.org/10.17159/1947-9417/2017/853]

Wilson, L.O. n.d. Types of Curriculum. The Second Principle: The work of Leslie Owen Wilson. [https://bit.ly/2ACV8N0]

Zidepa, L. 2015. #TransformWits Announces Manifesto. *Wits Vuvuzela*, 11 April. [https://bit.ly/2kQC3zy]

CHAPTER 4

Disrupting single stories through participatory learning and action

Kasturi Behari-Leak

Introduction

When student protesters demanded fee-free, decolonised, quality higher education in 2015 and 2016, universities catapulted into a whirlwind of panic. Students had attacked the very nature of higher education, asserting that universities had not changed in their cultural and knowledge practices since 1994, even though on the face of it, many looked like they had transformed. Students criticised teaching, learning and assessment practices that continued to domesticate students (and staff) into subservient roles in education and society and they demanded the development of responsive, decolonised and transformative curricula so that they could feel their lives mattered.

At the University of Cape Town (UCT), many initiatives were launched to respond to student calls for decolonisation and the university committed itself to an interrogation of coloniality to "lead us to addressing practices that are experienced as exclusionary by marginalised identities within UCT" (UCT, 2016). To this end, the University made funds available for each faculty to develop a set of strategies and interventions that "build on the best of UCT's present and past, while interrogating the historical values and assumptions that inform our institutional culture, and our ways of knowing, seeing and teaching" (UCT, 2016).

Using "curriculum" in its broadest sense, this chapter draws attention to a specific intervention to engage academic developers in conversations on what it means to decolonise knowledge, pedagogies and methodologies in the context of higher education change. The intervention, known as the Decolonisation Conversation Series (DCS), was designed to create a space for academic developers to have difficult conversations productively, about, for example, taken-for-granted assumptions of knowledge, uncritical reproduction of knowledge, and the need to contextual pedagogical practices across the university.

This chapter explores how the DCS created a space for disruption of traditional tropes, to raise awareness of representation and issues of visibility. Drawing on decolonial theory, and using examples of multiple modality texts such as visual, live and embodied texts, individual and collective memory, voice, dance and rap, this chapter will show that to "de-code" decolonisation, one cannot work only cognitively (with the head). One needs to work in a very grounded and affective way (with the heart) to access what decolonisation means. This chapter argues that how academics understand their disciplines, both ideologically and pedagogically, must be critically reflected on to identify practices and beliefs that keep the university stagnant and trapped, instead of open to change. Linking this to higher education classroom praxis, the author, who was project leader and facilitator of the DCS, explores in this chapter how academic developers and lecturers can create enabling spaces for students to express, articulate and enact values that allow them to come into their own, without fear of being erased, censored, alienated or marginalised.

Considering the context

The UCT 2016–2020 Strategic Planning Framework (UCT, 2016) is geared to steer the university in five priority areas, all of which explicitly focus on transformation and decolonisation. Parallel to the Framework, the vice-chancellor appointed the Curriculum Change Working Group (CCWG) to facilitate engagements and to shape strategies for meaningful curriculum change. As co-chair of the CCWG and member of the Centre for Higher Education Development (CHED) Transformation Committee, I embarked on a project called the Decolonisation Conversation Series (DCS) (mentioned earlier), to engage academic developers in critical reflection and dialogue about the academic development enterprise in CHED in relation to decoloniality and the curriculum. I conceptualised the DCS project design and focus, and presented it to the Transformation Committee for approval. The DCS aimed to induct academic developers in CHED and those working in faculties into the decolonial discourse in deliberate ways so they could participate fully as engaged scholars and practitioners. The project hoped to gain insight into how CHED could interpret the institutional strategic planning framework at a faculty level and transform pedagogies used by CHED's practitioners in line with the national call for decolonisation of the curriculum and what these attempts might mean for CHED as a development and support faculty at UCT.

Conceptualising the Decolonisation Conversation Series project

I conceptualised the Decolonisation Conversation Series (DCS) as an interwoven, participatory learning and action process (Chambers, 2007), with an explicit focus on "conversations", and drew on four ontological domains: Self, Other, Social and Community. The first consideration, using a decolonial frame, was to focus on the biographies and geographies of the Self in conversation with others, to recognise the interrelatedness and complexity of our intersectional identities and our multiple ways of being. The relational aspect, therefore, was important in building a sense of community amongst CHED's staff, where together we could start developing and incorporating positive gains from social movements into the organisational and teaching culture of CHED. The DCS was open to academic development staff across the academic, administrative and support divide, but participation was voluntary, based on availability and level of interest.

Another consideration was that protesting students and decolonial scholars draw on very deep theoretical and analytical frames to explore decolonisation, and for the most part, the language used in decoloniality is inaccessible to many people. An explicit design focus of the DCS was therefore to use the wide range of terms, vocabulary, concepts, and meanings used in decoloniality as "teaching-points" to unpack decolonisation in an accessible way.

The specific outcome of the DCS was to develop a social literacy regarding decolonisation, where literacy is a social practice, informed by critical social theory (Street, 1984). I envisaged that academic developers, who are already au fait with the benefits of using multiple literacies, would be keen to become better-versed in the discourse of decolonisation. The need for academic developers to understand the generative mechanisms that contribute to (un)transformed practices in different faculties is imperative if they are going to be key agents of curriculum change across the university.

Theorising "decoloniality"

Latin American and other decolonial scholars Wynter, Mignolo, Grosfoguel, Maldonaldo-Torres and Gordon have unpacked Power, Knowledge and Being in relation to coloniality and decoloniality, extending what had already surfaced through the works of Aime Césaire and Frantz Fanon. African scholars, Ndlovu-Gatsheni, Ramose and others have expanded on these terms, drawing on Biko, Mamdani, Mbembe and others on the continent. Based on this scholarship, the DCS focused on two concepts, Coloniality and Being, to explore the dispositions or attitudes needed to disrupt hegemonic spaces in CHED and to re-imagine how academic developers could work with mainstream curricula in ways that considered students and staff, in relation to knowledge and power. Our aim was to change how we relate to knowledge and each other by redefining our roles.

The concepts, power and being, will be discussed briefly now. The coloniality of power closely links to the notion of being, and what it means to be human, white, black, woman, young, and so on. In theorising "being", we draw on Fanon's (1986) zones of being, that point to the ontological resistance or ontological weight denied black/colonised people (1986). Explicated further by Grosfoguel (2011), the two zones are identified as the zone of being and the zone of non-being; each being mitigated or aggravated (respectively) by race. In the non-being zone, there is a general attitude of suspicion towards the humanity of the colonised (Grosfoguel, 2011). Mbembe (2015:181-189) describes coloniality as a form of violence: "the violence of being reduced to nothingness" and "the violence that one inflicts on Oneself: self-exhaustion, self-crucifixion". Du Bois (1999) discusses how difficult it is for those regarded as non-human to assert their right to be regarded as human. These ideas relate to marginalisation and alienation in the academy and why some academics and students, despite great effort, remain silent and invisible.

Our aim in the DCS was to break silences through dialogic conversations, to dislodge an internalised and normalised coloniality of being, and to invigorate a new sense of "being". It is discussed later, but we consciously "de-linked" (Mignolo, 2007) from traditional practices to open up spaces for previously silenced voices to be heard. Our pedagogy in the DCS, therefore, foregrounded plurality, multiplicity and difference (Dastile & Ndlovu-Gatsheni, 2013). To embrace a "decolonial attitude" (Du Bois, 1999), the DCS aimed to inspire responsibility and the willingness amongst academic developers to embrace the perspectives and points of view of those whose very existence is questioned and produced as insignificant.

A further theoretical consideration was to interrogate the concept of "being". Decolonial scholars have subverted Heidegger's notion of "Being" (note the capitalised 'B') by reconfiguring it as "being" (note the lowercase 'b') (Maldonaldo-Torres, 2007). Decolonial criticism rests on the assumption that Heidegger's Being was insufficient because who is considered a Being and which zone he/she articulates from is very different for colonisers and colonised subjects; for black and white; for men and women. Building on this ontological distinction, Torres further unpacks "being" as "be-ing", that is, being that is always in a state of being. It has a strong resonance with Mignolo's work on "epistemic delinking" from colonial power (2011:54) where the "de-" in decolonisation points to the performative gesture of actively resisting coloniality to assert a different way of knowing, being and doing. Delinking from coloniality shifts the colonised sense of self and voice (locus of enunciation) (Mignolo, 2007) from an emphasis on traditional power to the power of just showing up, being present and taking action to undo the damage (Ramose, 2003).

Theorising "conversations"

Conversations have been described as a process of two people understanding each other, opening up to each other and accepting points of view as worthy of consideration (Smith, 2001). Conversations by their nature suggest a relaxed and easy flow of information between people, in the process of talking, sharing, chatting, understanding each other, opening up to each other and truly accepting points of view as worthy of consideration (Smith, 2001). Decolonisation conversations are slightly more intense than ordinary ones, though, as they focus on underlying or unspoken assumptions that are oppressive and exclusive, and that influence interactions and practices in negative ways. One has to be present in ways that demonstrate a willingness to listen and to be heard, even when the topic and its unpacking is uncomfortable or awkward for the interlocutors.

Participants are usually involved in a conversation with their whole beings and carry the knowledge, continuity and memory of social interaction through time and space. Temporally, conversations are in the present flow of time, informed by the past (in its habitual aspect), but also oriented towards the future (as a capacity to imagine alternative possibilities) (Emirbayer &

Mische, 1998). Whether consciously or not, people exercise their agency in conversations when past understanding encounters present understanding and shapes what is taken into the future (Louden, 1991).

Spatial dimensions of conversations are significant too; not just in the geographical sense but in the spatiality of context and the materiality of "lived space" as a continuous struggle and contestation (Soja & Chouinard, 1999). Smith contends that "to each conversation, participants bring prejudices and unique understandings from their particular positionality and vantage point, with which participants engage. This does not mean that there is always agreement, but the conversation is an invitation to learn from the 'other', by opening up to the full power of what the 'other' is saying" (2001:20). This is not always easy, though, as meanings associated with words can produce different understandings to those that are intended (Holt, 2003).

"Conversations" is often used interchangeably with "dialogues" because they differ from seminars, symposia and meetings, that enact particular academic conventions and traditions. Protesting students, who say they privilege certain voices, now see these conventions as elitist and exclusionary. They call on the academy to explore other ways of "conversing". Rich, indigenous formats such as the lekgotla and the indaba (Behari-Leak, 2017), although not without their complexities, could be used to provide a sense of belonging, familiarity and comfort, specifically for black people who feel alienated from traditional academic conventions.

While conversations and dialogues share many similar features, they are different in purpose, form and articulation. The dialogue is a two-way, reciprocal conversation, prompted by a dialectic or critical question that must be explored (Freire, 1972). A conversation is an easy flow of information that does not explicitly address a problem or question. In the DCS, we chose to focus on conversations and not dialogues per se as we aimed to create a "safe space" that enabled people to interact in a non-threatening way and to mimic the natural flow of conversation between people. Our concern was that if academic developers saw dialogue as synonymous with debate or conflict, they would not attend or the process to enable shifts in understanding and perspective would be compromised.

At the same time, we wanted to converse in ways that were robust enough to disrupt the normalised ideas that shaped participants' cultural register and beliefs about students, knowledge, peers and higher education. The DCS called on participants to show an openness to exploring experiences that disrupted their sense of cohesiveness. But we were conscious of the need to work with disruption against a framework of care, where awkward topics could be explored, aired, discussed, critiqued, supported, and so forth. Even though there is much to "dialogue" about in decolonisation, we wanted to create a space where participants could bring themselves to open up in safe, yet vulnerable ways.

While the form of the conversation is less threatening than dialogue, as facilitators, we were not naïve about the difficulty of facilitating the content of our Conversation Series. Decoloniality is a difficult topic no matter how we soften it because it involves raising issues of marginalisation, representation and visibility (Wang, 1999). It is also about challenging hegemonic beliefs by becoming vulnerable insiders and outsiders. As facilitators, we are vulnerable too and bring in our insider knowledge or prejudgements. We knew we had to work purposefully to hold the space with trust, to enhance people's confidence, to enable them to share versions of their reality honestly and openly, without fear of censure.

Methods used in the Decolonisation Conversation Series

The DCS drew on a participatory learning and action methodology (Chambers, 2007) that involved participants working together to generate ideas and action for social change in the academy. Participatory learning and action methodology is a family of approaches, methods, attitudes, behaviours and relationships, that enable and empower people to share, analyse and enhance their knowledge of their life and conditions, and to plan, act, monitor, evaluate and reflect. Key principles include the right to participate, hearing unheard voices, seeking local knowledge and diversity, reversing learning and using diverse methods so that people are not just listened to but also heard and that their voices shape outcomes. This aspect connected very well with our conceptualisation of the DCS as a succession of "conversations" to seek out unheard voices and create the safe spaces that allow them to be heard (Wang, 1999).

As this was a transformation project, the DCS participants included academic developers from CHED, working in different departments such as language development, foundation courses, staff development, numeracy, multilingualism, technology-enhanced learning and so on. They attended a voluntary, monthly engagement and completed pre-tasks and pre-readings to enable them to participate in conversation circles, using storytelling and narrative techniques. The relatively small number of academics who attended (eight academics in the first month that increased to 10, 13 and 19 across all four conversations), does not represent CHED in any substantial way and belies the deep work achieved. There was an uneven representation as different conversation topics appealed to different people at different times. Given the timing of the conversations (Friday afternoons from 14:00–16:00), and challenges such as workload, interest, levels of comfort with the topic, it was inspiring to see that at least seven academics attended all events and served as "anchors" for the series. Other participants dipped in and out as they saw fit, but those who came back were able to engage and benefit from the series in myriad ways:

> What a joy and a privilege it was ... the conversation around decolonisation ... a deep theoretical understanding and incisive analysis of critical pedagogy. In addition to stimulating conversation, the session demonstrated the incorporation of multimodal texts, such as dance and rap music, into teaching, in recognition of learners' multiple literacies that are regularly marginalised or entirely eradicated. Both the experiential and participatory elements of the session distinguished it from traditional seminars and contributed to its effectiveness and my thorough enjoyment of it. (Participant 10)

The absence of others did not go unnoticed though, as one participant opined:

> What continues to be problematic for me is who is not in the room. Who chooses not to participate and be part of the conversation? That worries me – how can this work become a mainstream movement and who can take ownership? (Participant 3)

In some ways, it is understandable that there were many "empty seats" as this work is not easy, and many academics, even with good intentions, find it difficult to engage with difficult topics. Recognition that change is slow and needs percolation and fermentation is important so that those who do not show up are not ostracised. Instead, working with those who are willing might lead to them taking new practices into their contexts, by starting informal conversations of their own, stimulated by the DCS, that could grow the appetite for this work.

The DCS emphasised critically reflective practice, used in participatory processes to "undertake cycles of learning, reflection and action about experiences, with the aim of transforming people, their relationships within groups, organisations and social systems, and ultimately those systems themselves" (Fook, 2007). Apart from what they could take away, the DCS pedagogy encouraged participants to also give back – by reflecting on their experience in the "bookends" of each conversation. In the beginning, there was a group check-in to bring us to the room in full presence; and at the end of each session, a check-out or "de-brief" for the closure of the session. By building self-awareness, reflexivity and creativity of individuals in this way, we strengthened participants' sense of connection to each other to foster a collective consciousness and responsibility.

At the end of the series, participants were invited to complete written reflective narratives in response to a prompt that asked them to reflect on a particular moment that stood out for them and to discuss its meaning for their being in that moment. Participants' reflective pieces (n=10), as well as field notes, preparation notes, observations and reflections of the facilitators, comprise the data set for this study. Consent was received from participants, (whose names were anonymised to protect identities), to use their reflections in this study.

Analysing and reflecting on the Decolonisation Conversation Series

In her TED Talk, *The Danger of a Single Story*, Adichie (2009) tells of the danger of constructing people in stereotypically "single" ways, that rob them of their dignity and makes our recognition of our equal humanity difficult. Using the overarching theme of "the danger of a single story" (Adichie, 2009) for each conversation, the project explored curriculum work from the perspective of belonging, inclusion and marginalisation of students and staff. What follows is a discussion of some of the key issues that arose in each conversation in the DCS and how these critical aspects relate to decolonial theory and the overall goal of the DCS.

Conversation 1

The first conversation focused on the domain of the Self. We used different modalities to draw attention to texts and the authoring of texts. Even at this early stage, we sensed that some participants were uncomfortable with being in this space without the safety of the usual academic conventions. The smell of incense, for example, literally saw one person leave two minutes before we started. "Safety" is perceived as an emotional complementarity for conversations to be useful (Gayle, Cortez & Preiss, 2013), but we knew that creating a safe space would not necessarily be a comfortable space, as spaces open up differently: as an arena of trauma for some and healing space for others.

The politics of safe spaces juxtaposes safety and discomfort, relative to who is in the room. Many black students and staff, for instance, claim they feel unsafe all the time based on their race and class. Decolonial scholars would argue that this is coloniality of being, where structural markers of difference work in ways to marginalise and repress subjectivities (Quijano, 2000), causing them to feel "unsafe" under the colonial gaze. Gender works in the same way as we become aware of our complicit role in reproducing a heteronormative, cis-gendered society and academe. Ableism and age are further markers of safety/threat, as illustrated below:

> ... as one of the younger colleagues, it's always slightly intimidating being in a space with older colleagues that have been a part of the institution for much longer, as that niggling fear of whether or not I'd be able to voice my opinion in a way that was heard and understood, began to make itself comfortable in my stomach again. (Participant 1)

This first part of the session was deliberately designed to "read" each other and to read alternative texts and voices in the decolonial genre. We watched and worked through key ideas in the video text on *The Danger of a Single Story* and linked these to decolonial concepts such as erasure, invisibility and negation of identity (Gordon, 2006). Decolonial thought is alert to indigenous traditions of oral and verbal storytelling, erased in Western culture, and how this minimises self-esteem (Lugones, 2010). After collectively unpacking the (con)textual power and meaning of "single" and its "danger", and its role in the DCS, participants entered the conversation and shared stories: "The single story worked powerfully to hold the series together, I took it outwards in my teaching and thinking beyond our engagement" (Participant 2).

The second section focused on participants writing single stories from two points of view: either as readers of single stories of themselves or as writers of single stories of others. Participants then made masks and wrote their texts (single stories) on the masks from different points of view. We started the first round by putting all masks in a proverbial hat, with each person reading the story on the mask they chose. Using the mask as a metaphor, we linked every single story with the extent to which it masks, excludes and marginalises the Other. Masks are an important leitmotif in decolonial literature to focus on the need to disguise, whether in appearance, voice, accent, stature and identity, that which is read as inferior and unworthy. Similarly, Fanon (1986) in *Black Skins, White Masks* elucidates how masking black realities creates a psychic fracture in our sense of the whole being. Our invitation in the session was for people to unmask and bring themselves into play through different "readings" of the textual elements in the session:

> The activity with the masks in the first session stays with me ... There was a lot of discomfort in the room; I had misunderstood the activity and made the single story

about my own gendered and classed growing up ... I got caught up with the playing, but the aim was much more serious. This unfolded when we heard others' masked stories. It was a profound moment of empathy embodying someone else's single story .

(Participant 2)

Using techniques from the Augusto Boal's *Theatre of the Oppressed* (1993), participants were asked to respond to a story by bringing it into balance, to question further, affirm, placate or to challenge the story. The circle then opened up to discuss what had surfaced for them emotionally as they "experienced" the effects of the single shared stories. The group entered into the "conversation" and challenged their assumptions of the single stories they are exposed to:

> I know that I am part of the oppressive colonial heritage of UCT – even though I feel revulsion for colonialism, patriarchy and racism. But I still find it difficult to listen with an open heart when students make sweeping generalisations about race and coloniality that includes everyone white, everyone who is in a position of management, everyone with privilege.
>
> (Participant 4)

Here we see how a "double consciousness" (Du Bois, 1999) of a different kind, proves to be unsettling for someone who shares ideals of a free society but has to bear the brunt of being privileged. The masks allowed people to step into and out of internalised roles to surface the challenges of how single stories essentialise people to the detriment of their full potential. Here the zone of being and non-being are illuminated as loci of control for feeling included or alienated. People shifted their points of view based on the embodied experience of sharing others' stories:

> ... this unfolded when we heard others' masked stories. It was a profound moment of empathy embodying someone else's single story.
>
> (Participant 2)

For the masked role play, we decided to "disrupt" the spatial dynamics in the room by moving the desks away to the side to create a (symbolic) open space in the centre to converse. When the comfort of the barrier of a desk or table is taken away, people occupy the space differently. When the body is seated in a seat of power, it accrues all the benefits associated with the Being, but when dethroned and deseated, bodies move differently as beings. When power dynamics and relational aspects are refigured and recalibrated, the vulnerability of standing in a circle with nothing but your body disrupts the normalised and hegemonic tropes associated with learning; sitting still; being infantilised, domesticated and feminised (Snyman, 2015).

This echoes De Sousa Santos' "abyssal lines and abyssal thinking" (2007) through which he articulated two sides of the line for the coloniser and the colonised. He associates one side of the line (that is, metropolitan societies) with the paradigm of regulation/emancipation and the other side (that is, shifting colonial territories) with appropriation and violence. But entering the space and crossing the "abyssal lines" as vulnerable beings in this way enabled the conversation to deepen, as one participant observed.

> ... some of the participants began to speak from their hearts (not their heads) ... But the point is I remember thinking to myself I have NEVER heard people speaking like this – i.e. from their hearts and not their heads – at this place, before. (Participant 8)

Conversations can engage participants by evoking emotions such as concern, trust, respect, appreciation, affection and hope (Burbules, 1993). Emotions can be summoned in negative ways as well, where people feel anger, mistrust, pain, loss and shame. It is not surprising as we have profoundly different histories, positions and varied privileges with which we enter conversations.

Participants revealed that their sense of belonging and self-esteem eroded in the stories others had constructed of them, either as privileged white females, "incompetent" black males, or young and naïve students. White participants in the space shared the pain of feeling excluded and marginalised when black students constructed single stories of "race" about them:

> ... I feel like I no longer having a voice to speak, I have no legitimacy to speak as a lecturer, even when I want to help ... students shut you down just because you are white. (Participant 6)

This sharing was a powerful moment for those who were fully present in the conversation and highlighted a sense of knowing that comes when people are vulnerable. Vice (2010) asserts that there is moral damage by way of "habitual white privilege" for which white people need to take responsibility. These privileges are entrenched, making their eradication very difficult. Through this tension, though, there was a great empathy across the colour line in the room, where pain and truth shared a sacred space:

> This moment – a profound, extending being-in-the-middle ... have given me resources but also amplified some of the discomfort[s]. (Participant 2)

For others, the session had allowed them to reflect less emotively yet differently on systemic structures that make change slow and difficult:

> For me, the workshops unfolded and unfurled rather than disrupted my thinking ... a slower realisation about how pervasive our current structures are and how difficult the decolonisation process is. (Participant 3)

We ended the session by linking what was unpacked experientially with decolonial teachings, using an inside-out approach to knowledge building rather than being didactic. Each person reflected on the session and their feelings to debrief and close the session:

> What I have valued [are] the prompts that were provided to enable conversations to emerge, whether it was watching the Adichie video together and making notes or the mask activity. There didn't appear to be a fixed curriculum that the workshop facilitators needed to deliver, but there was enough scaffolding to ensure that conversations moved along. (Participant 5)

Conversation 2

The second conversation focused on the domain of the Other. Working again from a grounded and embodied position, this conversation looked at the single stories we create of students. We used the student theatre production, *The Fall*, as material to access some of the themes and challenges that students face at the university, especially when they feel alienated. *The Fall* is a well-known play written by a group of protesting students know as #RhodesMustFall, (RMF, 2015) about the protests of 2015. It completed a successful run at the Baxter Theatre, Grahamstown Arts Festival and the Edinburgh Festival. After reading a powerful extract from the play, we sat in silence and waited for someone to disrupt the silence. The facilitators held the space in silence, by looking around, being present and waiting. Then it began. People started sharing their stories of "reading" students negatively, based on their fears and internalised "scripts" of students as "trouble", "deficit", "incompetent", and so on:

> The second workshop ... that moment in the windowless classroom when we sat in a circle, prayer-like ... had just read from the script of *The Fall*, feelings welled up, and we talked about shame, and then I said something about the shame of 30 years of academic development work, wherefrom the beginning the shadow of the deficit model was there. (Participant 2)

Some felt that the issue of positionality needed to be dealt with more thoroughly as a way to understand how people were "positioned" as black, female, and so on, to tell particular single stories of students:

> ... I felt uncomfortable with not really knowing who the space was for, not knowing what was 'safe' to say or not and overthinking the power of my own positionality and not wanting it to infringe on the experiences of colleagues of colour. It just felt like addressing our own positionalities and how we understood ourselves in this space was a conversation that was needed. (Participant 8)

From deep within the energy of the group emerged the disclosure of "shame" associated with how they had constructed students in relation to their own identities:

> From the meaningful conversations and experiences that were shared, what stood out for me was the very moving recognition of shame that is experienced across all identities when engaging in the complexities of the current violent space that the institution is. (Participant 2)

Many black bodies in the DCS space recalled the shame of being (black) students and shared how "violent" it had been to be thought of as "less than" their counterparts. For others, it was the shame of being the beneficiary of heritage and legacy that had caused pain for others:

> For myself, as a white person, the conversation triggered the shame of my identity and heritage being one of a legacy of oppression. I was able to sit with that emotion, and also recognise the common experience of the emotion, but from different lived realities. (Participant 4)

The overall tenor was one of collective recognition and empathy, even though moments of truth-sharing were uncomfortable and made people feel very vulnerable:

> I left the session thinking a lot about the emotion of shame, what one does with it, how it can move one to the active process of decolonisation and how shame links to vulnerability … and connects vulnerability and shame to empathy. Empathy being something healing, that for me is part of the decolonisation process. (Participant 2)

The circle of voices that had shared deeply and felt deeply had been moved by listening to and feeling others' stories together as a collective:

> The shame of needing to perform a particular identity or acknowledging the shame of the institution were some of the sharings that came up, but it seemed to be an emotion that surprisingly brought the group together. (Participant 8).

We ended the session with a group reading of a passage from *The Fall* together, in the same way as is done in traditional Hindu prayers with a final group devotional song and prayer, the "aarti", to offer thanks and reverence:

> One final meaningful moment for me was how XXX introduced the closing group session by bringing an explanation of 'aarti'. It was the recognition of a particular cultural narrative and lived experience, that was brought into the space of an academic institution that unavoidably silences these narratives, that was particularly special. The moment stood out as a practical example of celebrating and honouring diverse traditions with honesty and respect and challenging the Eurocentric norm of XXX. (Participant 2)

Conversation 3

The third conversation focused on the domain of Society. Here, the attention turned to "discourses of development and deficit" and how these have influenced CHED's work institutionally and nationally. In the student protests, CHED received a fair amount of critique from protesting students who resisted the stigmatisation associated with being "developed". This critique challenged CHED's mission, and vision and its story of "relevance" in redressing and supporting educational issues and academic developers in CHED dealt with it difficultly. It was with this in mind that we thought a session focused on the "development discourse" could enable a space for discussion and debate.

We opened by showing that decolonial scholarship foregrounds the need to re-think language support and its current purpose, given the colonial heritage of English as a medium of instruction. The student protests had identified a relational gap between CHED and its students, expressed through CHED's work, its quality and the relevance of its scholarship. Unless it can tackle the issues, CHED and other academic development units might continue to receive charged critique, and perhaps, rejection, from the forward-moving decolonial turn waves that are underway nationally and globally. We hoped that we were shaping the reflection of CHED and practice towards remaining relevant and responsive in a rapidly changing milieu.

Using a participatory methodology known as the Knowledge Café, groups worked at tables and on flip chart paper, to explore the power of discourses to shape and mould practices, especially regarding the danger of the single stories of discourses. As academic development practitioners, we cannot afford to be complicit and naïve about what discourses do and how people draw on them to perpetuate practices that are uncritical and reductionist. When we brought the small group discussions to the plenary, we discussed the history, purpose, underpinnings, scope, challenges and affordances of academic development as a movement in the decolonial moment. The questions that arose focused on academic development in relation to Africa as the focal point to give recognition to the cultural contribution of Africa to world civilisation. A visiting academic from the University of Michigan joined this session, to offer perspectives on gender discourses in academia, based on her work as a post-colonial scholar in the diaspora.

This was a difficult conversation for the group because they were challenged to revisit the single story of "development" through the lens of decoloniality, and with the discourse of deficit that has come to be associated with academic development work, locally and abroad.

> I didn't like the third workshop. It became a jousting space, polarising around the deficit and development concepts. (Participant 2)

"Development" that had become attached to monetary handouts provided by the World Bank to bail Africa out of its financial predicament has lost traction by becoming linked to "charity", "missionary work" and domesticating pedagogies (McLaren, 1995). The heated debate and discussion that ensued left people feeling either energised or deflated.

> I found the first and third workshops most useful for my own thinking and development. The first was a reasonably gentle introduction to the space, facilitators and other people while I found the third intellectually stimulating with the discussion about what it means to 'develop' someone or to take a more critical approach to what is meant by 'development'. (Participant 3)

The facilitators noted that this third conversation's topic and methodology caused people to slip back into a debate mode; where the cognitive and intellectual prowess of those perceived as attacked and those perceived as doing the attacking overrode the heart and feeling spaces that the first two conversations had created. We left the session with a sense that an epistemological and cultural transformation was needed to bring the student critique and institutional response into greater clarity, parity, partnership and coherence with each other.

As facilitators, we felt that we had somewhat failed to balance the relationships between powerful and powerless people in the room to ensure that whoever was holding the floor, was doing so, not because the politics of privilege enabled them to, but because they had earned the right. But such is the nature of working in this organic way, and we had much to learn about how to enable others and ourselves to cross the threshold when conversations did not flow as we had anticipated. We had to learn how to maintain a balance between being provocative and conciliatory by leading from behind while also being willing to become redundant as quickly as possible (Bohm & Nicol, 1997).

Conversation 4

The fourth conversation focused on the domain of Community, where we highlighted the danger of a single story in representations of black bodies and black (hi)stories. Using multiple modes of video, rap, dance, slides and dance, guest presenters from the Rap Collective (a community-based group of rap artists) and the UCT Dance School explored the challenges that black bodies face in doing decolonial work. The session was a feast for the senses and participants drew the links between multiple texts in the session and the multiple texts that students bring with them to the classroom:

> In addition to stimulating conversation, the session demonstrated the incorporation of multimodal texts, such as dance and rap music, into teaching, in recognition of learners' multiple literacies that are regularly marginalised or entirely eradicated.
> (Participant 8)

We worked with the notion of a "decolonial attitude" and what Mignolo (2007) means by "de-linking" from the colonial project in what we do and how we do it. In this session, there was a creative flow of energy injected by both presenters, rendering the space different from the obsession in academia with the cognitive domain.

> Both the experiential and participatory elements of the session distinguished it from traditional seminars and contributed to its effectiveness and my thorough enjoyment of it.
> (Participant 9)

Again, the question of zones of being and who is considered human was foregrounded. Despite the gravity of the content, the mode made it entertaining and not nearly as disruptive as the previous conversations. In fact, for some participants, the input by the dance lecturer was "joyful":

> Most surprising was her way of communicating – she spoke to us with her heart, with her mind and with her body. She moved and talked expressively and warmly, reaching out to all of us as individuals ... I was most struck by her personal lightness and openness. Her presentation was positive, even joyful.
> (Participant 4)

But before the semblance of comfort invoked by the performance could seduce participants, we asked participants to be in the moment and watch with different eyes; to see what lay beneath the colonial narratives around rap and dance and how these constructed black and other bodies in exotic ways. The group was challenged to make the connection between what they saw and how they read their students; how their single stories of students "othered" them, making them special and exotic, under a colonial gaze:

> ... my reaction tends to defensiveness and withdrawal. My withdrawal is because I feel guilt, pain and distress – our history is so unbearable! And my privilege is built on this utterly terrible history, even if I didn't support what happened. Unlike XXX, I don't feel able to embrace the challenge as an opportunity to do things differently. But listening to her made me notice my defensiveness and think about other possible ways of reacting.
> (Participant 4)

The conversation deepened into culpability in reproducing tropes of black bodies in our social circles with our friends and families. In the reflective "bookend" of the session, participants were emotionally stretched to consider how they had created single stories of black dancers, artists and musicians without considering their being. There was still anger from those who felt they had been allies to the political struggle against oppression:

> ... we are cast as the enemy, and our progressive attitudes are denigrated as liberal salvos that perpetuate the status quo. (Participant 10)

Overall, the session generated a "confessional" type exchange where some white academics shared their vulnerability and sorrow in terms of remaining complicit in colonial reproduction in their classrooms and with their black colleagues.

The last session raised the bar regarding facilitation. We had to balance our own emotions and those of the circle, to hold the space in silence and with energy to allow the shifts to happen. We experienced first-hand that facilitating meaningful conversations requires one to establish rapport, "to know when not to speak and when to relinquish power for the sake of the group" (Bohm & Nicol, 1997). We found that to be authentic, the facilitator does not have to be a neutral "guide on the side" but must be respectful and responsible in terms of soliciting and "managing" all views and all the bodies in the room:

> I think what struck me the most from the session, was the way XXX and XXX held the space. Whether it was the video that we watched or an extract that we read, there was no direct prompt for the conversation and reflection that followed. It was left completely to us the group, and to [whoever] wanted to share. (Participant 8)

As facilitators, we realised we were obligated to be good leaders, to solicit reasons and evidence for the views held and to challenge some of those views when needed. Good facilitators have to know when to probe participants further, especially when the conversation becomes stuck or when what is said is not acceptable to the tenor or intention of the session.

> In the many ways that your leadership together offers invitation, challenge, rigour and warmth. This has become an invaluable space for us as peers to really hear each other and to think together about how we can individually and together grasp the opportunities for an authentic and effective decolonisation of teaching and learning.
> (Participant 9)

Conclusion

This chapter has discussed the value and richness of working in a generative and collaborative way on a specific intervention, that is, the DCS, to explore what is needed to bring the Self and the Other into conversation with each other, in the interest of sustainable and systemic change. By taking you on a memory walk of the DCS process, I explored what it means to engage with decoloniality as a space for disruption with care, by theorising how a decolonial methodology and alternative modalities can be used to this end.

What can be learned from this chapter is a way of working that can complement the existing ways of being and doing in academic development units, enacted by practitioners, staff developers and other roles. For example, the conversation methodology offered here could provide a counter-narrative to the traditional seminar-type engagement; the participatory approach could be used to foreground the importance of not only thinking but "being and feeling" in academic spaces.

We drew attention to the importance of the modality of conversation with its unique emergence and spontaneity and co-constructing understanding. We explored holding the space in ways that were "safe enough" to promote multimodal practices in the resources we generated and drew on. We aimed to enact the "un-seminar" and use the performative affordances of talking to one another in honest and open ways, as a way to ignite a response-ability in all those in the space. Our approach foregrounded the importance of *be-ing present and feel-ing present.*

Another take-home is the choice of the genre of "conversations" as a preferred pedagogy of practice. We witnessed how it enabled people to be and know from a different perspective. We saw the full gamut of emotions brought into play by participants, especially when the constitution of the group consists of unequal power relations between "those who want to name the world, and those who do not want this naming; or between those denied the right to speak, and those denying the right" (Freire, 1972:61). It would be important to include in an academic development repertoire of engagement strategies and could be equally useful for practitioners to explore regarding difficult emotions, relations and perspectives.

Linking this to student calls for the curriculum to be relevant, meaningful and authentic (Le Grange, 2016), the DCS experimented with pedagogies, teaching strategies and methodologies that are inclusive and representative of a pluriversal approach to knowledge (Ladson-Billings, 1995). It is also important as academic development can act as a broker between mainstream practices and alternative practices.

I hope that this chapter has provided a useful example of an alternative pedagogy to create spaces for disrupting the curriculum with care. In considering what the decolonial turn means for academic development, Vorster and Quinn (2017) identify useful strategies to enable academic developers to consider other ways of knowing and being. It might be useful to consider DCS engagements, facilitation and pedagogies highlighted in this chapter, to complement suggestions made by these authors, as a necessary precursor to activating the decolonial turn.

We are not naïve about the task of facilitation and the responsibility it carries. I hope that the discussion about facilitating meaningful conversations across a diverse group with differing worldviews supports academic developers in thinking through what is needed to find the right balance, where those usually powerful or who consider themselves the experts, are invited to relinquish the space for "others" to find their way. These gains can be strengthened further, to create similar spaces in other contexts so that a more experiential understanding of decoloniality is possible. This chapter concludes that "dialogic conversations" are a necessary disruption of colonial curriculum practices but need to be well planned, theorised, considered and facilitated in ways that enable, rather than shut down what can be a moving experience of disrupting our normality to make us more human.

Acknowledgements

A research assistant employed to support the DCS was also involved in the design and facilitation of the different sessions, although not a co-author of this chapter, his contribution to the project is acknowledged and appreciated.

References

ADICHIE, C.A. 2009. The danger of a single story. *TED: Ideas worth spreading*, July. [https://bit.ly/1kMOnud]

BEHARI-LEAK, K. 2017. Decolonising the curriculum: it's in the detail, not just in the definition. *The Conversation*, 9 March. [https://bit.ly/2mpwNDB]

BOAL, A. 1993. *Theatre of the Oppressed*. Translated by C.A. McBride. New York: Theatre Communications Group.

BOHM, D. & NICHOL, L. (ED). 1997. *On dialogue*. London: Routledge.

BURBULES, N. 1993. *Dialogue in teaching. Theory and Practice*. New York: Teachers College Press.

CHAMBERS, R. 2007. Whose Reality Counts? Notes for Participants. Participatory Learning and Action (PLA) and Participatory Rural Appraisal (PRA) Familiarisation Workshops, Institute of Development Studies, University of Sussex. [https://bit.ly/2koq7F2]

Dastile, N.P. & Ndlovu-Gatsheni, S. 2013. Power, knowledge and being: Decolonial combative discourse as a survival kit for Pan-Africanists in the 21st century. *Alternation*, 20(1):105-134. [https://bit.ly/2lYgddM]

De Sousa Santos, B. 2007. Beyond abyssal thinking: From global lines to ecologies of knowledges. *Review*, 30(1):45-89. [https://bit.ly/2lYg2PE]

Du Bois, W.E.B. 1999. The souls of black folk. In: H.L. Gates Jr & T.H. Oliver (eds). *Authoritative Text. Contexts. Criticisms.* New York: W.W. Norton & Co.

Emirbayer, M. & Mische, A. 1998. What is agency? *American Journal of Sociology*, 103(4):962. [https://doi.org/10.1086/231294]

Fanon, F. 1986. *Black Skin, White Masks*. London: Pluto Press.

Fook, J. 2007. *Reflective Practice and Critical Reflection.* In: J. Lishman (ed). *Handbook for Practice Learning in Social Work and Social Care: Knowledge and Theory*. London: Jessica Kingsley Publishers. Second Edition. 15 May, Ch. 26.

Freire, P. 1972. *Pedagogy of the Oppressed*. Harmondsworth: Penguin.

Gayle, B.; Cortez, D. & Preiss, R. 2013. Safe spaces, difficult dialogues, and critical thinking. *International Journal for the Scholarship of Teaching and Learning*, 7(2). [https://doi.org/10.20429/ijsotl.2013.070205]

Gordon, L.R. 2006. *Disciplinary Decadence: Living Thought in Trying Times*. Boulder, CO: Paradigm Publishers.

Grosfoguel, R. 2011. Decolonizing post-colonial studies and paradigms of political economy: Transmodernity, decolonial thinking, and global coloniality. *Transmodernity: Journal of Peripheral Cultural Production of the Luso-Hispanic World*, 1(1):1-38. [https://escholarship.org/uc/item/21k6t3fq]

Holt, R. 2003. Bakhtin's dimensions of language and the analysis of conversation. *Communication Quarterly*, 51(2):225-245. [https://doi.org/10.1080/01463370309370152]

Ladson-Billings, G. 1995. Toward a theory of culturally relevant pedagogy. *American Educational Research Journal*, 32(3):465-491. [https://doi.org/10.3102/00028312032003465]

Le Grange, L. 2016. Decolonising the university curriculum. *South African Journal of Higher Education*, 30(2):1-12. [https://doi.org/10.20853/30-2-709]

Louden, W. 1991. *Understanding teaching. Continuity and change in teachers' knowledge.* London: Cassell.

Lugones, M. 2010. Toward a decolonial feminism. *Hypatia*, 25(4):742-759. [https://doi.org/10.1111/j.1527-2001.2010.01137.x]

Maldonado-Torres, N. 2007. On the coloniality of being: Contributions to the development of a concept. *Cultural Studies*, 21(2-3):240-270. [https://doi.org/10.1080/09502380601162548]

Mbembe, A. 2015. *On the Postcolony*. Wits University Press: Johannesburg.

McLaren, P. 1995. *Critical pedagogy and predatory culture*. New York: Routledge.

Mignolo, W. 2011. *The darker side of Western modernity: Global futures, decolonial options*. Durham: Duke University Press. [https://doi.org/10.1215/9780822394501]

Mignolo, W. 2007. Introduction: Coloniality of power and de-colonial thinking. *Cultural Studies*, 21(23):155-167. [https://doi.org/10.1080/09502380601162498]

Quijano, A. 2000. Coloniality of Power, Eurocentrism, and Latin America. *Nepantla: Views from South*, 1(3)533-580. [https://bit.ly/2kVxAeZ]

Ramose, M. 2003. Transforming education in South Africa: paradigm shift or change? *South African Journal of Higher Education*, 17(3):137-143. [https://doi.org/10.4314/sajhe.v17i3.25413]

RMF (#RhodesMustFall). 2015. UCT Rhodes Must Fall Mission Statement. *The Salon*, 9(6-8). [https://bit.ly/2kEh9DX]

Smith, M.K. 2001. Dialogue and conversation. *The Encyclopaedia of Informal Education*. [https://bit.ly/2kVxV1f]

Snyman, G. 2015. Responding to the decolonial turn: Epistemic vulnerability. *Missionalia*, 43(1). [https://doi.org/10.7832/43-3-77]

Soja, E.W. & Chouinard, V. 1999. Thirdspace: Journey to Los Angeles and Other Real-and-Imagined Places. *Canadian Geographer*, 43(2):209-212. [https://doi.org/10.1177/030981689806400112]

STREET, B.V. 1984. *Literacy in theory and practice*. UK: Cambridge University Press.

UCT (UNIVERSITY OF CAPE TOWN). 2016. Distinguishing UCT: The University of Cape Town's Strategic Planning Framework, 2016-2020. [https://bit.ly/2N26Zco]

VICE, S. 2010. How do I live in this strange place? *Journal of Social Philosophy*, 41(3):323-342. [https://doi.org/10.1111/j.1467-9833.2010.01496.x]

VORSTER, J. & QUINN, L. 2017. The 'decolonial turn': What does it mean for academic staff development. *Education as Change*, 21(1):31-49. [https://doi.org/10.17159/1947-9417/2017/853]

WANG, C.C. 1999. Photovoice: A participatory action research strategy applied to women's health. *Journal of Women's Health*, 8(2):185-192. [https://doi.org/10.1089/jwh.1999.8.185]

CHAPTER 5

Re-imagining knowledge in the curriculum

Creating critical spaces for alternative possibilities in curriculum design

Sherran Clarence

Introduction

A central concern underpinning studies and practice in higher education over the last two decades is the curriculum: the design, manner of teaching, assessment and evaluation. Over the past three decades especially, innovative work has been done in the field of curriculum, notably constructive alignment (Biggs, 2011), integrated curricula (Drake & Burns, 2004), and within the sociology of knowledge (Maton, Hood & Shay, 2015; Muller, 2009; Shay, 2013; Wolff, 2015). These advances have brought conversations about how we design the curriculum, and teach, assess and evaluate it, to the centre of academic work. In South Africa these conversations, and the work of designing curricula that are responsive to students' lived sociocultural realities, as well as the "knowledge economy", have been made more challenging with recent calls to "decolonise" the curriculum under the banner of #FeesMustFall[1] (see Luckett, 2016; Shay, 2015). New Zealand, Canada, South Africa and the UK are all experiencing demands for curriculum transformation to include previously marginalised voices and knowledges (Curtis, Reid & Jones, 2014; Guraba, 2015; Lamb, 2015; Menon, 2015; NUSConnect, 2016).

Although there have been many moments of reconsideration in the past few decades, alongside societal and technological change, the potential disruptions to the status quo by student protests have created a space in higher education to consider curriculum and pedagogy anew. Specifically, now, there is an opportunity to re-imagine knowledge within the curriculum, and how this could be selected, taught and assessed in more socially and culturally responsive and inclusive ways (Luckett, 2016; Shay, 2015). This may go some way to responding to calls for curriculum change, primarily to those calls which ask for curriculum knowledge to be more connected to the world beyond the university, and more inclusive of a range of different voices and positionalities (Case, 2015; Ndlovu-Gatsheni & Zondi, 2016). The question addressed by this chapter is not *whether* the curriculum should be re-imagined at this crucial point in South African history – and this holds for many other post-colonial contexts as well. The question considered in this chapter is *how* we do this work, in practice, to ensure sustainable change.

This chapter offers a practical, yet theoretically sophisticated, tool that can be creatively used and adapted in academic staff development work to prompt lecturers to focus on knowledge, and questions of representation and inclusion in their curriculum design process. Using Basil Bernstein's Pedagogic Device, the chapter argues for understanding knowledge as created in, and moving between, three "fields" – production of discourse (research and development), recontextualisation (curriculum), and reproduction (teaching, learning and assessment). Specifically, the chapter uses the notion of the "discursive gap" between the fields of production and recontextualisation to suggest how academic staff development work can probe lecturers' ideology, personal insights, and tacit knowledge, especially the ways in which these influence curriculum design and delivery. Through this process, drawing on interview

---

[1] #FeesMustFall represents a loose coalition of student, and staff, movements that have staged rolling protests and other forms of demand for, amongst other things, free higher education, especially for poor students, a decolonised or Africanised curriculum, and changes in university staffing to reflect greater numbers of women and people of colour. The protests began in late 2015.

data from conversations with three lecturers teaching Political Studies at two different universities, the chapter demonstrates the value of the Pedagogic Device, and the discursive gaps in particular, in opening up and sustaining critical spaces for ongoing renewal in the field of curriculum design.

Curriculum development in higher education

Curriculum studies in higher education

Curriculum can be defined in a range of ways in higher education, from being seen as a set of topics or "contents" to be taught and learned, to be seen as something more profound in terms of orientations to different knowledges and ways of knowing (Shay, 2015). Drawing on the work of scholars such a Barnett, Parry and Coates (2001), Shay (2015) and Dall'Alba and Barnacle (2007), I use the following understanding of curriculum in this chapter: curriculum plays multiple roles in that, through its content, pedagogy and assessment, it should introduce students to, and develop their mastery of, different schools of thought, knowledges and ways of knowing. Further, it should encourage students to think critically and creatively about the world around them and their place within it, hence ensuring higher education's role in nurturing critical students and thinkers, aware of and responsive to their particular sociocultural contexts, rather than only narrow field specialists.

One such significant challenge lecturers face as curriculum "architects" is creating a pertinent, context-relevant balance between the concerns of mastery of disciplinary knowledge and knowing, and concerns that have wider social, cultural and personal relevance. The literature in this field, particularly studies published in the first decade of the 21st century on the "ontological turn", indicates that for a significant period of time, higher education curricula have focused too much on mastery of skills and disciplinary forms of knowledge, leaving the question of "what kinds of people or professionals are we educating?" relatively unanswered (Dall'Alba & Barnacle, 2007). In an increasingly complex world, in which crisis after crisis seems to provoke new ways of thinking about and responding to questions about how we live together – the global war on terror, and climate change, as examples – universities have been pressed to transform their curricula to focus on different forms of student learning and engagement. Key examples here are "service-learning" within the curriculum (see Lazarus et al., 2008; Waghid, 2002); "general education" courses with a mix of science and humanities subjects designed to get students working, reading, thinking and talking across race, class and gender lines (Timm, 2016; UFS, 2017); and a conscious consideration of the affective, political dimension of higher education, with academic staff development work becoming more focused on bringing post-colonial, critical discourses into engagements with academic staff (Manathunga, 2006; Vorster & Quinn, 2017).

Curriculum reform in higher education

Curriculum reform conversations are not new in higher education. At significant junctures in the different histories of countries and higher education systems these debates have arisen, such as in Hong Kong after their liberation from British Rule in 1997, or in South Africa after the end of apartheid in 1994 (Shay, 2015). What is somewhat recent, however, is the focus of curriculum renewal debates, which have moved from a focus on outcomes and student engagement (Biggs, 2011); to connecting students' knowledge and skills with deeper ontological engagements with the world and their place within in (Dall'Alba & Barnacle, 2007); to the role of knowledge, and the different kinds of knowledges and ways of knowing that are legitimated, or not, within universities (Maton, Hood & Shay, 2015; Wolff, 2015).

These debates all touch on the different roles curriculum should, and does, play in shaping the purpose and nature of higher education, and the teaching and learning cultures within universities, or national higher education systems. The outcome of higher education should be creative, critical, knowledgeable graduates, who are able to find a place in society, their community, and in the economy, and make contributions to the world in which they live on both fronts. If we can agree on this, then we have to take seriously the kinds of questions posed recently in protests and debates around the decolonisation of knowledge in several post-colonial contexts, including South Africa, the context for this chapter. These questions, at heart, are difficult: "Whose knowledge? Whose voices? Which knowledge traditions, and why those and not others? Whose histories and stories are legitimate and why? Whose histories, stories and voices are silenced?" (Case, 2015; Vorster, 2016).

Thus, curriculum reform conversations in post-colonial contexts, such as South Africa, need to begin with vital conversations about knowledge. It is crucial that academic staff developers be equipped to theorise ways of engaging lecturers in productive conversations about knowledge in their fields of study, and how this is selected into, and "recontextualised" as curriculum knowledge. A significantly emotional, psychological and intellectual challenge is to firmly question, disrupt, and shift problematic understandings of knowledge that bias the curriculum towards legitimating Western knowledge and ways of knowing, over contextually developed and relevant local and national bodies of knowledge. As Luckett argues, "it is ethically imperative in post-colonial contexts to re-create curricula that will recuperate and build black student agency for integrated identity formation, deep learning and academic achievement" (2016:424).

Decolonising knowledge in the curriculum

The debates on decolonising knowledge in the curriculum in the postcolony seem to centre largely around the inherent, and perhaps in many cases unconscious, privileging of Anglo- or Eurocentric knowledge. For the purposes of this chapter, and in line with the literature, I will term this "Western knowledge". In Sabelo Ndlovu-Gatsheni's terms, we could position this knowledge as discouraging thinking *about* Africa as a problem, and measuring African knowledge against the West, and rather encourage thinking *from* Africa, problematising and challenging other forms of knowledge and other contexts from African perspectives (2013, emphasis added). In her analysis of a Humanities curriculum, Luckett (2016) argues that if we do not take seriously the imperative to re-create the curriculum in the terms expressed above, we risk reproducing the unequal and unjust status quo. In essence, white students entering university with access to the cultural and intellectual bases on which curricula have been created will thrive, as black students continue to struggle, unable to recognise themselves in the curriculum which they have no choice but to study.

The calls for decolonising the curriculum need to be read as a powerful prompt for us to trouble and disrupt taken-for-granted authority of Western knowledges in the curriculum. Shay argues that whatever else curriculum must do, it must impart knowledge: "... knowledge [is] at the centre of ... [the] conceptualisation of curriculum ..." (2015:432). Further, as Barnett, Parry and Coate argue:

> For most academics, an institutional loyalty is secondary to a *disciplinary* loyalty and a working relationship within the institution is framed through the deep, underlying epistemological structures of the knowledge fields. Consequently, curricula will be shaped in significant degrees by the values and practices of the different knowledge fields. (2001:436, emphasis added)

These two quotations together point to the centrality of *disciplinary* knowledge fields in shaping lecturers' conceptualisations of their curriculum, as well as their sense of *what* they need to teach and perhaps *how* to train or educate students in their disciplinary traditions, epistemologies, and so on. Hence, any academic development work, as part of the whole university's labour, needs to marry the broader concerns of decolonisation of knowledge and social justice, with lecturers' concerns for their discipline and their related understandings of what counts as legitimate knowledge.

Basil Bernstein on knowledge in the curriculum and social justice

Basil Bernstein's work, in brief, focused on schools, and on how educational environments are structured and enacted. He was particularly interested in how schooling served to exclude the working classes in Britain from participation in further education (Bernstein, 1971, 2000). His work, particularly that on the Pedagogic Device and its rules for structuring the curriculum, has been used in research on school and university education (see, for example, Christie, 1999; Singh, 2002; Evans, Davies & Rich, 2009). Its application to academic staff development work, however, is fairly novel. As this theoretical model, or "tool for thinking with" is underpinned by a deeper concern with social justice, and access to the means for success and inclusion in education, it is well suited to academic staff development work, which in the South African context has always been underpinned by orientations to social justice and broader student success (see Boughey, 2007).

The Pedagogic Device as a model for curriculum design

The Pedagogic Device is a model visualising academic study that comprise three interconnected fields. The first is the field of production of discourse, where new knowledge in the field as a whole is created, debated and disseminated. Knowledge is then selected from this field through a process of recontextualisation in relation to the intended curriculum – this is the field of recontextualisation. This knowledge is then further transformed through pedagogy, assessment and evaluation in the field of reproduction (Bernstein, 2000:37). There are, according to Bernstein, rules that shape how consciousness, or meanings, are created and managed within each field, and these work to shape what knowledge, and forms of knowing, are legitimated, and which are not (see also Maton, 2014:Ch.3).

A key aspect of the Pedagogic Device, which will be focused on in the analysis in this chapter, is the "discursive gaps" between the three fields (see Figure 5.1).

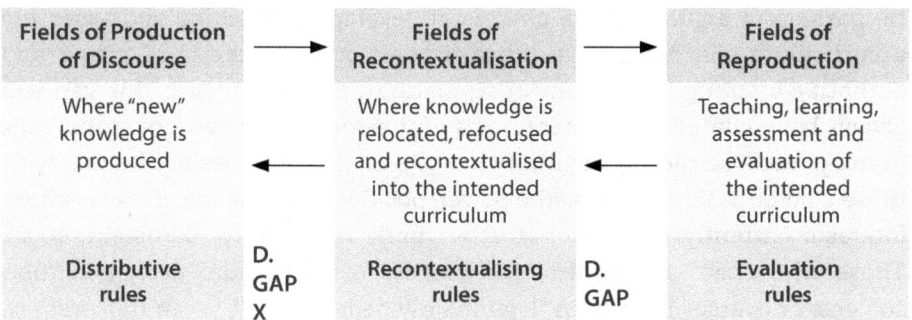

FIGURE 5.1 The Pedagogic Device
(Bernstein, 2000:37; Maton, 2014:48)

In Bernstein's account of the Pedagogic Device, there is a potential gap created by the indirect relation between meanings in the field of production of discourse, and the field of recontextualisation, and again by the indirect relation between meaning in the fields of recontextualisation and reproduction. I focus only on the first gap, marked with an X in Figure 5.1. Knowledge drawn from the field of production in Political Science – for example, data and information about an election cycle in a country and the enactment of democracy and other forms of political engagement through the course of an election – cannot be identical in the field of recontextualisation. It is transformed using a set of logics, or principles (see Maton, 2014; Bernstein, 2000) that shape not only the *what* that needs to be included in the curriculum, but also the *how*. In other words, the field of recontextualisation includes, as its set of principles by which knowledge is selected, transformed, and sequenced into a teachable curriculum, the purposes of the knowledge in service of educating students with certain sets of knowledge, skills and dispositions. These are informed by the nature of the discipline or field of study, and its underlying organising principles (Maton, 2014). Hence, the indirect relation between meanings in the field of production and meanings in the field of recontextualisation, and by the same token, between the field of recontextualisation and the field of reproduction.

Bernstein argues that this indirect relation of meanings creates what he calls a "potential discursive gap". He argues that this gap has within it the potential for:

> ... alternative possibilities, for alternative realisations of the relation between the material and the immaterial ... this potential gap or space ... is the site for the unthinkable, the site of the impossible ... It is the crucial site of the *yet to be thought* ...
> (2000:30, emphasis in original)

He goes on to argue that the process of developing, teaching and assessing a curriculum will have, as an intrinsic part of the exercise of power and authority, a strong investment in regulating this gap. Further, this gap will always be regulated with the interests of the dominant power, or status quo, in mind, because the gap signifies change – alternative possibilities and with those a potential challenge to the power, position or influence of those whose interests currently dominate, whether fairly or unfairly (Bernstein, 2000). Those who enact and control the process of curriculum design in their subjects or courses have been "legitimately pedagogised", yet in this process, possible contradictions and tensions can never be completely suppressed. For example, of a woman student reading texts and ideas on patriarchy and power written by men, but wondering if these ideas are challenged by women researchers. Or a black student, reading history through the lens of white researchers, while knowing this is a very partial and biased view of the world. These two students, when they become lecturers on the basis of their legitimacy being affirmed through earning a degree in Political Studies, or History, can then engage this "discursive gap", and harness its power and potential to challenge, and supplement, existing meanings. The unthinkable can, therefore become, the thinkable.

There are two aspects to draw out and summarise before I consider the data. The first is that the Pedagogic Device theorises possible interactions between three "fields" implicated in curriculum and in teaching and learning. It shows that no curriculum, or the ways in which it is taught and assessed, is "fixed" or immutable. It is possible, then, to take account of "contextual factors" when designing and enacting curriculum, to make necessary changes (Vorster, 2016:4). The second is that it is the discursive gaps that hold the potential power we need to re-imagine the curriculum design and teaching practices within our universities to account for and respond to, the contexts in which we live.

The chapter moves now to consider the discipline of Political Science, and the ways in which three lecturers working in two South African universities have made choices that can be reconsidered through the lens of the Pedagogic Device and the discursive gap.

The data

The data drawn on here comes from a larger qualitative study conducted at two universities, one a midsize, traditional, historically black institution, and the other a smaller, traditional, historically white institution. The contexts are different in that the former's student body largely comprises black and coloured students, many of them from poorer socio-economic backgrounds marked by underresourced homes and schools. The latter comprises a more mixed student body, but a significant percentage is white, middle-class students from relatively well-off socio-economic backgrounds. In interviews with lecturers during the study, it became clear that the backgrounds of students, and the university context and history itself, have some influence on what lecturers in these two departments choose to teach, that is, what knowledge they select for the curriculum and also on how they choose to sequence and pace the curriculum as they teach it.

The larger study concentrated in the main on the act of teaching itself, and how the lecturers sought to make meaning through enacting the curriculum in teaching (see Clarence, 2017a, 2017b). However, in the course of interviewing the lecturers at the close of the courses under observation in 2014 and 2015, data were also generated concerning curriculum design as it related to teaching. This data will be drawn on here, to consider afresh the notion of "alternatives" in designing curriculum, with particular reference to the calls made by the #FeesMustFall movements, for alternatives that acknowledge African knowledges and ways of knowing, and critiques of the West.

The respondents in the data quotes in the following section are given pseudonyms: there were two lecturers each in 2014 (Jane and Lee, from a historically black institution), and one lecturer in 2015 (Sarah, from a historically white institution).

Political Science, in both the historically white institution and historically black institution contexts, has a set of relatively core aims that transcend individual contexts, particularly in terms of the kinds of graduates the field wants to shape or educate. The "ideal" political science graduate is critical of received knowledges; can make a sound argument with relevant substantiation; has some grasp of, or appreciation for, nuance in terms of approaching knowledge and events critically; and can use political theory to make sense of, debate, and create knowledge across a range of problem scenarios (Goodin & Klingeman, 1998; Interview data). The kinds of knowledge that can be recontextualised from the field of production are somewhat open to debate and influenced by university context, and lecturers' ideologies and research, but the kind of graduate they want to shape is largely informed by the deeper logics of the field itself (see Clarence, 2017b).

It is difficult here to speak of a "Political Science canon", although in each sub-discipline[2] there are "classic" texts, such as Machiavelli, Hobbes, Plato and Jean-Jacques Rousseau in Political Thought, and perhaps Frantz Fanon, Kwame Gyeke, Achille Mbembe and similar on African Political Thought (which may be an area of Political Thought or part of Area Studies). It would be correct to consider each sub-discipline as having key texts it considers necessary for students to read to gain a firm foundation and sufficient historical and current perspectives on contemporary issues and events. Further, the field as a whole has particular concepts, such as power, democracy, and the state that carry with them key thinkers and their published works. As I will show, though, this is where possible spaces open up for re-imagination, and for alternative ways of thinking and responding to lived context; it is also in these spaces that lecturers' own unexamined beliefs about what is best, or right, for students to read and write can be more critically examined.

Analysis and discussion

Let us begin with Sarah, from a historically white institution (2015), who teaches Comparative Politics in the second semester of first year. In her interview, she talked about the core aims of the course, and how the course has evolved to achieve these, in relation to the country case studies used and the core concepts that drive a comparative analysis of the different countries' political systems.

> I think there are important questions to ask when you're doing Comparative Politics from somewhere outside of the West because it's really about comparing other bits of the world to the norm which is the West and where all the concepts are defined in relation to the West, and they're applied elsewhere, so I think I wanted students to think about that. So that's how I originally designed the course – was what is Comparative Politics, what are the problems with Comparative Politics? And then I used two concepts – democracy and development, and then we did comparatively those two.

She went on to add:

> We did have the US, South Africa, Brazil and India the last four or so years ... but I found that the students always end up doing the US and South Africa and they're very focused on being very critical about the US and very preoccupied with the US when I used the US as a case study. So to try to shift it from just being you know – the US is supposed to be a model of democracy, but it isn't – look at these problems, to shift them from that I replaced the US with Senegal just to mix it up a bit. So there's now the African country.

---

2 Comparative Politics, Area Studies (usually national politics), International Relations, and Political Thought (or Theory) are the four main sub-disciplines.

There was an interesting case in Senegal because what had happened a few years back was the president had changed the constitution so that he could serve a third term and then also tried to reduce the number of votes that he needed to become president in the presidential elections ... had he managed to lower the threshold that you needed in the first round of presidential elections to twenty-five per cent as he wanted to, he would've won the presidential elections. But because he withdrew that legislation because of how unpopular it was, he made the twenty-five per cent, but he needed to make fifty per cent. So he had to go to a second round, and he lost on the second round and conceded defeat ... and there was a new president from a different political party and what's interesting is Senegal has always had peaceful handovers of power ... So Senegal has some features that gets the students out of this kind of either viewing the West as the model but then being very resentful towards the Western models which is what a lot of our students feel. So, on the one hand, they want everything to be like the US, but on the other hand, they're very critical of the US. So, I just took the US out of the equation and then they had to use Brazil, which also has some very interesting things around democracy. And India ... South Africa ... in terms of democracy.

I now use the discussion of the Pedagogic Device in the previous section to position her initial comments about wanting her students to approach Comparative Politics from the angle of not accepting the West as the model and Africa/the global South as deficient in relation to the model. This would be positioned in the field of recontextualisation, because this underlying aim of the course is part of the recontextualising discourse that influences what knowledge is drawn from the field of production of discourse in Political Studies and even other allied social science fields, such as History or Philosophy. Her second set of comments about the four case study choices can be positioned in both the field of production of discourse, and the field of recontextualisation. Her comments about the elections in Senegal would be in the larger field of production, where the events happened, and where news reports, election monitoring reports, and academic analyses and critiques would have been written and published. In this field, too, are academic articles about the two concepts she has chosen to guide comparative analyses of the four country case studies: democracy and development.

Field of Production of Discourse		Field of Recontextualisation
Elections in Senegal, Senegalese realisation of democracy, academic writing on democracy and development, both applied and theoretical, published writing about all issues related to democracy, development, political and social engagement in India, Brazil, Senegal and South Africa. [This field is very broad, but the lecturer's approach will bear in mind the proposed course, and its design and outcomes, so not all of the possible literature will be considered.]	*Discursive gap* Which case study countries? Why these? Whose definitions or applications of democracy and development? From whose perspective? How do we weigh these perspectives and theories against one another in relation to the cases?	Selected academic (peer-reviewed, credible) writing about democracy and development in a more abstracted form (e.g., Joseph Schumpeter, Claude Ake, Rita Abrahamsen); Reading on the nature of comparing the West with developing parts of the world (Edward Said); Readings about the specific countries under study – history of these countries, demographic information, applied studies on democracy and development in these four countries.
Distributive rules here cover a range of possible positions and ideologies.		Recontextualising rules here may include the critique of dominant knowledge, as well as the education of a particular kind of knower, or thinker.

Figure 5.2 Possible Pedagogic Device model for "Comparative Politics"
(Sarah, Historically White Institution, 2015)

Key to this analysis is the discursive gap. Bernstein (2000) argues that no knowledge moves through these gaps without ideology at play. The ideology in question when we are looking at curriculum design could be that of the individual lecturer, but it could also imply the ideology of an academic department (aligned as liberals, critical of the current government, or for the current government, for example); a university context (for example, having a strong connection with the struggle against apartheid, or being closely aligned with the apartheid government); or even ideologies contained within national or international debates the curriculum is responding to (for example, more or less aligned with "knowledge economy and skills" understandings of higher education). In this case, for reasons of brevity, we will consider the ideology of the lecturer, and the context of decolonisation the current curriculum is being asked to respond to.

This lecturer included in the reading list an excerpt from Edward Said's classic text on post-colonial studies, *Orientalism*, first published in 1712. Commenting on the inclusion of this knowledge, related to our inquiry about ideology, she had this to say:

> I think I wanted them – maybe this is not a typical goal of a Comparative Politics course – I thought the Said ... the basic point that when we are making comparisons between countries, we need to be aware of **the relationship between power and knowledge** and how our knowledge about other countries and what's written about other countries is not just pure fact. That it's rather **always written from a particular perspective**, even

while you could have a set of lies in a country, but you could also have two perspectives that are more or less truthful, but very different. ... I think what I want them to start to think about is that there are **competing knowledge claims** as you put it, there isn't just one set of knowledges that I want you to learn. I want you to be able to see that there are many different ways of approaching democracy, for example. And to see that people have different views on what democracy is and that they provide arguments for those different views, and I want you to be able to understand and engage with those different arguments.

The sections highlighted in bold, speak to an underlying ideological position that values a critical, thoughtful approach to knowledge claims. Including Said was a deliberate choice to provide students with a foundation for the course that presented all the selected writing and knowledge about Brazil, India, Senegal and South Africa through this critical lens. This position also came through in the curriculum materials, where theorists making different arguments were actively compared with one another. For example, Joseph Schumpeter presenting a classical, Western argument about democracy was compared with Claude Ake's and Rita Abrahamsen's work that challenge and extend this conception from African and post-colonial perspectives.

I would argue that this lecturer has harnessed the power inherent in the discursive gap to include in her curriculum knowledge that coheres with an ideological position that values knowledge and positions that are critical of the West, and that present students with views from the global South that give them a fuller, more critical perspective of the concepts of democracy and development. In this way, alternatives to only studying texts written from the West about the West, holding it up as the model against which African and global South democracies are left wanting, are made possible. Lecturers, departments and universities' ideological positions and underlying values may be tempered by pragmatic contextual constraints, but they most certainly influence how knowledge is recontextualised into curriculum and legitimated through this, and the subsequent teaching and assessment process. The discursive gap, as Bernstein argues, can offer the potential to disrupt – "this is not a typical goal of a Comparative Politics course" – or to reinforce established bodies of knowledge and ways of thinking.

In the 2014 case, Lee and Jane, from a historically black institution, were interviewed together, as they co-taught a course combining Political Thought and International Relations. This is not typically done, but the combination of resource and staff constraints in this department created the necessity for a combined, introductory module at first-year level.

Speaking about the foundational nature of the first half of the course, *Political Thought*, taught in the first semester of the first year, Lee commented:

> ... in terms of content, it's an introduction to key concepts. Power especially, state, government, different institutions of government to some extent, those kinds of things. And then similar things but at an international level in the second similar foundational concepts in the second half of the semester. So, its foundational concepts I would say are all key, central concepts to political studies. ... We pretty much always talk about the state and we pretty much always talk about power and we pretty much always talk about sovereignty, anarchy at the international level.

Jane, who teaches the second half on International Relations (IR), commented:

> ... you can't put everything in IR in the first year; it's just too much so I took out stuff on international political economy. We decided to put in more of the evolution of world politics so that they could get a historical base because very few of them lived through these events like the Cold War. They just didn't know about Hitler and the World War. Political studies students should know about these things.

The conversation went on to talk about the nature of designing a curriculum at first-year level, and Jane commented in response:

> At undergraduate level, I don't think we get through enough foundation stuff. It's such a diverse discipline, it's got four sub-disciplines, and we only end up usually having two modules in each sub-discipline at an undergraduate level and often you scrape the surface. First-year is really – you're not going to learn anything terribly intellectual in first year ... first year is much more foundational. I mean you will learn about issues in the world, ... we're talking about Syria at the moment, or we will talk about elections in the first term so it will be topical, but you won't necessarily get into more intellectual debates, you won't necessarily be well grounded in the sub-discipline, it's foundational, it's some core concepts and approaches.

Two things are going on here which influence the design of this curriculum, and which could be probed further in the space offered by the discursive gap. The first is the constraints offered by the time given to the curriculum: there is limited time and space in this course, and in the undergraduate degree as a whole, to do more than offer students a foundation on which they could build in postgraduate or further study. This foundation, while it is notably important to these lecturers, seems not to be quite enough; their comments indicate a desire for more time to be "intellectual" and to delve deeper into key issues and related texts in the sub-disciplines. The second issue is a position on making the curriculum "topical" and linked to what students "should" know and what they do already know something about, such as Hitler, the Cold War, Syria and national elections. The first issue may be difficult to solve without significant structural changes to the curriculum and the undergraduate degree. But the second issue is more open to change and challenge: if there is a belief that students, as Jane puts it, "are not empty vessels when they come in, they actually do know some stuff, and we have to hook the content onto what they know", there is potential here for making the unthinkable, thinkable. In other words, it is possible to create a curriculum that is flexible enough to respond to students' lived realities, and to issues of both national and international significance, in ways that make the curriculum more inclusive of a range of perspectives, knowledges, and ways of knowing (see Figure 5.3).

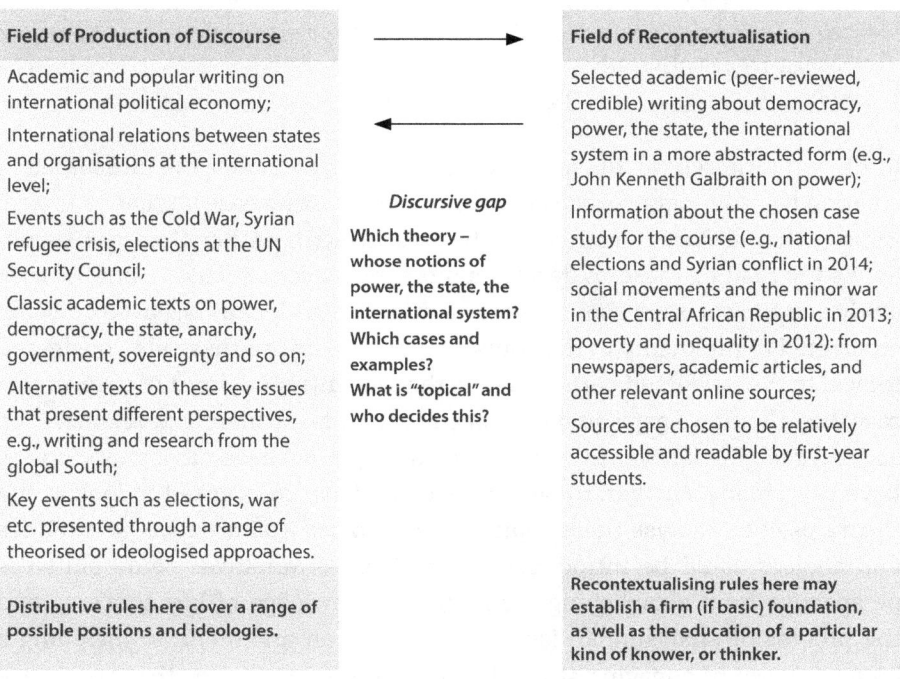

FIGURE 5.3 Possible Pedagogic Device model for "Political Thought and International Relations" (2014, Lee and Jane, Historically Black Institution)

Both lecturers commented that the choices of theory and cases are in service of the deeper recontextualising principles at play in Political Studies – at the local level creating the foundation they mention above, and at the broader level, educating the "ideal" critical, creative, argument-creating graduate discussed in the previous section.

> **Jane:** Hey, you learn this concept nationalism, and that's happening in the Ukraine – how cool is it that you've got the analytical tool to go and explain this to your parents. Hey, it's nationalism in the Ukraine, this is what I'm being taught, and actually,

I'm professionalising myself. In terms of the theory stuff for me, it's important to get them to know the dialectical words. You know A says this, B says this and then C comes and says this and then D says this – how do you synthesise this for yourself to explain a real-world problem?

Researcher: So, would you say that's one of the overall goals, and aims of your teaching is to try and cultivate more a sense of sort of interests and a sort of spark then giving them some sort of defined set of content and skills?

Lee: I think overall the aim of teaching, I mean that's part of it but it's cultivating a certain kind of thinker – a certain kind of intellectual agent. You can say to [student name], you know, what is the problem with the universe? Briefly, go away and come back tomorrow and give me an intelligent account of what Putin is doing in the Ukraine, and he would be able to do that ... And it doesn't matter what the topic is; he will be able to do it if I say to him – Ward committees in South Africa – he will be able to do it.

In the 2014 interviews, the lecturers spoke at length about the difficulties in creating this foundation and seemed focused on using case studies or topical issues, such as local elections or the war in Syria, rather than the theory applied to reading these, to develop a more inclusive curriculum. But the case study and topical issue choices were all made by the lecturers, based on being connected to the theory in the course, and also because these are considered topical to the field itself, rather than to the students studying it. Hence, in this case, the discursive gap could have been used by an academic developer, such as the researcher (above), to probe and challenge how these curriculum choices have been made. Further, the lecturers could have been asked to look at the theory used to analyse these topical issues, to see if alternative possibilities and choices could be introduced there. These alternatives could shift the perspective from establishing foundational knowledge of key concepts and the process of analysing an issue and making an argument, to including a broader sense of engaging students with theories and cases that encourage the kinds of critique more overtly present in the first example discussed in this section.

Academic development work within a discursive gap

Although they work in different sub-disciplines, and different institutional and departmental contexts, the data indicate that all three lecturers' choices in their curriculum design have been informed by both pragmatic and also deeper ideological, personal and professional influences. The challenge for academic developers is to try and engage lecturers at both levels: pragmatic and ideological. Often pragmatic concerns and complaints tend to win the day.

This is particularly so in an era of large classes, reduced contact time with students, and increased pressures on academics to publish their research, continually reinvent their teaching to respond to new trends and research, and engage in the life of the university as well as the surrounding community. Lecturers want, and need, help dealing with the practical concerns that arise from increasingly large classes, peopled with linguistically and socio-economically diverse groups of students.

However, academic development has a more crucial task. Through my academic development practice and research, I have learned that there is a deeper task underpinning assisting lecturers with these more immediate concerns. This task is twofold: in the first instance, academic development work needs to engage more critically with the often-tacit beliefs, ideologies and systems of power and authority at work within academic disciplines and departments. These need to be unpacked and held up to critique, because without this challenge, the ethical "imperative" Luckett (2016:424) speaks of, to recreate curricula in post-colonial contexts that "recuperate and build" the agency of previously marginalised students, will remain underrealised. In Bernstein's terms, curriculum, teaching and learning will serve to reproduce or serve the unequal and unjust status quo, instead of working to challenge and change it. In this part of the task, the model offered by the Pedagogic Device, and the conceptual power of the discursive gaps, can prove useful in highlighting the power of ideology in shaping the way curriculum is designed, taught and assessed. It can further hold tacit beliefs, ideologies and long-held practices up for scrutiny, and academic developers here, adopting a more critical, questioning approach, can ask important questions that need new answers, especially about knowledge in the curriculum.

This brings me to the second part of the task, which is introspective: academic development itself is a field that operates within a Pedagogic Device of sorts, where knowledge from the broader field of higher education research and practice is chosen, recontextualised and then utilised in practice. The ideologies and values academic developers hold need to be reflected upon, critiqued, and in many cases, changed (Manathunga, 2006). Academic developers need to broaden their knowledge base too, to create a more inclusive space in which a multitude of voices, from the West and the global South, can be brought into the conversation about the important work of higher education development (Vorster & Quinn, 2017). This work is more difficult, perhaps because in doing this, the light is shone on our practices instead of only outward on lecturers' or universities' work. The Pedagogic Device and its discursive gaps can thus be used to model, critique, and expand the knowledges and practices drawn on in academic development as well. This reflexive work will only serve to enhance the ability of academic developers to engage lecturers empathetically and critically in the difficult work of imagining and enacting new and alternative possibilities in their curriculum and teaching.

Transforming curriculum is more complex than changing reading lists. It requires us to reflect on the positions and identity we hold, and roles we play, whether as students, as lecturers, or as academic developers. The approach offered in this chapter can aid the important disruptive, creative role of academic development by opening up a space that could become one that invites a more mutual engagement around crucial and difficult questions about knowledge, social inclusion, and social justice in education. Through working consciously to make this a shared space, we can move away from negative spaces of blame, shame and self-doubt, towards a critical understanding of the epistemic and ontological logics of the disciplines, and how they relate to the social contexts in which we live and teach. If the ideal graduate of any higher education system is a full citizen, capable of realising their best life – as argued by Case (2015) and Luckett (2016) – then we need to take seriously the disruptive, critical role of academic development, and harness theorised tools and approaches that make the practical work of engendering and sustaining change possible.

References

BARNETT, R.; PARRY, G. & COATE, K. 2001. Conceptualising curriculum change. *Teaching in Higher Education*, 6(4):435-449. [https://doi.org/10.1080/13562510120078009]

BERNSTEIN, B. 1971. *Class, Codes and Control*, 1. London: Routledge & Kegan Paul. [https://doi.org/10.4324/9780203014035]

BERNSTEIN, B. 2000. *Pedagogy, symbolic control, and identity: Theory, research, critique*. Revised Edition. London: Rowman & Littlefield.

BIGGS, J.B. 2011. *Teaching for quality learning at university: What the student does*. New York: McGraw-Hill Education.

BOUGHEY, C. 2007. Educational Development in South Africa: From Social Reproduction to Capitalist Expansion? *Higher Education Policy*, 20(1):5-18. [https://doi.org/10.1057/palgrave.hep.8300140]

CASE, J.M. 2015. Reimagining the curriculum in a postcolonial space: engaging the public good purposes of higher education. Keynote address at HELTASA conference, 17-20 November. [https://bit.ly/2m2wSgs]

CHRISTIE, F. 1999. The pedagogic device and the teaching of English. In: F. Christie (ed). *Pedagogy and the shaping of consciousness: Linguistic and social processes*. London: Bloomsbury, 156-184.

CLARENCE, S. 2017a. Surfing the waves of learning: enacting a Semantics analysis of teaching in a first-year Law course. *Higher Education Research and Development*, 36(5):920-933. [https://doi.org/10.1080/07294360.2016.1263831]

CLARENCE, S. 2017b. Knowledge and knowers in teaching and learning: an enhanced approach to curriculum alignment. *Journal of Education*, (66):65-84. [https://bit.ly/2krmDlb]

Curtis, E.; Reid, P. & Jones, R. 2014. Decolonising the academy: the process of re-presenting indigenous health in tertiary teaching and learning. In: F. Cram, H. Phillips, P. Sauni & C. Tuagalu (eds). *Maori and Pasifika higher education horizons (Diversity in Higher Education)*, 15. Bingley, UK: Emerald Group Publishing Limited, 147-165. [https://doi.org/10.1108/S1479-364420140000015015]

Dall'Alba, G. & Barnacle, R. 2007. An ontological turn for higher education. *Studies in Higher Education*, 32(6):679-691. [https://doi.org/10.1080/03075070701685130]

Drake, S.M. & Burns, R.C. 2004. *Meeting standards through integrated curriculum*. Virginia: ASCD.

Evans, J.; Davies, B. & Rich, E. 2009. The body made flesh: embodied learning and the corporeal device. *British Journal of Sociology of Education*, 30(4):391-406. [https://doi.org/10.1080/01425690902954588]

Goodin, R.E. & Klingemann, H.D. (eds). 1998. *A new handbook of Political Science*. Oxford: Oxford University Press. [https://doi.org/10.1093/0198294719.001.0001]

Guraba, H. 2015. What is an African curriculum? *Mail & Guardian Online*, 17 April. [https://mg.co.za/article/2015-04-17-what-is-an-african-curriculum]

Lamb, C. 2015. *(Neo)Liberal scripts: settler colonialism and the British Columbia school curriculum*. MA thesis, Queen's University, Canada.

Lazarus, J.; Erasmus, M.; Hendricks, D.; Nduna, J. & Slamat, J. 2008. Embedding community engagement in South African higher education. *Education, Citizenship and Social Justice*, 3(1):57-83. [https://doi.org/10.1177/1746197907086719]

Luckett, K. 2016. Curriculum contestation in a post-colonial context: A view from the South. *Teaching in Higher Education*, 21(4):415-428. [https://doi.org/10.1080/13562517.2016.1155547]

Manathunga, C. 2006. Doing educational development ambivalently: Applying post-colonial metaphors to educational development? *International Journal for Academic Development*, 11(1):19-29. [https://doi.org/10.1080/13601440600578771]

Maton, K.; Hood, S. & Shay, S. (eds). 2015. *Knowledge-Building: Educational studies in Legitimation Code Theory*. London: Routledge.

Maton, K. 2014. *Knowledge and knowers: Towards a realist sociology of education*. London: Routledge. [https://doi.org/10.4324/9780203885734]

Menon, N. 2015. Why our universities are in ferment. *The Hindu*, 15 February. [https://bit.ly/2mlO6Fr]

Muller, J. 2009. Forms of knowledge and curriculum coherence. *Journal of Education and Work*, 22(3):205-226. [https://doi.org/10.1080/13639080902957905]

Ndlovu-Gatsheni, S.J. & Zondi, S. (eds). 2016. *Decolonizing the university, knowledge systems and disciplines in Africa*. Durham: Carolina Academic Press.

Ndlovu-Gatsheni, S.J. 2013. Decolonising the university in Africa. *The Thinker*, 51:46-51.

NUSConnect. 2016. Why is my curriculum white? *NUSConnect*, Wednesday, 11 March. [https://bit.ly/2UM7t79]

Said, E. 1978. *Orientalism*. New York: Pantheon Books. [https://bit.ly/2ntCpHG]

Shay, S. 2015. Curriculum reform in higher education: a contested space. *Teaching in Higher Education*, 20(4):431-441. [https://doi.org/10.1080/13562517.2015.1023287]

Shay, S. 2013. Conceptualizing curriculum differentiation in higher education: A sociology of knowledge point of view. *British Journal of Sociology of Education*, 34(4):563-582. [https://doi.org/10.1080/01425692.2012.722285]

Singh, P. 2002. Pedagogising Knowledge: Bernstein's Theory of the Pedagogic Device. *British Journal of Sociology of Education*, 23(4):571-582. [https://doi.org/10.1080/0142569022000038422]

Timm, D. 2016. General Education at DUT: Building Communities of Practice. PowerPoint presentation. [https://bit.ly/2m1egNF]

UFS (University of the Free State). 2012. Newsarchive: UFS101 prepares new students for life. [https://bit.ly/2lWooY1]

Vorster, J.A. 2016. Introduction. In: J.A. Vorster (ed). *Curriculum in the context of transformation: reframing traditional understandings and practices*. Rhodes University: CHERTL.

Vorster, J.A. & Quinn, L. 2017. The 'decolonial turn': what does it mean for academic staff development? *Education as Change*, 21(1):31-49. [https://doi.org/10.17159/1947-9417/2017/853]

Waghid, Y. 2002. Knowledge production and higher education transformation in South Africa: Towards reflexivity in university teaching, research and community service. *Higher Education*, 43(4):457-488. [https://doi.org/10.1023/A:1015211718131]

Wolff, K. 2017. Insights into conceptual and contextual engineering problem-solving practices in the 21st century: some implications for curriculum redesign. Paper presented at 3rd Biennial Conference of the South African Society for Engineering Education. Durban, 13-15 June, 189-198. [https://bit.ly/2lXsgIr]

CHAPTER 6

Transforming curriculum development through co-creation with students

Alison Cook-Sather, Kelly E. Matthews & Amani Bell

Introduction

Many calls for curriculum transformation focus on how academic developers can work with academic staff to reconceptualise curriculum as a space of disruption, rather than replication, of dominant perspectives and practices. Fewer of these calls focus on how academic developers might challenge the widespread assumption that curriculum reconceptualisation is the sole purview of academic staff. Drawing on a growing body of literature and our own experiences as academic developers, we describe one way to challenge this assumption: by reconceptualising curriculum development as a relational and reciprocal process through which students have a fundamental right to have a voice and to take an active role. Expanding curriculum design and redesign to include partnerships amongst students, academic and professional staff, and academic developers fosters radically and productively disruptive co-creation; it upends traditional and normative notions of hierarchy and power within curriculum development in higher education. This approach affirms Quinn's argument (2012) that academic developers have a critical role to play in disrupting hegemonic notions of who gets to shape the curriculum.

In this chapter, we put ourselves in conversation with existing literatures and scholars, which we acknowledge through traditional academic citations, and we also write informally to our fellow academic developers about our own experiences. First, we evoke arguments regarding student voice work in primary and secondary school contexts that underpin much student-staff collaboration in higher education. Next, we summarise the premises of a rapidly expanding body of scholarship on staff engaging students as partners in learning and teaching in higher education. We then discuss curricular co-creation as a relational process. After that, we offer examples drawn from essays published by staff and student partners and from our respective practices as academic developers that transform curriculum design and redesign work through the creation of partnership spaces that are inclusive of students. Based on these examples, we offer some recommendations for how academic developers can support such work, and we conclude with implications for academic developers, particularly those working in neoliberal contexts.

Student voice and the rights of students in shaping their education

That students have a fundamental right to assert the power of their voice and to take an active role in dialogue and partnership with educators has been argued through student voice work in the context of primary and secondary schools for decades. For instance, prefacing their edited collection of chapters focused on student voice work in Canada, the United Kingdom, and the United States, Pollard, Thiessen and Filer (1997:2) claimed that "children are citizens who arguably have as much right to consideration as any other individual". Similarly, Thomson (2007:780, citing Wyn, 1995), argued that young people are already citizens "whose rights to participate in decisions that affect them are daily violated in schools". Whether within the frame of international mandates such as the United Nations Convention on the Rights of the Child or according to more local commitments, students' rights underpin virtually all student voice efforts (Cook-Sather, 2006).

Building on these assertions of students' rights, early arguments for students taking an active role in dialogue with educators about teaching and learning focused on how such partnership can directly improve educational practice. These arguments suggested that when teachers listen to and learn from students, they can: begin to see the world from those students' perspectives (Heshusius, 1995); make what they teach more accessible to students (Johnston & Nicholls, 1995); and contribute to the conceptualisation of teaching, learning, and the ways we study teaching and learning as more collaborative processes (Wilson & Corbett, 2001). More recently, scholars have focused on how to involve young people actively and meaningfully in decisions about their participation in informal as well as formal educational settings (Bourke & Loveridge, 2018).

These arguments have been taken up in higher education practice and research as well. For instance, in the context of the United States, Ferguson, Hanreddy and Draxton (2011) argued for giving students a voice as a strategy for improving teacher practice. Writing in the United Kingdom, Seale, Gibson, Haynes and Potter (2015:550) asserted that we must wrestle with issues of power concerning ownership and expertise in educational research if we are to enact "the vision of student engagement and the ideals of strong participation and expression of student voice". Frison and Melacarne (2017) identified a strongly felt need in Italy to support "student voice" approaches and partnerships between students and teachers.

These and many more arguments have been presented in support of students' right to assert the power of their voice, and yet young people's perspectives are still typically excluded from the arenas of curricular and pedagogical practice (Lundy, Welty, Blanchet-Cohen, Devine, Smith & Swadener, 2015). Lundy and Cook-Sather (2016:274) have argued that "the core principles of both children's rights and student voice call for a kind of respect and shared responsibility – a partnership, in essence – that the traditional hierarchies and power imbalances structured into educational institutions do not easily allow or support". This call for partnership has been taken up in higher education through a wide range of approaches, some of which focus on how students can "become full participants in the design of ... curricula" (Bovill, Cook-Sather & Felten, 2011:133).

The emerging "students as partners" movement in higher education

Gärdebo and Wiggberg (2012:9) have predicted that "if there is to be a single important structural change during the coming decades, it is the changing role of students who are given more room in defining and contributing to higher education". As one way of defining and contributing to higher education, students engaging in co-creation with staff, faculty or academics, administrators, and professional staff can take many forms, all of which build on approaches developed through student voice work: (1) learning, teaching, and assessment; (2) subject-based research and inquiry; (3) curriculum development and pedagogic consultancy; and (4) the scholarship of teaching and learning (Healey, Flint & Harrington, 2014).

Regardless of the form such co-creation takes, scholars have contended that mutual respect, reciprocity, and shared responsibility for learning and teaching should inform the partnership, defined as "a collaborative, reciprocal process through which all participants have the opportunity to contribute equally, although not necessarily in the same ways, to curricular or pedagogical conceptualization, decision-making, implementation, investigation, or analysis" (Cook-Sather, Bovill & Felten, 2014:6-7). Such work "challenges traditional assumptions about the identities of, and relationships between, learners and teachers" (Matthews, 2017:1).

Students also describe the potential of this reconceptualisation of student and staff roles and relationships. For instance, drawing on his experience as an undergraduate student and student partner in Australia, Dwyer (2018:1) has suggested that partnership between students and staff can be a "relational and transformative pedagogic space" that "can allow participants to act outside the role-boundaries that typically confine their teaching and learning activities". In Canada, McMaster University's "student scholars" programme illustrates this potential. The programme invites students' perspectives on course/curriculum design or pedagogical research and offers students meaningful roles through which they "contribute intellectual property to the project" and have "some autonomy and voice in decision-making processes" (Marquis, Puri, Wan, Ahmad, Goff, Knorr, Vassileva & Woo, 2016:5).

While we recognise a wide variety of partnership practices and the diverse range of people who can be involved, our focus here is on students and tertiary educators, typically academic staff, working together on the design and redesign of college and university curriculum. Thus, building on student voice work, we bring into conversation the emerging movement of students and staff as partners in higher education that privileges collaborative relationships in pedagogical practice with existing scholarship on curriculum as a dynamic, relational, and co-created lived experience.

Theorising curriculum as a process of co-creation

Curriculum has been conceptualised in many ways, from a "blueprint for achieving restricted objectives" (Egan, 1978:65), to a perspective on content (Schubert, 1986), to a course designed through the running of it (Pinar, 2004). Each of these, and any notion of curriculum, "frames knowledges in particular ways. Some frames are visible, while others are not" (Anwaruddin, 2016:433). Co-creation has the unique potential not only to make visible but also to challenge these frames by "actively involving students in learning development and processes of co-creation," which can challenge "existing learning relationships and power frames [and deconstruct] dominant pedagogical frames that promote only Western worldviews" (Ryan & Tilbury, 2013:7).

When students become partners with staff in this work, they inform the development and revision of curriculum with a diversity of identities and experiences as well as their unique perspectives from their positions as both knowers and learners. Curriculum becomes understood as the co-construction of knowledge between learner and teacher (Fraser & Bosanquet, 2006; see also Bovill, Bulley & Morss, 2011), taking the form of *currere* – the Latin infinitive form of curriculum, which means "to run the course", or, in the gerund form, "the running of the course" (Pinar, 2004). Such a notion of curriculum is consistent with Bron and Veugelers' (2014:134) argument that "to consider involving students in curriculum design, we need to see the curriculum, not as a product or a fixed set of requirements, but as a process wherein external aims give direction but also where teachers and students influence what is actually experienced in class".

As efforts to co-create curriculum have expanded, scholars have developed ways to distinguish different forms and extents of curricular co-creation. Bovill and Bulley's (2011) ladder of student participation in curriculum design shows how students can become increasingly active in such work, and Moys, Collier and Joyce (2018) explore how to expand student agency in curriculum design. Bovill and Woolmer (2018) offer the distinction between co-creation *of* the curriculum (co-design of a programme or course, usually *before* it is taking place) and co-creation *in* the curriculum (co-design of learning and teaching within a course or programme usually *during* the teaching period). Cook-Sather, Bahti and Ntem (in press) add making explicit and challenging the hidden curriculum of a course. One of the key distinguishing factors amongst these various kinds of curricular co-creation is whether the design and redesign are undertaken with students who are enrolled in the course, or with student partners who are not enrolled.

Co-creating a course before it is taught can make it more likely that the course will meet the needs and address the interests of students who enrol (Shore, 2012) and is, by definition, undertaken with students not (yet) enrolled. Co-creation and revision of a course as it is unfolding have the potential to maximise learning, build on the power of multiple perspectives, realise a more democratic approach, or some combination (Bergmark & Westman, 2016; Bunnell & Bernstein, 2014; Cates, Madigan & Reitenauer, 2018). Such co-creation can unfold with the students enrolled in the course or with a student partner not enrolled in the course. Curricular revision after a lecturer teaches a course brings to bear student perspectives on how, for instance, the course activities and assessment might be brought into greater alignment (Charkoudian, Bitners, Bloch & Nawal, 2015; Delpish, Holmes, Knight-McKenna, Mihans, King & Felten, 2010; Mihans, Long & Felten, 2008; Moore, Altwater, Mattera & Regan, 2010). Such co-creation typically involves students who had been enrolled but have completed a course. And finally, co-creation of curriculum focused on navigating challenging or controversial content (Brunson, 2018; Daviduke, 2018) focuses on revealing and interrogating the hidden curriculum that resides in the "gaps or disconnects between what faculty intend to deliver (the formal curriculum) and what learners take away from those formal lessons" (Hafferty, Gaufberg & O'Donnell, 2015:35; see also Jackson, 1968; Ong, Smith & Ko, 2017; Perez, 2016). This form of co-creation can be undertaken with students enrolled in a course or with student partners not enrolled.

All of these forms of co-creation can help expand what has typically been created for upper and middle-class students into a curriculum that is more inclusive for equity-seeking students. They all require academics and students to rethink and revise their traditional institutional positions, roles, and responsibilities in relation to the curriculum created and the process of that creation. Research and reflections on efforts to co-create curriculum suggest that it is demanding, can be destabilising, and can be deeply rewarding. Much research focuses on the challenges to academics of co-creating curriculum, including concerns about power, authority, responsibility, coverage, standards, and more (Bovill, Cook-Sather, Felten, Millard & Moore-Cherry, 2016). But students may also be wary of co-creation, because they are "accustomed to, and often comfortable with, assuming a relatively powerless role in the classroom" (Delpish et al., 2010:111).

These disruptive aspects of co-creation, prominent enough in Western contexts, can be even more so in Eastern contexts, where, as Kaur, Awang-Hashim and Kaur (2018:3) explain, cultural values, "rooted in respect for hierarchy, humility, polite attitude, and tolerance (Nguyen, 2005) inhibit students from questioning, contradicting, or challenging teachers' knowledge or perspective" (Cheng, 2000; Pagram & Pagram, 2006). Preliminary findings suggest, however, that, like students in Western contexts who have participated in pedagogical partnership, students in an Eastern context experience deeper learning, a more engaging classroom environment, a sense of empowerment, increased competence, and enhanced relationships with instructors (Kaur, Awang-Hashim & Kaur, 2018).

Such radical disruption of the curriculum design process and institutional hierarchies can, in the South African context, "engage students, particularly those from marginalised groups, in meaning-making activities to enable them to develop coherent accounts of their lived experiences" (Anderson, 2012, cited in Quinn & Vorster, 2017:135). Partnership in the design and redesign of the curriculum is particularly well suited "to ensure that the lived realities of all students are acknowledged" and to support students feeling included and able "to thrive academically and as human beings" (Quinn & Vorster, 2017:137).

The practices and possibilities of curriculum development through partnership

Academic developers have a critical role in supporting the transformation of curriculum design and redesign by re-imagining those as developed in a partnership space. Through creating spaces and support for student-staff partnership, academic developers can facilitate curriculum development and revision processes that value students and academics as human beings who enact learning and teaching through a dialogic understanding of curriculum and curriculum development. To illustrate such an approach, we provide selected examples from essays published by staff and student partners. These describe processes of curriculum co-creation through partnership focused on: collaborating on course design as a course is unfolding; re-designing a course in the semester before teaching it again; and deconstructing the hidden curriculum. After presenting these examples of student-staff co-creation of curriculum, we draw on our own experiences as academic developers to offer examples of: influencing courses and university-wide curriculum renewal; partnering with students in a whole-of-degree programme curriculum review; and co-creating an institution-wide, pedagogical partnership programme.

Collaborating on course design as a course is unfolding

A Psychology course that was initially designed and taught by Dan Bernstein at a large, research-intensive university in the midwestern region of the United States was opened up to co-teaching and co-design when Bernstein met Sarah Bunnell, a doctoral student and graduate teaching assistant. They explain that "this collaboration was further enhanced through ongoing partnerships with undergraduate students who had previously completed the ... course". Bernstein and Bunnell invited several students to contribute their insights to the design of the course:

> We met weekly with our undergraduate collaborators, in both the semester leading up to the offering of the course and while the course was being taught. We discussed in detail the goals that we had for student learning for each section of the course, what was working well (and not as well as we would like), and ways in which we could maximise student learning and engagement with the material.
>
> (Bunnell & Bernstein, 2014:1)

Changes they made based on students' suggestions included redesigning assessment tasks and introducing interesting examples, readings, and videos that were relevant to students' lives. In so doing they took steps towards ensuring "that the lived realities of all students are acknowledged" and supporting students in feeling included and able "to thrive academically and as human beings" (Quinn & Vorster, 2017:137).

Re-designing a course in the semester prior to teaching it again

At a small, selective liberal arts college in the mid-Atlantic region of the United States, a new academic in the Chemistry Department and three undergraduate students who had taken her first-semester *Organic Chemistry* course engaged in a semester-long redesign process through which they revised course content, assignments, and methods of assessment for the course (Charkoudian et al., 2015). During their first meeting, they identified seven different themes, decided to dedicate two weeks to each theme, and scheduled weekly meetings to discuss the needs they identified within each theme and actions to meet those needs. The themes were:

1. the general organisation of the course;
2. poster presentations;
3. pre-lecture quizzes;
4. problem sets;
5. exams;

6. lecture notes; and
7. reflection on the re design process.

The academic noted that "as the professor, I was able to see the class with beginners' eyes" (Charkoudian et al., 2015:7), and she was able to work with the students enrolled in her course as "a part of a team ... to achieve the course objectives" (ibid.:9). One of the student partners who worked on the course redesign commented that:

> I did not foresee ... the extent to which participating in this process made me feel more connected to the course and the Chemistry Department as a whole. I think that student participation in course design could be a powerful pedagogical tool that urges students to invest in their education and take responsibility for their learning.
> (Charkoudian et al., 2015:7-8)

Deconstructing the hidden curriculum

In a year-long pedagogical partnership with an experienced academic, an undergraduate student partner at a small, selective, liberal arts college for women in the mid-Atlantic region of the United States worked with her staff partner through the challenge he faced when, based on student feedback, he realised that "[f]or the first time in his thirty plus year career, he was unsure about whether he was fit to teach his subject matter" (Brunson, 2018:2). Teaching a course that included underrepresented perspectives in a discipline that is typically amongst the most inclusive, this academic nevertheless "worried that his class was not inclusive enough and that he lacked an understanding of what his students were experiencing that was necessary to create a successful learning environment" (Brunson, 2018:2). He realised that he could not "continue to design curricula and teach as before", and he "wanted to know if there was a way that he could create a curriculum that would make him more 'in touch' with his students" (Brunson, 2018:2).

Together, Brunson and her staff partner worked to name, explore, and conceptualise how to create curricular structures through which he and the students enrolled in his course could engage with the course content, which positioned him and his students very differently. Brunson had not taken this course, and she was not completing a major in the discipline. Nevertheless, she was able to work with her staff partner to analyse and revise the course in ways that reassured him and improved the experience of the students enrolled in the course, partly through embracing their "discomfort in the unknown" (Brunson, 2018:1).

Programme- and institution-wide approaches to supporting curricular co-creation

As academic developers, each of us has not only supported curricular design and redesign efforts by individual student and staff partners, such as those described above, we have also worked to support co-creation in programme- and institution-wide efforts. We offer an example of such efforts from each of our contexts.

Amani: Influencing courses and university-wide curriculum renewal

As an academic developer at a large research-intensive university in Australia, I have worked with staff and students in a range of ways to facilitate partnerships for curriculum renewal. My initial foray into the area was with a group of 500 business students, where a deliberative democracy process was used so that all students could have a say in changing the course, midway through the semester (Bell, Carson & Piggott, 2013). The process enabled the students to agree on and suggest three changes to the course coordinator, who implemented them immediately.

I then worked with a fellow academic developer, Tai Peseta, and with a different group of students each year over two years to inform university-wide discussions about curriculum renewal. Through the partnership, we worked together to gain a better understanding of each year's theme (assessment in 2014, cultural competence – the ability to work in cross-cultural settings – in 2015). The student ambassadors presented their findings in provocative and creative ways at the university's annual learning and teaching colloquia, resulting in changes in thinking for both staff and students (Peseta, Bell, Clifford, English, Janarthana, Jones, Teal & Zhang, 2016; Bell, Peseta, Barahona, Jeong, Lan, Menzies, Trieu & Wen, 2017).

The following year, I supported staff-student pairs to explore and make changes to the teaching and assessment of cultural competence in five courses. Working at this scale had some challenges: at times it felt less coherent than all working together on one project, but it was also rewarding to share the diverse ways cultural competence was experienced in different disciplines (Bell, Barahona, Beg, Coulson, Eymont, Hartman, Hubble, Leung, McDonnell, Ni, Peseta, Sakhaee & Uptin, 2017). The student partners gained interpersonal interaction skills, research skills, an improved understanding of cultural competence, insights into the specific ways the university is undertaking to promote cultural competence, and new-found confidence to work alongside academics. Besides, the student partners gained skills in cultural competence that they saw would be useful in their careers. The academics gained a deeper insight into what was working and not working in their units and were keen to continue to expand their efforts to embed cultural competence in their courses.

Kelly: Partnering with students in whole-of-degree programme curriculum review

In 2015–2016, I worked half-time in the Faculty of Science to collaborate with the Associate Dean Academic (ADA) and other curricular leaders on a Review of the Bachelor of Science (BSc) at the University of Queensland. Because of our existing relationship, the ADA was open to my suggestion that we draw on student feedback (students as a source of data), while *also* including students more actively in the review planning process. (I used the language of collaborators instead of partners.) Despite his concerns about the appropriateness of engaging "students as partners" in the curriculum review processes, he went along with my plan.

The student partners enriched the analysis of broader quantitative data sets informing the review process by offering insights through their lived experience of the science curriculum. I observed how the students acquired knowledge and language about the science curriculum while also gaining a new sense of agency to shape the curriculum review process. As an example, I partnered with an international student, Sam Dvorakova, pursuing a dual degree in Science and Arts that felt disjointed and fragmented (Dvorakova & Matthews, 2017). Being a part of the review planning process with me, Sam learned that 35 per cent of science students were in dual degrees, and it seemed many others shared Sam's experience. Sam signed up to talk to the external review panel when they visited the University of Queensland and drew on the review data, using the new language learned, and shared a personal story about the BSc feeling disjointed and fragmented. The committee responded to Sam and included a specific recommendation to enhance the curriculum for dual degrees in the BSc – a student-generated change to curriculum policy enabled by engaging with students in the review process.

The experience was personally transformative for Sam, who saw that having a voice could effect change for a larger cohort of students. The experience also disrupted my thinking about a partnership with students in traditional academic development work. I was not acting through a formal structure supported by the University. I was acting against the preference of the ADA.

Through the ordinary act of bringing students into conversations about the curriculum, I was taking a stance as an academic developer when I easily could have maintained the status quo by excluding students from curricular decision-making.

Alison: Co-designing a pedagogical partnership programme

in 2006, I unexpectedly moved into the role of an academic developer when administrators at Bryn Mawr College in Pennsylvania, USA, asked me to conceptualise a programme to support our academic staff in pedagogical reflection. I agreed, on condition that the programme would be a pedagogical partnership programme like the one I had facilitated in the context of our secondary teacher preparation programme since 1995 (see Cook-Sather, 2002). In collaboration with undergraduate students as well as academics and administrators, I developed the Students as Learners and Teachers (SaLT) programme, through which academics are paired for semester-long partnerships with undergraduate students to explore, affirm, and, where appropriate, revise pedagogical approaches and curriculum.

The pilot phase of the programme supported five faculty and five students of colour working to develop more culturally responsive classrooms (see Cook-Sather & Des-Ogugua, 2018). The programme then expanded to include pedagogy seminars linked with semester-long pedagogical partnerships with undergraduate students. Currently, all incoming academics at Bryn Mawr and Haverford Colleges may choose to participate in a variety of partnership experiences as part of their orientation and development, including a semester-long seminar and pedagogical partnership with an undergraduate student in exchange for a reduced teaching load in their first year (see Cook-Sather, 2016, 2018).

Either as an extension of or independent from this work, any academic at Bryn Mawr and Haverford Colleges can work in curriculum design or redesign projects with individual students or groups of students, and, as in all SaLT partnerships, the students are paid by the hour for their work. Through all these projects I aim to fulfil my "moral responsibility to work towards not just formal access to university, but also academic success for the majority of students" (Vorster & Quinn, 2017:11).

Recommendations for supporting curricular co-creation

When both students and academics develop the capacity and confidence to co-create, they can experience outcomes such as: shared responsibility, respect, and trust; learning from each other within a collaborative learning community; and individual satisfaction and development (Lubicz-Nawrocka, 2018). To engage in the work of co-creation, both academics and students need to develop a mindset, vocabulary, and confidence to collaborate (Cook-Sather, Bovill & Felten, 2014; Mihans, Long & Felten, 2008). They also need structures to engage in and reflect on the process of curriculum design and redesign.

Developing a co-creation mindset

As our discussions of student voice, students' rights, student-staff partnership, and curricular co-creation illustrate, the mindset required for this work is one of receptivity to a range of perspectives, willingness to share power and responsibility, and commitment to engaging in a messier, less predictable process of curriculum design and redesign than the inherited model. Such a mindset requires confidence and humility, tolerance of uncertainty, willingness to let go of canonical assumptions, and excitement about discovery. The results of embracing such a mindset are not only the development and revision of more inclusive and responsive curriculum but also, as a student partner put it, inspiration to students "to invest in their education and take responsibility for their learning" (Charkoudian et al., 2015:8).

Developing a vocabulary

To make the most of partnership, students and staff need to develop ways of naming what they are doing and ways of communicating with one another from their respective positions. While staff and students are regularly required to communicate in the language of whatever subject matter they are exploring together, they less often talk with one another about the structures and processes that support that engagement – the curriculum. Discussing in detail "the goals that we had for student learning for each section of the course", for instance, as Bunnell and Bernstein (2014:1) describe, necessitates finding language for those goals. Kelly's example of partnering with students in whole of degree programme curriculum review and the new language her student partner, Sam, developed about the science curriculum as well as the new sense of agency Sam gained to shape the curriculum review process provides another illustration.

Developing confidence

Curricular co-creation has the potential to inspire confidence because those engaged in it know that the result will be more informed. Student and staff partners can build confidence through the process of co-creation by actively seeking to understand one another's perspectives and affirming one another's contributions. Equally important to developing confidence is embracing one's "discomfort in the unknown", as Brunson (2018:1) put it – a capacity to sit with uncertainty such that it is generative and energising, prompting constructive action, rather than destabilising and debilitating, prompting withdrawal and retreat to established ways of students and staff engaging with one another and curriculum development.

Developing structures

The structure that Charkoudian and colleagues (2015) developed – creating a meeting schedule, identifying themes, and revising course organisation, activities, and assessments – allowed their student-staff team to move collaboratively and efficiently through the co-creation process with all voices contributing to every phase. The university-wide discussions about curriculum renewal and cultural competence work Amani describes also offer examples of structures that support co-creation. Finally, the institution-wide structures that Alison co-created and further developed in collaboration with students and others to scaffold curricular as well as pedagogical co-creation not only support the particular participants in any given co-creation effort but also create space and support, through modelling and inviting, for other staff and students to enter and use. Such structures, both within partnerships and in wider institutions, are most effective when they achieve a balance between being supportive and being flexible.

In conclusion: The potential of academic developers to shape the co-creation of curriculum

The examples above show the diverse ways in which academics and academic developers can work in partnership with students to enact curriculum development and renewal that is more inclusive of and responsive to students. While such ways of working bring challenges, the benefits are well documented. However, most academics and students may not be aware of the possibilities of engaging with students as partners, curriculum co-creation through partnership, and how this work can differ from student engagement more generally.

We recommend that academic developers introduce academics to partnership practices, share information about their history, and provide support for different ways of conceptualising and enacting forms of partnership focused on curriculum development and revision that supports "academic success for the majority of students" (Vorster & Quinn, 2017:11). Several studies have explored how academic developers might support partnership work (e.g., Bovill, Cook-Sather & Felten, 2011; Curran & Millard, 2016), and as Bovill and Felten (2016:2) argue, academic developers "have the opportunity and the responsibility to advise and support people and institutions in navigating new roles and creating new spaces to make partnerships strong and sustainable". Academic developers can build bridges between students and staff (Barrineau, Schnaas, Engström & Härlin, 2016) and challenge traditional student and academic roles to make way for partnership (Bergmark & Westman, 2016).

Many academic developers are working in institutions that are increasingly influenced by neoliberal forces that seem to be at odds with partnership practices "as locations for the negotiation of power and to ground our continuing efforts in the possibilities for redistributing power in ways that change us, that deepen our bonds, and that intervene towards social justice in our world" (Cates, Madigan & Reitenauer, 2018:44). Dwyer (2018:12), from his perspective as an undergraduate student, raises concerns about neoliberal appropriation where the language of partnership is evoked and yet the practice enacted "prioritises high achieving students", "prioritises students who are financially stable", and "exacerbates the disparities between certain types of individuals and both implicitly and explicitly encourages peer competition amongst staff and student", because the underlying intent "is the advancement and development of the university as a business". Therefore, as academic developers we have to ask ourselves how we want to use the power we might have (Cousin, 2013) to work against these potential effects of partnership even as we recognise that we are entangled in the power structures of our institutions, which are shaped by neoliberal forces that could diminish or silence our beliefs about the purposes and role of higher education (Peseta, 2014; Roxå & Mårtensson, 2017).

Expanding curriculum design and redesign to include partnerships amongst students, academic staff, and academic developers upends traditional and normative notions of hierarchy and power within higher education curriculum development processes through radically and productively disruptive co-creation. Such an approach has the potential to challenge neoliberal forces but can also be appropriated by them. While supporting such co-creation processes could position academic developers in conflict with institutional leadership and policies that value products, outcomes, and self-interest, where students are positioned and treated as customers, curriculum co-creation offers a counter-narrative to traditional models of education (Matthews, Dwyer, Hine & Turner, 2018) that makes possible alternative ways of being and interacting.

We have focused in this chapter on expanding curriculum design and redesign to include partnerships amongst students, academic staff, and academic developers to foster radically and productively disruptive co-creation. We welcome further research that brings pedagogical partnerships into conversation with decolonisation literature and practices – explorations of how partnerships might contribute to decolonising the curriculum. By transforming curriculum development into a process that emphasises dialogue and reciprocity between students and academics, ensuring that students of all experiences and identities have a right to their voice and to active participation in curriculum design and redesign, academic developers can model a form of democracy in action that enriches the teaching and learning experience in higher education while also modelling and supporting the development of a more equitable and inclusive world.

References

ANWARUDDIN, S.M. 2016. Contesting the violence of Tylerism: Toward a cosmopolitan approach to the curriculum of second language teacher education. *Teaching in Higher Education*, 21(4):429-441. [https://doi.org/10.1080/13562517.2016.1155550]

BARRINEAU, S.; SCHNAAS, U.; ENGSTRÖM, A. & HÄRLIN, F. 2016. Breaking ground and building bridges: A critical reflection on student-faculty partnerships in academic development. *International Journal for Academic Development*, 21(1):79-83. [https://doi.org/10.1080/1360144X.2015.1120735]

BELL, A.; BARAHONA, S.; BEG, G.; COULSON, S.; EYMONT, R.; HARTMAN, J.; HUBBLE, T.; LEUNG, N.; McDONNELL, M.; NI, J.; PESETA, T.; SAKHAEE, E. & UPTIN, J. 2017. Curriculum transformation for cultural competence: Students and academics working in partnership to embed a new graduate quality. Paper presented at the Higher Education Research and Development Society of Australasia Conference, Sydney, 28-30 June.

BELL, A.; CARSON, L. & PIGGOTT, L. 2013. Deliberative democracy for curriculum renewal. In: E. Dunne & D. Owen (eds). *The student engagement handbook: Practice in higher education*. Bingley: Emerald, 499-508.

BELL, A.; PESETA, T.; BARAHONA, S.; JEONG, S.; LAN, L.; MENZIES, R.; TRIEU, T. & WEN, A. 2017. Conversation together: Student ambassadors for cultural competence. *Teaching and Learning Together in Higher Education*, 21. [https://repository.brynmawr.edu/tlthe/vol1/iss21/5]

BERGMARK, U. & WESTMAN, S. 2016. Co-creating curriculum in higher education: Promoting democratic values and a multidimensional view on learning. *International Journal for Academic Development*, 21(1):28-40. [https://doi.org/10.1080/1360144X.2015.1120734]

BOURKE, R. & LOVERIDGE, J. (EDS). 2018. *Radical collegiality through student voice: Educational experience, policy and practice*. Singapore: Springer.

Bovill, C. & Woolmer, C. 2018. How conceptualisations of curriculum in higher education influence student-staff co-creation in and of the curriculum. *Higher Education*, 78(3):407-422. [https://doi.org/10.1007/s10734-018-0349-8]

Bovill, C.; Cook-Sather, A.; Felten, P.; Millard, L. & Moore-Cherry, N. 2016. Addressing potential challenges in co-creating learning and teaching: Overcoming resistance, navigating institutional norms and ensuring inclusivity in student-staff partnerships. *Higher Education*, 71(2):195-208. [https://doi.org/10.1007/s10734-015-9896-4]

Bovill, C. & Felten, P. 2016. Cultivating student-staff partnerships through research and practice. *International Journal for Academic Development*, 21(1):1-3. [https://bit.ly/2m1up5J]

Bovill, C. & Bulley, C. 2011. A model of active student participation in curriculum design: Exploring desirability and possibility. In: C. Rust (ed). *Improving student learning: Global theories and local practices: Institutional, disciplinary and cultural variations*, 18. Oxford: Oxford Brooks University (Centre for Staff and Learning Development), 176-188. [https://eprints.gla.ac.uk/57709/1/57709.pdf]

Bovill, C.; Bulley, C.J. & Morss, K. 2011. Engaging and empowering first-year students through curriculum design: Perspectives from the literature. *Teaching in Higher Education*, 16(2):197-209. [https://doi.org/10.1080/13562517.2010.515024]

Bovill, C.; Cook-Sather, A. & Felten, P. 2011. Students as co-creators of teaching approaches, course design and curricula: Implications for academic developers. *International Journal for Academic Development*, 16(2):133-145. [https://doi.org/10.1080/1360144X.2011.568690]

Bron, J. & Veugelers, W. 2014. Why we need to involve our students in curriculum design: Five arguments for student voice. *Curriculum and Teaching Dialogue*, 16(1/2):125-139.

Brunson, M. 2018. The formation and power of trust: How it was created and enacted through collaboration. *Teaching and Learning Together in Higher Education*, 1(23). [https://bit.ly/2kpxufq]

Bunnell, S. & Bernstein, D. 2014. Improving engagement and learning through sharing course design with students: A multi-level case. *Teaching and Learning Together in Higher Education*, 1(13). [https://bit.ly/2kWFpRD]

Cates, R.; Madigan, M.R. & Reitenauer, V.L. 2018. 'Locations of possibility': Critical perspectives on partnership. *International Journal for Students as Partners*, 2(1):33-46. [https://doi.org/10.15173/ijsap.v2i1.3341]

Charkoudian, L.K.; Bitners, A.C.; Bloch, N.B. & Nawal, S. 2015. Dynamic discussion and informed improvements: Student-led revision of first-semester organic chemistry. *Teaching and Learning Together in Higher Education*, 1(15). [https://bit.ly/2krP7LL]

Cheng, X. T. 2000. Asian student's reticence revisited. *System*, 28:435-446. [https://doi.org/10.1016/S0346-251X(00)00015-4]

Cook-Sather, A. 2018. Developing 'Students as Learners and Teachers': Lessons from ten years of pedagogical partnership that strives to foster inclusive and responsive practice. *Journal of Educational Innovation, Partnership and Change*, 4(1). [https://doi.org/10.21100/jeipc.v4i1.746]

Cook-Sather, A. 2016. Undergraduate students as partners in new faculty orientation and academic development. *International Journal of Academic Development*, 2(2):151-162. [https://doi.org/10.1080/1360144X.2016.1156543]

Cook-Sather, A. 2006. Sound, presence, and power: Exploring 'student voice' in educational research and reform. *Curriculum Inquiry*, 36(4):359-390. [https://doi.org/10.1111/j.1467-873X.2006.00363.x]

Cook-Sather, A. 2002. Re(in)forming the conversations: Student position, power, and voice in teacher education. *Radical Teacher*, 64:21-28. [https://bit.ly/2m4FAui]

Cook-Sather, A.; Bahti, M. & Ntem, A. In press. Pedagogical partnerships: A how-to guide for faculty, students, and academic developers in higher education. Center for Engaged Learning Open Access Series. Elon University.

Cook-Sather, A.; Bovill, C. & Felten, P. 2014. *Engaging students as partners in learning and teaching: A guide for faculty*. California: John Wiley and Sons.

Cook-Sather, A. & Des-Ogugua, C. 2018. Lessons we still need to learn on creating more inclusive and responsive classrooms: Recommendations from one student-faculty partnership programme. *International Journal of Inclusive Education.* [https://doi.org/10.1080/13603116.2018.1441912]

Cousin, G. 2013. Evidencing the value of educational development by asking awkward questions. In: V. Bamber (ed). *Evidencing the value of educational development.* London: Staff and Educational Development Association, Special 34:19-22.

Curran, R. & Millard, L. 2016. A partnership approach to developing student capacity to engage and staff capacity to be engaging: Opportunities for academic developers. *International Journal for Academic Development,* 21(1):67-78. [https://doi.org/10.1080/1360144X.2015.1120212]

Daviduke, N. 2018. Growing into pedagogical partnerships over time and across disciplines: My experience as a non-STEM student consultant in STEM courses. *International Journal for Students as Partners,* 2(2). [https://doi.org/10.15173/ijsap.v2i2.3443]

Delpish, A.A.; Knight-McKenna, H.M.; Mihans, R.; Darby, A.; King, K. & Felten, P. 2010. Equalizing voices: Student-faculty partnership in course design. In: C. Werder & M.M. Otis (eds). *Engaging student voices in the study of teaching and learning.* Virginia: Stylus, 96-114.

Dvorakova, S.L. & Matthews, K.E. 2017. Graduate learning outcomes in science: Variation in perceptions of single- and dual-degree students. *Assessment and Evaluation in Higher Education,* 42(6):900-913. [https://doi.org/10.1080/02602938.2016.1208804]

Dwyer, A. 2018. Toward the formation of genuine partnership spaces. *International Journal for Students as Partners,* 2(1):11-15. [https://doi.org/10.15173/ijsap.v2i1.3503]

Egan, K. 1978. What is curriculum? *Curriculum Inquiry,* 8(1):65-72. [https://doi.org/10.1080/03626784.1978.11075558]

Ferguson, D.; Hanreddy, A. & Draxton, S. 2011. Giving students voice as a strategy for improving teacher practice. *London Review of Education,* 9(1):55-70. [https://doi.org/10.1080/14748460.2011.550435]

Fraser, S.P. & Bosanquet, A.M. 2006. The curriculum? That's just a unit outline, isn't it? *Studies in Higher Education,* 31(3):269-284. [https://doi.org/10.1080/03075070600680521]

Frison, D. & Melacarne, C. 2017. Introduction – Students-faculty partnership in Italy: Approaches, practices, and perspectives. *Teaching and Learning Together in Higher Education,* 1(20). [https://bit.ly/2knaX2O]

Gärdebo, J. & Wiggberg, M. 2012. Importance of student participation in future academia. In: J. Gärdebo & M. Wiggberg (eds). *Students, the university's unspent resource: Revolutionising higher education using active student participation.* Uppsala, Sweden: University of Uppsala, 7-14. [https://bit.ly/2lWFVzj]

Hafferty, F.W.; Gaufberg, E.H. & O'Donnell, J.F. 2015. The role of the hidden curriculum in 'on doctoring' courses. *AMA Journal of Ethics,* 17(2):129-137. [https://doi.org/10.1001/virtualmentor.2015.17.2.medu1-1502]

Healey, M.; Flint, A. & Harrington, K. 2014. *Engagement through partnership: Students as partners in learning and teaching in higher education.* York, UK: The Higher Education Academy. [https://bit.ly/2s5UYbF]

Heshusius, L. 1995. Listening to children: 'What could we possibly have in common?' From concerns with self to participatory consciousness. *Theory into Practice,* 43(2):117-123. [https://doi.org/10.1080/00405849509543668]

Jackson, P W. 1968. *Life in classrooms.* New York: Holt, Rinehart and Winston.

Johnston, P.H. & Nicholls, J.G. 1995. Voices we want to hear and voices we don't. *Theory into Practice,* 43(2):94-100. [https://doi.org/10.1080/00405849509543665]

Kaur, A.; Awang-Hashim, R. & Kaur, M. 2018. Students' experiences of co-creating classroom instruction with faculty. A case study in eastern context. *Teaching in Higher Education,* 24(4):461-477. [https://doi.org/10.1080/13562517.2018.1487930]

Lubicz-Nawrocka, T.M. 2018. Students as partners in learning and teaching: The benefits of co-creation of the curriculum. *International Journal for Students As Partners,* 2(1):47-63. [https://doi.org/10.15173/ijsap.v2i1.3207]

Lundy, L.; Welty, E.; Blanchet-Cohen, N.; Devine, D.; Smith, K. & Swadener, B.B. 2015. What if children had been involved in drafting the United Nations Convention on the Rights of the Child? In: A. Diduck, N. Peleg & H. Reece (eds). *Law in society: Reflections on children, family, culture and philosophy essays in honour of Michael Freeman*. Leiden: Brill, 223-242. [https://doi.org/10.1163/9789004261495_013]

Lundy, L. & Cook-Sather, A. 2016. Children's rights and student voice: Their intersections and the implications for curriculum and pedagogy. In: D. Wyse, L. Hayward & J. Pandya (eds). *The SAGE handbook of curriculum, pedagogy and assessment*. London: SAGE Publications, 2.

Marquis, E.; Puri, V.; Wan, S.; Ahmad, A.; Goff, L.; Knorr, K.; Vassileva, I. & Woo, J. 2016. Navigating the threshold of student-staff partnerships: A case study from an Ontario teaching and learning institute. *International Journal for Academic Development*, 21(1):4-15. [https://doi.org/10.1080/1360144X.2015.1113538]

Matthews, K.E. 2017. Five propositions for genuine students as partners practice. *International Journal for Students as Partners*, 1(2):1-9. [https://doi.org/10.15173/ijsap.v1i2.3315]

Matthews, K.E.; Dwyer, A.; Hine, L. & Turner, J. 2018. Conceptions of students as partners. *Higher Education*, 76(6):957-971. [https://doi.org/10.1007/s10734-018-0257-y]

Mihans, R.J. II, Long, D.T. & Felten, P. 2008. Power and expertise: Student-faculty collaboration in course design and the scholarship of teaching and learning. *International Journal for the Scholarship of Teaching and Learning*, 2(2): Article 16. [https://doi.org/10.20429/ijsotl.2008.020216]

Moore, J.L.; Altvater, L.; Mattera, J. & Regan, E. 2010. Been there, done that, still doing it. In: C. Werder & M. Otis (eds). *Engaging student voices in the study of teaching and learning*. Virginia: Stylus, 115-129.

Moys, J.L.; Collier, J. & Joyce, D. 2018. By design: Engaging graphic design students in curriculum development. *The Journal of Educational Innovation, Partnership and Change*, 4(1). [https://doi.org/10.21100/jeipc.v4i1.752]

Nguyen, T. H. 2005. Cultural background for ESL/EFL teachers. Cuyahoga Community College. Paper appeared in a multicultural project at Northeast ABLE Resource Center (Ohio).

Ong, M.; Smith, J.M. & Ko, L.T. 2017. Counterspaces for women of color in STEM higher education: Marginal and central spaces for persistence and success. *Journal of Research in Science Teaching*, 55(2):206-245. [https://doi.org/10.1002/tea.21417]

Pagram, P. & Pagram, J. 2006. Issues in e-Learning: A Thai case study. *EJISDC*, 26(6):1-8. [https://doi.org/10.1002/j.1681-4835.2006.tb00175.x]

Perez, K. 2016. Striving toward a space for equity and inclusion in physics classrooms. *Teaching and Learning Together in Higher Education*, 1(18). [https://bit.ly/2m5yUMt]

Peseta, T.L. 2014. Agency and stewardship in academic development: The problem of speaking truth to power. *International Journal for Academic Development*, 19(1):65-69. [https://doi.org/10.1080/1360144X.2013.868809]

Peseta, T.L.; Bell, A.; Clifford, A.; English, A.; Janarthana, J.; Jones, C.; Teal, M. & Zhang, J. 2016. Students as ambassadors and researchers of assessment renewal: Puzzling over the practices of university and academic life. *International Journal for Academic Development*, 21(1):54-66. [https://doi.org/10.1080/1360144X.2015.1115406]

Pinar, W. 2004. *What is curriculum theory?* New Jersey: Lawrence Erlbaum Associates.

Pollard, A.; Thiessen, D. & Filer, A. (eds). 1997. *Children and their curriculum*. London: Falmer Press.

Quinn, L. (ed). 2012. *Re-imagining academic staff development: Spaces for disruption*. Stellenbosch: African Sun Media. [https://doi.org/10.18820/9781920338879]

Quinn, L. & Vorster, J. 2017. Connected disciplinary responses to the call to decolonise curricula in South African higher education. In: B. Carnell & D. Fung (eds). *Developing the higher education curriculum research-based education in practice*. London: UCL Press, 131-144. [https://doi.org/10.2307/j.ctt1xhr542.15]

Roxå, T. & Mårtensson, K. 2017. Agency and structure in academic development practices: Are we liberating academic teachers or are we part of a machinery suppressing them? *International Journal for Academic Development*, 22(2):95-105. [https://doi.org/10.1080/1360144X.2016.1218883]

Ryan, A. & Tilbury, D. 2013. *Flexible pedagogies: New pedagogical ideas*. London: Higher Education Academy.

Seale, J.; Gibson, S.; Haynes, J. & Potter, A. 2015. Power and resistance: Reflections on the rhetoric and reality of using participatory methods to promote student voice and engagement in higher education. *Journal of Further and Higher Education*, 39(4):534-552. [https://doi.org/10.1080/0309877X.2014.938264]

Schubert, W.H. 1986. *Curriculum: Perspectives, paradigms and possibilities*. New York: Macmillan.

Shore, S. 2012. 'Changing education': Helping to conceptualize the first 360. *Teaching and Learning Together in Higher Education*, 1(7). [https://bit.ly/2lXVMhc]

Thomson, P. 2007. Making it real: Engaging students in active citizenship projects. In: D. Thiessen & A. Cook-Sather (eds). *International handbook of student experience in elementary and secondary school*. Dordrecht, The Netherlands: Springer, 775-804. [https://doi.org/10.1007/1-4020-3367-2_31]

Vorster, J. & Quinn, L. 2017. The 'decolonial turn': What does it mean for academic staff development? *Education as Change*, 21(1). [https://doi.org/10.17159/1947-9417/2017/853]

Wilson, B.L. & Corbett, H.D. 2001. *Listening to urban kids: School reform and the teachers they want*. New York: State University of New York Press.

CHAPTER 7

Integrating academic literacies into the curriculum in Occupational Therapy

Currents of disruption and congruence in a collaborative process

Arona Dison & Lucia Hess-April

Introduction

The literacies required for academic engagement are often taken for granted in curriculum design and implementation, in spite of their integral role in students' learning within academia generally and in particular disciplines. In this chapter, we reflect on an ongoing research-based collaborative process undertaken by lecturers in an Occupational Therapy department at the University of the Western Cape (UWC) together with an academic developer to integrate academic literacies into the curriculum. The themes of disruption and congruence in the lecturers' interactions and emerging understandings of academic literacies within the context of the ongoing shaping, implementing and researching of the Occupational Therapy second year curriculum are explored. Following a brief background to the project, an outline of some of the theory about academic literacies is provided. Currents of disruption where different understandings and concepts came into interaction with each other as well as currents of congruence are explored. Finally, small-scale changes made in the curriculum that arose out of the process, are highlighted. The authors of this chapter are Arona, the academic developer in the Faculty of Community and Health Sciences at the time, and Lucia, a lecturer in the Occupational Therapy department, who initiated and led the project in the department together with Arona.

Disruption and congruence

The term "disruption" is used by Quinn (2012:1) to mean "adopting a stance of questioning, challenging and critiquing taken-for-granted ways of doing things in higher education". Provoked by the theme of this book, this chapter offers an exploration of how the theme of disruption manifested itself in the collaborative process that the Occupational Therapy lecturers engaged in relation to the Occupational Therapy curriculum. This collaborative process was characterised by currents of cohesion, continuity and familiarity pushing against currents of disruption, thus illustrating both congruence and disruption, equally in the interactions between the participants and in the understanding of concepts related to academic literacies.

There was a parallel between the concepts of congruence and disruption and that of normative and transformative approaches to academic literacies which will be discussed in more detail in the conceptual framework section of the chapter. A normative approach aims to induct students into dominant academic and professional literacies. A transformative approach engages with students' literacies, aiming to challenge the status quo (Lillis & Scott, 2007). Consequently, the latter resonates with the concept of disruption in the sense of "critiquing taken-for-granted ways of doing things". Initially, Arona's approach to students' development of academic literacies was framed within a normative approach. During the project, she extended her conception of academic literacies to include transformative approaches. Although transformative literacies was not an overt focus of the project, there were discussions about transformative pedagogies which lecturers in the Occupational Therapy department used. The academic developer and the Occupational Therapy lecturers came with different academic frames of reference and used different language regarding students' learning and literacies. During the project, they negotiated meaning across these perspectives, that generated a rich process of mutual learning (Wenger, 1998).

The Occupational Therapy department has developed what they identify as an emancipatory curriculum with the key focus of equipping students to become agents of change (UWC, 2013). Thus the curriculum inherently lent itself to disruption in the sense of challenging the status quo. However, social justice education (Moje, 2007) also requires the induction of students into the established discourses of the university and the profession for them to succeed in their university and professional careers. During the project, the lecturers grew to realise how much they took for granted about students' learning and development of academic and professional literacies. The project enabled them to address the development of students' literacies in the second year Occupational Therapy curriculum with more understanding and intent.

In the introduction to Lillis, Harrington, Lea and Mitchell's (2015:15) book on transformative practices in academic literacies, Mitchell describes transformation as "an inclination towards envisaging understandings of, and actions within any particular context [which are alternative to the] normative and the status quo". Transformative thinking, according to Geertz (1993), involves:

> ... translation, how meaning gets moved, or does not, reasonably intact from one sort of discourse to the next; about intersubjectivity, how separate individuals come to conceive, or do not, reasonably similar things; about how thought frames change ... how thought norms are maintained [and] thought models acquired.
> (Geertz, 1993:154, cited in Lillis et al., 2015:15)

The focus of this chapter is the collaborative process that all the participants experienced in the exchange of ideas, practice and reflection on practice in the Occupational Therapy project on integrating academic literacies into the curriculum. In reflecting on how understandings and beliefs about students' learning, development of academic and professional literacies and practices washed against each other, shifted and changed, we offer examples of how, in small ways, existing curriculum practices were reshaped or strengthened. We trace how moments and currents of disruption led to changes in understanding, learning and growth and how these intersected with currents of congruence, arising out of shared history and understandings, collaboration and familiarity in the department.

Background

The Occupational Therapy department at UWC has a diverse group of students from a range of socio-economic and educational backgrounds. They include first language speakers of English and multilingual students whose first language is not English. The faculty academic developer, Arona, extended an invitation for participation in a project on integrating academic literacies into the curriculum. Lucia was interested in initiating a collaborative research project in the department as she "was noticing the valuable things that they [the lecturers] were doing and thought that they should share these practices". The lecturers were motivated to become involved in the project because of their concern about the quality of their students' writing within the Occupational Therapy programme. We chose the second year of the programme for the project focus, and all the second-year lecturers participated in the project. Lecturers' expected a certain level of academic literacy from the students, who had done a stand-alone academic literacy module and experienced their first year of university study. Lecturers wanted to explore why these expectations were not being met and develop strategies to address this.

We intended that the project would take three years, from 2015 to 2017. The goal for the first year was for participants (the lecturers) to develop a theoretically informed understanding of academic literacies, to unpack what literacies were required in Occupational Therapy and consider how the department was facilitating the development of these literacies already, and uncover possible areas for development. By the end of the first year, small-scale curriculum changes were introduced for the second year, incorporating more intentional building of academic literacies development into the modules. These changes were to be implemented and researched in the second year. In the third year, curriculum changes would be reiterated, informed by the research, conducted in the second year. The project exceeded the planned time frame because of the #FeesMustFall student protests of 2015 and 2016 which took place towards the end of both years.

Occupational Therapy, defined by the World Federation of Occupational therapists (WFOT, 2012), is a profession that promotes health and well-being through occupation. Occupation enables people to meet their needs and refers to the ordinary activities that people do daily and the way they use their time, energy, interests and skills in meeting their needs for health and well-being (Christiansen & Townsend, 2004). Historically, Occupational Therapy education in South Africa was not responsive to societal needs. Postapartheid developments around health reform and higher education in South Africa, however, facilitated the review of the UWC curriculum. This resulted in the adoption of a socially responsive programme and a critically oriented curriculum that would assist Occupational Therapy students to understand their role as critical practitioners.

The Occupational Therapy department provided an environment conducive to a participatory, collaborative project of this kind. It is a small department composed of eleven full-time lecturers and about 220 students. From the perspective of the academic developer, initially an outsider to the department, it was a close-knit group. This is not to say it was necessarily harmonious, but there was congruence in the lecturers' commitment to the development of competent and critical professionals and to teaching and learning which facilitated this. It was evident that there was a high level of substantive interaction about teaching and learning in the Occupational Therapy programme and an openness to the contribution of the academic developer. There was a schedule in place with times for administrative meetings alternating with "scholarship" sessions (engagement with research and teaching and learning) throughout the year. For the duration of the project, a portion of the scholarship time was allocated to the academic literacies project, thus providing space for it to be sustained.

In the first year of the project, we conducted a focus group discussion with all Occupational Therapy lecturers about what academic literacies students needed and how the lecturers developed these literacies in their modules. A focus group discussion was also conducted with second-year Occupational Therapy students to elicit their views on their development of academic reading and writing abilities and to what extent these were facilitated and within the Occupational Therapy curriculum. We presented the preliminary analysis of the focus groups to the department. There were learning opportunities scheduled in the form of a discussion about an article on academic literacies, and a seminar presented by Cecilia Jacobs, a leading South African scholar on academic literacies. All of the lecturers in the department participated in the initial focus group discussion, subsequent member-checking session and the seminar by Jacobs. Thus the project was firmly located in the department from the start. At the end of the first year, there was a planning workshop for changes for the following year. The second and third years of the project involved discussion of plans for integrating academic literacy into modules, reflections on the implementation of the changes and writing. In the fourth year, the participants planned a programme focused on writing about the implementation of changes in their modules and the accompanying research.

Conceptual framework

Two broad theoretical approaches inform this chapter – an academic literacies approach to students' reading and writing (Lea & Street, 1998; Jacobs, 2005; Lillis & Scott, 2007) and an approach to learning centred on critical reflexivity

(Giroux, 1988; Freire, 1990). There is a rich body of research on the socially constructed nature of academic literacies both internationally and in South Africa. An academic literacies approach views literacies as social practices embedded in socially and culturally situated contexts. Academic literacy theorists reject a skills-based, deficit model of student writing which locates problems with individual students and highlights the complexity of writing practices required at university (Lea & Street, 1998). As Lea and Street (1998:158) argue, "academic literacy practices constitute central processes through which students learn new subjects and develop their knowledge about new areas of study". Literacies are seen as being contextualised in disciplines rather than generic skills that students can learn out of context and then apply within disciplinary reading and writing. Furthermore, there are implicit academic writing conventions linked to disciplinary practices. The term academic conventions refer here to "generally accepted discipline-specific rules of writing, such as use of the first person, structure, validity and use of evidence and rules of referencing" (Rai, 2004:151). The use of the plural form for literacies comes out of the recognition that there is not one generic form of academic literacy, but rather many different literacies since they are embedded in different social or disciplinary contexts (Gee, 2008).

Lea and Street (1998:158-159) in their seminal article, identify three models of (or approaches to) students' writing in higher education namely the "study skills", "socialisation" and "academic literacies" models. The models are not seen as mutually exclusive, and the academic literacies model encapsulates the other two into "a more encompassing understanding of the nature of student writing". The study skills approach view literacy as "a set of atomised skills which students have to learn and which are then transferable to other contexts". The focus is on attempting to "fix" students' problems with language and learning. The socialisation approach focuses on the need to induct students into the culture of the academy. Although there is some level of acknowledgement of disciplinary differences, Lea and Street argue that this approach treats the norms and practices of the institution as homogeneous and does not sufficiently theorise processes of change and the exercise of power within institutions. An academic literacies approach sees literacies as social practices, which are located within institutions and disciplines and constituted within these sites of discourse and power. Students need to develop a repertoire of literacies which are appropriate to different settings and to "handle the social meanings and identities that each [setting] evokes" (Lea & Street, 1998:159).

Lillis and Scott (2007:13) distinguish between a normative and transformative approach to academic literacies. The aim of a normative approach is to "identify and induct" through identifying academic conventions in relation to discourse, structure or genre and exploring how students might be taught to become proficient in particular academic literacies, in other words, become socialised into academic discourse communities. A transformative approach involves a critical engagement with academic conventions and an ability to locate these conventions within "contested traditions of knowledge making" (Lillis & Scott, 2007:13). It requires questioning by writers of how these conventions may affect their meaning making. It explores alternative ways of meaning making in academia, valuing the resource that students bring to the university as "legitimate tools for meaning making" (Lillis & Scott, 2007:13).

As mentioned above, the UWC Occupational Therapy department offers what is described as emancipatory curriculum or a "curriculum for transformation, as its key focus is equipping students to become agents of change" (UWC, 2013). This implies shaping graduates who are able to participate in critical or transformative action through building their critical consciousness (Freire, 1990). The curriculum, therefore, facilitates critical reflexivity and develops the participants' capacity for questioning and challenging the status quo regarding the occupational rights of individuals, groups and communities. Critical reflexivity is pro-active, as its focus is on providing practitioners with a tool that will make them aware of the assumptions that shape their interaction with others (Jones, 2009). Occupational therapists are constantly challenged to reflect on contextual factors as they relate to the world of their practice and the lives of their clients (Kinsella, 2001). Influenced by Giroux (1988), Kinsella (2001:2) argues that by reflecting on the ideological factors and the politics that inform their workplaces, occupational therapists can begin to "rethink and reform the traditions that may prevent us from becoming active reflective practitioners". Kinsella (2001) asserts that reflection on practice leads occupational therapists to a closer examination of the contexts of their clients' lives, the contexts of their practice, and the systemic factors that influence both of these. The insight gained through reflection can provide a foundation for occupational therapists' actions, as they advocate for their clients and for systemic change.

Since the 1980s, reflective practice has been increasingly recognised as one of the necessary attributes of competent health professionals generally (Schön, 1983, 1987; Epstein & Hundert, 2002). Reflective writing is a widely used genre for assignments in practice learning modules in Occupational Therapy.

It requires students to draw on their personal values and past experiences and to "make links with relevant theoretical knowledge" (Rai, 2012:270). It is both a means of developing reflective capability and is used for the assessment of students' capability. Mann, Gordon and MacLeod (2009:610) understand reflection to fulfil several functions, including "helping to make meaning of complex situations and enabling learning from experience". It can potentially influence the choice of how to act in difficult or morally ambiguous circumstances (Wald et al., 2012). Expectations of reflective writing are significantly different from the conventions of the "essay" genre required in theory courses. Moreover, the expectations are implicit rather than clearly stated (Rai, 2006). During the project, a student's comment about reflective writing provided a significant disruptive moment. This will be discussed below.

Conceptual understandings and insights: Currents and moments of disruption and congruence

In this section, we reflect on the currents of disruption and congruence that the lecturers experienced on the project, and identify particular moments that acted as catalysts for disruption and renewal of thinking. Themes that arose from the evidence are highlighted, consisting mainly of transcripts of an initial staff and student focus group, as well as several further discussions by the lecturers, together with the academic developer.

The main currents of disruption are elucidated in the theme of critiquing unexamined assumptions about students' learning and integrating academic literacies into the curriculum. Under this theme, lecturers' perceptions of their role in developing students' academic literacies; lecturers' expectations of students' literacies and how explicit lecturers were in communicating their expectations to students are examined. The theme was, however, not only characterised by disruption. There were also movements towards congruence through the process of discussion, sharing and reflection.

The main currents of congruence were centred on the deepening of lecturers' understandings of academic literacies and their integration into the curriculum. In analysing the project data, converging currents surfaced – a transformative approach to academic literacies aligned with the concept of critical literacies espoused by the Occupational Therapy department.

Currents of disruption: Critiquing unexamined assumptions about students' learning and literacies

Lecturers had different understandings of their role in developing students' academic literacies. In the first focus group session with all the lecturers in the department, it appeared that some of the lecturers approached academic literacy from a "study skills" perspective (Lea & Street, 1998). Students who were regarded as weak in writing and reading comprehension were seen to be lacking specific study skills and therefore required support to "learn" these skills. Within this perspective, the "problem" is seen as largely being that of the student (Boughey, 2002), with support only considered once students submitted work and were in danger of failing a course. There were three issues that emerged with regard to the role of disciplinary lecturers in developing students' academic literacies: firstly, whether it was part of a subject specialist's responsibility to facilitate students' development of academic literacy; secondly, the availability of time and space in the curriculum; and thirdly, expertise for integrating academic literacies on the part of the lecturer.

One of the lecturers in the initial focus group expressed the view that it was not her job to teach academic literacy in her first-year module "because there're so many other things that need to be covered in my course" (February 2015). In a subsequent discussion session, this point was expanded, bringing in the issues of the capacity of lecturers as well as space in the curriculum. She said, even if "there was space and time for me to do all of that in class" she didn't have the skills and the training to make reading and writing "part of the curriculum – [even something] as simple as how to write an essay…" (July, 2015). In contrast to this view, another lecturer expressed the opinion that developing academic literacies was a matter of "integrating it into what we do in our course", but said: "I don't know how to do that." This was echoed by a comment that they were "already kind-of making the changes" and their concern was "how do we develop our capacity so that we integrate both without adding on [which was] a tough call".

In the initial lecturers' focus group the issue of Occupational Therapy content and development of academic literacies was also approached from the perspective of whether one could identify distinctive *academic* literacies and *professional* literacies, particularly with regard to practising as an occupational therapist and how these literacies related to each other. Lecturers agreed that it was crucial for an occupational therapist to be able to integrate theory into practice, for example, when working with a client or a community. One of the lecturers pointed out that:

> ... in teaching students, one is focusing on how to be an occupational therapist, how to think and reason like one, but by doing that, you're going to have to address [academic literacy] at some level in order ... for the student to be able to reason or critique [or translate practice into theory]. It's still academic literacy but its discipline-specific academic literacy ...

The lecturers' emerging understanding arising out of engagement in the process, appeared to shift from the first focus group to the discussion after the analysis of the staff and student focus groups. They started acknowledging that academic literacy practices differed from school literacy practices and needed to be explicitly "taught" in the curriculum. This was compounded by the South African context and the diversity of students entering higher education. Lecturers agreed that students needed to develop Occupational Therapy specific literacies, and began to recognise that these were connected to the development of academic literacies. In the early stages of the project, there was emerging recognition that academic literacies needed to be integrated into the curriculum, but there was concern about how to integrate literacies development in terms of time and space in the curriculum and lecturers' own capacity to do this. One of the lecturers in a scholarship meeting in August 2016 indicated the extent of the shift when she said: "We have actually adopted the responsibility for academic literacies whereas before it was assumed to have been done outside of the professional curriculum maybe [in the first-year academic literacy module]."

During the project, there were shifts in the lecturers' expectations about what levels of academic literacies students should have at various levels of the Occupational Therapy programme. In the initial focus group, some of the lecturers articulated their frustrations because they assumed that students should have basic levels of academic literacies on entering the university which most of them did not. Furthermore, they expressed frustration that students did not seem to transfer academic skills that they had been taught previously.

One of the lecturers outlined what she saw as basic literacies that she expected of students. She expected that they should be able to write a basic essay with an introduction, body and conclusion and should know "how to keep bits together ... from topic to topic". She expected them to be able to write a basic argument. She acknowledged that some of the lecturers teaching at a first- and second-year level were explicitly teaching students basic academic literacies, such as essay writing and referencing, but were frustrated that the students were still not meeting the requirements of academic writing expected of them. Referencing was a great concern for the lecturers. During the project, there was a shift from exasperation directed at students to more understanding of why referencing is challenging for students and discussion about how they could support students in learning how to reference.

In a scholarship meeting in August 2016, lecturers were sharing initial stages of interventions that they had made in their modules that they intended to research. At this point, there is evidence of them questioning some of the assumptions that had been expressed before about students' learning and literacies development and suggesting ways of addressing some of these issues. For example, one of the lecturers who had expressed frustration before about unmet expectations and lack of transfer articulated more understanding and acceptance of these conditions, as well as ways of dealing with them. She no longer assumed that "once students had learned a skill they should be competent in it", which implies a shift from a skills-based approach to more of a socialisation approach. Furthermore, she said that the project had made her pay more attention to the detail of her teaching:

> ... not that I necessarily changed that much in my semester, but I am more aware of academic literacies and I'm listening to what the students are saying and adding things ... not just assuming that the students have it.

The assumption on the part of the lecturers that students should enter university with the required literacies to engage in university studies could be seen to shift significantly during the project. This is articulated in the August discussion. A clear moment of disruption and clarification of the issues was Cecilia Jacobs' presentation in May 2016. Her presentation influenced the lecturers, and they often referred to it later:

> What for me stood out very boldly ... was the meeting we had with Cecilia and when she spoke about the 80 per cent of school children that do not come to university but the 20 per cent that do come – we expect them to be ready for university and we complain they are not prepared and it's very difficult.

At the start of the project, lecturers expressed the view that they were very clear and explicit in communicating their expectations of what was required from students. From the initial post-analysis session, the lecturers became aware that at times there were gaps between their expectations and students' interpretations of what lecturers required from their writing.

Lecturers thought that they clearly communicated their expectations of students' writing. However, some of the students in the student focus group indicated that in many cases they found the expectations of writing in the different modules unclear. They expressed a view that the requirements for writing were not made explicit by lecturers but were frequently left hidden, causing uncertainty. They were, therefore, often unsure as to how they were not meeting staff expectations and wanted explicit feedback to identify their weaknesses.

In the focus group with students, the point was made most strongly about the genre of reflective writing. The following comment made in the students' focus group was challenging for the lecturers:

> I think that in a way it's the hardest thing ever to do even though they say it's reflective – whatever you feel, whatever you think, but at the back of your mind, you're still like, I should say this, I should say that. So, you're not really saying exactly what you want to say because you're scared you're going to be marked down on your opinion because you're scared it's wrong.

This student's comment provided a moment of disruption when we presented the preliminary analysis of the focus groups to the lecturers (July 2015). One of the lecturer's immediate responses was: "These are the second years – they don't even get marked on the reflections ... only in their fourth year." She focused on the detail where the student expressed her anxiety about being marked down. However, at that point, she seemed to miss the insight that the student was providing, which was that the genre of reflective writing was harder than the lecturers realised and that some students experienced ambiguity and anxiety about what the lecturers required of them.

Although the immediate response from one of the lecturers when hearing this student's point appeared to be defensive, the quotation had a significant impact on the lecturers. Reinforced by discussion in the student focus group, this comment pointed to the mismatch that sometimes occurred between lecturers' perceptions of the extent and clarity of their communication to students about expectations and the students' perceptions. The point was referred to at times throughout the project and originating from the point of disruption; it became a strong current of congruence amongst the lecturers.

The particular genre of reflective writing is one which is susceptible to being misunderstood both by students and lecturers. It tends to be misunderstood by lecturers in that it can be seen as a straightforward form of writing as it draws on students' own experience, but in contrast to this it is difficult for students to manage the different voices required, particularly the personal experience voice, and the analytical voice which relates theory to their own experience.

The student in the focus group received an ambivalent message, the requirement of expression of her personal voice and opinion, which conflicted with her fear that there was a required point of view which may be in contrast to hers. Mitchell (2017) observed an overt strategy by a group of first-year medical students. They admitted to strategically "deviating from the truth [their own experiences, observations and opinions] to comply with the task criteria to successfully achieve the course directives". The two situations differ in that the Occupational Therapy student was expressing her uncertainty about what was required, and the medical students made a strategic choice based on a strong belief that there was a "right answer". Nevertheless, both of these expressions point to complexity and ambiguity in the requirement of reflective writing.

Critically reflective practice is both a central process and the desired graduate attribute which informs the curriculum and pedagogy of the Occupational Therapy programme. The question that was highlighted by the student's comment about the genre of reflective writing and the impact on the lecturers' understandings suggested that the department needed to engage in more critical ongoing reflection on their pedagogical practices.

Currents of congruence: Embedding and aligning academic literacies in the curriculum

We discussed above how in the first lecturers' focus group, there was a diversity of views expressed regarding lecturers' role in facilitating students' development of academic literacies. There was also discussion about the need for deliberate teaching of academic literacy skills in the curriculum and how this could be made more explicit and coordinated between the modules in the second year, and within the context of the whole programme.

In response to some lecturers' concerns about lacking capacity to integrate academic literacies into subject teaching, Lucia suggested that the lecturers "examine each module and look at ... what specific skills of academic literacy [they] are eliciting in that module so that [they] are aware of it and it could be incorporated". She said that they were already doing it, but it was not coherent, it was "hit and miss" and needed to be more streamlined in the programme and more explicit.

The ensuing discussion involved lecturers grappling with these ideas about their modules and exploring the implications of the integration of academic literacies for assessment. While the department had always communicated with each other about the content of their modules, one of the benefits of the project was the intensity of interaction about the second-year curriculum, particularly regarding the development of academic literacies and students' learning.

One lecturer emphasised the need to communicate to students what academic literacies were being focused on in a particular module or assignment so "[students] must know that, you need to make sure that in your arguments these are the [literacies], you must incorporate them, then you will be getting marks for that as well". She said that that would motivate them to put more effort into searching for relevant information and incorporating supporting literature into their assignments (Lecturers focus group, February 2015).

In the scholarship meeting in August 2016, lecturers discussed what they had been doing on their interventions in their modules so far. One of the lecturers reflected that through the project, they had been informally developing principles for integrating academic literacies. For example, they had used scaffolding before in their teaching, but as part of the project, they had spoken about it and thought more about it than before. She said:

> ... now we are actually planning scaffolding into the module, being a lot more explicit and clear with our instructions and guiding the students a lot more, explaining why things are important ... contextualising the things with the students and not just assuming they are on the same page as us.

Lecturers also discussed how students found it difficult to make connections between different parts of the course and suggested that they constantly point out the links between the different modules in terms of theory and practice, content and academic literacies. They suggested using concept maps to show the conceptual structure of modules and how they fitted into the programme more broadly.

Accordingly, as a result of the project, the second-year lecturers came to a shared understanding that academic literacies needed to be embedded in the curriculum design to support students' acquisition of professional as well as academic literacies through a process of explicitly building literacies development into the curriculum in a coordinated way.

Curriculum interventions

As part of the project, lecturers explored various curriculum interventions that involved designing their modules and related learning tasks and assignments with the aim of facilitating students' development of academic literacies. Attention was given to module outcomes and expectations, learning tasks and formative assessments. Lecturers engaged in a collaborative process in which they drew on the group's combined reflections and developing understandings of academic literacies to implement related interventions in their modules. In the third year of the project, they gave informal presentations to the group about small-scale interventions that they were introducing in the different modules and researching. This section reflects on some of the changes which were implemented, drawing on lecturers' presentations.

Lecturers selected modules where they would focus on particular academic literacies. In two of the modules the emphasis was on working with literature. Lecturers guided students on how to write a literature review in stages. They provided scaffolding in the process of searching for literature, selecting a journal and article, reading an article and incorporating articles in their writing. Students then needed to combine these literacies in an assessment task.

One of the lecturers described how she coached her students in the writing of an assignment:

> ... the students are still very insecure with formulating arguments and constructing sentences and constructing of thoughts, taking content out of an article and turning it into something that is actually their own. So we work through those and then summarise articles and write sections of essays, and they submit that to me, and I provide feedback ... that worked quite nicely in terms of preparing for their assignment.

Lecturers who required students to submit drafts for formative feedback found that it fostered students' engagement with the content of their writing. It assisted with the interpretation of case studies as well as the integration of literature sources and formulating arguments and reaching conclusions. Another lecturer described how she mediated students' sourcing, reading and understanding of articles, using collaborative learning. Students worked in groups, where each group had to search for one article explaining a particular concept which was significant for their case study. Once they had developed an understanding of the concept, they shared it with the rest of the class. They then drew on the pool of literature to write up their case study.

In the module, *Occupational Therapy and Chronic diseases*, students were required to search for literature using the search engines and databases available in the library. They learned to use literature appropriately, evaluating its relevance and applying it to different pathologies and contexts discussed in their writing. The lecturer described how he directed students to search for literature:

> We once watched a video in class and then showed them that they need to think about the occupation that the person does and the skills the person needs. For example, if this person has an amputation, search literature that speaks about amputation. Search literature that speaks to [the] community – because this person also belongs to a community. They learn how to use [the] information for effective intervention – in the lives of people with the aforementioned conditions.

Currents of disruption and congruence: Grappling with transformative and critical literacies

The concept of critical literacies and its role in the Occupational Therapy curriculum was one of the currents that ran through discussions in the project. Arona pointed to links between the concept of transformative literacies (Lillis & Scott, 2007) and critical literacies (Luke, 2004; Galvaan, 2015). With regard to academic literacies, the project predominantly took a normative approach to literacies development as it focused on students' mastering the academic literacies required in Occupational Therapy.

As discussed above, the department had taken on an emancipatory approach to the curriculum oriented to educating critically reflective professionals which would require the students to developed critical literacy. There was an assumption that the lecturers had a shared understanding of critical literacy. However going back to the initial lecturers' focus group transcript it was evident that there were divergent concepts of critical literacy and in some cases, critical literacy was used interchangeably with critical thinking, reading and writing. When lecturers discussed critical literacy in the focus group, one of them spoke of the ability of students to integrate quotations from literature into their writing appropriately. Another lecturer referred to the need for students to consider the author's perspective and how that influenced the article as well as the contexts in which research was located and how that related to the South African context. One lecturer described how third-year students read an article about bipolar veterans in the United States. She said that they could get information from the article about the bipolar condition but they "could not correlate that that was a veteran population and what that meant, and that is completely different to what we see in South Africa".

These "critical reading and writing literacies" which were described could be seen as part of academic literacies and not critical literacy specifically, depending on one's understanding of "critical".

In the same focus group, Lucia described critical literacy in the following way:

> ... understanding involves not just the words but ... what is beneath the words ... it is also about understanding the context in which [it has been] written ... so that you can identify that ... this comes from a particular frame of reference, or a particular discourse is being followed. [It involves trying to] identify the worldview that is being utilised in the piece of writing ... I think it is something that develops over the years.

Goodfellow (2011) argues that the concept of critique within much conventional academic literacy teaching has been diluted to a "soft" form of critical thinking. Such an understanding of critical thinking focuses primarily on the conventions of academic argument such as "maintaining a disinterested stance and presenting evidence for more than one point of view" (Goodfellow, 2011:138). According to such an understanding, critical thinking is not used to engage with matters of "political, cultural and individual significance" (Goodfellow, 2011:138).

In Occupational Therapy education, developing critical literacy entails helping students to recognise political factors that impact on occupational engagement and well-being. The term "critical literacy" refers to a deepened consciousness of a situation that allows students to recognise, reflect on and challenge hegemonies that impact on occupational well-being (Galvaan, 2015). The process is one that entails "asking hard questions, seeing underneath, behind, and beyond texts to understand how these texts establish and use power over us, over others, on whose behalf, in whose interests" (Luke, 2004, in McLaughlin & Devoogd, 2004:4). Thus, it is a practice involving disruption of what is on the surface.

In a workshop at the end of 2015, the lecturers discussed the development of critical literacy in the curriculum, which was emphasised mainly in the fourth year. This was particularly pertinent to developing students' competencies in community development practice, emphasised in the fourth year. One lecturer said:

> They cannot do community development without critically looking at systems and structures in communities. If they address occupational rights, then they have to look at that, they look at occupational apartheid and injustices. For me, that is what critical literacy is. It really encompasses [an] understanding of those issues – it is a political understanding.

Lecturers agreed that elements of critical literacy were, however, infused in the whole curriculum in which students were made aware of power issues. An awareness of differential power relations furthermore comes to the fore in the adoption of client-centred practice, which is an approach that fosters the active participation of clients by drawing on their strengths and ensuring that practice is relevant to their context, goals, values and interests (Townsend, Polatajko, Craik & Davis, 2007).

It was pointed out that students and practitioners needed to be able to negotiate power relations when working in a multidisciplinary team, where different professionals were more or less empowered through societal structures. For example, an occupational therapist could find herself in a challenging situation with regard to a patient if her viewpoint differs from a professional nurse or medical doctor.

Luke's (2004) interpretation of critical literacy resonates with Lillis and Scott's (2017) conceptualisation of a transformative approach to academic literacies in which students (and lecturers) engage critically with academic conventions and locate these conventions within "contested traditions of knowledge making" (Lillis & Scott, 2007:13). A transformative approach to literacies requires questioning by writers of how these conventions may affect their meaning making. It explores alternative ways of meaning making in academia, valuing the resources that students bring to the university as "legitimate tools for meaning making" (Lillis & Scott, 2007:13).

As mentioned above, the project was not approached from a transformative literacies perspective with regard to students' academic literacies development. However, there are practices which we looked at through a transformative literacies lens in retrospect when analysing the data. *Health promotion and youth wellness* is a community-based module focused on youth at risk. As part of this module, the students needed to do a community intervention in a school. Based on their experience, the students identified a social injustice that they had seen in the school or community. They were required to identify the occupational risk, occupational rights that are violated, occupational injustices that the community experiences and propose interventions that can address the occupational injustices.

The assessment for this learning activity was a graphic mind map. The students represented their interventions through mind maps in which they integrated text and visual images. The lecturer said, "it's not about plunging a lot of words on a piece of paper – but using their understanding through what they have experienced [in the fieldwork] and in-class and integrating their learning". This could be seen as a way of drawing on students' multimodal resources where students could choose "how to represent meaning from a range of possibilities" (Archer & Breur, 2016:7), including images created from their life-world, without being constrained to write academic discourse.

Educators, need to see critical literacy as an attribute that students need to develop but can, however, be complacent about their own practices. When the student (in the focus group) questioned whether the lecturers expected her to write what she thought or what they wanted to hear, it disrupted the complacency of the lecturers about the transparency of their expectations. It led them to be more aware of the power dynamics which played out in lecturer-student interactions. This comes through in a reflection written by a lecturer in response to the student's comment:

> If students are not free to truly express themselves, are they fully learning? If the power dynamic changes enough for them [not] to fear to raise an opinion that differs from mine, then might we lose our ability to mould them into the therapists we need them to be? Or is this my fear of losing my power as the 'expert'?

The lecturers aimed to develop critically reflective professionals equipped to contribute to social justice. The programme, therefore, required students to understand and experience reflexivity. Similarly, lecturers needed to understand and practice reflexivity regarding issues of power between themselves and students if they were to address critical literacy more effectively.

Conclusion

In conclusion, we return to Mitchell's exploration of a version of transformation in the introduction of this chapter. Drawing on Geertz (1993), she describes it as "an inclination towards envisaging" understandings and actions within a particular context, which are alternative to the normative and the status quo (Lillis et al., 2015:15). While we recognise the need for large-scale institutional and curriculum transformation, like Mitchell, we wish to acknowledge the value of small-scale changes, where "meaning gets moved ... thought frames change" (Geertz, 1993:154, in Lillis et al., 2015:15) through the ongoing engagement of a community of practice engaged in the mutual endeavour of teaching and learning. The process described here was deeply embedded in the particular context, approaches of individuals, relationships and the organisational culture and ethos of the Occupational Therapy department, so we are not suggesting that it is replicable in the same form. However, we found value in exploring and sharing what happened at a micro-level in this process and suggest that aspects of this process might be implemented in different contexts, even if it is with a few lecturers in a department who can gradually assert more of an influence in that context.

The role played by the academic developer and the strategies utilised to facilitate a reciprocal project of mutual learning enhanced the value and effectiveness of this collaborative project. All involved were able to deeply engage with and develop their practices in ways that exceeded their expectations. Through asking relevant questions, being a resource, actively seeking to understand diverse perspectives and being sensitive to lecturers' responsibilities and workloads, Arona, as the academic developer, was instrumental in assisting lecturers to contribute to the discussions according to their levels of comfort and expertise. In this space, they were able to challenge each other, try new things in practice, report back, and seek feedback. The acknowledgement and feedback that they received enabled them to derive more meaning about the value of what they were doing as well as to expand and deepen individual and collaborative practices of integrating academic literacies into the curriculum.

During the project currents of congruence, arising from familiarity, collaboration and shared meaning, washed against currents of disruption. We challenged taken-for-granted ways of thinking that led to mutual learning, the forming of new understandings, and the implementation of small-scale changes. It is likely to continue to have an impact on the department and the overall curriculum through the ongoing practices of the lecturers and their contribution to departmental processes. Based on our experience of this project, we argue that there is a need to open up more spaces for engagement in higher education institutions that facilitate this kind of transformative work.

References

Archer, A. & Breur, E. 2016. Introduction: A Multimodal Response to Changing Communication Landscapes in Higher Education. In: A. Archer & E. Breuer (eds). *Multimodality in Higher Education*. Brill: Leiden, 1-17. [https://doi.org/10.1163/9789004312067_002]

Boughey, C. 2002. Naming' Students' Problems: an analysis of language-related discourses at a South African university. *Teaching in Higher Education*, 7(3):295-307. [https://doi.org/10.1080/13562510220144798]

Christiansen, C.H. & Townsend, E. 2004. *Introduction to occupation: the art and science of living*. Saddle River, NJ: Prentice-Hall.

Epstein, R.M. & Hundert, E.M. 2002. Defining and assessing professional competence. *Journal of the American Medical Association*, 287:226-235. [https://doi.org/10.1001/jama.287.2.226]

Freire, P. 1990. *Pedagogy of the Oppressed*. New York: Continuum.

GALVAAN, R. 2015. Embracing an occupational perspective to promoting learning in context. *South African Journal of Higher Education*, 29(3):281-293. [https://doi.org/10.1111/1440-1630.12268]

GEE, J. 2008. *Social Linguistics and Literacies. Ideology in discourses*. 3rd Edition. Milton Park: Routledge. [https://doi.org/10.4324/9780203944806]

GEERTZ, C. 1993. *Local knowledge*. London: Fontana Press.

GIROUX, H. 1988. Teachers as transformative intellectuals. In: H. Giroux (ed). *Teachers as intellectuals: Towards a critical pedagogy of learning*. Granby, MA: Bergin & Garvey, 121-128.

GOODFELLOW, R. 2011. Literacy, literacies and the digital in higher education. *Teaching in Higher Education*, 16(1):131-144. [https://doi.org/10.1080/13562517.2011.544125]

JACOBS, C. 2005. On being an insider on the outside: new spaces for integrating academic literacies. *Teaching in Higher Education*, 10(4):475-487. [https://doi.org/10.1080/13562510500239091]

JONES, M. 2009. Transformational Learners: Transformational Teachers. *Australian Journal of Teacher Education*, 34(2):14-27. [https://doi.org/10.14221/ajte.2009v34n2.2]

KINSELLA, E.A. 2001. Reflections on reflective practice. *Canadian Journal of occupational therapy*, 68(3):195-198. [https://doi.org/10.1177/000841740106800308]

LEA, M.R. & STREET, B.V. 1998. Student writing in higher education: An academic literacies approach. *Studies in Higher Education*, 23(2):157-172. [https://doi.org/10.1080/03075079812331380364]

LILLIS, T. & SCOTT, M. 2007. Defining academic literacies research: issues of epistemology, ideology and strategy. *Journal of Applied Linguistics*, 4(1):5-32. [https://doi.org/10.1558/japl.v4i1.5]

LILLIS, T.; HARRINGTON, K.; LEA, M.R. & MITCHELL, S. 2015. *Working with Academic literacies: Case studies towards Transformative practice*. Anderson, South Carolina: Parlour Press.

LUKE, A. 2004. In: M. McLaughlin & G. Devoogd (eds). *Critical Literacy: Enhancing students' comprehension of text*. New York: Scholastic.

MANN, K.; GORDON, J. & MACLEOD, A. 2009. Reflection and reflective practice in health professions education: A systematic review. *Advances in Health Science Education*, 14:595-621. [https://doi.org/10.1007/s10459-007-9090-2]

MITCHELL, V. 2017. Diffracting Reflection: A move beyond reflective practice. *Education as Change*, 21(2):165-186. [https://doi.org/10.17159/1947-9417/2017/2023]

MOJE, E. 2007. Developing Socially Just Subject-matter Instruction: A Review of the Literature on Disciplinary Literacy, *Teaching Review of Research in Education*, 31:1-44. [https://doi.org/10.3102/0091732X07300046001]

QUINN, L. 2012. *Re-imagining academic staff development: Spaces for disruption*. Stellenbosch: African Sun Media. [https://doi.org/10.18820/9781920338879]

RAI, L. 2004. Exploring Literacy in Social Work Education: A Social Practices Approach to Student Writing. *Social Work Education*, 23(2):149-162. [https://doi.org/10.1080/0261547042000209170]

RAI, L. 2006. Owning (up to) Reflective Writing in Social Work Education. *Social Work Education*, 25(8):785-797. [https://doi.org/10.1080/02615470600915845]

RAI, L. 2012. Responding to emotion in practice-based writing. *Higher Education*, 64:267-284. [https://doi.org/10.1007/s10734-011-9492-1]

SCHÖN, D. 1987. *Educating the reflective practitioner*. San Francisco: Jossey-Bass.

SCHÖN, D. 1983. *The reflective practitioner: How professionals think in action*. New York: Basic Books.

TOWNSEND, E.A.; POLATAJKO, H.J.; CRAIK, J. & DAVIS, J. 2007. Canadian model of client-centered enablement. In: E.A. Townsend & H.J. Polatajko (eds). *Enabling occupation II: Advancing an occupational therapy vision for health, well-being, and justice through occupation*. Ottawa: Canadian Association of Occupational Therapists, 87-151.

UWC (University of the Western Cape). 2013. Mission Statement. Unpublished document. [https://www.uwc.ac.za/Pages/Mission.aspx]

Wald, H.S.; Borkan, J.M.; Taylor, J.S.; Anthony, D. & Reis, S.P. 2012. Fostering and evaluating reflective capacity in medical education: Developing the REFLECT rubric for assessing reflective writing. *Academic Medicine*, (87)1:41-50. [https://doi.org/10.1097/ACM.0b013e31823b55fa]

WFOT (World Federation of Occupational Therapists). 2012. *Occupational Therapy Definition.* [http://www.wfot.org]

Wenger, E. 1998. *Communities of Practice. Learning, Meaning, and Identity.* Cambridge: Cambridge University Press. [https://doi.org/10.1017/CBO9780511803932]

CHAPTER 8

Uncovering the complicit

The disrupting interview as a decolonising practice

*Lee Easton, Roberta Lexier,
Gabrielle Lindstrom & Michelle Yeo*

Introduction

The final report of Canada's Truth and Reconciliation Commission (TRC, 2015) which addressed the legacy of Canada's residential school system and its (often brutal attempts) to assimilate Indigenous peoples, created an urgent need for Canadian educators to consider their complicity with Canadian colonialism and its profound consequences to Indigenous peoples. As the report showed, the state created residential schools with "the purpose of separating Aboriginal children from their families, to minimise and weaken family ties and cultural linkages, and to indoctrinate children into a new culture" (TRC, 2015:v). As part of the path forward, the Commission issued 94 Calls to Action, including detailed direction for education and educators. However, the Calls to Action pose particular challenges to postsecondary educators because, following Eve Tuck and Wayne K. Yang's (2012) arguments, we contend that the university and the disciplines that comprise it are deeply complicit. With the epistemological structures of a Eurocentric hetero-patriarchal worldview that helped erase, discredit and overwrite Indigenous worldviews and thus overtly and covertly supported the aims of the residential school system. As a team of settler and Indigenous scholars we have come to see that, from that perspective, our disciplines are a party to this project, especially through the silencing and erasing processes of what we call "complicit knowledge production". If Canadian postsecondary educators wish to engage the 94 Calls to Action, we believe as a first step faculty, and academic developers must identify the specific ways that their disciplines have been complicit in colonialism; it is to that task this chapter is devoted. We recognise that our work emanates from our specific location and experiences on the lands of the Blackfoot Confederacy, but we believe our decolonisation project will resonate with educators in other colonial contexts, who have, in various ways, attempted to address their specific legacies of colonialism. We, therefore, offer our Canadian experience in the hope that it may prove useful for addressing similar issues elsewhere.

Our work begins with Indigenous scholar Willie Ermine's (2007) notion of "ethical space", which provides an appropriate starting point to theorise widely about what it may take to decolonise the disciplines in the university. As Ermine theorises, ethical space rests at the intersection of Western and Indigenous epistemologies. The disparate histories, experiences, and interpretations of Indigenous and Western paradigms informed the creation of ethical space, but, as Ermine (2007:195) argues, this area is dynamic and in a state of constant flux. Moreover, although these superficial differences create the ethical space, "What remains hidden and enfolded are the deeper level thoughts, interests and assumptions that will inevitably influence and animate the kind of relationship the two can have. It is this deeper level force ... that needs to be acknowledged and brought to bear in the complex situation produced by confronting" and making transparent the epistemic clashes that define Indigenous and Western thought-worlds. Battiste, Bell and Findlay (2002:84) note that decolonisation within the academy "requires multilateral processes of understanding and unpacking the central assumptions of domination, patriarchy, racism, and ethnocentrism that continue to glue the academy's privileges in place". Curriculum development, then, offers one site for this ethical space to emerge, especially when we frame curriculum broadly as "a process and a practice active in the production of subjectivities, of knowing subjects...whose engagement with curriculum is relational, that is based on relations of power into the which subjects are (re)positioned differently and inequitably" (Kelly, 1997:24). There is then a dual focus to decolonising curriculum that must happen on the local level of the classroom, the syllabus and teaching practices and the larger disciplinary structures to which Ermine (2007) points.

In response, we turned to Decoding the Disciplines, a process developed by Scholarship of Teaching and Learning (SoTL), scholars Joan Middendorf and David Pace (2004), to help university teachers, who are disciplinary experts, deal with student bottlenecks to learning. Often, these places where students become consistently stuck relate to difficult disciplinary concepts or processes that have become so internalised and familiar for the expert that we have a difficult time explaining them to students or do not realise we need to explain since they are so obvious to us. In this model, a key step in addressing this problem is a Decoding interview, whereby interviewers help teachers unpack crucial mental operations and the origins of their knowledge (Middendorf & Pace, 2004:6). What becomes clear through this process is, in part, the way that students must be socialised to "thinking, practicing, and being" in specific disciplinary ways (Miller-Young & Boman, 2017:23). The Decoding Process has been fruitfully employed by academic developers working with faculty members interested in curriculum transformation. The interview assists in making visible what was previously hidden to the expert in terms of their own tacit knowledge, which then helps them to see how to better structure learning for their students (Boman, Currie, MacDonald, Miller-Young, Yeo & Zettel, 2017).

Undoubtedly, Decoding the Disciplines' focus on curricular practice offers important insights; however, the approach is cognitivist (and functionalist) in its orientation (Yeo, 2017:49) and can be strikingly apolitical. Certainly, "finding" the historical moment of learning may provide the instructor with an epiphany that can then make for better teaching. But, lost in the moment of improvement is the more difficult critical question of "complicit" knowledge, which is entangled with disciplinary knowledges that have often "served the purpose of promoting an imperialist view of the world that justifies colonisation premised on European epistemological supremacy" (Tuck & Gaztambide-Fernández, 2013:75). As Indigenous scholars emphasise, colonial ideologies indoctrinated through education, specifically inherent within curriculum development processes, have marginalised Indigenous knowledges and practices and categorised their epistemologies as a hindrance to progress (Mcmurchy-Pilkington, 2008). A writing curriculum, for example, is neither a value-neutral process, nor is it a practice that is free from cultural influences.

Instead, as Mcmurchy-Pilkington (2008) asserts, developing curriculum is an act that instils specific values and norms that Eurocentric culture deems as desirable or worth knowing. Educational theorist Michael Apple's (2004) Marxist conceptualisation of curriculum helps to frame this exploration more precisely. Apple defines curriculum to include not just the "explicit" documented ideas and day-to-day practices in classrooms but also draws particular attention to the "hidden" curriculum which he identifies as deeply ideological and ontological. Given that the hidden curriculum is produced by the assumptions that also produce capitalism (and its associated structures of heterosexuality and patriarchy), we believe the hidden curriculum also includes "complicit" knowledge that sustains colonialism.

Reflecting on how Decoding the Disciplines surfaces tacit knowledges, we wondered if a repurposed Decoding interview might be helpful to uncover the expert's unintentional/unconscious complicity with colonial structures, practices, and subjectivities. Following the path of the Decoding the Disciplines interview, our decolonising interviews also reside in confronting, and making transparent tacit knowledges, but here we look for the implicit colonial ideologies that are reproduced in curriculum development to serve as starting points for decolonising our thinking. Our repurposed Decoding interviews, drawing on Western methods of auto-ethnography, critical pedagogical theory and Indigenous theories focused on context and relationality, offered us an opportunity to render the ethical space of curriculum development transparent. As we show, the interviews and the reflections on them also revealed more in-depth levels of thought which enabled us to explore and acknowledge how Western knowledge systems (and the university) have led to the cognitive colonisation of Indigenous peoples (Battiste, 2013). Our goal is to model for faculty and academic developers an approach to curriculum development that can illuminate how complicit knowledges function in their specific contexts.

Locating ourselves

This chapter is structured in part with our individual voices evident, as we have come to understand the importance of personally locating ourselves, creating relationships with each other and the reader, and taking responsibility for personal transformation. Notably, the approach of locating oneself within the conceptual and cultural landscape of Indigenous perspectives is a recurring theme in the literature (Wilson & Restoule, 2010) and aligns with an "Indigenous presence that is surfacing within Western universities" (Kovach, 2009:156). So, we begin by introducing ourselves and how we came to this process.

Michelle Yeo

I am a settler scholar born in Treaty[1] 7 territory in Calgary, Alberta, Canada. My great grandparents all came from Europe to Saskatchewan, Treaty 6 territory, where they farmed land that I only recently understood was not simply uninhabited land for the taking. I grew up in the urban environment of Calgary, attending school, becoming literate in a school environment that seamlessly matched my middle-class upbringing. Until my undergraduate years in early childhood education, I was almost entirely oblivious to the Tsuut'ina First Nations reserve bordering on our city.

In my role as an academic developer, at our midsized, teaching-focused university, I have worked for the past five years or so with Decoding the Disciplines as a fruitful process to assist disciplinary experts in breaking through blind spots in their practice. The work done by a group of us at Mount Royal University moved beyond the traditional cognitive focus of Decoding to attend to interpretive elements, for example, of identity (MacDonald, 2017) and the body (Currie, 2017). At a conference where we demonstrated the Decoding process, Lee and Roberta were in the audience and asked some troubling questions about the embedded Enlightenment framework assumed by the Decoding model. This got me thinking about how Decoding might be shifted to disrupt disciplines, not merely to uncover their inner workings to socialise students into disciplinary norms better.

Lee Easton

I, too, am a settler scholar. I hail from Sudbury, Ontario, a hard-rock mining city, located on Treaty 9 territory, where I lived until I moved to Southern Ontario to attend university. My perspectives are shaped from being raised in a single-parent family and from my identification as a gay man who found postsecondary education provided an exit route from my working-class background. Over the past decade, the scholarship of teaching and learning projects I have undertaken with my long-time collaborator, Kelly Hewson, have focused on how affect, Canadian identity, and film studies pedagogy raise questions about Indigeneity and decolonisation in Canada (Easton &

---

1   Eleven numbered treaty agreements were signed between the colonial Canadian government and First Nations between 1870 and 1921. Primarily seen as land sales from the perspective of Canada, treaties remain a contentious issue today because of the misunderstanding, language barriers, and misinterpretations between both parties. We honour our respective treaty regions as an act of reconciliation and to acknowledge First Nations perspectives on treaty-making.

Hewson, 2014, 2018). Our findings have led me to consider ways to change my pedagogy to unsettle the comfortable Canadian identity that many students bring to class.

This background provoked my initial discomfort when I heard David Pace talk about Decoding the Disciplines at the 2016 Banff Centennial Symposium for SoTL. I was already ambivalent about the Decoding approach, but as I listened to Dr Pace, I wondered whether Decoding the Disciplines could work when we considered Indigenous ways of knowing that are radically and, perhaps, irreducibly different from those epistemologies that emerge from the European Enlightenment project and which have formed the basis of the modern University since the 1800s (Derrida, 1983). After some discussion with Roberta, we agreed to begin work on a project that would explore these questions.

Roberta Lexier

Lee's questions about and discomfort with Decoding the Disciplines, a method I was familiar with from a collaborative project investigating reciprocity in Community-Service Learning courses (Pettit, Rathburn, Calvert, Lexier, Underwood, Gleeson & Dean, 2017), inspired me to think more fully and critically about the assumptions at its core and the possibilities of its use for decolonisation.

I am a settler scholar originally from Regina, Saskatchewan (Treaty 6 territory), now living in Calgary, Alberta (Treaty 7 territory). I have, since at least high school when we learned about residential schools, been aware of and concerned about the history and legacy of colonialism in Canada and around the world. Although I trained as a historian of post-World War II social movements in Canada, I have always been uncomfortable in the discipline; I am conscious of the complicity of historians in colonisation and the oppression of Indigenous peoples in Canada, and I have found the methods and approaches of the discipline constraining and limiting.

Inspired by the Truth and Reconciliation Commission report and my own politics, I have engaged extensively with the Indigenisation process at Mount Royal University by attending public lectures and events, participating in a Faculty Learning Community (Yeo, Haggarty, Ayoungman, Wida, Pearl, Stogre & Waldie, 2019), and rigorously re-examining my research and teaching in an effort to better reflect Indigenous content and ways of knowing. Thus, when Lee raised his concerns about Decoding the Disciplines, I was immediately intrigued.

Gabrielle Lindstrom

As a First Nations woman born and raised on the largest reserve in Canada and a scholar of national and international Indigenous studies, critical cultural studies, and anti-racist pedagogy, I know all too well the oppressive contexts of colonisation. For many who do not have direct experience with what it means to have your own humanity defined for you, it is difficult to comprehend what life might be like for Indigenous peoples living within a social and cultural context of oppression. The power to define what constitutes truth and how reality is interpreted, essentially the ontological foundation of a culture, has been undeniably stripped from Indigenous cultures the world over. Our history has become myth, and our stories relegated to folklore. Our education, political, and social systems have been deemed primitive. Our knowledge and philosophies have been categorised as superstitious or reduced to ecological matters.

Directly informed by my Indigenous perspective which can be defined as a distinct paradigm that is culturally determined, it has taken me many years to critically recognise the unilateral arrangement that comprises Indigenous/Canadian relationships and to look back to my ancestral teachings as equally valid and valued sources of knowledge. I have come to appreciate that it is a journey of healing that requires I continually reflect on my experiences as a learner. From my perspective, the act of decolonisation occurs when we explore and understand the other ways of coming to know the world that extend beyond the Western paradigm. Because of its emphasis on critical reflection and personal growth, the current project offers a space for me to contribute to processes of decolonisation as well as the opportunity to build strong relational connections with other scholars who are deeply invested in confronting colonial complicity.

Indigenous philosophical perspectives

Indigenous perspectives originate from Indigenous knowledge. Indigenous knowledge is different from Western knowledge systems in that Indigenous knowledge privileges the sourcing of knowledge from multiple epistemological wellsprings such as dreams, visions and the spirituals components related to human experience as opposed to books and written documents. Moreover, Indigenous scholars often observe that it is difficult to conceptualise theory from an Indigenous perspective given that Indigenous philosophical stances, meaning our epistemological and ontological understandings, originate from our direct experiences in relation to others and the natural world

(Bastien, 2004). However, theory is a fluid and dynamic concept. Simply because theory can be thought of as a tool to better help us interpret experiences – a lens through which we can view the world around us – theorising from an Indigenous perspective can be traced back to the oral tradition and the metaphors and symbols we used to help locate ourselves within a web of relational connections (Cajete, 1994). Today, the similarities found in Western and Indigenous theoretical stances hold valuable opportunities to realise intersecting beliefs, values, and ethics which potentiate the ways we interpret our learning experiences from those perspectives.

Indigenous scholar Marie Battiste (2002) argues that epistemology from a Western perspective can be defined as a theory of knowledge and its resulting pedagogy by which we come to learn about the world around us. Indigenous epistemology, on the other hand, encapsulates the philosophies, ceremonies, histories, and experiences with the sacred as specific ways of knowing which in turn reflects multiple sources of knowledge. Indigenous pedagogy includes practices such as talking or sharing circles, dialogue, experiential learning, role-modelling, ceremony, storytelling, and meditation (Battiste, 2002). Further, Indigenous scholars such as Betty Bastien (2003, 2004, 2016) and Ermine (1995, 2007) posit that Indigenous epistemology is premised within a pursuit of personal self-development and growth through which individuals aim to reach their full potential in life through acts of inward reflection (Ermine, 1995). However, our responsibilities are also conceptualised within a network of relational alliances with others and with the natural world (Bastien, 2016). Hence, from an Indigenous perspective, self-reflection is always engaged in within this relational framework and enacted through reciprocal exchanges (Bastien, 2016). Indigenous pedagogical approaches involve strategies that affirm and validate relational alliances in which deep introspection define an individual's contributions and responsibilities to the collective. Within this dynamic of self-in-relation (Graveline, 1998), ethical spaces of engagement emerge in a process through which members of disparate cultures come together in dialogue to realise a vision of reconciliation and transformation (Ermine, 2007). Reconciling the disparity in worldviews involves recognising and confronting our thought-worlds as possible sites of colonial complicity and this is no easy task; it is an act of decolonisation which requires intentionally re-evaluating from a critical perspective what we value as sources of knowledge and truth. Below, we offer some insights into how our thinking was transformed in those moments of struggle as we grappled with our disciplinary bottlenecks. We considered this an experiment on ourselves, which, if successful in helping us to rethink our disciplines, might model a way for academic developers to support faculty members in their rethinking and growth.

Methodology: The disrupting interview

Our overall goal in the process was to determine if an adapted Decoding interview could be used to disrupt disciplinary assumptions and unsettle our practices. To begin this process, Michelle, Lee, and Roberta took turns as interviewers and interviewees in what we have come to refer to as "disrupting interviews". We each approached the process with a necessary willingness to examine our disciplines critically, and indeed, each had been doing so through our academic work in the past. Before each interview, the three of us were asked to identify a bottleneck, some aspect of our discipline that reinforces and supports colonialism. Michelle hoped to examine the ways literacy, a central tenet of her discipline of Education, reinforces Western ways of knowing and being (Willinsky, 1998); Roberta explored how the dismissal of evidentiary sources, especially oral history, marginalises Indigenous peoples and others; and Lee identified essay writing, taught in English Studies or Composition courses, as potential colonial practices.

Once the bottlenecks were identified, we met and participated in interviews; two of us would act as interviewers and the other as interviewee. Like a traditional Decoding interview, the interviewee was asked to explain their bottleneck in as much detail as possible. Then, diverging from the traditional process, the interviewee was asked to consider the colonial aspects of that bottleneck. Once we had established some sense of how our disciplines might be complicit in the colonial project, the interviewers encouraged the interviewee to think about the ways they remain personally complicit in these concepts. In the Decoding interview, the key question is typically, "How do *you* do that?"; in the disrupting interview, the key question became, "Can you *imagine* an alternative?" Similar to the Decoding interviews, the interviewers continued to push interviewees deeper until they reached a point of surprise or resistance. It was this moment that led to insights about, not only our disciplinary, but also, our personal complicity in the colonial project.

The interviews were then transcribed, and we each reviewed the three texts. We hoped to identify moments of disruption and surprise in each interview to begin an analysis of the process as a way to unsettle ourselves and our disciplines. Below we quote extensively from our role as the interviewee, though also refer to exchanges in the others' interviews. Upon further reflection, we realised that decolonisation requires the establishment of reciprocal relationships with Indigenous scholars, and we asked Gabrielle to join our team. She did not participate in the interviews themselves but read the transcripts, offered an interpretive analysis and participated in all discussions that emerged from those documents.

Uncovering complicity: Repurposing the decoding interview

Drawing on the Decoding idea of the bottleneck, Michelle, Lee, and Roberta tried to identify a disciplinary "blind spot" that reproduces colonialism – the overt domination, consumption, and erasure of Indigeneity (Tuck & Yang, 2012; Tuck & Gaztambide-Fernández, 2013; Battiste, 2013). Drawing on the notion of the hidden curriculum (Apple, 2004), we were looking for places in the discipline where colonial structures are embedded and to which academics are often oblivious. We describe how we each reached a moment of surprise and resistance, where we found, in our thinking, deeper embeddedness of the bottlenecks and some invisible line that we felt unwilling to cross. First, Gabrielle contextualises this struggle within an Indigenous framework.

Gabrielle Lindstrom

Within the academic landscape of our current project, my discipline of Indigenous Studies is located within a critical sphere that confronts the socio-historical contexts of nation-building and political organising, gendered and cultural hierarchies, and pedagogical, philosophical, and ideological foundations of oppression – to name but a few. As such, critical scholars within the field of Indigenous studies are free to interrogate and problematise issues from a multitude of disciplinary perspectives. I, too, have been afforded the flexibility to offer my students a rich learning experience that not only honours their own human experiences but also enables me to draw on the wisdom contained within my ancestral knowledge. It informs both my pedagogy and my relationship with the students I teach and learn from, as well as the institution within which I foster my criticality. As I reviewed the transcripts of my colleagues' disrupting interviews in relation to their respective disciplinary contexts and how these disciplinary knowledge systems may contribute to the continued colonisation and marginalisation of Indigenous peoples, I became critically aware of how the interplay between Indigenisation and decolonisation is one in which we must all be active participants in at institutional and personal levels. Thus, our work contributes to "new currents of thought that flow in different directions and overrun the old ways of thinking" (Ermine, 2007:203).

From my perspective, the process of repurposing the Decoding interviews is about disrupting common beliefs around what constitutes truth within one's own discipline. As I reviewed the interview transcripts, I realised that personal and professional growth is found in the struggle. Notably, as my colleagues were grappling with their sense of what constitutes truth, what is not important becomes apparent, and what is not truth is revealed in the sense that inert knowledge and practices are questioned and other ways of knowing are explored. With regards to the essay as a bottleneck, for example, my colleague, Lee, observed how essay writing practices reinforced hierarchies and specific linearity in thinking and interpreting the world that may be consistent with a Eurocentric mindset. In contrast, he remarked how, "from a disciplinary perspective, we have to rethink some key things, and perhaps a decolonising view could help us understand what some of our investments are", especially in promoting print literacies to the exclusion of other literacies.

The interview data concerned with the bottlenecks that occur in the disciplines of history, and of early childhood education, led me to realise that Indigenous oral histories require us to do the interpretive work – they call us into a creative process that asks us to see the enchantment in our world and that relationships with all things, both animate and inanimate, are possible, that life does not start with us, that we are not the centre of the world. These ideas of relationality are best reflected in Indigenous scholar Leroy Littlebear's (2000) claim in the sense that "[i]f everything is animate, then everything has spirit and knowledge. If everything has spirit and knowledge, then all are like me. If all are like me, then all are my relations" (n.p.). In this worldview, the nature of knowledge is dynamic and accessible through the exchange of relational energies and vastly different when compared to written knowledge, which Indigenous scholars critiqued as a static epistemology, often privileged by Western empirical knowledge-keepers.

Michelle Yeo

My first discipline is education, specifically, early childhood education, and I started my career as a kindergarten teacher. For my bottleneck, I chose literacy, one of the central priorities of early education. In my interview, I described how we teach reading and writing in the early years of school with missionary zeal, with "the faith that there simply must be some good that comes from what we all know to be good" (Stuckey, 1991:33). Indeed, I argued that while the main explicit purpose of schools in those years is literacy, the hidden curriculum is socialising patriarchal control of the child's body (Grumet, 1988). Literacy practices are not value-free, and within my interview, we explored how literacy can act as a technology of colonisation (Willinsky, 1998), a "technology whose nature is always social, or, at least, always socially derived and socially defined" (Stuckey, 1991:26). We talked about the evangelical aspect of literacy learning (Mathieson, 1975), particularly in relation to what the system sees as "disadvantaged" or "culturally impoverished" children – by which we mean children who are growing up without books or robust literacy practices in their homes. Literacy then becomes a moral imperative for Western educators.

In my interview, I wanted to address a more subtle yet powerful element. In our approaches to literacy, there are complex webs of cultural assumptions – around what it means to be an educated citizen, about the "natural" development of a child, and about how learning occurs. As I described my bottleneck, I foregrounded what I was already comfortable with, in describing aspects of colonised practice in early learning:

> ... there is a prevailing idea that if kids don't learn to read by seven, they are in big trouble ... they start to get remediated, and those remedial programmes are very technical and rote, and not based on kids making meaning of the world, and so then they are further marginalised.

Adding to this, I discussed the history in residential schools of punishing children for speaking their Indigenous language – languages which were not written down, and they were forced instead to speak, read, and write in English, the language of the coloniser, so *then that project of teaching them to read English becomes very destructive.*

As an academic developer, I have conducted many traditional Decoding interviews, and usually there is the hoped-for "ah-ha" moment where the interviewee comes to some realisation or breakthrough about their tacit knowledge and teaching practices. In our disrupting interviews, uncomfortably, we each found instead an "unsettlement" moment, where we hit a cognitive barrier. That moment, for me, occurred when Lee asked: "Can you imagine a kindergarten without books?" This produced a surprising and troubling discomfort, as I tried to think about what this would look like:

> **Lee:** Could you imagine a primary classroom that never taught literacy at all?
> **Michelle:** No.
> **Lee:** Why? I am not saying ... to be clear, I am not suggesting that they don't learn anything, I am just asking, could you imagine a primary education world where there are no books?
> **Michelle:** That would be very ... okay, so can I imagine it in the current context, do you mean? Or just in my wild imagination?
> **Lee:** No, no. Like you, personally, would you ever advocate for a bookless primary classroom?
> **Michelle:** [*laughs*] I could advocate for a bookless kindergarten. Yeah, that would be really hard; that would be really hard for me.
> **Lee:** Why?

Michelle: Uh ... I think because I see ... I see that as being the central task of early education, I mean to a large extent. So it is very hard for me to imagine ... huh. I ... like, it would be hard for me to imagine how I would teach that way, without books ... to imagine teaching without me reading anything would be very challenging.
Lee: But you could imagine the students not reading? ... We should be videotaping, the non-verbals are good!
Michelle: Yeah, that would be really challenging, and I would have to rethink everything about how I taught.

This section of the transcript illustrates powerful discomfort, the painful unsettlement as I encountered a line that would be very difficult for me to cross. What I learned from this was the extent of my colonisation, and indeed, how literacy functioned and continues to function in buttressing the framework. I discovered through this that despite my critique of literacy, the depth of my continued commitment to it. I also discovered or re-discovered, what David Abram (1996) contends is the ultimate result of the written word – to cut us off from the "breathing" world as it phenomenologically exists. The only way I could imagine a book-less kindergarten would be to take it outside, out to the natural world.

Roberta Lexier

As a historian, I am conscious of the ways my discipline perpetuates colonialism by attempting to erase Indigenous peoples from the history of Canada. Most of these are obvious to historians. For example, the use of Confederation in 1867 as the primary marker of Canadian history, the emphasis on Europeans (and men) as the founding fathers of the nation, the conception of Canada as a colony rather than an active participant in the colonial project, the active silencing of Indigenous voices and experiences and the glossing over of colonial policies and practices (Ottawa, 2017).

For my turn as an interviewee, however, I wanted to examine a different, and perhaps less obvious, way the historical profession is complicit in colonialism: the privileging of written documentation over all other potential evidentiary sources. A recent keynote lecture by Indigenous historian Blair Stonechild (2018) in which he challenged the dismissal of oral history sources and the ways this marginalises and excludes Indigenous peoples from the historical record, inspired me. I have long used oral history in my research, initially as a way to supplement documented history and later as my main source of evidence. However, motivated by Stonechild, I hoped to use the decolonising interview to uncover my complicity in the colonial project by questioning my use of and resistance to alternative sources of evidence.

The interview allowed me to, first, identify the "bottleneck" and, second, to deeply analyse my perspectives on and justifications for my use of evidence in historical research. Through this process, I more fully understood the ways I resist the methods of my discipline, whether consciously or subconsciously. Being questioned by Lee and Michelle about how and why I use oral history in my research projects made this clear. Initially, I hoped to supplement documentary sources with interviews, solely to add some interest and personal anecdotes to my narrative; I never planned for oral history to supplant extensive documentary evidence. And yet, participating in oral interviews highlighted what is missing in documents and provided insights into the motivations and actions of individuals in the past. Thus, becoming increasingly conscious of my resistance to dominant historical methods, I now prioritise oral history over an analysis of the documents. As I said in my interview:

> I am sort of seeing the archival documents, in a way, now as a supplementary source, rather than the reverse of that. I think unintentionally, I think it was subconsciously first, but now that I am thinking about it more, I think it is an intentional attempt to subvert the methods of the discipline in some ways. I want to say that oral history actually is useful on its own.

This also allows space for greater inclusion of Indigenous voices and ways of knowing in my research and my teaching.

The disrupting interview also provided an opportunity to consider the issues of objectivity and subjectivity. Explaining historical methods to academics in other disciplines forced me to consider the ways that documents are assumed to be truthful, unbiased, and impartial while oral history is viewed as biased, prejudiced, and unreliable. In explaining my bottleneck, I argued:

> … you could do oral interviews and talk to people, but the argument is that their memories are faulty and will be reconstructed by the time and the context, and all those things that come afterwards, and, so to really get to the truth you need to use the archival material, and then you can kind of use the oral interviews to add some extra nuance. Or some fun stories or extra kind of things, but [t]here is no way that oral history can be factual; it is problematic.

While historians have long acknowledged the limits of their interpretations of the past, and have questioned their ability to reconstruct a factual representation of prior events, the trust in documents over other potential sources is nevertheless deeply ingrained in the profession. Challenging these assumptions about objectivity and subjectivity allows for a wider critique of the discipline and greater participation by marginalised groups.

However, the interview also forced me to confront the limits of my willingness and ability to resist the dominance of documents as historical sources. Although I easily referred to "ghosts of the people who wrote" the documents, when the interviewers continued to ask questions, I found it difficult to accept that similar "ghosts" could be found in oral interviews. "I think that highlights again this obsession with documentation that there are ghosts in the documents, but not in people!" I am still fully enmeshed in Western thinking that prioritises the material and observable over the spiritual world. As Indigenous ways of "knowing" include the spiritual world, this challenges me to consider my complicity in devaluing and dismissing a different way of seeing the world. My interview, then, forced me to confront the ways that I, as someone dedicated to decolonisation, remains complicit in colonisation, the places where our disciplines reinforce existing colonial strategies, and the need for personal transformation as well as institutional change.

Lee Easton

I came to the disrupting interview to examine how and why writing the essay and its cousin, the research paper, retain such a central role in the discipline of English and specifically within its aligned (and subordinate) activity of teaching university-level writing skills, often in composition classes. In my interview, Michelle asked what made the essay a colonial practice. I noted the origins of the essay in 17th-century French writing: "That is the interesting thing, to say it in French means 'to try', it is an experiment; it is a way to think, right?", and emphasised that my teaching focus is on encouraging students write essays which are well structured and coherent. Michelle offered an observation which I found useful:

> The little bit I do know about the way there is a completely different kind of rhetoric … just verbally from Indigenous community members, a more circular way of talking.

This perspective underscored how teaching students to write the academic essay based on European thinking inculcated in my students a specific approach to the wor(l)d but more disturbingly *maintains* a set of settler-colonial relations that, for example, over-write Indigenous storytelling practices or, as Michelle's comment emphasises, dismisses more circular forms of thinking and communicating.

Similar to Michelle and Roberta's interviews, I also encountered my moment of "*No!*". When asked about the importance of coherence in writing, especially formal school assignments such as essays and research papers, my personal investments (and personal empowerment as a writer) were such that I could not easily relinquish my commitments to this concept because it seems so central my concept of what constitutes "good writing". Through the interview, however, I see more clearly how English Studies and my investments in learning/teaching to write an effective essay both position the written word as a better way to communicate and crucially as a divider between the primitive and the civilised. Privileging the written essay can marginalise other ways of recording, communicating and validating official knowledge. These values are deeply imbricated into composition's hidden curriculum and are evident in marking rubrics that value attributes such as the essay's organisation, logic and coherence, or the writer's grammar and style.

The interview also opened a place to state my intuitive hunches about the discipline:

> So I guess what I am trying to say, and to go back to that broader sense of what is colonial, well I think I can't help but feel everything I am talking about goes back to sort of, you know, antiquity and sort of the study going back to Greece, right? The study of rhetoric and the importance of logic and how these are values that are best found and transmitted through this genre of writing.

A quick literature search easily turned up an intellectual history of American composition studies (Nystrand, 1993). The study, which emphasised the foundational theorists of composition studies, is a veritable who's who of European philosophy: Aristotle, Kant, Marx and Locke.

However, upon further reflection, I am struck that I did not explore in my disrupting interview my investments in two key disciplinary practices: close reading and insisting on appropriate pronoun usage in their writing. Close reading assumes a particular relationship between the text and reader where the reader can work out the meaning of the "words on the page". Similarly, third-person pronoun-use in essay writing positions the writer as an objective rational observer, explaining a particular point. My students often ask if they can use the first-person pronoun in their essays since such use has often been discouraged in earlier grades.

During my interview, I talked about pronoun-use in academic writing, and to my surprise, I too subscribe to this convention about pronouns, albeit with some flexibility:

> [Essay writing must be] Impersonal, the third person, please! ... I tell my students I don't mind if you use 'I' or 'we' or 'they'; it doesn't matter to me, but do not use 'you'! – You are not talking directly to the reader.

In conversation with Gabrielle, I see that my insistence on an objective third-person pronoun or my grudging acceptance of the subjective first-person pronoun might be interpreted, through an Indigenous lens, as a rejection of relationality and ultimately a means to exclude other ways of speaking and writing found amongst post-colonial writers such as Jamaica Kincaid. When you use the second person to speak directly to the reader, you break down the clear subject-object relationship that the essay promotes.

Taken together, our interviews underlined how enmeshed we are within the micro aspects of teaching – the classroom, the bureaucratic disciplinary apparati of our disciplines such as books, archives, desks, and essays – even if we are ambivalently attached to them. Gabrielle mentions the struggles she observed in our interviews; in some ways these struggles emerge from our understanding of our knowledges, about how deeply complicit we are in maintaining settler-colonial relations.

The potential of disrupting interviews

We undertook this process in the hope that a repurposed Decoding interview – what we are calling a disrupting interview – might help academic developers assist faculty members in identifying the ways their disciplines, and more importantly how they as individuals, are complicit in colonialism. This interview process encourages individuals to engage more fully and personally with the decolonisation project and contribute to the transformation of universities. As it is, decolonisation at the institutional level is sometimes easier: we can create policies and processes that acknowledge colonial structures and practices and attempt to ameliorate them. However, the decolonisation of institutions of higher learning also requires individual faculty members to reconsider how their courses and pedagogical practices are complicit in colonial structures that lie at the core of universities. Anything that pushes us beyond this safety is a test of our cultural allegiance (Ermine, 2007) which is, in turn, based on the values and ethics surrounding our sense of self, and relation to others and the natural world. This is the more important work in the decolonisation project; without it, we continue to, often subconsciously, reinforce colonialism in our curriculum and pedagogies.

Following the lead of Bastien (2016) and Ermine (1995), we argue that relationships are central to the decolonisation process. It is essential, for instance, that settler scholars work directly with Indigenous scholars and communities to gain greater understanding of and respect for different epistemologies and ontologies. Only through reciprocal relationships can any progress be made towards reconciliation. The disrupting interview has the potential to foster the spirit of relationality to begin unravelling our complicity in colonisation. Gabrielle's involvement, her generous reading of our struggle, and articulation of the importance of the ethical space helped us to envision the possibility of transformation. We believe academic developers adopting the disrupting interview will benefit most when Indigenous voices and contributions are an integral part of the process; the local issues and theories related to specific colonial projects will vary according to the specific cultural, historical realities that influence relationships in specific geographic locations.

The decolonising interviews encouraged each of us to identify and confront the ways our disciplines remain complicit with the colonial project. For each of us, our struggle with our complicity, and the places we continue to resist alternative ways of thinking and doing provided what Michelle referred to as the "unsettlement" moment. While struggle can be uncomfortable, and clearly, we still resist some alternatives, finding and exposing our limits to accepting other ways of thinking and doing is an important step along the path to decolonisation. We agree with De Leeuw, Greenwood, and Lindsay (2013:391) when they argue:

> Unsettling colonialism and indeed troubling good intentions, must similarly never be comfortable. It is, we suggest, at the very moment when something ascends to a position of normative comfortableness that it most desperately needs troubling. It is exactly at the moment when we, especially those of us who are settler colonists, feel good about having reached a place of comfort and stabilization about unsettling colonialism that we should be feeling most troubled.

When uncovering complicit knowledge, academic developers and faculty will need to be attuned to the affective dimensions of complicity. Associated feelings of settler guilt, helplessness, and grief require time and a willingness to explore their implications; however, these emotions cannot then become an excuse to evade accountability or action. In our experience, this exploration can also be gratifying, relational, and filled with hope. We recognise too that some academic developers and faculty may not arrive at a moment of unsettlement. However, this apparent failure need not be discouraging.

Both the academic developer and the faculty member might pause and reflect on what barriers have arisen in unearthing complicity. What happens if they do not proceed? Perhaps they could reflect on surprises or unexpected absences in the interview, all of which might generate another conversation. Reflection and discussion, albeit less direct, may help arrive at a different unpredicted element of complicit knowledge. When stuck, more reflection, more questions and most importantly, more listening is a good idea.

Still, although the decolonisation process requires that we discover points of compatibility, we must be open to the points of difference and irreconcilability. We might find "decolonisation is fundamentally rendered impossible and that something new and different must be imagined" (De Leeuw, Greenwood, & Lindsay, 2013:391). The decolonisation process requires that institutions, disciplines, and, more importantly, individuals grapple with these limitations and acknowledge the importance of alternative ontologies and epistemologies. We must learn to accept difference while we acknowledge the limits to transformation. As we search for ways to change, we must accept that change is not always possible or even desirable. So, then, for academic developers and for us personally, hard questions arise in the ethical space we have described: What are we willing to leave behind and how do we move forward? How do we transform our practices to better reflect multiple ways of knowing and doing? How do we learn to live well with radical differences, honouring them, while resisting the urge to assimilate, whether into an Indigenous or Western paradigm? With practices such as the disrupting interview, we take our responsibility towards disciplinary accountability and the road to reconciliation seriously.

References

ABRAM, D. 1996. *The Spell of the Sensuous*. New York: Vintage Books.

APPLE, M.W. 2004. *Ideology and Curriculum*. 3rd Edition. New York: Routledge. [https://doi.org/10.4324/9780203487563]

BASTIEN, B. 2016. Indigenous pedagogy: A way out of dependence. In: K. Burnett & G. Read (eds). *Aboriginal history: A reader*. Don Mills, Ontario, Canada: Oxford University Press.

BASTIEN, B. 2004. *Blackfoot ways of knowing: The worldview of the Siksikaitsitapi*. Calgary: University of Calgary Press.

BASTIEN, B. 2003. The cultural practice of participatory transpersonal visions. *Revision*, 26(2):41-48.

BATTISTE, M. 2013. *Decolonising education: Nourishing the learning spirit*. Saskatoon, Canada: Purich Publishing Inc.

BATTISTE, M. 2002. *Indigenous knowledge and pedagogy in First Nations education: A literature review with recommendations*. Ottawa, Ontario, Canada: Indian and Northern Affairs Canada.

BATTISTE, M.; BELL, L. & FINDLAY, L.M. 2002. Decolonising education in Canadian universities: An interdisciplinary, international, Indigenous research project. *Canadian Journal of Native Education*, 26(2):82-95.

BOMAN, J.; CURRIE, G.; MACDONALD, R.; MILLER-YOUNG, J.; YEO, M. & ZETTEL, M. 2017. Overview of decoding across the disciplines. In: J. Miller-Young & J. Boman (eds). *New Directions for Teaching and Learning*, 150. San Francisco: Jossey-Bass, 13-18.

CAJETE, G. 1994. *Look to the mountain: An ecology of Indigenous education*. Durango, Colorado: Kivaki Press.

CURRIE, G. 2017. Conscious Connections: Phenomenology and Decoding the Disciplines. In: J. Miller-Young & J. Boman (eds). *New Directions for Teaching and Learning*, 150. San Francisco: Jossey-Bass, 37-48. [https://doi.org/10.1002/tl.20236]

DE LEEUW, S.; GREENWOOD, M. & LINDSAY, N. 2013. Troubling Good Intentions. *Settler Colonial Studies*, 3(3-4):381-394. [https://doi.org/10.1080/2201473X.2013.810694]

DERRIDA, J.; PORTER, C. & MORRIS, E.P. 1983. The principle of reason: The university in the eyes of its pupils. *Diacritics*, 13(3):2-20. [https://doi.org/10.2307/464997]

EASTON, L. & HEWSON, K. 2014. How, exactly, does the beaver bite back? The case of Canadian students viewing Paul Haggis' *Crash*. In: G. Roberts & D. Stirrup (eds). *Parallel Encounters: Culture at the Canada-US Border*. Waterloo, Ontario, Canada: Wilfrid Laurier University Press, 91-110.

EASTON, L. & HEWSON, K. 2018. From border pedagogy to treaty pedagogy: Canadian exceptionalism in the Canadian film studies classroom. *Canadian Review of American Studies*, 48(1):63-83. [https://doi.org/10.3138/cras.2017.011]

ERMINE, W. 2007. Ethical Space of Engagement. *Indigenous Law Journal*, 6(1):193-203. [https://bit.ly/2krWnqR]

ERMINE, W. 1995. Aboriginal Epistemology. In: M. Battiste & J. Barman (eds). *First Nation education in Canada: The circle unfolds*. Vancouver, British Columbia, Canada: UBC Press.

GRAVELINE, F.J. 1998. *Circle works: Transforming Eurocentric consciousness*. Michigan: Fernwood Publishers.

GRUMET, M. 1988. *Bitter Milk: Women and Teaching*. USA: The University of Massachusetts Press.

KELLY, U. 1997. *Schooling Desire: Literacy, Cultural Politics and Pedagogy*. New York: Routledge.

KOVACH, M. 2009. *Indigenous methodologies: Characteristics, conversations, and, contexts*. Toronto: University of Toronto Press.

LITTLEBEAR, L. 2000. Jagged worldviews colliding. [https://bit.ly/2msbPnC]

MACDONALD, R. 2017. Intuitions and Instincts: Considerations for Decoding Disciplinary Identities. In: J. Miller-Young & J. Boman (eds). *New Directions for Teaching and Learning*, 150. *Using Decoding the Disciplines Framework for Learning Across the Disciplines*. San Francisco: Jossey-Bass, 63-74. [https://doi.org/10.1002/tl.20238]

MATHIESON, M. 1975. *The Preachers of Culture: a Study of English and Its Teachers*. Totowa, New Jersey: Rowman and Littlefield.

MCMURCHY-PILKINGTON, C. 2008. Indigenous peoples: Emancipatory possibilities in curriculum development. *Canadian Journal of Education*, 31(3):614-638. [https://files.eric.ed.gov/fulltext/EJ809263.pdf]

MIDDENDORF, J. & PACE, D. 2004. Decoding the disciplines: A model for helping students learn disciplinary ways of thinking. In: D. Pace & J. Middendorf (eds). *New Directions of Teaching and Learning*, 98. *Decoding the Disciplines: A Model for Helping Students Learn Disciplinary Ways of Thinking*. San Francisco: Jossey-Bass, 1-12. [https://doi.org/10.1002/tl.142]

NYSTRAND, M.; GREENE, S. & WIEMELT, J. 1993. Where did composition studies come from? An intellectual history. *Written Communication*, 10(3):267-333. [https://doi.org/10.1177/0741088393010003001]

PACE, D. & MIDDENDORF, J. 2017. Foreward. In: J. Miller-Young & J. Boman (eds). *New Directions for Teaching and Learning*, 150. San Francisco: Jossey-Bass, 9-11.

PETTIT, J.; RATHBURN, M.; CALVERT, V.; LEXIER, R.; UNDERWOOD, M.; GLEESON, J. & DEAN, Y. 2017. Building Bridges from the Decoding Interview to Teaching Practice. *New Directions for Teaching and Learning*, 150. San Francisco: Jossey-Bass, 75-85. [https://doi.org/10.1002/tl.20239]

STONECHILD, A.B. 2018. Misunderstanding Indigenous Spirituality in Mainstream History. Keynote Address at the Canadian Historical Association Annual Meeting. [https://cha-shc.ca/_uploads/5bd210c4f277b.pdf]

STUCKEY, J.E. 1991. *The Violence of Literacy*. Portsmouth, NH: Cook Publishers.

TRC (Truth and Reconciliation Commission of Canada). 2015. *Honouring the Truth, Reconciling for the Future: Summary of the Final Report of the Truth and Reconciliation Commission of Canada*. Winnipeg: Truth and Reconciliation Commission of Canada.

Tuck, E. & Wayne Yang, K. 2012. Decolonisation is not a metaphor. *Decolonisation: Indigeneity, Education* and *Society*, 1(1):1-40. [https://bit.ly/2Dfcn5D]

Tuck, E. & Gastambide-Fernández, R.A. 2013. Curriculum, replacement, and settler futurity. *Journal of Curriculum Theorizing*, 29(1):72-89. [https://bit.ly/2m1qeHf]

Ottawa, M.D. 2017. Why is Canada's 150th Birthday Controversial. *The Economist*, 29 June 2017. [https://econ.st/2kUoCPf]

Willinsky, J. 1998. *Learning to Divide the World: Education at Empire's End*. Minneapolis: University of Minnesota Press.

Wilson, D. & Restoule, J. 2010. Tobacco ties: The relationship of the sacred to research. *Canadian Journal of Native Education*, 33(1):29-45. [https://bit.ly/2kUoQpz]

Yeo, M. 2017. Decoding the disciplines as a hermeneutic practice. In: J. Miller-Young & J. Boman (eds). *New Directions for Teaching and Learning*, 150. San Francisco: Jossey Bass, 49-62. [https://doi.org/10.1002/tl.20237]

Yeo, M.; Haggarty, L.; Ayoungman, K.; Wida, W.; Pearl, C.; Stogre, T. & Waldie, A. 2019. Unsettling faculty minds: A faculty learning community on Indigenization. *New Directions for Teaching and Learning*, Special Issue 157. San Francisco: Jossey-Bass, 27-41. [https://doi.org/10.1002/tl.20328]

CHAPTER 9

Reconfiguring academic development through feminist new materialist and posthuman philosophies

Vivienne Bozalek

Introduction

> To think is to experiment, but experimentation is always that which is in the process of coming about – the new, remarkable, and interesting that replaces the appearance of truth and are more demanding than it is. (Deleuze & Guattari, 1994:111)

> Radical pedagogies are taken here to be experimental forms of learning that are on-going and passionately protesting inert ideas. It is education of and for vitality – learning how to intensify one's capacity to live affirmatively, and with singularity of style. (Ednie-Brown, 2015:20)

I started doing academic development formally in 2008 when seconded from being Chairperson of the Department of Social Work at the University of the Western Cape (UWC), to a newly created position of Director of Teaching and Learning at the institution. I had been working at UWC since 1989 and was delighted to work with colleagues from the then newly established Academic Development Centre, as I felt that I knew very little about how teaching and learning worked at a university level. I worked closely with academic development colleagues, who all made various contributions and inputs into the courses I was teaching at the time. I remember one colleague working with me in the classroom and helping to give feedback in the form of polite questions to the students doing freewriting in class, about the central concepts in the course. We would then base the following lecture on the assumptions that the students had expressed in their writing about these concepts – a very responsive form of teaching. I was also interested in notions of feminist pedagogy and was involved in the design, development and teaching of the Postgraduate Women's and Gender Studies Programme that started in 1995 at UWC.

Since my assumption of the role, together with other colleagues, we have become involved in several professional development teaching and learning courses for academics at UWC:

- Induction courses for new academics;
- Courses for chairpersons of departments;
- An inter-institutional Postgraduate Diploma in Teaching and Learning in Higher Education taught across three higher education institutions in the Western Cape; and
- Short Quality Teaching and Learning courses run by academic development people from the four higher education institutions in Cape Town for academics from these institutions under the auspices of the regional Cape Higher Education Consortium (CHEC).

The professional development programme has primarily been conventional, focusing on curriculum alignment of graduate attributes, learning activities and outcomes, and assessment tasks and evaluation. Of late we have begun to experiment with new ways of engaging with academics through inter-institutional courses – particularly two recent ones on Multimodal Pedagogies that involves conceptual work with several arts-based pedagogies, and another on Reconfiguring Scholarship in Higher Education – that will be elaborated on in this chapter.

My scholarship in teaching and learning and collaboration with colleagues through research projects have also led me to new ways of thinking about how to do pedagogies. I have been associated with and also the principal researcher on a number of National Research Foundation (NRF) projects which have investigated alternative ways of thinking about higher education pedagogies, including a focus on critical posthumanism and feminist new materialism and how these could be put to work in the field. These projects have given rise to alternative ways of engaging with PhD students, as project members have initiated weekly reading groups run along the lines of communities of enquiry. I discuss these reading groups as examples of academic development in this chapter. I will now go on to introduce feminist new materialism and posthumanism, examining how they change the way that academic development is thought about and done.

Feminist philosophies such as "new materialism" and "posthumanism" point to the impossibility of separating *epistemology* (theories of knowing) from *ontology* (being and becoming) and *ethics* – proposing an *ethico-onto-epistemological* entanglement. This ethico-onto-epistemological entanglement ruptures conventional ways of doing academic development, where epistemology is usually foregrounded at the expense of ontology and ethics. Academic development work prominently focuses on "epistemological access" and assumes that students need access to "powerful knowledges" rather than focusing on becoming, and what matters to students. As a different way of configuring academic development, this chapter considers how feminist new materialism and posthumanism might be put to use, where *knowing*, *becoming* and *doing* are all mutually implicated for inspiring what really matters in academic development at this troubled juncture in higher education. The chapter illustrates how feminist new materialism and posthumanism might help to re-imagine the relationships of academic developers, academics and the material world.[1] Feminist new materialism and posthumanism are based on a relational ontology where entities and agency do not pre-exist relationships, but rather come into being through relationships. This means that academic developers, academics and the material world are co-constituted through their entangled connections, rather than being separate and individual beings and entities. The term "academic development" can be seen as problematic in that it does not do justice to the viewpoint of posthumanism and feminist new materialism. This is precisely because being predicated on a relational ontology, the focus shifts away from the *subject* and *object* to their co-constitution or entanglement (Barad, 2007). Here, an

---

[1] According to post-humanists and feminist new materialists such as Karen Barad, the material world or matter is not passive or inert but vibrant (has agency) and comes about through entanglements. New materialists do not distinguish between the physical and social world, but also do not see things as having fixed essences or properties, but as coming into being through relationships. Barad (2007:151) refers to matter as "*not a thing, but a doing, a congealing of agency*" [emphasis in the original]. As Keller and Rubenstein (2017) point out, humans are not only entangled in matter – they are also materialisations who are entangled with other materialisations. Similar to Barad, they see matter as a process rather than a thing. New materialists move beyond the binaries of spirit/matter, sentience/non-sentience (Keller & Rubenstein, 2017).

academic developer and those who are being worked with, as well as materials such as curricula, all come into being through entanglement, becoming-with each other as accomplices through collaborative processual acts of creative, experimental practice that capacitate all involved in accessing their potential. Perhaps the notions of "cultivating collective knowing and being", "sympoiesis (making together)" (Haraway, in Davis & Turpin 2015:257), "rendering each other capable" (Despret, 2004, 2016), "a cross-fertilisation of capacitations" (Massumi, 2015a:68) and co-composing (Manning, 2009) would be more apt descriptions for this sort of collective work. Feminist new materialism and posthumanism would thus think of education as the creation of events where *all* transform in terms of knowing, doing, and becoming, including teachers, students, curriculum, as well as concepts that are being reworked. Drawing on the work of Deleuze, Ina Semetsky (2013:82-83) explains how education might be envisaged and enacted from the perspective of these approaches:

> Deleuze insists that we learn nothing from those who say: 'Do as I do.' Our only teachers are those who tell us to 'do with me' and can emit signs to be developed in heterogeneity rather than propose gestures for us to reproduce.

Another major challenge for using the concept "development" in academic development is that it has been associated with colonialism (see Bozalek & Dison, 2013). The chapter also provides some ideas as to how feminist new materialism and posthumanism might move beyond Western Subject/Object dichotomies and reductive curricula and methodologies which produce packageable content, predictable, measurable outcomes and deliverable products (Lenz Taguchi, 2010; Massumi, 2015). Contesting the assumption that knowledge is located in an autonomous rational, middle class, able-bodied, male Western subject, the chapter shows how this unstated normative subject is problematic in that it detracts from the creative development of new patterns of thought for academic development today. The chapter provides some practical ideas about how academic development can be done differently by using the ideas of feminist new materialism and posthumanism, focusing on several instances where these ideas have been put to work. It also provides the reader with some central concepts for enacting academic development from a posthumanist and feminist new materialism perspective.

The chapter is organised in the following way: Firstly, I describe what feminist new materialism and posthumanism are and how they pertain to academic development. Secondly, I describe central concepts underpinning this sort of work and provide some examples of "academic development" activities that illustrate the enactment of feminist new materialism and posthumanist ethico-onto-epistemological perspectives. Using these examples, I also consider how other approaches to pedagogy, which are not necessarily located in higher education, such as the Reggio Emilia approach, hold promise for academic sympoiesis and intra-active pedagogy of feminist new materialism and posthumanism.

The chapter focuses specifically on work that has been done on teaching and learning short courses with academics as well as reading groups with PhD students. It is not to say that such an approach could not be applied or is not valuable in the undergraduate curriculum, but it is not the focus of this chapter.

What is "feminist new materialism" and "posthumanism"?

Feminist new materialism and posthumanism are relational ontologies that use ideas from process philosophers such as Baruch Spinoza, Alfred North Whitehead, Niels Bohr, Isabelle Stengers, Gilles Deleuze and Felix Guattari. Feminist new materialist or posthumanism authors such as Karen Barad, Rosi Braidotti, Erin Manning and Brian Massumi, amongst others, have taken ideas from these process philosophers forward in various ways, using feminism, quantum physics and queer theory. Process philosophy is concerned with relationality and creativity and sees the world as being in a state of constant change (Massumi, 2015a). Feminist new materialism and posthumanism question assumptions that entities such as humans or objects are bounded, discrete and stable. These approaches challenge human-centred views of the world as well as Western Cartesian assumptions of binary oppositions nature/culture, human/animal, mind/body – which are present in most social and political thought. These binary oppositions are separate and are hierarchical with one side being inferior and the other superior. Feminist new materialism and posthumanism regard matter or objects in the material world as vital, alive, active, dynamic and indeterminate, rather than as passive, inert, measurable and predictable. The human, non-human and more-than-human[2] are seen as having vital forces, indeterminate boundaries, being entangled or inseparable, and as coming into being *through* relationships. Barad uses the neologism *intra-action* to show how identities or entities do not exist *a priori* but come into being through their relationships or entanglement with each other. Interaction, on the other hand, is different in that it assumes a relationship between already existing independent entities. The difference between "intra-action" and "interaction" is crucial to understanding the

---

2 The entanglement of humans and non-humans such as human and non-human animals, as well as humans and events, humans and affects (Manning, 2012).

relational ontology of feminist new materialism and posthumanism, that call for intra-action, not interaction (Barad, 2017b). Coming into being through relationality means that there is no pre-existing subject or object and that entities do not have an essence or a fixed identity.

Consequently, "matter" is ontologically indeterminate[3] and lacking in inherent characteristics or identity. According to Barad (2007), through quantum physics, under different experimental conditions, "matter" can be either a particle or a wave, which contests the notion of essentialised identities. Individuals or entities thus come to be through relationships rather than through wilful or intentional humans acting on passive objects. Consequently, "agency" is not seen to reside in human beings but rather occurs in *enactments* or the *event* or *occasion*.

Feminist new materialism also provides an alternative to the linguistic or cultural turn that focused solely on language, texts and discourses, excluding the importance of the material world (Braidotti, 2013). In feminist new materialism and posthumanism, the material is as important as the discursive and they cannot be separated – but should be considered together as material-discursive – matter and meaning are thus mutually implicated – hence the notion onto-epistemology (Barad, 2007; De Freitas & Sinclair, 2014; Lenz Taguchi & St. Pierre, 2017).

At the heart of feminist new materialism and posthumanism is a concern with *mattering* or *what matters* – weaving together an inseparable ethico-onto-epistemology. In addition to this, space and time are not seen as determinate givens, but as coming into being intra-actively through phenomena – Barad (2007) refers to *spacetimemattering*[4] as a reconfigured entanglement of space, time and matter with no pre-given boundaries between them. Also,

---

3   Being ontologically indeterminate means the undoing of identity in that entities or objects do not exist independently and do not have fixed, distinct or determinate properties or boundaries (Barad, 2007). This is because nothing exists outside of relationships or intra-actions – where entangled agencies are mutually constituted. Representationalism believes that independent entities exist outside of representing them, that you need representations to mediate these independently existing entities.

4   Quantum physics unmoors and disrupts the notions of space, time and matter because of indeterminacy, a superposition of here-there, then-now, through quantum entanglements showing dis/continuity – neither continuity or discontinuity, but what Barad (2007) refers to as a "cutting together-apart" (Barad, 2017a:84). Space, time and matter are "intra-actively produced in the ongoing differential articulation of the world. Time is not a succession of evenly spaced intervals available as a referent for all bodies and space is not a collection of preexisting points set out as a container for matter to inhabit" (Barad, 2007:234). Space and time are intra-actively produced in the making of phenomena – they don't exist outside phenomena. Past, present and future are threaded through each other and bleed into each other (Barad, 2017a).

central to these approaches is the notion of micropolitics elaborated upon by Massumi (2014), which refers to ethics and politics produced through encounters and forces that impact on situations. A relational ontology presumes a radically different approach to ethics (Bozalek & Zembylas, 2017a) that as Barad (2007:93) suggests, is "not about right responses to a radically exteriorised other, but about responsibility and accountability for the lively relationalities of becoming of which we are a part".

Language is also seen as having a material effect and as an intervention which brings about learning – a catalytic force for bringing out the new, rather than a means of communication or representation – here there is no distinction between matter and meaning (De Freitas & Sinclair, 2014). De Freitas and Sinclair (2014:52) ask the question: "How might an inclusive materialism allow us to rethink learning as an indeterminate act of assembling various kinds of agencies rather than a trajectory that ends in the acquiring of fixed objects of knowledge?", which this chapter will attempt to go some way towards answering in thinking with some concepts and propositions, which are drawn from feminist new materialism and posthumanism. These concepts and propositions will be considered through some examples of activities used when working with academic staff and postgraduate students in their scholarly practices. This question is unpacked further below in its relation to posthumanism and feminist new materialism.

The first thing that De Freitas and Sinclair's (2014) question alerts us to is that feminist new materialism and posthumanism value *process* or *enactment* for engaging in learning rather than a product which represents learning. Secondly, that being *indeterminate*, much of what is valuable in learning happens *fortuitously* and cannot be predicted. Thirdly, that learning happens *relationally in assemblages*, rather residing in individuals or entities. Finally, the purpose of learning is not to transmit or acquire fixed objects or bodies of knowledge, but that learning is rather concerned with experimentation and the creation of concepts (a pedagogy of the concept). Various stakeholders and theorists in higher education might vigorously contest these approaches to rethinking learning in higher education, however, there is increasing interest now developing in approaches, such as Slow scholarship (Bozalek, 2017), post qualitative inquiry (St. Pierre, 2018), Deluezian (Masny, 2013) and new materialist approaches to higher education curricula (Snaza, Sonu, Truman & Zaliwska, 2016). Feminist new materialism and posthumanism hold that learning is ontological, concerned with the materiality of knowledge and that concepts and other material forms of learning exist on the same plane of immanence as physical bodies (De Freitas & Sinclair, 2014), supporting

Barad's material-discursive entanglement and inseparability. De Freitas and Sinclair (2014:84) propose inventive acts for creative mathematics pedagogy that are both indeterminate and ontological and involve four characteristics. They propose that a creative act:

- introduces or catalyses the new – quite literally, it brings forth or makes visible what was not present before;
- is unusual, in the sense that it must not align with current habits and norms of behaviour;
- is unexpected or unscripted – in other words, without prior determination or direct cause;
- is without given content, in that its meaning cannot be exhausted by existent meanings, bringing forth new uses of language.

De Freitas and Sinclair's (2014) work is concerned specifically with mathematics, but the above four characteristics also form part of what I propose a feminist new materialism and posthumanist approach might offer, as will become apparent in the examples that are provided in this chapter. Feminist new materialism and a posthumanism approach foreground curiosity and wonder, being open to the world's liveliness, becoming together/apart through experimenting in in/determinacy, and moving away from what Whitehead (1967:2) refers to as "inert ideas". Barad's (2015:154) idea that "[t]heories are living and breathing reconfigurations of the world" is a useful one to bear in mind for academic development courses using feminist new materialism and posthumanism, as will become clear later in this chapter. In the next two sections, I discuss some significant concepts associated with feminist new materialism and posthumanism – that of affect, event, thought, concept and proposition, after which I describe practices where these concepts are put to work in academic development courses and activities.

Affect

The Spinozist view of affect is used in feminist new materialism and posthumanism. This is a philosophical rather than psychologised conception of affect, so dominant in the academy, which contests the fact that affect resides in the body, as an internal personal feeling or emotion possessed by an individual but sees affect as happening in the in-between. From a Spinozist view, affect is a pre-personal force or intensity impacting on what a body can be and do. Affect is both relational and dispersed. It is also transversal, traversing or cutting across traditional categories, and mutually inclusive – affect includes both subjective and objective, internal and external, body and mind, freedom and constraint (Massumi, 2015a). According to Spinoza, affect implies an openness to the world, being an active part of the world and as being response-able to the world – he sees affect as the body's capacity "to affect and be affected" (Massumi, 2015a:3). A body, according to Spinoza, is "what it can do as it goes along", "the capacities it carries from step to step". Massumi (2015a:4) discusses affect in terms of the concept of "manoeuvrability", the "where we might be able to go and what we might be able to do in every present situation". Affect also involves a transition of moving from one state of capacitation to the next – either an augmenting or a diminishing of capacity. Affect has to do with the potential available to us in situations and supersedes both emotion and conscious thought. From a Spinozist view, affect is also a way of connecting to others and other situations, participating in processes (Massumi, 2015a:6). This means that the micropolitics of the event – the next steps in experimentation, are what matters in working with academic staff, rather than the big utopian picture. Massumi (2015a) posits that affect cannot be separated from microshocks which occur with shifts in attention, interruptions, and so on, and are happening continually in our lives, and can sometimes pass by unnoticed – it may be felt without being registered consciously. Affect refers to being inducted into or attuned to tendencies and potential (Massumi, 2015b:57). Rotas (2016:187) reports on how curriculum theorist Ted Aoki (1993, 2005) "uses the term 'attunement' to express the bodily potential of learning in relation with environments". In terms of relation, the event will play out differently every time. From an affective position, pedagogy is about triggering cues and activating bodies in different ways, through microshocks or interruptive signs that attune bodies to activate potential.

Event, thought, concept, proposition

Erin Manning and Brian Massumi established an alternative space for doing education with "a laboratory for research-creation … that operates transversally between philosophy, creative practice and activism" called the SenseLab, based in Montreal (Massumi, 2015a:xi). For over a year they considered how to set up an event, what constitutes an event (an intellectual encounter that creates the opportunity for something to happen) and how to enable concept-creation through creative techniques and experimentation (Manning, 2009). An event is carefully planned with what Massumi (2015a:73, 79) refers to as "enabling constraints" and "techniques of relation" – by which he means the conditions for creative interaction, exploration, intensity and invention that focus on the *process* rather than the content, issue or outcome.

The SenseLab involved artists, dancers and philosophers in processes to develop concepts where education, research and artistic creation were expressly tied to philosophy (Colebrook, 2017). It brought together art to intensify perception and rigorous verbal expressions of concepts from the academic side in symbiosis for these creative events, where people were invited in a hospitable way to bring what mattered to them or what moved them and work with that. Massumi and Manning view philosophy as the creation of concepts, a philosophy of doing, which is how Deleuze and Guattari envisaged philosophy, too. Concepts are created "to augment capacities to act, feel and perceive, and also to think" (Massumi, 2015a). Thought is also not seen to be located in the mind, but as what moves through the body – as creative movement. Thought is also seen as ontogenetic – as propelling more thought ("from force to form to force"), reorientating thinking (Lenz Taguchi & St. Pierre, 2017), focusing on becoming rather than being (Manning, 2009:6).

Regarding concepts, Manning (2009:6) explains how they are "forces that take form at the junction between the emergence and expressibility of thought", and concepts provide the potential forces of events. Events do not precede time and space but create them, and are process-orientated – rather than outcomes-based or goal-oriented (Rotas, 2016). Furthermore, events are entangled with the human and more-than-human, intra-acting experimentally in ways that are conducive to intensive curiosity, rather than seeking to find solutions to problems framed prior to encounters (Rotas, 2016). As Lenz Taguchi (2010:137) explains:

> If we embrace an onto-epistemological perspective of immanence and one-ness, then learning in a pedagogical space cannot be isolated to a simple cause and effect relationship. We cannot think that if we do exactly *this*, *that* is what will be the learning outcome that can then be correctly measured. This is because *this* material that we use, or *that* way of explaining or talking, is never isolated from a lot of other things going on *in-between* and *through* other things in the learning event in a specific moment [emphases in the original].

There is a multiplicity of forces and intensities swirling through the actual event of the process of learning. Propositions that are "theories in the making" are also ways of making "thought felt" and moving "the concept into action", "cutting through the event", creating potential and possibilities (Manning, 2009:226). An important consideration for academic development informed by feminist new materialism and posthumanism is how assessment and an assessable product can be seen to stop potential and possibility in its obsession with success or failure, mastery and judgement. Assessment practices mitigate against taking risks, making mistakes, experimentation or indeterminacy. Assessment involves pinning something down and separating, which according to Massumi (2015:14) is "a weakness in judgement because it doesn't allow for these seeds of change, connections in the making that might not be activated or obvious at the moment". The implications that this would have for higher education would be a much stronger emphasis on formative rather than summative assessment, and of being rendered capable through dialogical feedback and the affordances of different spaces such as Google Docs (Bozalek & Zembylas, 2017a).

Slow and diffractive readings

"Slow reading", according to Boulous Walker (2017) is reading against the institution. It is an alternative way of engaging with texts which involves attentiveness, re-turning (turning over and over again) to the same texts to find new insights in them and engaging care-fully with texts. As an academic developer, I have been in various reading groups in my higher education institution, my international research projects focusing on feminist new materialism higher education pedagogies, as well as for inter-institutional spaces that have engaged with "slow reading". Each week a reading is set, or we may go through a whole text, meeting weekly to follow on where we have left off – this is indeterminate and depends on the needs and desires of the group members. The groups are run as communities of inquiry, where we read the text before coming to the group, discussing questions of clarification and issues that particularly struck the readers in pairs or threes in the group. We then meet in plenary and share the questions we have of the text and what was particularly striking and then collectively decide which questions or issues to zoom in on and focus on in the text. We then engage in collaborative reading practices (Truman, 2016; Bozalek, 2017), reading sections of the text to each other, taking it in turns to read aloud, after which we discuss what we have read, trying to stick closely to the text and not bringing in comparisons or critiques of the text (Massumi, 2017).

"Diffractive reading" is like slow reading in that it involves attending to the fine details of the text and doing justice to the ideas of the author (Barad, 2007). It also involves reading the ideas of one or more theory/approach/text/oeuvre *through* another, rather than juxtaposing one *against* another or foregrounding one and holding it as foundational while comparing it to others, as usually is the case in literature reviews or academic arguments. A diffractive reading is different from a comparison in that neither body of knowledge, theory or oeuvre, that is being read through the other is regarded as a fixed entity to begin with, and neither takes preference, but in reading one through the other, new insights and provocations are reached. In interviews with Barad (Dolphijn & Van der Tuin, 2012; Juelskjær & Schwennesen, 2012), she distinguishes diffractive reading from critique, the latter which she regards as doing epistemological damage. Massumi (2015a, 2017) also warns against an over-reliance on critique, that he sees as being demobilising in its reliance on reason, and discouragement of potential through an underappreciation of affect. For Barad (2007), a diffractive reading is an affirmative methodology that is different from reflection, which assumes a position of exteriority and distance from thinking. A diffractive methodology is used to read theories and oeuvres through each other, produce new insights, imaginaries and patterns of thought (Bozalek & Zembylas, 2017b).

Concept creation

For Deleuze and Guattari, philosophy is about creating concepts, and pedagogy is about experimentation, encounters that reorientate thought, forcing "thinking in thought" (Deleuze, 1994:139). This is not a process which can be taught as it does not rely on rationality but comes about through the unexpected in experimental and creative encounters. In a primer she wrote about Deleuze, Claire Colebrook (2002:15), writes that "concepts are not labels or names that we attach to things; they produce an orientation or a direction for thinking". The process-oriented nature of pedagogy means that it should, as it goes along, involve a further complexification of concepts, rather than finding answers or seeking solutions. Concept as method notes that concepts take on different meanings in different historical periods and different disciplines and can also become transdisciplinary. Foucault, Deleuze and Guattari did philosophy using the concept as a method (Taguchi & St. Pierre, 2017). As a method, the way concepts affect and are affected in the world cannot be predicted but are rather experienced as a shock to thought.

In some of my research project meetings on higher education pedagogies, I have used Massumi's (2017) ideas of speed-dating with concepts, for example when reviewing the work of Nancy Fraser (2008) in an NRF project meeting, the project members engaged in conceptual speed-dating about the concepts *distribution*, *recognition* and *representation* – three central concepts in Fraser's work.

Massumi and Manning introduced the notion of conceptual speed-dating in their SenseLab, to enable participatory parity in discussions about concepts in the text, where artists, dancers and philosophers come together to learn and encounter each other. They did this because Massumi and Manning realised that these groups of people were in very different places with regard to engaging verbally with concepts. In academic development courses and research projects, participants also come with different needs and from different contexts. Conceptual speed-dating allows everyone to participate, focusing on the specificities of the text rather than generalising about it (Massumi, 2015, 2017). In Massumi's (2015, 2017) conceptual speed-dating, the participants and facilitators were given the following instructions:

1. Choose a generative text with enough richness (Dawkins, 2017).
2. Choose a minor concept[5] weaving through the generative text.
3. Ask each person in the group to count off as a 1 or a 2.
4. Instruct the 1s that they are "posts".
5. Instruct the 2s that they are "flows".
6. Ask the Posts to find a post: a spot in the room where they would like to have a conversation.
7. Ask the Flows to pair up with a post.
8. Direct everyone to a page in the text where the minor concept occurs.
9. Ask the participants to discuss the function of the minor concept, staying as close as possible to the text, with detailed attention to its construction.
10. Notify participants that when exactly five minutes are up, they will hear a signal and that when they hear the signal, they must end their conversation immediately, even if they are in the middle of a word.
11. When the five-minute signal sounds, ask all Flows to move to the next Post in a clockwise direction.
12. Repeat 8–10 times.
13. Bring the group back together and discuss in plenary session what they discovered about the minor concept and the text (Massumi, 2015:59-60; 2017:111).

Engaging in this way allows disparate groups of people from different backgrounds the opportunity to encounter each other in what Massumi refers to as an "unacknowledged mutual miscomprehension" (Massumi, 2015:61).

---

5 A minor concept is a lesser-known concept that is important in the text, but that the reader does not grasp, a concept not generally concentrated on in hegemonic literature but a central concept that helps make the text and recurs in the text (Dawkins, 2017). A close reading is done of the minor concept, of the work it does in the text.

The chosen text for the conceptual speed-dating needs to be a generative and open one, where it can be read again and again without exhausting its potential and hospitality for new thoughts.

Another example of where we used conceptual speed-dating was on the short course, *Reconfiguring Scholarship: Writing, Reviewing and Publishing Differently*, one of the 2018 Quality Teaching and Learning in Higher Education short courses run under the auspices of the Cape Higher Education Consortium (CHEC, 2018, 2017). For a session in this short course, the facilitators and participants decided to focus on the concept "ontology of immanence" to do conceptual speed-dating using the reading by St. Pierre (2018).

What such alternative academic development courses attempted to do was to facilitate a reorientation of thinking by focusing on what mattered for the academics who attended the course – encouraging them to bring an unfinished piece of work they were working on. The curriculum involved engaging in various experimental and creative practices of thinking-doing-making in transdisciplinary events. It made it possible for the participants to reconfigure or re-imagine concepts that were important to them. Part of the course was alerting academics to how they can use concepts as methods, and how they can be both transformative and inventive, fostering experimental thought (Colebrook, 2017). As Lenz Taguchi and St. Pierre (2017:3) put it:

> Instead of thinking about education as the production of the perfectly enlightened, harmonious, and thus subjected individual, the ideal becomes the enactment of inventive and experimental processes that make possible potentially new and different kinds of human subjects.

Propositions

Feminist new materialism and posthumanism pedagogies use propositions to activate thought (Manning & Massumi, 2014) and emanate from the work of Alfred North Whitehead (1978). Propositions are "thoughts in motion" and "oscillate between potential and actualization", not knowing in advance what might happen or be produced (Manning, 2008:17-18). They are thus speculative, emphasising what may be, through chance, improvisation, and experimentation. Propositions are process-oriented, focusing on events, rather than being sets of instructions, judgements or prescriptive rules to follow (Springgay & Truman, 2018b; Truman & Springgay, 2016). Propositions thus give rise to experimentation, as "speculative-eventing" (Springgay & Truman, 2018b; Truman & Springgay, 2016:204), "propulsing an event toward what it can do" (Manning, 2008:18), creating enabling constraints, that are both productive and limiting, rather than prescriptive strategies. According to Deleuze, events are expressed through propositions (Olsson, 2009). The use of propositions in research, pedagogical practice and other creative endeavours have been taken forward in the work of Erin Manning (2008) and Brian Massumi (Manning & Massumi, 2014), and more latterly by Stephanie Springgay and Sarah Truman (see Springgay, 2016; Springgay & Truman, 2018a, 2018b; Truman & Springgay, 2016).

An example of an exercise involving propositions was in the CHEC short course, *Reconfiguring Scholarship: Writing, Reviewing and Publishing Differently* (CHEC, 2018), mentioned above concerning speed-dating. The course participants were introduced to the work of Springgay and Truman, who use propositions for walking in their various publications (Springgay & Truman, 2018a, 2018b; Truman & Springgay, 2016). Walking as a methodology allows taking ideas/thinking for a walk or "thinking-in-movement" (Truman & Springgay, 2016:204). The participants, who were attending the residential part of the course at a semi-rural venue located in the Winelands of Cape Town, engaged in an exercise on decolonial orientations to writing place, introduced to the participants by Fikile Nxumalo from the University of Toronto, whose work is on an exercise involving propositions. She provided participants with a brief overview of her work using Adobe Connect, to intra-act with them and explained the exercise as follows:

Activity: Decolonial orientations to writing place

Writing place

Take a walk around, nearby (preferably outdoors). Search for evidence of Black/Indigenous, settler, and immigrant presences. These could be signs, sculptures, artwork, monument, a building, a body of water, a tree/plant, a patch of earth, an animal (that is, human and more-than-human storying of places).

Come back in 30 minutes.

Select one subject/site (e.g., one that connects to Indigenous presences). Take a photo, then practice writing a responsive, creative, detailed and descriptive piece about this site paying attention to the writing propositions we discussed and noting why you selected this site. While you may not know the specific past-present histories of the site you have chosen, your writing can pose questions/wonderings/imaginings about and (re)story the site.

The writing propositions were the following:

1. De-romanticising "nature" by attending to anthropogenically (human-caused) "damaged places".
2. Paying attention to the ways that the more-than-human world actively "stories" places.
3. Restoring places and paying attention to and "presencing" marginalised (such as Black, Indigenous, Immigrant) place stories.
4. Paying attention to uneven/inequitable human geographies of place.
5. Paying attention to the "affects"/embodied emotions evoked by a place.

Participants responded very creatively to this exercise and produced interesting photovoice pieces, including poems, and so on.

Art explorations of the propositions

After doing the walk in the CHEC (2018) short course, the following day one of the facilitators, a professor in Fine Arts from Stellenbosch University, took the participants (and other facilitators) through working with maps and opening up the possibilities of engaging with the propositions in different ways. Five pieces of tracing paper and a map of the area (a rural area in Stellenbosch) were provided for participants to draw on and consider five of the propositions suggested by Fikile.

On another day in the CHEC (2018) short course, a professor of English and an expert in poetry from Wits University, discussed poetry with the other facilitators and participants. The professor read some examples of poems for inspiration and invited participants/facilitators to write poems about any issue they felt like writing about, for example, their research or concepts.

What was interesting in this CHEC (2018) short course and another CHEC short course, *Multimodal Pedagogies and Post-Qualitative Scholarship in Higher Education*, held the year before in 2017 (CHEC, 2017), was that the facilitators participated in the activities together with the participants – the relational processes of rendering each other capable, as well as the provocations of the various art forms – the walking methodology and photovoice exercise of Fikile's; the map and tracing exercise for Fikile's propositions as well as the Wits professor's poetry exercise; and the conceptual speed-dating.

These all activate potentials, which is not only dependent on the humans involved, but which is event-based. The enabling constraints of the event, for example, structured improvisation which Erin Manning uses in the SenseLab, make possible conditions for experimentation which generate intensities and new thoughts to be expressed. As Nikki Rotas (2016:184) notes, "[t]he potential of the event is embodied in the relational (more-than-human) practices that the proposition activates".

Pedagogical documentation

Throughout the process of the CHEC (2018, 2017) short courses, the facilitators were both doing or making-with alongside the participants, as well as doing pedagogical documentation, a methodological tool that comes from the Reggio Emilia movement in early childhood development (Edwards, Gandini & Foreman, 1998). The Reggio Emilia approach was developed by Loris Malaguzzi for impoverished children as a response to fascism after the war in Italy. Edwards, Gandini and Foreman (1998:12) describe pedagogical documentation, the visual, graphic audio and video recordings of children's comments and discussions as serving three functions:

1. Providing children with conscious memory of what they said and did to establish the next steps for learning and facilitation of their work;
2. Serving as a research tool for the educators to understand the pedagogical work and the capacities of the children; and
3. Serving as a record for parents and the public.

In the visualising process and content of pedagogical documentation, during which the pedagogical work is materialised, the teachers and children are co-constructors and co-producers, using multiple perspectives for experimenting, learning and democratic participation (Dahlberg, Moss & Pence, 2007). Pedagogical documentation also involves listening and sharing – as Vea Vecchi explains it: "One of the foundations of our work is the careful, respectful, tender 'listening' with solidarity to children's strategies and ways of thinking and avoiding predetermined results" (Vecchi, 2010:xvii). The emphasis in the Reggio Emilia approach is also on new ideas and original thinking, creativity, relationship, invention, affirmation, intensity and "affect"; the unpredictability of learning; process rather than product or predetermined outcomes; working with the aesthetic and the poetic, in-depth and unhurried rather than superficial and rushed; attentiveness and care; active engagement rather than transmission as well as transdisciplinarity, rejecting preconceived categories and disciplinary boundaries, which all can be seen to be very similar to feminist new materialism and posthumanist approaches to curriculum and education.

Pedagogical documentation has been used by Lenz Taguchi (2010) as a central tool in professional development with teachers researching their practice. Based on Barad's (2007) thinking, Lenz Taguchi (2010:63) refers to pedagogical documentation as a material-discursive apparatus used for observing something, understood as "taking part in a process of 'material' (re)configurations or discursive practices" (2007:184). Pedagogical documentation is thus seen as an active and lively agent in "generating discursive knowledge" (Lenz Taguchi, 2010:63) and constructing meaning through material such as notes, photographs, videos, and so on, that are seen to matter, and that become vibrant actors in the learning process. The documentation constructs "space where intra-active phenomena between children, concepts and materials can emerge and be actualised (that is, made visible and readable to us)" (Lenz Taguchi, 2010:66).

Liselott Olsson (2009:20) explains how she uses pedagogical documentation with teachers, researchers and children, not as a form of representation, but in bringing forces and intensities for opening possibilities of multiple vital, open-ended collective ways of becoming-with issues of interest for all involved. Listening, observing and recording each other are important parts of pedagogical documentation, as ways of making visible what was not visible before as Lenz Taguchi (2010) makes clear and De Freitas and Sinclair (2014) note when describing creative acts in *Mathematics and the Body*, alluded to earlier in this chapter.

On the two CHEC short courses described in this chapter, people's abstracts, concept writing, artwork, intra-actions, poetry, were videoed and photographed along the way and made available to all participants and facilitators in a folder on Google Drive. During the *Reconfiguring Scholarship* course, participants used pedagogical documentation to select parts of their work they used for a collaborative book which two graphic artists made from the project. Each person had a two-page spread in the book – that was published by African Sun Media in 2018. In the previous CHEC (2018) short course, group members, giving feedback to each other in weekly meetings, as well as annotated comments on the multimodal artefacts developed by participants on their concepts. These learnings were forceful in assisting participants to re-think and re-turn to their concepts.

In another writing group, with PhD students and colleagues in a research project, we used a Google Doc to write about a concept that emerged from our conversations each time we met. We did freewriting on the concept simultaneously on the same Google Doc and then read our pieces to each other, after which further discussions on the subject ensued. One of us also always audio recorded the sessions and uploaded the recordings of this in the Google folder. We also took many photographs of our talking, walking, writing and used the montage of recorded talking, writing, videos and photographs to present our work at a conference. See video[6] below:

We were thus using pedagogical documentation as collaborators of events of learning and invention, becoming anew through doing justice to what was happening. As Lenz Taguchi (2010:94) expresses it: "Pedagogical documentation in an intra-active pedagogy goes beyond the theory/practice divide, in that it embraces the interdependence of thinking and living."

Conclusion

This chapter has attempted to provide examples that incorporate an ethico-onto-epistemological approach as highlighted in feminist new materialism and posthumanism, rather than a myopic focus on epistemology (Barad, 2007; Braidotti, 2013; Haraway 2016). Indeed, feminist new materialism and posthumanism involve far more than a critique of epistemology – they are radically different approaches to doing academic development emanating from a relational ontology, that holds that knowledge, identities or entities do not pre-exist relationships, but come into being through relationships. In this chapter, through the examples of academic development that I have shared, I have tried to show the importance of different sorts of practices or enactments that are experimental, affirmative and inclusive. Formalised and pre-existing approaches to academic development are thus not seen as particularly helpful in engaging with colleagues to enhance academic practices. This chapter has attempted to provide some ways of doing what De Freitas and Sinclair (2014:52) suggest, which is alluded to at the beginning of this chapter: "How might an inclusive materialism allow us to rethink learning as an indeterminate act of assembling various kinds of agencies rather than a trajectory that ends in the acquiring of fixed objects of knowledge?"

6   https://youtu.be/zPnph_L45tl

Feminist new materialism and posthumanist approaches thus change practices commonly used by academic developers from engaging in "thinking about" to "thinking-doing" (Springgay, 2016). Rendering each other capable and making-with each other, pedagogy becomes emergent, rather than pre-existent to the encounter or the event (Barad, 2007; Truman, 2016). Feminist new materialism and posthumanist approaches to academic development might be like what Truman (2016:95) refers to as critical public pedagogies that involve interventions that employ "noncanonical knowledge, defamiliarization, artistic interventions, and perhaps marginalia or additions to an existing text on a page". They are generative, playful and inventive aesthetic practices of knowledge-creation (Rotas, 2016). This way of working undoes many of the assumptions employed in academic development professional courses that focus on learning to teach. Such approaches, also used with undergraduate students – that many authors in higher education have written about (see De Freitas & Sinclair, 2014; Ednie-Brown, 2015; Snaza et al., 2016; Masny, 2013) but it is beyond the scope of this chapter which focuses mainly on staff development and working with postgraduate students.

Concept creation, Slow, diffractive reading, walking, creative aesthetic/artistic and propositional methodologies, are some of the experimental process-oriented modes of doing curricula I have suggested in this chapter. These can be possible ways for reconfiguring academic development as sympoiesis and co-composition to activate event potential and new directions for learning for all involved. These processes involve pedagogical enactments of aspects of science, art and philosophy. This creates intensive orientations for trans-individual co-composition and thinking in events or encounters that do not prescribe specific outcomes, in this way providing a process of potentiation for reconfiguring academic development.

References

BARAD, K. 2017a. Troubling time/s and ecologies of nothingness: re-turning, re-membering, and facing the incalculable. *New Formations*, 92. [https://doi.org/10.5422/fordham/9780823279500.003.0010]

BARAD, K. 2017b. What flashes up: Theological-political-scientific fragments. In: C. Keller & M. Rubenstein (eds). *Entangled Worlds: Religion, science and new materialisms*. New York: Fordham University Press, 21-88. [https://doi.org/10.2307/j.ctt1xhr73h.4]

BARAD, K. 2015. On Touching – The Inhuman That Therefore I Am (v1.1). In: S. Witzgall & S. Kerstin (eds). *Power of the material/Politics of materiality*. Zurich: Diaphanes, 153-164.

BARAD, K. 2014. Diffracting diffraction: Cutting together apart. *Parallax*, 20(3):168-187. [https://doi.org/10.1080/13534645.2014.927623]

BARAD, K. 2007. *Meeting the universe halfway: Quantum physics and the entanglement of matter and meaning*. London: Duke University Press. [https://doi.org/10.1215/9780822388128]

Boulous Walker, M. 2016. *Slow Philosophy: Reading against the institution*. London: Bloomsbury.

Bozalek, V. 2017. Slow Scholarship in Writing Retreats: A Diffractive Methodology for Response-Able Pedagogies. *South African Journal of Higher Education*, 31(2):40-57. [https://doi.org/10.20853/31-2-1344]

Bozalek, V, & Dison, A. 2013. Using institutional strategic interventions to enhance teaching and learning at UWC. *South African Journal of Higher Education*, 27(2):383-400.

Bozalek, V. & Zembylas, M. 2017a. Towards a response-able pedagogy across higher education institutions in post-apartheid South Africa: An ethico-political analysis. *Education as Change*, 21(2):62-85. [https://doi.org/10.17159/1947-9417/2017/2017]

Bozalek, V. & Zembylas, M. 2017b. Diffraction or reflection? Sketching the contours of two methodologies in educational research. *International Journal of Qualitative Studies in Education*, 30(2):111-127. [https://doi.org/ 10.1080/09518398.2016.1201166]

Braidotti, R. 2013. *The Posthuman*. Cambridge: Polity Press.

Colebrook, C. 2017. What is this thing called education? *Qualitative Inquiry*, 23(9):649-655. [https://doi.org/10.1177/1077800417725357]

Colebrook, C. 2002. *Gilles Deleuze*. New York: Routledge.

CHEC (Cape Higher Education Consortium). 2018. *Reconfiguring Scholarship: Writing, Reviewing and Publishing Differently*. Short course. CHEC.

CHEC (Cape Higher Education Consortium). 2017. *Multimodal Pedagogies and Post-Qualitative Scholarship in Higher Education*. Short course. CHEC.

Dahlberg, G.; Moss, P. & Pence, A. 2007. *Beyond Quality in Early Childhood Education and Care: Languages of Evaluation*. Second edition. London: Routledge.

Dawkins, R. 2017. Tools for jimmying experience: Conceptual speed dating on Facebook. *First Monday*, 22 [https://doi.org/10.5210/fm.v22i111.7746]

De Freitas, E. & Sinclair, N. 2014. *Mathematics and the Body: Material Entanglements in the Classroom*. New York: Cambridge University Press. [https://doi.org/10.1017/CBO9781139600378]

Deleuze, G. 1994. *Difference and repetition*. Translated by P. Patton. New York: Columbia University Press.

Despret, V. 2016. *What would animals say if we asked the right questions?* Minneapolis: University of Minnesota Press.

Despret, V. 2015a. We are not so stupid ... animals neither. *Angelaki*, 20(2):153-161. [https://doi.org/10.1080/0969725X.2015.1039855]

Despret, V. 2015b. Who made Clever Hans stupid? *Angelaki*, 20(2):77-85. [https://doi.org/10.1080/0969725X.2015.1039843]

Despret, V. 2004. The body we care for: Figures of anthropo-zoo-genesis. *Body and Society*, 10:111-134. [https://doi.org/10.1177/1357034X04042938]

Dolphijn, R. & van der Tuin, I. 2012. *New Materialism: Interviews and Cartographies*. University of Michigan Library: Open Humanities Press. [https://doi.org/10.3998/ohp.11515701.0001.001]

Ednie-Brown, P. 2015. Critical Passions: Building Architectural Movements Toward a Radical Pedagogy (in 10 steps). *Inflexions*, 8:20-48.

Edwards, C.; Gandini, L. & Foreman, G. 2002. *The hundred languages of children. The Reggio Emilia approach – Advanced reflections*. London: Ablex.

Grosz, E. 2008. *Chaos, territory, art: Deleuze and the framing of the earth*. New York: Columbia University Press.

Haraway, D. 2016. *Staying with the Trouble: Making kin in the Chthulucene*. London: Duke University Press. [https://doi.org/10.1215/9780822373780]

Juelskjær, M. & Schwennesen, N. 2012. Intra-active entanglements: an interview with Karen Barad. *Kvinder, Koen og Forskning*, 21(1-2):10-23. [https://doi.org/10.7146/kkf.v0i1-2.28068]

Keller, C. & Rubenstein, M. 2017. Introduction: Tangled matters. In: C. Keller & M. Rubenstein (eds). *Entangled Worlds: Religion, science and new materialisms*. New York: Fordham University Press, 1-20. [https://doi.org/10.2307/j.ctt1xhr73h]

Lenz Taguchi, H. 2010. *Going beyond the theory/practice divide in early childhood education*. London: Routledge. [https://doi.org/10.4324/9780203872956]

Lenz Taguchi, H. & St. Pierre, E.A. 2017. Using Concept as Method in Educational and Social Science Inquiry. *Qualitative Inquiry*, 23(9):643-648. [https://doi.org/10.1177/1077800417732634]

Manning, E. 2012. *Always more than one: Individuation's dance*. London: Duke University Press. [https://doi.org/10.1215/9780822395829]

Manning, E. 2009. *Relationscapes: Movement, art, philosophy*. Cambridge: The MIT Press. [https://doi.org/10.7551/mitpress/9780262134903.001.0001]

Manning, E. 2008. Creative Propositions for Thought in Motion. *Inflexions: A Journal for Research-Creation*, 1(1):1-24. [www.inflexions.org]

Manning, E. & Massumi, B. 2014. *Thought in the act: Passages in the ecology of experience*. Minneapolis: Minnesota University Press. [https://doi.org/10.5749/minnesota/9780816679669.001.0001]

Massumi, B. 2017. *The Principle of Unrest: Activist Philosophy in the Expanded Field*. London: Open Humanities Press. [https://doi.org/10.26530/OAPEN_630732]

Massumi, B. 2015a. *Politics of affect*. Cambridge: Polity.

Massumi, B. 2015b. Collective Expression: A Radical Pragmatics. *Inflexions: A Journal for Research-Creation, Radical Pedagogies*, Spring:59-88. [https://bit.ly/2mrxmNd]

Olsson, L.M. 2009. *Movement and experimentation in young children's learning: Deleuze and Guattari in early childhood education*. London: Routledge. [https://doi.org/10.4324/9780203881231]

Rotas, N. 2016. Moving Toward Practices that Matter. In: N. Snaza, D. Sonu, S.E. Truman & Z. Zaliwska (eds). *Pedagogical Matters: New Materialism and Curriculum Studies*. New York: Peter Lang, 179-196.

Semetsky, I. 2013. Learning with Bodymind. In: D. Masny (ed). *Cartographies of Becoming in Education: A Deleuze-Guattari perspective*. Rotterdam: Sense Publishers, 77-92. [https://doi.org/10.1007/978-94-6209-170-2_7]

Springgay, S. 2016. Meditating with Bees: Weather Bodies and a Pedagogy of Movement. In: N. Snaza, D. Sonu, S.E. Truman & Z. Zaliwska (eds). *Pedagogical Matters: New Materialism and Curriculum Studies*. New York: Peter Lang, 59-74.

Springgay, S. & Truman, S.E. 2018a. *Walking Methodologies in a More-than-Human World: Walking Lab*. London and New York: Routledge.

Springgay, S. & Truman, S.E. 2018b. On the Need for Methods Beyond Proceduralism: Speculative Middles, (In)Tensions, and Response-Ability in Research. *Qualitative Inquiry*, 24(3):203-214. [https://doi.org/10.1177/1077800417704464]

St. Pierre, E.A. 2018. Post Qualitative Inquiry in an Ontology of Immanence. *Qualitative Inquiry*, 1-14. [https://doi.org/10.1177/1077800418772634]

Truman, S.E. 2016. Intratextual entanglements: Emergent pedagogies and the productive potential of texts. In: N. Snaza, D. Sonu, S.E. Truman & Z. Zaliwska (eds). *Pedagogical Matters: New Materialism and Curriculum Studies*. New York: Peter Lang, 92-107.

Truman, S.E. & Springgay, S. 2016. Propositions for Walking Research. In: K. Powell, P. Bernard & L. Mackinley (eds). *International Handbook for Intercultural Arts*. New York: Routledge, 259-267.

Vecchi, V. 2010. *Art and Creativity in Reggio Emilia Exploring the role and potential of ateliers in early childhood education*. London: Routledge. [https://doi.org/10.4324/9780203854679]

Whitehead, A.N. 1978. *Process and Reality*. New York: Free Press.

CHAPTER 10

Academic developers as disruptors

Reshaping the instructional design process

Keisha Valdez & Dianne Thurab-Nkhosi

Introduction

Education plays a significant role in how citizens are socialised and what they value. Frequently in higher education, Western-centric perspectives are idealised and dominate ways of understanding the world and how knowledge is produced and shared (Thaman, 2003). Decolonisation of curriculum creates an opportunity to acknowledge the dominance of Western-created knowledge and pedagogies and invites indigenous and non-Western ways of knowing and understanding the world (Thaman, 2003). In the quest for curriculum transformation in both developed and developing contexts, decolonisation of the curriculum should be considered. Disruption of marginalising practices and the opening of spaces for learning from multiple perspectives can contribute to the decolonisation of the curriculum.

In the twenty-first century, we cannot describe higher education without mentioning online learning and its ability to create these inclusive spaces by connecting students with the world far beyond the walls of a classroom and static textbooks. As online learning has been gaining ground within higher education, academic developers who work in instructional design are increasingly charged with the responsibility of providing support and guidance as faculty members design, develop and teach their courses. If curriculum transformation requires a radical change to course design (De Lissovoy, 2010), then it may be useful for academic developers to critically examine their role and influence in the online course design process. This has led us to adopt the position that we, as academic developers, have the potential to be disruptors. In our roles as instructional designers operating in the United States and the Caribbean, we worked collaboratively to propose an alternate curriculum transformation model of instructional design. We are hoping that this alternative model can re-shape instructional design practice towards decolonised curriculum. Because we work in a cross-disciplinary environment, we are approaching the development of the model from a more generic perspective rather than a specific subject area.

Our proposed Fifth Dimension Curriculum Transformation Model (5D-CTM), elements of which have only been implemented informally to date, builds on the frequently-used ADDIE instructional design model (Analysis, Design, Development, Implementation and Evaluation) along with other existing alternative course design frameworks. These models will be described in more detail later in the chapter. Our model is intended to address issues of decolonisation. This chapter first explores online and blended learning as a space for transformation. We then present decolonisation of the curriculum as a disruption of marginalising practices in instructional design and explore the academic developer's role in supporting this transformation in an online course design context. We argue that the 5D-CTM creates authentic opportunities for academic developers to act as disruptors as they implement new ways of working with academic colleagues. The chapter concludes with some recommendations for implementing the 5D-CTM as a means of disrupting marginalising course design practices.

Positioning online and blended learning to disrupt practices and open spaces

Online and blended learning has the potential to open spaces for learning. It can be a means of providing increased access and knowledge sources. It requires educators to explore the identities of their students, rethink the content and the ways in which this content is presented. This new way of thinking about courses, students and knowledge, strategically positions online and blended learning course design as an opportunity for reform. The transformative capacity of online and blended learning in higher education institutions is linked to the potential to provide more inclusive and authentically connected learning experiences for students. Online and blended learning can make it possible for teachers and students to explore their disciplines by creating expanded ways of defining, sourcing, and sharing knowledge. The ubiquitous nature of online and blended learning has allowed this mode of teaching and learning to open spaces for teaching and learning and has positioned online and blended learning as a potential disruptor.

Disruptive innovation has a role to play in stimulating transformation in higher education. The ideas of disruption and transformation can be closely tied to various conceptions of online and blended learning (Christensen & Horn, 2013; Garrison & Kanuka, 2004). Garrison and Kanuka's rationale for the transformative capacity of online and blended learning relates to the potential of this learning to provide more learner-centred, individualised learning and more access through convenience and affordability for students:

> What makes blended learning particularly effective is its ability to facilitate a community of inquiry. Community provides the stabilizing, cohesive influence that balances the open communication and limitless access to information on the internet. Communities also provide the condition for free and open dialogue, critical debate, negotiation and agreement – the hallmark of higher education. Blended learning has the capabilities to facilitate these conditions. (Garrison & Kanuka, 2004:97)

In exploring disruptive innovation, it should be recognised that blended learning is subject to varied definitions in the literature (Bates, 2018; Poon, 2013; Twigg, 2003). These definitions range from an understanding of blended learning as a combination of learning experiences that integrate some use of educational technology, to approaches that focus on a combination of online instruction and face-to-face experiences (Watson, 2008). Both online and blended learning design, therefore, represent a significant departure from face to face teaching and "represent(s) a fundamental reconceptualization and reorganisation of the teaching and learning dynamic" (Garrison & Kanuka, 2004:97). It is this departure and requirement for reconceptualisation that allows for the potential for online and blended learning to serve as a disruptor of traditional ways of thinking about disciplinary knowledge and approaching teaching and learning.

It would be naïve to assume that this opportunity to disrupt and transform the curriculum will be easily recognised and acted upon by those who are in the position to do so. Without guidance or intervention, it may be tempting for academics/course designers to return to their familiar sources of disciplinary knowledge that may be Western-dominated and continue the familiar culturally exclusive curriculum even within an online and blended learning mode.

As online and blended learning is ubiquitous and more academic programmes take on online and blended learning formats supporting the reconceptualisation of the curriculum to incorporate new ways of designing curriculum is particularly problematic. This is especially so if those who are intimately involved in course development are applying instructional design frameworks, which are inherently conservative (De Lorme, 2014).

While it has been suggested that online and blended learning can be transformative and can foster student reflection, dialogue and community building (Bates, 2018), these benefits can only occur with thoughtful design. This thoughtful design can capitalise on the spaces created by online and blended learning and allow for recognition of dominant ways of knowing and the invitation of other ways of understanding the world. Thoughtful design, however, needs a guiding philosophy or principles. In our quest for "transformation", we are proposing that principles relevant to the decolonisation of the curriculum may be appropriate.

Decolonisation of curriculum as transformation: Inviting other ways of knowing

Decolonisation of curriculum and the invitation of other ways of understanding the world can begin with deep reflection on sources of knowledge, the content selected, and, the pedagogies and instructional approaches employed by the instructor. All these elements are important in the design of the curriculum. Through the design of the course curriculum, the disciplinary experts signal what and whose knowledge is valuable enough to be investigated, passed on to others, and preserved for future generations. This power may be at the heart of questions about the influence of universities (Brennan, King & Lebeau, 2004).

If we entertain the notion of higher education institutions having a hand in whose sources of knowledge ultimately are perceived as dominant, then we can more easily see curriculum as a medium for social transformation and decolonisation. This is supported by Heleta's (2016) assertion that academics who are interested in socio-economic transformation must change the "what and how" of their teaching practice. Decolonisation of the curriculum can be an opportunity to invite alternative ways of thinking about the world to promote cultural inclusivity (Thaman, 2003) and decentralising Western knowledge systems (Le Grange, 2016)

In his call for a "pedagogy of lovingness", De Lissovoy (2010) sees decolonisation of the curriculum as possible through the creation of a renewed curriculum that is aware of, and sensitive to cultural differences and aims to develop a global community. We see co-creation involving students, lecturers and other community stakeholders as critical to the development of a renewed curriculum regardless of the subject matter. Thus, our proposed instructional design model, which will be described later in the chapter will have as a feature the element of co-creation and collaboration.

De Lissovoy (2010) acknowledges that while we need to confront colonialism, and in particular Eurocentrism, we also need to recognise that we live in an increasingly connected world, and we must, therefore, forge relationships of interconnectedness and solidarity. This involves a decentring of Western-perspectives and broadening the focus to include the contributions which emerge from more societies and experiences. De Lissovoy argues that we must ensure that historically marginalised people and indigenous struggles should be prioritised. His "pedagogy of lovingness", calls for a reconceptualisation of social relationships and the fostering of a condition of kindredness through recognition of human relations over academic and cognitive relations.

A "pedagogy of lovingness" is aligned with Le Grange's (2016:9) four Rs, summarised below, which he sees as essential elements of a decolonised curriculum:

- Relational accountability – the curriculum parts are holistically interconnected to human beings and their beliefs.
- Respectful representation – provisions are made for all voices, knowledge and experiences to be represented.
- Reciprocal appropriation – the outcomes and benefits of the knowledge are shared with the wider community.
- Rights and regulations – the curriculum shows respect for the cultural customs and protocols that guide how knowledge is owned and credited.

In our earlier discussion of the role of online and blended learning as a strategic point for change, we proposed that it can expand how knowledge is defined, sourced and shared. Built into the online and blended learning design process is the opportunity to embrace a wider variety of students and expand perspectives that value and preserve far more identities, culture and knowledge. Course/curriculum design, particularly with online and blended learning, requires participation in a thoughtful process.

Researchers have pointed to the importance of academic staff development to enable thoughtful curriculum development and course design (Kim & Bonk, 2006; Kenney & Newcombe, 2011; Badawood, Steenkamp & Al-Werfalli, 2013). According to Kenney and Newcombe (2011), academics must be supported to design and deliver blended instruction effectively. This involves making the necessary provisions for knowledge and skills development and actively creating the space to encourage the exploration of transformative thinking. To consider the application of a transformative model of course design, we as academic developers should consider our professional position and interactions with mainstream academics.

This lays the foundation for us to argue for the role of academic developers as disruptors and change agents, particularly those charged with course or instructional design responsibilities. Academic developers can serve as, not only the source of course design training, but also as supporters and collaborators in a course design process, aimed at promoting decolonised curriculum with relational accountability, respectful representation, reciprocal appropriation and rights and regulations (Le Grange, 2016).

Shifting assumptions of neutrality in academic development to support change

As academic developers who work in faculty development units in higher education, we take on roles and responsibilities which have been described as varied, specialised and complex (Bath & Smith, 2004; Land, 2001; Vorster & Quinn, 2015) and filled with tensions and fragmentation (Hicks, 2005). Often the role is that of a service provider, of supporting academics or administration, positioned as their "clients". Rathburn and Newcombe (2012) use the adjective of "go-betweens" to describe the consultancy nature of the role. Academic developers become a mediator for problem-solving, change and negotiation for academics and administrators; and their assignments often originate from or are highly influenced by external forces, resulting in an inclination of academic developers to present themselves as being collegial, neutral agents with a singular focus on the deliverables requested.

Researchers have questioned the idea of neutrality in academic development work (Wuetherick & Ewert-Baur, 2012; Rathburn & Newcombe, 2012). Rathburn and Newcombe (2012) explain that there is often a subconscious connection between the approaches taken to consultation, and the developer's, intentions, perception of his/her role and allegiance. They describe academic development practices as either practised domestication or liberation. In practising domestication, academic developers are concerned with remaining true to institutional goals, policies, academic norms or prescribed professional standards. In our experience in the United States and the Caribbean, many academic developers have taken a domestication stance when it applies to instructional design. We have heard it said time and again: *While we support the instructional design process, it's not really our course. Our job is to support the work academics want to get done in their online and blended learning course. Afterall, as the subject matter experts, they would know what is best for their students.*

This domestication approach is juxtaposed with liberation, where academic developers are driven by a transformation agenda, a desire to challenge the status quo, and they align themselves with academics as peers. In the online and blended learning context, this would not mean denying the faculty designers as subject matter experts but also recognising the academic developer's accountability, voice and responsibility for the ways pedagogical decisions are made in the courses. Either way, whether an academic developer takes a domestication or liberation approach to academic development and instructional design work, in particular, neutrality is unlikely. The academic developer's actions in the course design process are tied to the stances he/she takes and how authority and agency of all stakeholders are perceived. This, therefore, has implications for how academic developers guide the instructional design process.

Campbell, Kanuka and Schwier (2009) espouse similar ideas in their descriptions of how academics engage with instructional designers. The symbiotic relationship between the instructional designers, academics, students and the course has the potential to be transformative for the institution, the individuals and society. In consultation with the academic, each recommendation offered, the framework adopted, or design developed, is connected to a deliberate position of academic developers and conceptions under which they operate. In essence, if the academic is relying on academic developers' pedagogical and design expertise to shape a final product, then the academic developers have a responsibility to recognise and own their influence and agency in the relationship.

Academic developers as disruptors owning agency

Many researchers have written about the identity of academic developers (Land, 2001; Green & Little, 2013; Neame & Forsyth, 2016). The questions that linger are those that relate to agency. Whose role is it to effect change? Is the responsibility shared? What is the authority of the academic developer? The academic developers' liaison-like role "enables them to carry out mixed portfolios in [the] third space between professional and academic domains. They are characterised by an ability to build common ground with a range of colleagues, ... and to develop new forms of professional space, knowledge, relationships and legitimacies associated with broadly based institutional projects" (Whitchurch, 2009:13).

Questions we could ask ourselves are: Do we as academic developers hide within this third space, attempting to insulate it with objectivity and neutrality? Or do we take advantage of this third space and capitalise on opportunities to create new ways of thinking and interacting with all constituents and stakeholders? If we recognise the agency that the academic developer position affords us and accept the potential we have to influence the transformation of courses, the experiences of students, academics, and the larger institution, then it becomes easier to see that academic developers can in fact be disruptors.

From change supporters to change agents

The role of academic developers as change agents seems to lie in our readiness or desire to use our sphere of influence for disruption. As academic developers, we may be faced with histories, social structures and geopolitics that devalue some of us, while privileging others. We may find that many higher education practices reinforce this status quo. In such situations, consideration could be given to creating more inclusive academic and institutional practices, and curricular reform that is responsive to the needs of the global society. As academic developers, we have considered that inherent in the criticism of the beliefs and biases that underpin colonial and Western-centric pedagogies, is an equally heavy critique of the very practices and structures that operationalise these beliefs. In their discussion on the practices of academic developers and decolonisation, South African researchers Vorster and

Quinn (2017:35) highlight: "The structural and cultural conditions of a specific context influence ways in which people can or cannot exercise their agency. How people respond to structural and cultural constraints and enablement depends on their personal properties and powers."

They describe these tensions as the experiences of academics and further identify that academic developers must be aware of the structural factors that may lead to academics' resistance to transform their practice. As academic developers, we recognise that this tension also applies to us. We too need to be cognisant of the mechanisms that can facilitate or inhibit change. There is some onus on academic developers to embrace our responsibility for *some* of that intentional work of facilitating change. This is not to suggest that the academic is a free agent and can easily navigate the political landscape of higher education; rather, we propose that in our influential *third space*, academic developers can help academics to exercise their agency or academic freedom, to introduce and legitimise new knowledge forms, and introduce new ways of accessing knowledge. This, we argue, may require a rethinking of the course design process.

Rethinking the course design process to allow for decolonising curriculum

Mathers (2015) suggests that when design is ultimately concerned with user needs and is approached from a high-level systemic view and less incrementally, "We could find the solutions to some of the most 'wicked' problems of our time" (Mathers, 2015:28). If we apply Mather's hypothesis to instructional design frameworks, we start to see that we can risk missing the opportunity for disruption and transformation and end up simply muddling through the motions of course design in ways that reinforce the status quo. Addressing design too linearly using frequently employed instructional design processes, such as ADDIE, may put developers at risk of using disjointed incrementalism and focusing on step-by-step progress through the design process. We suggest using an alternative design model to transform the curriculum. Several alternative design models have been proposed which seem to have more potential for the decolonisation of the curriculum. While these models focus on process, some on multiculturalism and others on accommodating online learning, we suggest there may be a need for a model that specifically focuses on decolonising curriculum. Such a model we believe can be formed through a combination of the traditional ADDIE and two of the existing alternative models, namely the Third Dimension Model and AMOEBA.

Moving from ADDIE to a curriculum transformation model

ADDIE is an acronym, representing the five interconnected phases of the instructional design process, namely:

- *Analysis* – Based on a needs analysis course designer will identify any problems to be addressed through the curriculum, and identify desired outcomes for the course.
- *Design* – This phase largely focuses on blueprinting of a specific plan and strategy for meeting the needs identified in the analysis phases.
- *Development* – The development phase advances the analysis and design phases to a more concrete form. Content resources and lessons may be created at this phase. Software and hardware are sourced and set up.
- *Implementation* – The instruction is delivered to students and students are supported through instruction to meet the identified outcomes.
- *Evaluation* – This phase is thought to be ongoing monitoring and evaluation of the effectiveness at all phases of the design process.

From our interactions within the field, ADDIE is commonly used by academic developers to guide the course design process. In early planning meetings where the analysis and design are done, academics usually drive the process as the "content or subject matter experts". We assume that the academics know the desired outcomes of the course and their students. In the design phases, academics are thought to know what the best knowledge sources are, and what perspectives students should be exposed to. During the critical points of evaluation, it is the academics who are expected to determine if their previously established student needs were met and the outcomes addressed. Throughout most of the process, the instructional designer is positioned as a technology consultant and project manager, supporting the online development or technical "mounting" of the course and ensuring that the progress is steady. Often the academic does not know what the instructional design process will be and is open to guidance. As academic developers, we may offer ADDIE as the framework to be used, but later we step aside to position ourselves as supporters of the process, deferring to the knowledge of the content experts. Although as academic developers intimately engaged throughout the stages, we may not actively point out systemic problems at the beginning of the process. We may be hesitant to question the decisions made by the academics around what is to be learned, the needs of students or the implications of the content selected. Academic developers defer to the content expert and may only take the lead at the development phase or advising on ways of operationalising the course activities in the various design phases.

From our experience, the academic developer serves to focus on commonly accepted good practices in online course design and teaching, guiding in what is considered the more "neutral" areas of pedagogy and education technology.

Alternative course design frameworks

To allow for decolonising curricula, including pedagogy, course design frameworks need to be, not only flexible, but also allow for understanding and appreciation of cultural differences (De Lorme, 2014; Parrish & Linder-VanBerschot, 2010). Decolonising pedagogy cannot be realised without accounting for culture and recognition of alternative ways of knowing in instructional design. Several researchers have proposed instructional design models that consider culture in the design process, and which can serve as frameworks for decolonising pedagogy. With the rise in online and blended learning, researchers such as McLoughlin (1999:231) highlighted the fact that "[w]eb-based instruction often appears to be tailored to the needs of a particular cultural group, recognising the specific learning needs, preferences and styles of a single, perhaps homogeneous, group of learners".

It is this realisation and the work of McLoughlin (1999) and others that has stimulated the development of several alternative instructional design models, which take into account the need for inclusivity. Two of these models include the Third Dimension Model (Thomas, Mitchell & Joseph, 2002) and AMOEBA (Gunawardena, Wilson & Nolla, 2003).

Third Dimension Model

The Third Dimension Model emphasises "culture", which Thomas et al. (2002) state are omitted from the ADDIE model. They see culture as not only critical to knowledge building but to all phases of the design process. Thomas et al. recognise various definitions of culture and acknowledge its dynamic nature. Their concept of culture is in keeping with Powell (1997), who defines culture as:

> ... the sum total of ways of living, including values, beliefs, aesthetic standards, linguistic expression, patterns of thinking, behavioural norms, and styles of communication, which a group of people has developed to assure its survival in a particular physical and human environment ... (in Thomas et al., 2002:41)

Recognising that instructional designers and academics, cannot concentrate only on content, Thomas et al. propose that a "third dimension" of culture be added to the 5-phase ADDIE process. This third dimension consists of three parameters, namely intention, interaction and introspection, which are intended to generate considerations of multiculturalism as they are applied to each of the five ADDIE phases.

- *Intention* involves a constant questioning of intention using a culturally sensitive lens during all the phases of design;
- *Interaction* proposes a more "constructionist" perspective where instructional designers, content experts and student/end users collaborate on the design; and
- *Introspection* involves instructional designers reflecting and considering thoughts, beliefs, attitudes and feelings including their own biases, throughout the process.

The model calls for mindfulness of our cultural biases and the effects of these biases on the courses we create. The significant elements of this model are the reflection in each of the dimensions which requires a continuous questioning of self and the process, in relation to culture.

The visual representation of the Third Dimension Model found in Figure 10.1 highlights its potential in its representation of the three parameters as orbiting around and embracing the dimensions of ADDIE.

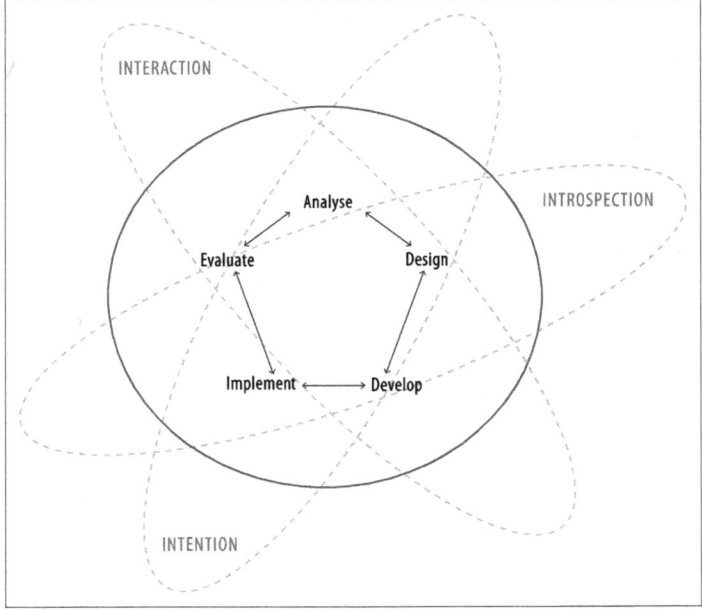

Figure 10.1 Third Dimension Model
(Thomas, Mitchell & Joseph, 2002:43)

While the model addresses the need for introspection, it does not explicitly account for the need to adapt to changing conditions, in particular when one considers constantly changing technology and the need for adaptability in such an environment. Thomas et al. (2002) also do not guide how the model should be applied or operationalised.

AMOEBA

Gunawardena et al. (2003) propose another alternative instructional design model. The Adaptive, Meaningful, Environmental-based Architecture for online course design model uses an AMOEBA as a metaphor, based on the single-celled organism. "The AMOEBA is adaptive to its environment; it is meaningful because it provides meaningful learning opportunities for students; it is organic because it is alive and can grow, change, and recycle; it is environment-based because it depends upon the environment for nutrition and support" (Gunawardena et al., 2003:794).

Similar to other alternative models that are focused specifically on online learning, AMOEBA emphasises interaction and collaboration amongst instructional designers, students, the academic and other constituents. This model suggests a highly participatory role for students in course decisions where firstly, the needs and characteristics of students will be identified, and options for teaching and learning will be considered based on these needs. The model proposes the idea of students as co-designers and advocates for course changes to be made as situations emerge, in response to feedback from students.

These two models present opportunities for curricula change through systemic considerations. They suggest a need for a framework that looks at operations within a process that involve constant reflection, meaning-making, questioning and representing broader views.

If we look at these frameworks through the lenses of De Lissovoy's "pedagogy of lovingness" and the opportunities allotted for Le Grange's four Rs of a decolonised curriculum (relational accountability, respectful representation, reciprocal appropriation and rights and regulations), we can see there is some alignment. We found that the overlapping concepts of collaboration, negotiation and accountability, are significantly woven throughout the design process as evident in the "intention, interaction and introspection" of the Third Dimension Model. We also found these spaces in the AMOEBA model, where adaptability is explicitly addressed. The elements or parameters of these two models have the potential to guide the instructional design process in a manner that allows for decolonising pedagogy, particularly in an online and blended learning context. This led us to bring together these elements in what we have termed the Fifth Dimension Curriculum Transformation Model (5D-CTM), which we propose may enable decolonising pedagogy and curriculum transformation.

The Fifth Dimension Curriculum Transformation Model

Instructional design that facilitates disruption, transformation or decolonising pedagogy requires a model that enables course design teams to adjust their approaches in several ways. The Fifth Dimension Curriculum Transformation Model (5D-CTM) may provide the framework within which to do this.

Firstly, all members of the design team need to acknowledge their positions on how they interact with the dominant culture of the institution and the wider environment, and its role in how courses are designed and delivered. This requires a level of *interrogation* of systemic and individual practices and beliefs, that calls for practitioners to reflect on and respond to specific questions before, during and after courses are designed. These questions should tease out what guides perceptions on knowledge and how it is shared. We will elaborate on this element of interrogation in a subsequent section.

Secondly, there needs to be the development of a pattern for reflection and constant questioning during the instructional design phases. This is where the Third Dimension of ADDIE is relevant. As we move through the phases of instructional design, each step of the process requires a series of critical questions as we seek to move forward.

Thirdly, there must be allowances for responsiveness in an ever-changing environment. There must be collaboration amongst all stakeholders in the course design process, and space and ability to allow for changes to be made to accommodate perhaps unanticipated needs or circumstances. This is where the AMOEBA model provides a place for cognisance of adaptability.

These adjustments to approaches suggest consideration of an alternative model of instructional design that builds on the Third Dimension and AMOEBA models and accounts for interrogation, intention, introspection, interaction and adaptability. These parameters are represented as orbitals around and through the ADDIE design process in our Fifth Dimension Curriculum Transformation Model depicted in Figure 10.2.

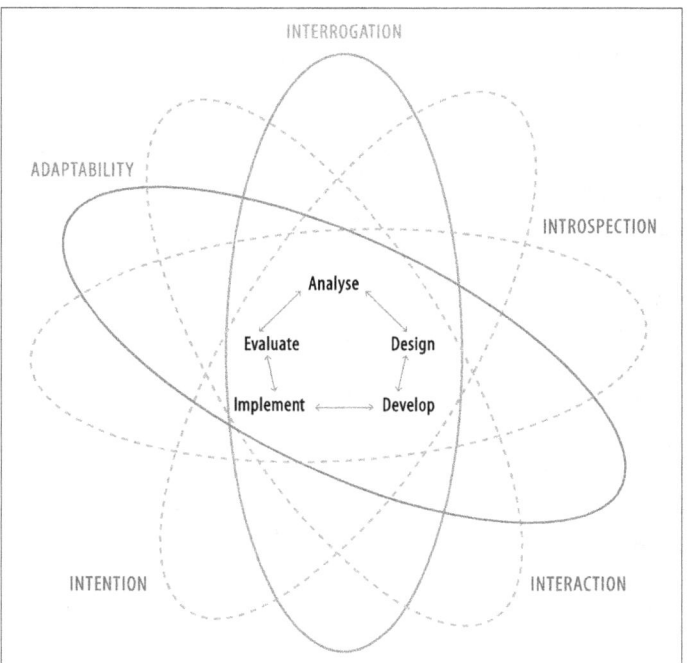

FIGURE 10.2 Fifth Dimension Curriculum Transformation Model
(Adapted from the Third Dimension Model –
Thomas, Mitchell & Joseph, 2002)

Orbitals of the Fifth Dimension Curriculum Transformation Model

Interrogation (of Practices and Beliefs) – One can argue that an interrogation is an aggressive act evoking images of "policing" the content and pedagogical decisions of academics. In this vein, it may even be perceived as questioning the ideals and values of academics themselves. We recognise this interpretation and invite an alternative way of perceiving interrogation. To interrogate is also to ask the difficult questions (see Table 10.1) and to drill down to the core of the matter. In this alternative design model, we are suggesting that when ADDIE is employed, interrogation demands a thoughtful rationale for the decisions and the assumptions we are making in course development. For example, in the analysis phase when the needs of the student and the context of the course are being considered, the academic developer in the role of instructional designer can take this opportunity to interrogate the mechanisms that are used to collect information about the students and their environment and the assumptions that colour the interpretation of findings. This process of interrogation is to be applied through all the stages of course design and the phases of ADDIE. Interrogation complements the introspection, interaction, and intention that the Third-dimensional model promotes by providing the critical lens to support deep reflection.

Introspection in our model calls for members of the course design team to engage in a process of inward facing, rich analysis. This places the course design team in a position to reflect on action and thinking, as well as allowing themselves to be accountable for their ideas and beliefs. Introspection is internal and self-regulatory, but when partnered with an external process of interrogation, it can also support interaction.

Interaction requires shared accountability and responsibility for pedagogy. This makes the course culturally relevant and inclusive. As noted by Thomas, et al. (2002) interaction assumes that culture is derived from human interaction and socialisation and thus requires all stakeholders to collaboratively ask the questions which tease out cultural relevance to students, the context of the institution and the wider community.

Intention drives any activity, and as course designers, we should question our intention in a manner that ensures that the integrity of our intentions remains true. Intention calls for us to continuously seek to address inequities and practices which have the potential to disadvantage students. We need to remain respectful of the ethical protocols around knowledge creation and sharing. "Intention", supported by "interrogation", requires us to keep in focus the core *raison d'être* for the courses and programmes we design.

Adaptability calls for us to encourage flexibility to meet the demands of a dynamic, volatile environment. It requires us to draw on the whole community as relevant stakeholders to keep on the pulse of the changing environment. Adaptability allows us to gauge the changes required to remain relevant and culturally sensitive.

There are challenges and vulnerabilities that come with applying interrogation, introspection, integration, intention and adaptability as a part of the online and blended learning design framework. Upon sharing the construct of interrogation with some academic developer colleagues, their knee-jerk reaction was: *How do you plan on getting academics on board with all this, especially the interrogation?* That question feeds into the tensions around the role of the academic developer. These tensions include questions around whether academic developers are allies, coaches or partners in the course design process and to whom they are accountable. We believe that in the absence of a systematic, institutional mandate for decolonising curriculum, academic developers can take the lead and they can be the source of motivation for individual lecturers in the design of courses and programmes. This type of bottom-up approach to incremental change in higher education can stimulate further action towards transformation. Campbell, Kanuka and Schwier (2009) see instructional designers as agents of design and position the process as being personally and professionally transformative for all stakeholders. Our 5D-CTM builds on the Third Dimension Model, so it incorporates both the systemic and the systematic. Therefore, we see the element of interrogation, for example, not as something that is done *to* academics; rather, it is done *with* academics. In a symbiotic fashion, the academic and the developers and the rest of the design team are all accountable for their assumptions and practices. The 5D-CTM positions the developer to be transformed and equally subject to intention, introspection, integration and adaptability, complemented by interrogation. He/she is expected to engage as an equally responsible and accountable stakeholder in the course design process.

Enacting the Fifth Dimension Curriculum Transformation Model

Our 5D-CTM aims to capture the essentials of curriculum decolonisation and transformation. We recognise that when proposing any radical shift in approach, it is critical to provide concrete strategies for enacting it. Therefore, we offer some actionable starting points. There is always a danger of becoming too rigid or prescriptive in trying to provide a blueprint, so we are proposing that the process be treated with some flexibility in respect for the dynamic nature of the course design process.

Setting expectations and relationship building

There is an initial step of both trust and relationship building to create a culture of shared responsibility between the academic developer and academics in their working relationship, to respond to concerns about academics buying into this rigorous and potentially vulnerable design approach. In the early planning meetings well before getting into complexities of the design process, or even talking about content, we as academic developers, need to provide clear intentionality around relationship building and expectation setting. As alluded to earlier, as academic developers, we are often relegated, sometimes willingly, to a seemingly "neutral" position. In supporting and facilitating transformation, we may need to disrupt that practice and openly position ourselves as a partner, ally *and* critical friend from the beginning. This means that there should be a candid conversation about time commitments, roles and responsibilities, a shared understanding of the rationale behind this approach, transparency about beliefs about inclusive and decolonised curriculum along with a negotiation of the process. This candid conversation should include an agreement from academics that they would try to be open to new ways of approaching course design. This is not to suggest that these professional working relationships will be forged overnight, nor is there the expectation that lecturers will commit blocks of undivided time to it. Rather, expect the processes to be thoughtfully and deliberately integrated into the established course design timeline. With the 5D-CTM, we believe that the nature of the relationship and interactions are what will be changed most.

Building in time and space for all perspectives

The 5D-CTM is meant to support the de-centring of Western perspectives, and widen what constitutes knowledge. Academic developers need to consider several important factors as part of the course design process such as:

- whether the core development team is fluid enough to allow for adaptability.
- whether members are amenable to reciprocal interrogation.
- whether members of the indigenous community should be asked to come to the university or student leaders asked to participate in select planning meetings.
- what the selection of the meeting location outside the university might communicate about what is valued.

In keeping with Le Grange's rights and regulations elements of curriculum decolonisation, the design project timelines should build in time and care for authentication checking with the expanded team in culturally appropriate ways.

Asking questions at key phases

One practical approach to implementing the 5D-CTM is applying the model to instructional design within three broad stages, namely the pre-design, design and implementation stages, as depicted in Table 10.1. The three broad stages allow course design teams to visualise where the various elements in the model may fall within the course design process and provides the flexibility for the use of instructional frameworks other than ADDIE. In the first row of Column 1, for example, pre-design is aligned with the analysis stage of course design. This is the conceptualisation stage of the course team's work, and it is envisioned that the relevant elements of the curriculum design model within this stage are *interrogation, introspection, intention* and *interaction*. The final column provides a sample of relevant questions which the course design team could pose to each other to confront preconceived notions of knowledge, design, teaching and learning which can act as a barrier to transformation. The questions, which relate to elements/orbitals of the 5D-CTM represent the ways of thinking that the academic developer/instructional designer may ask the academic to explore. These questions are intentionally broad samples that are meant to initiate dialogue and continue critical thought throughout the design cycle. They are by no means exhaustive and are intended to stimulate critical thought and discussion. They might be adapted in response to different disciplines and specific course contexts.

At a glance, the questions may seem to put much of the responsibility for critical thinking and reflection on the academic; but in reality, they are designed to be asked by/of anyone on the design team. Academic developers themselves are encouraged to use thought-provoking questions and dialogue about the students, and the selection of disciplinary knowledge for there to be disruption in everyone's practices. The academic developer can continuously think about how the academics' answers to these questions can serve as a torch throughout the design process, illuminating the way forward. They are guiding them to very deliberate and responsive decision-making. The questions are meant to initiate reflection in each stage of the course design process, at the point of development and design where the team engages in working through pedagogy and assessment, these questions will form a backdrop, guiding decisions.

TABLE 10.1 Key questions for operationalising the Fifth Dimension Curriculum Transformation Model (5D-CTM)

Stages of Operation	Instructional Design Phases (based on ADDIE)	Elements of the 5D-CTM	Relevant Questions corresponding to the 5D-CTM elements
PRE-DESIGN	Analysis	Intention	What are our students' backgrounds beyond the usual demographics of discipline, gender and age?
		Interrogation/ Introspection	Is there any inherent bias in the sources of information that I am using?
		Intention	How do I intend to use the information gathered about the students and the larger community to support transformative, culturally relevant learning?
		Intention/ Interrogation	Through what cultural lens am I interpreting the learning needs and backgrounds of students?
		Intention	What will be our sources of disciplinary knowledge?

Stages of Operation	Instructional Design Phases (based on ADDIE)	Elements of the 5D-CTM	Relevant Questions corresponding to the 5D-CTM elements
PRE-DESIGN (cont.)	Analysis (cont.)	Intention/ Interrogation/ Introspection	To what extent do my preconceived notions about the sources of disciplinary knowledge impact on my design thinking?
		Intention/ Interrogation/ Introspection	How can disciplinary knowledge be shared, and how will it impact my design thinking?
		Interrogation/ Introspection	How can I include the voices and experiences of students and other stakeholders in my curriculum development decisions?
		Adaptability	What are the developmental needs of the communities in which the students are expected to serve?
		Interrogation/ Introspection	How did I determine my initial sources of information? What did I not choose as a source, and why?
		Introspection/ Interrogation/ Adaptability	What is my interest in transformation and disruption? What are the systemic boundaries within the institution, department etc. that may facilitate or constrain my goals?
		Introspection	Where are my knowledge gaps related to the culture of my students? How do I plan to fill them?
		Introspection	What is my power and agency within the communities from which my students originate or with non-Westerngroups?
		Introspection/ Interrogation	How might this impact on my relationship with students and on transformative outcomes?
DESIGN	Design and Development	Intention/ Introspection	To what extent do my preconceived notions about the sources of knowledge and how knowledge should be shared impact my design decisions?
		Intention/ Introspection/ Adaptability	To what extent are my identified outcomes aligned with the development needs of my students and the wider society?
		Interaction/ Introspection/ Interrogation/ Adaptability	Where is there space provided for the students and other stakeholders to engage in the design process?

Stages of Operation	Instructional Design Phases (based on ADDIE)	Elements of the 5D-CTM	Relevant Questions corresponding to the 5D-CTM elements
DESIGN (cont.)	Design and Development (cont.)	Adaptability	Is my course design sufficiently flexible for a blended/online environment and changing conditions?
		Inspection	What do my selected resources say about what I value?
		Introspection/ Interrogation	Have I designed in ways that I hold myself accountable for the student experiences and disruption?
		Interrogation	What are the systemic boundaries within the institution, department etc. that may facilitate or constrain the design?
DELIVERY/ IMPLEMENTATION	Implementation and Evaluation	Introspection/ Interaction/ Adaptability	To what extent do my preconceived notions about the sources of knowledge and how knowledge should be shared impact my implementation/ delivery? What strategies allow for universal access?
		Introspection/ Adaptability	How can my implementation strategies take advantage of the affordances of new technology?
		Introspective/ Interaction/ Interrogation	Am I transparent about my transformative ntentions?
		Introspection/ Interaction/ Adaptability	How am I learning from students?
		Intention/ Interaction	How do I regularly and authentically check for impact on individuals and the larger community?

The role of the academic developer is therefore critical in the implementation of such a model, and in developing the model it was necessary to consider the assumptions around our role and the need to reconsider our positions and how we negotiate the relationships to encourage transformation and disruption.

Conclusion

Through the design of our 5D-CTM, we present an opportunity for greater openness and the possibility for a more flexible approach to course design which would better serve the responsive nature of online and blended learning and course design in general. While we have not yet implemented the model in its entirety, this presentation of the 5D-CTM represents our move towards changing the nature of our course design process and how our work as academic developers is conceptualised. We hope that the application of the model and the experiences of the academic developers, lecturers, students and community stakeholders who use it will form the basis of future research and assist in the development of decolonising curriculum.

Responsiveness to change is a core requirement of our century where institutions of higher education must grapple with the tension of coping with many ongoing social, economic and political changes. Any call for change or disruption to the status quo begins with a re-evaluation of existing goals and priorities, a rethinking of prevailing practices and a re-examination of what is valued as part of the process. With the ongoing debates and challenges that come with transformations in higher education to include the role and impact online and blended learning formats, we need curriculum processes that are receptive to transformation. To be disruptive, academic developers and those working in course design teams should think and practice in ways which demonstrate such sensitivity, in a continuously reflective and collaborative way.

References

BADAWOOD, A.; STEENKAMP, A. & AL-WERFALLI, D. 2013. A Systematic Approach to Faculty Development – Capability Improvement for Blended Learning. *Information Systems Education Journal*, 11(3):101-114. [https://files.eric.ed.gov/fulltext/EJ1145041.pdf]

BONK, C.J.; KYONG-JEE, K. & TINGTING, Z. 2006. Future Directions of Blended Learning in Higher Education and Workplace Settings. In: C.J. Bonk, C. Graham, R. Charles & J. Cross (eds). *The Handbook of Blended Learning: Global Perspectives, Local Designs*. San Francisco: John Wiley and Sons. [http://publicationshare.com/bonk_future.pdf]

BATES, T. 2018. Why is innovation in teaching in higher education so difficult? *Online Learning and Distance Education Resources*, 19 July 2018. [https://bit.ly/2m7xxwM]

BATES, T. 2014. Is the ADDIE Model Appropriate for Teaching in a Digital Age? *Online Learning and Distance Education Resources*, 9 September. [https://bit.ly/2mtN36A]

BATH, D. & SMITH, C. 2004. Academic developers: An Academic Tribe Claiming Their Territory in Higher Education. *International Journal for Academic Development*, 9(1):9-27. [https://doi.org/10.1080/1360144042000296035]

BRENNAN, J.; KING, R. & LEBEAU, Y. 2004. *The Role of Universities in the Transformation of Societies: Synthesis Report*. London: Association of Commonwealth Universities and the Open University.

CAMPBELL, K.; KANUKA, H. & SCHWIER, R.A. 2009. A Preliminary Study and Research Protocol for Investigating Sociocultural Issues in Instructional Design. Paper presented at annual conference of the American Educational Research Association, San Diego, April.

CHRISTENSEN, C.M. & HORN, M.B. 2013. Innovation Imperative: Change Everything. Online Education as an Agent of Transformation. *The New York Times*, 1 November. [https://nyti.ms/2mltjBU]

De Lissovoy, N. 2010. Decolonial Pedagogy and The Ethics of the Global. *Discourse: Studies in the Cultural Politics of Education*, 31(3):279-293. [https://doi.org/10.1080/01596301003786886]

De Lorme, C.M. 2014. *Decolonizing Instructional Design Through Auto/Ethnography*. PhD thesis, North Dakota State University of Agriculture and Applied Science.

Garrison, R.D. & Kanuka, H. 2004. Blended learning: Uncovering its Transformative Potential in Higher Education. *Internet and Higher Education*, 7:95-105. [https://doi.org/10.1016/j.iheduc.2004.02.001]

Graham, C. 2006. Definition, Current Trends and Future Directions. In: C. Bonk & C. Graham (eds). *The Handbook of Blended Learning: Global Perspectives, Local Designs*. San Francisco, CA: John Wiley and Sons, 3-21.

Green, D. & Little, D. 2013. Academic Development on the Margins. *Studies in Higher Education*, 38(4):523-537. [https://doi.org/10.1080/03075079.2011.583640]

Gunawardena, C.N.; Wilson, P.L. & Nolla, A.C. 2003. Culture and Online Education. In: M.G. Moore & W.G. Anderson (eds). *Handbook of Distance Education*. Mahwah, NJ: Lawrence Erlbaum Associates, 753-775.

Heleta, S. 2016. Decolonisation of Higher Education: Dismantling Epistemic Violence and Eurocentrism in South Africa. *Transformation in Higher Education*, 1(1):1-8. [https://doi.org/10.4102/the.v1i1.9]

Hicks, M. 2005. Academic Developers as Change Agents: Caught in The Middle. Paper presented at 28th Higher Education Research and Development Society of Australasia Annual Conference, Sydney, 3-6 July. [https://bit.ly/2kN9WBB]

Kenney, J. & Newcombe, E. 2011. Adopting A Blended Learning Approach: Challenges Encountered and Lessons Learned in an Action Research Study. *Journal of Asynchronous Learning Networks*, 15(1):45-57. [https://doi.org/10.24059/olj.v15i1.182]

Kim, K. & Bonk, C.J. 2006. The Future of Online Teaching and Learning in Higher Education: The Survey Says … *Educause Quarterly*, 29(4):22-30. [https://bit.ly/2kMfH2s]

Land, R. 2001. Agency, Context and Change in Academic Development. *International Journal for Academic Development*, 6(1):4-20. [https://doi.org/10.1080/13601440110033715]

Le Grange, L. 2016. Decolonising the University Curriculum. *South African Journal of Higher Education*, 30(2):1-12. [https://doi.org/10.20853/30-2-709]

Mathers, J. 2015. Design Intervention. *RSA Journal*, 161(5561):24-29. [https://bit.ly/2lYx2Fr]

McLoughlin, C. 1999. Culturally Responsive Technology Use: Developing an On-Line Community of Learners. *British Journal of Educational Technology*, 30(3):231-243. [https://doi.org/10.1111/1467-8535.00112]

Neame, C. & Forsyth, R. 2016. Identifying Needs and Opportunities for Academic Development. In: D Baume & C. Popovic (eds). *Advancing Practice in Academic Development*. Oxon, UK: Routledge, 17-31.

Parrish, P. & Linder-VanBerschot, J.A. 2010. Cultural Dimensions of Learning: Addressing the Challenges of Multicultural Instruction. *International Review of Research in Open and Distributed Learning*, 11(2). [https://doi.org/10.19173/irrodl.v11i2.809]

Poon, J. 2013. Blended Learning: An Institutional Approach for Enhancing Students' Learning Experiences. *Journal of Online Learning and Teaching*, 9(2). [https://bit.ly/2m6v31l]

Rathburn, G. & Newcombe, N. 2012. Authenticity in Academic Development: The Myth of Neutrality. *International Journal for Academic Development*, 17(3):231-242. [https://doi.org/10.1080/1360144X.2012.679273]

Thaman, K.H. 2003. Decolonising Pacific Studies: Indigenous Perspectives, Knowledge and Wisdom in Higher Education. *The Contemporary Pacific*, 15(1):1-17. [https://doi.org/10.1353/cp.2003.0032]

Thomas, M.; Mitchell, M. & Joseph, R. 2002. The Third Dimension of ADDIE: A Cultural Embrace. *TechTrends*, 46(2):40-45. [https://doi.org/10.1007/BF02772075]

Twigg, C.A. 2003. Improving Learning and Reducing Costs: New Models for Online Learning. *Educause Review*, September/October:28-38. [https://bit.ly/2kywgyI]

VORSTER, J. & QUINN, L. 2017. The 'Decolonial Turn': What Does It Mean for Academic Staff Development? *Education as Change*, 2(1):31-49. [https://doi.org/10.17159/1947-9417/2017/853]

VORSTER, J. & QUINN, L. 2015. Towards Shaping the Field: Theorising the Knowledge in a Formal Course for Academic Developers. *Higher Education Research and Development*, 34(5):1031-1044. [https://doi.org/10.1080/07294360.2015.1070126]

WATSON, J. 2008. *Blended Learning: The Convergence of Online and Face-to-Face Education*. North American Council for Online Learning. [https://bit.ly/2m1oduw]

WHITCHURCH, C. 2009. The rise of the blended professional in higher education: A comparison between the UK, Australia and the United States. *Higher Education*, 58(3):407-441. [https://doi.org/10.1007/s10734-009-9202-4]

WUETHERICK, B. & EWERT-BAUER, T. 2012. Perceptions of neutrality through a post-colonial lens: institutional positioning in Canadian academic development. *International Journal for Academic Development*, 17(3):217-229. [https://doi.org/10.1080/1360144X.2012.700896]

CHAPTER 11

"I've got a deep, complicated relationship with technology"

Towards an understanding of the interplay of barriers and agency in academics' educational technology practices

Nompilo Tshuma

Introduction

The integration of educational technology into teaching and learning in higher education has, for decades, been lauded as the panacea for a range of curriculum and pedagogical issues. Governments, higher education institutions and popular media have acclaimed technology's "ability" to disrupt learning as we know it and transform the structure and purpose of universities. This view points to a possible utopian optimism that technology will accomplish what it says it will accomplish (Webster, 2017) despite the fact that for over 40 years researchers have pointed to technology's uncanny ability to frustrate human "ends and intentions ... [by] enhancing certain ends, [while] denying or even destroying others" (Winner, 1977:29). This utopian view of technology in general – and learning technologies in this particular instance – has been driven by the unprecedented explosion of mobile and desktop applications and devices, as well as the adaptation of other technologies for learning like robotics, wearable devices and many others. It has also been fuelled by the assumption that our students are digital natives – having grown up with technology all around them. The assumption is that students will find the integration of technology exciting and engaging because learning will now take place in spaces already familiar to them.

While researchers present evidence of technology's potential to transform the way we teach and how students access and engage with knowledge (Flavin, 2012; Ng'ambi & Bozalek, 2015), the predicted large-scale disruption of teaching and learning practices has not happened as expected. Instead, while higher education has been "on the brink of being transformed through learning technologies, ...it has been on that brink for some decades now" (Laurillard, 2008:1). Research shows that while there are academics who are innovating and disrupting their curriculum using technology, there are still signs of low-level usage which duplicate the traditional sage-on-stage teaching model, and, in some instances, there seems to be a complete avoidance of the use of any form of educational technology by academics (Blin & Munro, 2008; Gregory & Lodge, 2015).

In an attempt to explain this disparity in the way academics integrate technology for teaching, researchers tend to label academics as resistant to technology as a result of a range of barriers to technology use (Reid, 2014). Different variations of the technology acceptance model have also been utilised to frame these barriers further in terms of the usability of, and academics' attitudes towards, specific technologies for teaching and learning (Harrati, Bouchrika & Mahfouf, 2017; Schoonenboom, 2014). As such, this "barriers" narrative has become the dominant explanation for the poor uptake of educational technology in higher education. In this chapter, I discuss the impact of this dominant perspective on both academic developers' practices as they support academics with integrating technology into their teaching, as well as academics' perspectives of their practices. I argue that while a range of contextualised barriers has the potential to impact academics' educational technology choices and practices, an exclusive focus on barriers ignores the agency of academics to act "so rather than otherwise" (Archer, 2003:3) by resisting or defying this dominant narrative even in highly constrained environments. Thus, I argue that academic developers who focus on the "interplay of barriers and agency" can better align their support for educational technology integration with academics' needs, than those who focus mainly on overcoming barriers to technology integration.

Methodology

For this chapter, I use some of the findings from a larger study that employed critical ethnography. This is a methodology that seeks to examine, understand and explain a social and cultural context through the use of a variety of data collection methods. Seeking to understand the culture of a particular social group is the distinguishing element of this methodological approach (Creswell, 2012), a culture which "can only be inferred" (Wolcott, 1999:253) as it refers to socially constructed values, beliefs and accepted norms of behaviour. With critical ethnography, the careful excavation of this covert culture also focuses on opening up to scrutiny the constraining politics and hegemonies in the social context. This agenda-driven methodology does this by embracing the impact that I, as the researcher, have on the data collection process (Davies, 2008), the contentious process of authentically representing another's culture through my own (Madison, 2012), as well as using knowledge from the research to bring about social change in the form of emancipation from, or transformation of, a marginalising social context (Thomas, 1993).

I utilised three data collection methods: participant observation, in-depth interviews and informal and work-related interactions. Although triangulation of data sources helped me to better understand academics' reality in terms of their perceptions and practices with educational technology, I also realised that even with triangulation, my perception of their culture and context would be incomplete and value-laden (Carspecken, 1996; Madison, 2012). This led me to engage in self-reflection throughout the data collection process as I sought to understand themes emerging from my data analysis and to deal with how these conflicted with my pre-research understandings of academics' reality of educational technology use. This reflexive process is part of the iterative nature of ethnographic data analysis which should ideally happen throughout the research project and inform further data collection (Carspecken, 1996). The purpose of the data analysis phase was to make meaning of the culture under study by repeatedly immersing myself in the data to help me find patterns and build connections to the social context (Hammersley & Atkinson, 2007).

The research project discussed here was undertaken at Rhodes University, a small South African research-intensive university where I support academics as they integrate technology into their teaching. For this chapter, I used data generated from interactions with three academics. Respondent 1 has been teaching in higher education for about 19 years and currently teaches postgraduate students in a professional social science discipline. She was selected as a research participant because she used the institutional learning management system extensively but did not seem to venture beyond the learning management system course structure followed by her departmental colleagues. Respondent 2 has been teaching mostly undergraduate students in a pure science discipline for over 30 years. She was selected as a research participant because she has been an early adopter of innovative learning technologies adapted from other departments or institutions. Respondent 3 teaches at both undergraduate and postgraduate level in a social science discipline and has been in academia for about nine years. She was selected to be part of this study because, in my informal conversations with her, she had expressed strong views *against* using technology for teaching.

The next section presents the theoretical lens used to analyse the data.

Scott's public/private transcript

James Scott is an anthropologist who has studied the resistance displayed by marginalised groups and the impact of this resistance in counteracting the power of superordinate groups (Scott, 1987, 1990). His representation of resistance emphasises a quiet, everyday lived resistance in the form of subterranean and mundane acts like "passive noncompliance, subtle sabotage, evasion and deception" (Scott, 1987:31). He uses what he terms the public and private transcripts to explain the interaction between the two groups (Scott, 1990).

The "public transcript" is the dominant perspective (in this instance, the "barriers narrative" alluded to earlier) perpetuated by the superordinate group (Scott, 1990). In this chapter, I only focus on the dominant perspective, rather than the members of the superordinate group – although I do allude to the power that academic developers have in the higher education space and how they could at times be considered the "more powerful other" by some academics. This public transcript shapes the perspectives and actions of members of the social context in different ways. The public transcript reflects the opinions of the dominant group and hence drives their actions. On the other hand, the public transcript impacts on the perspectives of the subordinate groups, particularly when they are in the presence of those they perceive as the more powerful other. However, their perspectives and actions change when they are in private spaces.

This changed perspective is what Scott terms the *private or hidden transcript*, and is often expressed only to "trusted" others (1990). It represents the reality of the subordinate groups and plays out as resistance to the "hegemonic appearances" of the public transcript (Scott, 1990:xii). As the discussion of the data in the following sections will show, the hidden transcript represents the complex mix of factors that motivate academics to integrate technology into their teaching despite the constraining barriers. While this hidden transcript shows agency in action, it is often hidden from the dominant group and needs careful excavation. As I will argue, instead of reinforcing the dominant barriers narrative as the major constraint to educational technology integration, academic developers should rather seek to understand this hidden transcript to inform the support they offer academics. To do this, they need to find ways to position themselves as the trusted, rather than the more powerful, other.

Public transcript: Barriers to educational technology integration

Researchers are often inclined to place the blame on constraints and barriers to account for the disparity in the way academics use educational technology (Reid, 2014). These barriers tend to focus on the academics themselves or the institution and include a high academic workload; the failure of institutions to adequately reward educational technology initiatives; academics' lack of technological skills to complement their pedagogical and content knowledge; technical mishaps or breakdowns and the risk of unexpected outcomes of educational technology innovations; and the autonomous nature of academics' work which may result in resistance to either institutional directives about educational technology use or the position of power adopted by educational technology implementers (Gregory & Lodge, 2015; Howard, 2013; King & Boyatt, 2015; Reid, 2014).

Research in the African context highlights some of the same barriers but also introduces a different dimension linked to the continent's colonial history and economic status. These additional barriers include: inadequate infrastructure (buildings, internet bandwidth and erratic power supply); the high cost of technological resources sourced from the global North; Western-developed technologies that fail to acknowledge African culture and approaches to teaching and learning in the local context; lack of policies at institutional and national level to guide the implementation of educational technologies; lack of technology support and skills; and negative attitudes towards technology for teaching (Cross & Adam, 2007; García Almiñana et al., 2012; Makokha & Mutisya, 2016; Sife et al., 2007; Ssekakubo et al., 2011; Unwin et al., 2010).

While I concede that the above barriers do have the potential to impact the educational technology choices and practices of academics, I maintain that a strictly barriers narrative is problematic in several ways. Firstly, it places the blame on either the academics or resource-deficient universities and fails to consider the complex socio-political context within which both academics and universities operate. Besides these structural and cultural issues, this view denies or ignores the agency of academics to integrate technology into their teaching even in highly constrained and regulated university environments.

Secondly, a strictly barriers narrative is also problematic because it perpetuates *which* stories are accepted as valid in the educational technology field, as cautioned by Bromley (1997:57):

> The way we describe any phenomenon, the stories we tell about it, shape what we do and do not see in it. Some stories highlight social dynamics obscured by other stories. If one's project is to help equalize the distribution of power in society, stories that illuminate the workings of oppression are essential. Stories which ignore, or downplay, the role of conflict and difference in history imply that what is good for the most visible members of society is good for everyone (as all of us purportedly have interests that are primarily shared), and thereby provide support – not necessarily intentional – for efforts to maintain that group's position of privilege. It is important to ask what such stories omit (and therefore imply is non-existent or insignificant), and what assumptions must be accepted in order to see the world in such a way.

These dominant stories can result in researchers becoming preoccupied mainly with those conjecturally relevant areas of study and fail to address the messy complexity of educational technology integration. The same stories are then perpetuated in future research because, as researchers we are only "noticing (or not noticing)" what is dictated by the field as worthy of our attention, rather than "what *there actually is* to notice" (Bigum & Rowan, 2015:16, italics in original). Furthermore, these relevant topics shape what is noticed by future researchers, and, particularly in educational technology, those un-told or "irrelevant" topics are counted as hypothetical or at best inconsequential (Bigum & Rowan, 2015; Bromley, 1997).

And thirdly, as academic developers driving and supporting the integration of educational technology in higher education, we are in danger of failing to offer academics the support they need to integrate technology effectively into teaching. These "relevant stories" referred to earlier, lock us in an "ed-tech bubble" which is out of touch with academics' lived experiences (Kerr, 1989; Selwyn, 2012). Our rhetoric and excited animations about the success of new technology are rarely in touch with what is happening on the ground (Selwyn, 2012). We are also accused of often maintaining an over-engaged status as technology "elites" which has desensitised us to the needs and values of what we consider as the underengaged "masses" (Morozov, 2011) and we sometimes even presumptuously label academics as "inhibitors" (Watty, McKay & Ngo, 2016) or barriers to be overcome (Kerr, 1989) for educational technology innovation to happen. As a result, our approach to supporting academics as they integrate new technologies tends to focus on managing barriers to mitigate their impact and fails to consider the complex interaction of structure, culture and the agency of academics.

This barriers narrative can be viewed as the public transcript, as elaborated in the previous section because it signals the accepted assumptions about educational technology integration. In this instance, both academic developers and the academics they support in using educational technology, accept this barriers narrative as representative of their practice (or lack thereof) with educational technology. While this public transcript may not have originated from academic developers, the literature presented in this section suggests that they may be perpetuating it in several ways – including their elitist attitudes towards the "masses" who are resistant to technology and their propensity to keep recounting the same barriers story.

Impact of public transcript (barriers narrative) on academics' perceptions

The barriers narrative seems to be a widely accepted way of viewing how academics interact with technology for teaching. And this accepted view (the public transcript) has an impact on the way academics view their choices and practices in relation to technology for teaching. In the early stages of this research study's data collection, most of the research respondents were critical of their non-use or underusage of technology for teaching and often pointed to some of the same barriers discussed in the literature as constraining their practice. Respondent 1 was fairly confident in her use of the institutional learning management system until she inherited a course from another colleague. This course was different from the standard template of the other courses in the department and combined a complex mix of computer applications and resources that students had been engaging with both in and out of the classroom. Respondent 1 felt there was pressure for her to continue with the same kinds of online activities.

> I have completely let the site [*referring to the LMS*] down. We had an agreement [to maintain the site] … Comes to me and I see her site, and I think I can't, I just felt overwhelmed with all of it – it's like, I can't deal. So I'm so, at this point I don't know what my capacity needs are because I just have looked and just found no I can't, *yaz' uk'thini, ngizokhala* [you know what, I'm going to cry]. (Respondent 1)

The barrier that Respondent 1 confirmed about her practice with educational technology was the lack of technological skills. As a result of the pressure to carry on a complex set of online activities, she was overwhelmed and ended up doing what she terms "the bare minimum".

Respondent 2 labels herself as a "lagger" who will wait until others have been using technology successfully in their teaching for a while before she is prepared to try and introduce it into her teaching:

> So, I think I went to [a Moodle] workshop once I'd heard that people were using [Moodle] quite extensively and then I said ok well let me go. And then … I know I don't use it to its full capacity. But if I hear other people are doing something nice then I kind of tap into it, but always only in a limited way. … I'm not very good [at] clicking new buttons and seeing what's there. I never ever play … But if someone comes to me and gives me a good idea, I'm very happy to implement it. But I don't play with technology to find those new things. [*Speaking about a Teaching with Technology Showcase*] And sometimes it takes me to go to 2 or 3 of those before I even think about it. So, I literally, yah, so I got someone to show me exactly which buttons to press and how to press them and … I wrote down all the instructions and then I could do it. And I still follow those instructions, and I don't do anything different from that. (Respondent 2)

She believes her lagger status is because of her attitude towards technology – fear.

> I always see myself as a bit of a technophobe … not technophobe, but I am scared of technology, so I always try a little bit. I'll always wait for people to kind of try [then] convince me. (Respondent 2)

Respondent 2 reflects two barriers to technology discussed in the literature: lagging behind because of a lack of technological skills and a negative attitude towards technology – in this instance, fear. Adding a different facet to the negative attitude barrier, Respondent 3 expresses her frustration with the way technology changes the learning space and makes it difficult for her to create a social learning space. Her opening comment – "I have a deep, complicated relationship with technology" – alludes to the existence of a complex, nuanced and maybe even fragile relation to technology, not just with this particular respondent, but with other academics as well. This is the relationship (hidden transcript) that academic developers should ideally seek to uncover. Respondent 3 goes on to express how this complexity has come about:

> The issue, the complicated relationship now comes when the technology in itself becomes the end and be it all for the students, because remember my principles on teaching: teaching is not just for me about transferring knowledge.... For me, teaching is about; it's a social space whereby we can engage as ... individuals and also, we actually have a direct dialogue ok. For me that's, that is what it's about. Not that I can't have a dialogue on [a] forum in [Moodle], but there's something that changes in the room when we're having a dialogue and other students are also changed by that particular dialogue ok. So it's not just very individualised it's a collective. Learning becomes a collective effort, ok. So sometimes I feel like technology kind of individualises learning and also depersonalises the space of learning. (Respondent 3)

In reflecting on the way the academics in this research study seemed to support the barriers narrative when elaborating on their interaction with technology, I found this aligning with Scott's description of how marginalised groups will uphold the public transcript when in the presence of those perceived as the more powerful other. My positionality as an academic developer supporting academics as they integrate technology may have had an impact on how the respondents chose to frame their relationship with technology initially. Two issues came to the fore as I reflected on this positionality. Firstly, I realised that the respondents could have made assumptions about my expectations in terms of their technology practices. They seemed to be justifying why they were not using technology as they should be – or at the very least, how they thought I expected them to be using technology. This happened mostly at the start of the data collection process. Secondly, the fact that I got to choose "how" their stories were immortalised on paper further augmented my position of power – through my inherently subjective and prejudiced lens. As Hall (1996) points out, representing a culture has a "constitutive" and "formative" role, which gives me as the researcher the power to shape how the readers will conceive the meaning of the respondents' stories (Bar-On, 1996).

As the data collection process progressed, however, the respondents' narrations of their relationship with technology shifted. I elaborate on this in the next section, as well as my reflections on why they may have changed.

Hidden transcript: Why do academics integrate educational technology?

The public transcript has an impact on the perspectives and actions of academic developers, as well as how academics frame their use (or lack thereof) of educational technology. However, I argue that this public transcript (barriers narrative) tells only part of the story about what impacts academics' educational technology choices and practices. While barriers do have an impact – as the narratives in the previous section show – an exclusively "barriers narrative" ignores the agency of academics to act in ways contrary to the causal powers of the structural constraints in their contexts. As part of a larger research study that showed a complex and messy mix of structural forces as having an impact on the educational technology choices and practices of academics, this chapter only reports on the hidden transcript – the reasons academics give for using particular technologies even in contexts where there is a dearth of resources, skills and support.

The national student protests that rocked South African higher education in 2015 and 2016 (highlighted in several chapters in this book) opened pathways for dialogue around decolonising the curriculum and culture of South African higher education – particularly in previously white institutions like Rhodes University (where this study took place). While the protests had a positive impact, there were also some unintended consequences. One of these was the strong affective reactions which accompanied public discussions that dealt with the issues raised in the student protests (Costandius, Nell, Alexander, Mckay, Blackie, Malgas & Setati, 2018). These inevitably led to the polarisation of staff and students, where some feared aggravating the volatile situation and chose to remain silent, while others became even more outspoken as a result of the silence of others (Costandius et al., 2018). Aware of this situation, Respondent 1's teaching approach was aimed at creating a safe space for her postgraduate students to have critical dialogues about the climate of higher education and its impact on the university. Students had previously requested that the classroom sessions be audio recorded and made available in case some of them were unable to attend the face-to-face sessions. Because of the critical and reflective nature of those classroom dialogues, her students would sometimes request that she pause the recording. As Respondent 1 elaborates:

> There would be times though because that's the thing with that module is that when you've got people in a safe space, they can then talk about stuff that they wouldn't want repeated outside of yah. So they'd be times where you hear people say you need to press stop, and so I press stop, and then we have that discussion, and then we can

> resume again. So if you weren't there, you'd missed out on that part of the conversation, but if you were there, you would have been privy to that. So it's not like kukhulunywa ngabany' abantu [*talking about other people*] it's just yah. So all I did was ... I just used my phone, press record.   (Respondent 1)

Respondent 1 started recording the classroom dialogues because her students requested her to. Hence her integration of this technology served the students' needs if they happened to miss a class or wanted to go over the classroom discussions in their own time. As a teacher, her main values centred around enabling and maintaining a safe space because of the nature of the critical and reflective conversations she prompted, as well as the fact that some of the students did not have any other space to reflect on their experiences and opinions about the volatile university climate during the student protests. Although the learning management system where the recordings were posted was a closed course accessible only to the course participants, these security features did not allay the students' fears about the conversations being shared in other spaces. Respondent 1 managed this critical balance by responding to the need to create safe spaces where students could "be authentic", as she called it. Secondly, she allowed the students to decide how and when the recordings would happen, thereby giving them agency to determine which conversations ended up on the learning management system.

In Respondent 2's instance, she was concerned that her students focused on cramming solutions and answers and lacked discipline-specific problem-solving skills, and in her teaching, she sought ways to help her students comprehend the thinking behind solutions. While in the previous section she expressed her fear of technology, how she had to be convinced before experimenting with technology, and the step-by-step instructions she would need to write out before trying out any technology, she found a technology that could complement what she was trying to accomplish with her students.

> As soon as I come across something that I know they find very difficult, I do a podcast. ... And there are lots of tutorial or test-based questions that they've really struggled with but that I do the explanation to show the thinking behind how the problem should be tackled. So now just before the exams, before swot week there was one question that they had lots of, oh I was going to, for the last week of lectures I was going to do revision. And of course, there was no revision week because there was no lecture week [*suspended because of the student protests*]. So what I did was, I knew that there were questions from previous exam papers that they have come to me a lot with. So I did podcasts on those showing them the thinking behind it but not giving them answers to the actual questions. Just showing them how the problem solving behind it happens.   (Respondent 2)

In this instance, Respondent 2's fear of technology did not prevent her from learning to use technology to support her students. And the way that she used the technology supported how she taught – guiding her students to understand the problem-solving process in a pure science discipline.

Despite Respondent 3's frustration with how technology depersonalises and individualises the learning space (see the previous section), she found a way to integrate it into her teaching such that it aligned with what she wished to accomplish in her class. As highlighted earlier, she strove to create an engaging social learning space with her students and found that technology could help her do that and bring a diverse student body together.

> You look for examples that they tend to share because I tend to follow things on social media. I know, for example … what is happening in the pop culture? And I know currently people are debating about Beyonce's video you know. You bring that into the conversations within the classroom. … Those are the things that they tend to share. For us in [a social science discipline] we are, I can say that social sciences are privileged in that sense that we can bring such popular culture into the classroom in making examples. So those are the examples that tend to bridge the divide. (Respondent 3)

Respondent 3 used technology by browsing on social media to keep abreast with what was happening in popular culture. She believes that whether her students are "in the US or Britain or in Lusikisiki [*a small town in South Africa*], [they] know what is …trending". Thus, she uses technology (social media in this instance) to research trending topics and then brings them into her teaching.

The above narratives show that while academics lamented that common barriers constrained how (or if) they integrated educational technology; on closer examination it became clear that these same academics exercised their agency in spite of these barriers. In the next section, I will discuss the impact that this understanding of academics' practices could have on educational technology support.

Re-imagining educational technology support

As highlighted at the start of this chapter, the barriers narrative has become a popular explanation when examining the disparity in academics' choices and practices with educational technology. While it is true that a range of barriers has a constraining effect on educational technology integration, this narrative does not tell the whole story as it ignores academics' agency to act contrary to those barriers. In this chapter, I use Scott's public and private (hidden) transcripts to frame three aspects: (1) the barriers narrative, which is the accepted view (public transcript); (2) its impact on academics' perceptions of their practice with educational technology (acceptance of the public transcript); and (3) how their agency enables them to reject this public transcript and integrate technology in ways that align with their teaching values (hidden transcript).

If academic developers believe that barriers are the main constraint to the integration of educational technology into the curriculum, then the support they give academics will focus mainly on eliminating these barriers. This barriers narrative will also be perpetuated in institutional documentation, policies, research and publications. As such, the accepted narrative (public transcript) will likely have an impact on the way academics view their practice with educational technology, particularly in their conversations with an academic developer. As an academic developer myself, this was the view that I held prior to the commencement of this research study, and, in retrospect, this view had been perpetuated by what I had read in the literature (the relevant stories referred to earlier) as well as informal conversations with academics. However, undertaking this research not only gave me access to the hidden transcript but also challenged my views about the barriers narrative and showed its interplay with academics' agency. This has changed the way I interact with academics about educational technology (asking questions that seek to uncover the hidden transcript) and how I think about my role and my practice. Therefore, one of the arguments I make is that, as academic developers, we need to research our practice, be open to our perceptions and assumptions being challenged, and learn from that research.

As this chapter has shown, the hidden transcript opens to scrutiny several pertinent issues that academic developers need to take into cognisance as they re-imagine how they support the integration of educational technology into the curriculum. Firstly, it may take time to excavate the private transcript. Academics will usually initially express the public transcript (barriers narrative) and how it has constrained their practice with educational technology. However, over time, probably as they perceive the academic developer as a trusted other rather than the more powerful other, they may begin to share their educational technology practices. Secondly, when they start revealing the hidden transcript, academics display a "reflective awareness" that rejects the popular hegemonic narrative (Anderson, 2008:254).

Interestingly, in this research study, this process was not a conscious or deliberate rejection of the public transcript, but rather a matter-of-fact expression of what they were doing – a kind of lived, every day, quiet resistance. When I presented the research results to the research respondents, it was both a revelation and an affirmation – a revelation because they were not conscious of their resistance, and an affirmation because of the recognition that they were integrating technology into the curriculum to complement what they valued as academics. Hence, their teaching values guided their reflective awareness as they integrated technologies into their teaching in spite of constraining barriers.

Should this hidden transcript (and how it could be brought to light) have an impact on the re-imagining of educational technology support? I argue that it should. Because of diverse institutional contexts, this re-imagining will proceed differently. However, there are a few general considerations that could inform this process. Firstly, academic developers need to be critically reflective about their position of power as they interact with academics, and particularly as they have conversations with them about their teaching with technology practices. Academics may assume that there are expectations about what they *should* be doing with technology, and this may be reflected in how they choose to respond to these conversations. Secondly, academic developers should have these conversations in what I choose to term "safe spaces", where academics have grown comfortable with sharing their challenges, and where the academic developers have become accepted as a trusted other. These conversations could also be facilitated by other academics (who already have the status of the trusted other).

An example of this is teaching with technology showcases where other academics share their innovations with educational technology, the challenges that led them to explore these innovations and the constraints they have experienced using them in their teaching. Respondent 2 highlights how she heard from several academics during such showcases before she considered implementing podcasts in her class. And in her instance, she did not come to our office (academic development) for help but contacted the specific academics to teach her how to use Camtasia.

Conclusion

While technology for teaching and learning can disrupt the curriculum, its uptake has been less than ideal in higher education institutions in South Africa and internationally. One of the main reasons put forward for this is the wide range of barriers to technology integration which have a constraining impact on academics' practices. The argument that I make in this chapter is that this dominant perspective can be considered the public transcript because it is the most widely accepted narrative when explaining the disparity in educational technology use. Its impact has been felt in several ways: academic developers focusing on technical skills development and overcoming barriers to technology integration in their support of academics, and academics expressing these barriers as constraining their educational technology practices. However, closer inspection shows that academics integrate technology into their curricula in ways that complement their teaching values, notwithstanding the constraining barriers. Through their agency, they develop a reflective awareness and act contrary to the dictates of these barriers. As such, I recommend educational technology support that shifts the focus from the barriers narrative to one that seeks to understand the hidden transcript through the creation of safe spaces for academics to have conversations about their practices with educational technology. These safe spaces will allow academic developers to have a better understanding of the socio-political context within which academics operate, as well as their teaching values and how they are striving to engage their students. Hence, academic developers will be better placed to recommend and introduce educational technologies that align with specific academics' teaching values, and maybe even challenge them to disrupt the way they teach and engage their students.

References

ANDERSON, G. 2008. Mapping academic resistance in the managerial university. *Organization*, 15(2):251270. [https://doi.org/10.1177/1350508407086583]

ARCHER, M.S. 2003. *Structure, agency and the internal conversation*. Cambridge: Cambridge University Press. [https://doi.org/10.1017/CBO9781139087315]

BAR-ON, D. 1996. Ethical issues in biographical interviews and analysis. In: R. Josselson (ed). *Ethics and Process in the Narrative Study of Lives*. Thousand Oaks: Sage, 9-21. [https://doi.org/10.4135/9781483345451.n2]

BIGUM, C. & ROWAN, L. 2015. Gorillas in their midst: Rethinking educational technology. In: S. Bulfin, N.F. Johnson & C. Bigum (eds). *Critical Perspectives on Technology and Education*. New York: Palgrave Macmillan, 15-34. [https://doi.org/10.1057/9781137385451_2]

BLIN, F. & MUNRO, M. 2008. Why hasn't technology disrupted academics' teaching practices? Understanding resistance to change through the lens of activity theory. *Computers and Education*, 50(2):475-490. [https://doi.org/10.1016/j.compedu.2007.09.017]

BROMLEY, H. 1997. The social chicken and the technological egg: Educational computing and the technology/society divide. *Educational Theory*, 47(1):51-65. [https://doi.org/10.1111/j.1741-5446.1997.00051.x]

CARSPECKEN, P.F. 1996. *Critical ethnography in educational research: A theoretical and practical guide*. New York: Routledge.

COSTANDIUS, E.; NELL, I.; ALEXANDER, N.; MCKAY, M.; BLACKIE, M.; MALGAS, R. & SETATI, E. 2018. #FeesMustFall and decolonising the curriculum: Stellenbosch University students' and lecturers' reactions. *South African Journal of Higher Education*, 32(2):65-85. [https://doi.org/10.20853/32-2-2435]

CRESWELL, J.W. 2012. *Qualitative inquiry and research design: Choosing among five approaches*. Los Angeles: Sage.

CROSS, M. & ADAM, F. 2007. ICT policies and strategies in higher education in South Africa: National and institutional pathways. *Higher Education Policy*, 20(1):73-95. [https://doi.org/10.1057/palgrave.hep.8300144]

DAVIES, C.A. 2008. *Reflexive ethnography: A guide to researching selves and others*. 2nd Edition. London and New York: Routledge.

FLAVIN, M. 2012. Disruptive technologies in higher education. *Research in Learning Technology*, 20:102111. [https://doi.org/10.3402/rlt.v20i0.19184]

GREGORY, M.S. & LODGE, J. M. 2015. Academic workload: the silent barrier to the implementation of technology-enhanced learning strategies in higher education. *Distance Education*, 36(2):210-230. [https://doi.org/10.1080/01587919.2015.1055056]

HALL, S. 1996. New ethnicities. In: D. Morley & K. Chen (eds). *Stuart Hall: Critical dialogues in cultural studies*. Abingdon: Routledge, 442-451.

HAMMERSLEY, M. & ATKINSON, P. 2007. *Ethnography: Principles in practice*. 3rd Edition. Abingdon: Routledge. [https://doi.org/10.4324/9780203944769]

HARRATI, N.; BOUCHRIKA, I. & MAHFOUF, Z. 2017. Investigating the uptake of educational systems by academics using the technology to performance chain model. *Library Hi Tech*, 35(4):629-648. [https://doi.org/10.1108/LHT-01-2017-0029]

HOWARD, S.K. 2013. Risk-aversion: Understanding teachers' resistance to technology integration. *Technology, Pedagogy and Education*, 22(3):357-372. [https://doi.org/10.1080/1475939X.2013.802995]

KERR, S.T. 1989. Teachers and technology: An appropriate model to link research with practice. Paper presented at the Annual Meeting of the Association for Educational Communications and Technology, Dallas, Texas, 221-247. [https://eric.ed.gov/?id=ED308823]

KING, E. & BOYATT, R. 2015. Exploring factors that influence adoption of e-learning within higher education. *British Journal of Educational Technology*, 46(6):1272-1280. [https://doi.org/10.1111/bjet.12195]

LAURILLARD, D. 2008. Digital technologies and their role in achieving our ambitions for education. Report. London: University of London, Institute of Education. [https://bit.ly/2lX2BiM]

MADISON, D.S. 2012. *Critical ethnography: Method, ethics, and performance*. 2nd Edition. Los Angeles, California: Sage.

MOROZOV, E. 2011. What do we think about? Who gets to do the thinking? In: J. Brockman (ed). *How is the Internet Changing the Way You Think? The Net's Impact on Our Minds and Future*. London: Atlantic Books, 228-231.

NG'AMBI, D. & BOZALEK, V. 2015. Editorial: Massive open online courses (MOOCs): Disrupting teaching and learning practices in higher education. *British Journal of Educational Technology*, 46(3):451454. [https://doi.org/10.1111/bjet.12281]

REID, P. 2014. Categories for barriers to adoption of instructional technologies. *Education and Information Technologies*, 19(2):383-407. [https://doi.org/10.1007/s10639-012-9222-z]

SCHOONENBOOM, J. 2014. Using an adapted, task-level technology acceptance model to explain why instructors in higher education intend to use some learning management system tools more than others. *Computers and Education*, 71:247-256. [https://doi.org/10.1016/j.compedu.2013.09.016]

SCOTT, J.C. 1990. *Domination and the Arts of Resistance: Hidden Transcripts*. New Haven: Yale University Press.

SCOTT, J.C. 1987. *Weapons of the weak: Everyday forms of peasant resistance*. Reprint Edition. New Haven: Yale University Press.

SELWYN, N. 2012. Bursting out of the 'ed-tech' bubble. *Learning, Media and Technology*, 37(4):331-334. [https://doi.org/10.1080/17439884.2012.680212]

SIFE, A.S.; LWOGA, E.T. & SANGA, C. 2007. New technologies for teaching and learning: Challenges for higher learning institutions in developing countries. *International Journal of Education and Development Using ICT*, 3(2):57-67. [https://bit.ly/2mlsxoN]

SSEKAKUBO, G. SULEMAN, H. & MARSDEN, G. 2011. Issues of adoption: have e-learning management systems fulfilled their potential in developing countries? Paper presented at the South African Institute of Computer Scientists and Information Technologists Annual Conference on Knowledge, Innovation and Leadership in a Diverse, Multidisciplinary Environment, 3-5 October, Cape Town, South Africa, 231-238. [https://doi.org/10.1145/2072221.2072248]

THOMAS, J. 1993. *Doing critical ethnography*. Newbury Park: SAGE. [https://doi.org/10.4135/9781412983945]

WATTY, K.; MCKAY, J. & NGO, L. 2016. Innovators or inhibitors? Accounting faculty resistance to new educational technologies in higher education. *Journal of Accounting Education*, 36:115. [https://doi.org/10.1016/j.jaccedu.2016.03.003]

WEBSTER, M.D. 2017. Questioning technological determinism through empirical research. *Symposion*, 4(1):107-125. [https://doi.org/10.5840/symposion2017416]

WINNER, L. 1977. *Autonomous technology: Technics-out-of-control as a theme in political thought*. Cambridge: MIT Press.

WOLCOTT, H.F. 1999. *Ethnography: A way of seeing*. Lanham: Altamira Press.

CHAPTER 12

Re-imagining curriculum development and the role of academic developers in a university of technology in the post-colonial setting

*'Mabokang Monnapula-Mapesela,
Ntsoaki Malebo & Isaac Ntshoe*

Introduction

Debates around the transformation of society and higher education globally are discussed using terms, such as massification, opening and widening access to education, and redressing historical inequities and inequalities. In South Africa, the main purpose of transformation is to transition the country from the apartheid to the post-apartheid system. However, transformation conversations continue because there are diverse conceptualisations of what constitutes a socially just and transformative, non-racial, non-sexist higher education system (Ntshoe, 2003).

While a significant measure of progress has been achieved regarding some of the issues relating to transformation, there is growing uneasiness about the extent to which transformation as initially conceptualised has not addressed the less obvious forms of inequity. As the world becomes more global, and as South Africa enters its third decade of democracy, there continue to be calls to interrogate the more covert forms of racism. There are also questions raised about the current quality and relevance of provision of higher education, and the need to create a socially just and transformed higher education system. The call to transform the curriculum in decolonial and post-apartheid settings is unlikely to yield any different results while still trapped in the original discourses of transformation. While these narratives were key post-1994, the decolonial agenda requires alternative ways of thinking, particularly concerning how knowledge is acquired and distributed by higher education.

In this chapter, we propose an alternative framework for re-imagining the development of socially just curricula in the post-colonial and post-apartheid context of higher education in general, and in our institution particularly. This framework involves creating disruptive spaces in existing curricula to advance socially just higher education. The question with which this chapter wrestles is: *To what extent do academic developers in partnership with disciplinary experts, have the necessary capabilities to engage with curriculum theory and participate in the creation of disruptive spaces to respond to the calls for decolonising curricula?* We argue that the roles of academic developers in creating disruptive spaces for academics and students will not materialise unless alternative frameworks are imagined and developed.

Firstly, we reflect on the influence of institutional culture on the agency of academic developers and disciplinary experts for developing a shared understanding of a transformed decolonised curriculum. Secondly, we critically reflect on the role of academic developers in partnership with disciplinary experts to create disruptive spaces for analysing, critiquing and navigating complex curricula practices for a socially just transformative curriculum. Thirdly, we propose a curriculum framework for ways in which academic developers can contribute to creating spaces to disrupt traditional curriculum practices. We believe that without curriculum design practices grounded on strong curriculum theory, academic developers will not be able to exercise their agency to contribute to disrupting traditional curriculum practices.

Contributors to the chapter

The contributors to this chapter work at a university of technology[1] in South Africa. Two are academic development professionals, while one is a disciplinary expert. We draw on our experiences of curriculum transformation and development in our context. Although this reflective piece comes at the end of a two-decade-long era of curriculum change at universities of technology, we hope it will provide a fresh lens through which our academics and perhaps academics at other universities of technology can respond to students' calls for the decolonisation of curricula. This is an aspect of curriculum transformation that has received little attention in our context.

Towards responding to the curriculum decolonisation agenda

Curricula in South African universities have been criticised for, "reflecting colonial and apartheid worldviews, and being disconnected from African realities, including the lived experiences of the majority of black South Africans (students)" (Ramoupi, 2014:271). Current curricula seem to privilege colonial and Western epistemologies that are at odds with the decolonial agenda (De Sousa Santos, 2001).

While demands to decolonise higher education date back to post-colonial discourses of the 1960s followed by current decolonial debates (Fataar, 2018; Heleta, 2016), these calls became more pronounced during the #FeesMustFall and #RhodesMustFall student protests in 2015 and 2016. Students were calling for the deliberate disruption of existing curriculum practices by invoking decolonisation narratives to propose alternative epistemologies in post-colonial contexts (Mbembe, 2015; Ndlovu-Gatsheni, 2013). These narratives maintain that post-colonial and post-apartheid curricula in South Africa continue to promote white supremacy and dominance, as well as stereotyping of Africa, which merely worsen rather than redress the injustices of the past (Badat & Sayed, 2014).

---

1 Universities of technology focus on technology innovation and transfer and offer technological career-directed educational programmes. They engage with industry to produce innovative problem-solving research. Many of the programmes offered include work-integrated learning that requires students to complete a structured programme while working in an organisation (Knowledge Hub, 2015).

We argue that succeeding at university has up to now remained a distant dream for the majority of black university students, largely because university communities have neglected the role of engaging students in learning the disciplines in ways that meet their legitimate learning needs (Scott, 2009). Responding to some of these challenges requires that curricula, teaching, and assessment in post-colonial settings should be designed in ways that induct students into the knowledge of the field, including ways of knowing that will contribute to academic success.

Key questions in the conversation on the discourse of curriculum decolonisation should include:

- From what knowledge traditions are the content of courses drawn, and why those knowledge traditions and not others?
- Is it possible, given a particular field, to draw knowledge from other traditions?
- Can examples of how the knowledge relates to African contexts be included?
- Is it possible to show how the knowledge links to the histories/experiences of different students in the class?
- In what ways does the knowledge validate or challenge students' experiences/lives?
- Who teaches and why?
- Are there aspects of the curriculum, pedagogy and assessment practices that some students may find alienating? (Vorster, 2016:5)

We argue that academic developers and academics need to understand what these questions mean as they take steps to address the specific demands of the curriculum decolonisation agenda.

As a response to some of the concerns raised, there have in recent years been increasing calls to critique the original transformation agenda by introducing the discourse of decolonisation of the curriculum, and therefore of knowledge (Ndlovu-Gatsheni, 2013). These calls highlight the concern that the transformation of higher education as conceptualised in 1994 has not uncovered and eradicated covert practices, based on race and class, of excluding students from participating meaningfully in higher education. Our experience of higher education and curriculum development has clearly shown that many higher education policies developed after 1994, including our institutional policies, intended to enable transformation, have not yet created a platform for universities to address specific issues related to the decolonisation of curriculum. While we agree that social justice is now acknowledged as being an integral part of curriculum transformation, we argue that there is no agreement at national policy and institutional levels about what curriculum transformation in the decolonial context is in practice. Thus, what a decolonised curriculum is or should be, which stakeholders are to drive the decolonial project, and especially the role of students in this process, remain contested.

We argue that the National Qualifications Framework (NQF) (RSA, 2008), and the subsequent Higher Education Qualifications Sub-Framework (HEQSF) (CHE, 2013) could not, on their own, lead to the proposed curriculum transformation. The NQF is not based on theories to guide curriculum transformation, but rather on frameworks adopted as part of the global move to facilitate smooth articulation and credit transfer amongst institutions. Thus, key elements of the global trends embraced by the NQF include an emphasis on generic modes, including outcomes-based, soft-skills, core-skills, competence-based as starting points in designing curricula. This emphasis on generic modes has resulted in shifting the focus away from the disciplinary and knowledge bases of fields of professional and sectoral fields of practice of qualifications and programmes offered by universities of technology. Sectoral fields refer to programmes of study that provide students with knowledge and skills that prepare them for jobs and careers in specific sectors, for example engineering technologists and technicians, radiographers, and so on. This shift has resulted in drifting away from interrogating other important issues such as what is taught, whose knowledge is taught, and to whom it is taught (Ntshoe, 2012). Even though the HEQSF has had an impact on curriculum change in the last decade in South Africa, especially at universities of technology, it has not been sufficient to stimulate debate or led to the changes needed for the post-colonial curriculum (Monnapula-Mapesela, 2017).

The role of academic developers in relation to curriculum in our context and perhaps in other contexts has been contested. In some cases, academics feel that academic developers are encroaching on their territory. These contestations relate to the tension between the expertise and domains of academic disciplines and the domains and expertise of academic developers. Even more challenging is that higher education in the post-apartheid and post-colonial context is being challenged to think much more critically about the effects of coloniality on all aspects of the curriculum. At the institutional level, there is also a concern that discussions about decolonising the curriculum are the preserve of academics, to the exclusion of students who themselves are rightful stakeholders, who have powers to influence higher education change. Demands by students for a decolonised higher education curriculum have magnified the problems of those tasked with the role of curriculum development in all universities because curriculum design now needs to be understood within a particular context – a decolonial context, which many academics, academic developers and researchers are yet to conceptualise. The continued negative effects of coloniality on curriculum, pedagogy and assessment practices still need to be investigated, understood, and then changed (Maldonado-Torres, 2007: 243).

In post-apartheid South Africa, institutions originally designed for specific population groups have been abolished and all institutions are theoretically open to everyone, but institutional cultures remain set and often reflect previous ideologies, policies and practices. This is particularly evident in curricula. What is being called for is the disruption of existing curriculum practices. Academic developers are unlikely to be able to contribute to this disruption unless they actively engage academics and students in discussions about how curricula can be decolonised in the various disciplines and fields. Furthermore, as partners, academic developers must play a critical role in mediating between academics and students by bringing them together to debate curriculum transformation possibilities.

Curriculum transformation at universities of technology: Enabling and constraining structural, cultural and agential factors

The call for decolonising curriculum in South Africa should be understood within a particular history of the country where institutions before 1994 were categorised in terms of race, colour and ethnicity.

Universities of technology, formerly known as technikons, have a different purpose and mission, as well as distinctive culture (tradition, values) from traditional universities. They typically have three mandates, namely, to offer career-focused programmes, engage in applied research, and develop strong links with industry (Du Pre, 2010). These relatively new universities were created by the Higher Education Act (RSA, 1997) which emphasised knowledge types produced by traditional universities as distinct from those by universities of technology as criteria for distinctiveness. The HEQSF (CHE, 2013) makes a distinction between two types of curriculum and qualifications: one which is formative or research-based and aimed at producing disciplinary experts; the other to produce knowledgeable professionals. The latter qualifications are thus oriented more closely to the demands of the workplace (Muller, 2009:14).

In terms of this categorisation, universities of technology offer primarily sectoral knowledge for the various occupational fields and the applied side of knowledge and qualifications; while traditional universities offer disciplines primarily as sources of knowledge and therefore award research-based qualifications (RSA, 2007). However, traditional universities also prepare graduates for specific occupations and professions such as accountants, architects, dentists and lawyers.

Since their establishment, universities of technology have been on a journey of transformation that requires them to develop a new identity as a "university". This means redefining their roles and functions to align with what is required of universities while avoiding "mission drift". Mission drift, as used here, refers to the tendency of universities to move away from their intended mandates, focus and purpose, to mandates and purposes of other institutional types. As part of the transition, universities of technology were required to overhaul their curricula and academic programmes aligning them to the prescripts of the HEQSF. The transformation of technikons to universities of technology, therefore has, what Mbembe (2016) describes as *a double character* – a phase of closure as well as the time for possibility. However, for this possibility to become a reality, academic development centres had to be established to support students and academics, to respond to the teaching and learning challenges that arose from this new university of technology mandate.

Historically the purpose of academic development/ support in most historically white universities was to assist the minority of black students who had been admitted to their institutions with their studies. Few historically black universities had formal academic development structures before 1994. When universities of technology were established, it was recognised that academic developers could contribute to helping them to define their identities and meet their mission and vision goals. Much of the work academic developers were and still are required to do is linked to curriculum development and review.

Understandably, academic developers in universities nationally are facing challenges regarding their role in creating disruptive spaces for collaboration in dealing with curriculum transformation, as well as the decolonisation of curriculum. Amongst the challenges are, firstly, the fact that the majority of black students wishing to enrol at universities do not have adequate high school-leaving scores. A well-coordinated partnership between academic developers and academic staff is, therefore, pivotal to offer academic staff support to interrogate their current curriculum practices to ensure that they meet the needs of their students.

Secondly, before changing their designation to universities of technology, the former technikon curricula were centrally developed by "conveners" who were a select group of lecturers from different technikons (Du Pre, 2010). Thus, the rest of the lecturers saw their roles as implementers of curricula developed centrally. The seeming reluctance on the part of academics in our institution to engage with curriculum could be attributed to a culture inherited from this technikon convener system.

In spite of these reservations, at universities of technology, there are still expectations that academic developers should adopt the role of conveners. These conflicting expectations have unfortunately resulted in the dearth of lecturers with curriculum design expertise at universities of technology and consequently a general lack of capacity and enthusiasm to interrogate curriculum.

Thirdly, in the last few years, we have experienced challenges meeting the CHE's tight time frames for phasing out old technikon programmes and revising curricula in line with the HEQSF requirements. At the outset, the CHE required all institutions to categorise each of their programmes as either: a category A programme, which meant they only had to change the naming of the programme in accordance with the HEQSF; a category B programme, which required content changes of 50% or less; or a category C programme, which entailed the development of completely new programmes (CHE, 2011). Although this policy created an ideal opportunity for all institutions and academics to engage in meaningful curriculum work, there was a tendency for some academics to opt for only making technical changes and as a result they denied themselves a chance to truly transform their programmes, and only ensured that the basic requirements for accreditation were met.

Since universities of technology prepare students for particular vocations and professions, it is expected that relevant industries and professional bodies would have an interest in the curriculum design of different professional and sectoral fields offered by this sub-sector of higher education. Roles of professional bodies in the curricula of universities of technology include the following: Firstly, ensuring that curricula cover the appropriate theoretical knowledge of specific disciplines related to the vocation/profession in question. Secondly, professional bodies endorse the CHE's accreditation of certain programmes of fields of study in universities of technology and prescribe the time students need to spend in practice through work-integrated learning. The purpose is to ensure that curricula of different fields of study meet acceptable quality standards. Those academics nominated by their institutions as curriculum advisors on these bodies such as the Engineering Council of South Africa, the South African Institute of Chartered Accountants and the Health Professional Council of South Africa, rarely see themselves as curriculum theorists. These advisors consider themselves as contributing to (and in some cases requiring) curricula that reflect the expectations and interests of the government, employers and professional bodies *that mediate curriculum interests.* Despite the general belief that professional bodies impose strict restrictions on what should go into the curriculum of professional and sectoral fields, we argue that academics, academic developers and students have a pivotal role to play in selecting what goes into the curriculum in collaboration with the professional bodies. The perception about the imposition of curriculum by professional bodies could be attributed to the seeming paralysis on the part of academics and academic developers regarding the power they have to influence curriculum transformation.

We, therefore, argue that the inability or lack of awareness of the need, on the part of academics and academic developers, to participate meaningfully in curriculum transformation debates could be attributed to the lack of recognition of the role of strong curriculum theory. We also argue that engagement in curriculum to create spaces for disruption will not be realised unless academics, academic developers and students recognise, not only their power in curriculum matters but also the diverse spaces from which they can participate actively in the decolonial agenda. Furthermore, the envisioned role of academics and academic developers can only materialise if they give cognisance to research, theories and epistemologies from the North (rational, technicist, process-product theories), and South (theories of subaltern studies and post-colonial epistemologies, including critical and radical pedagogies), amongst others. They must also critically deconstruct theories of the North and use these to develop curricula relevant to the post-colonial and post-apartheid settings in the South (Tyler, 1949; Stenhouse, 1975; De Sousa Santos, 2001; Gatsheni-Ndlovu, 2013; Manathunga, 2018).

Expecting academic developers in our institution to drive the process of developing new curricula, and especially persuading academics to undertake an overhaul and transformation of their programmes has been a tall order, as many academics opt to implement only the bare minimum of changes to their programmes instead of developing new qualifications altogether (Monnapula-Mapesela, 2017). We have to work closely with academics to change this culture, by discouraging the recycling of old technikon programmes rather than the intended in-depth transformation that is required. Exercising authority for many academic developers, particularly at universities of technology, has been met with many challenges. One reason for this is that academic developers are frequently unable to make convincing claims regarding their academic development professionalism (Blackmore & Blackwell, 2006). As in traditional universities, many academic developers at universities of technology migrated to academic development from other disciplines with no particular knowledge of academic development work. They have not had the opportunity to build the curriculum knowledge and practices they need to work with academics in revising and developing curricula, particularly in a context of calls for decolonising curricula and all that this entails.

In our institution, and perhaps at other universities in South Africa and beyond its boundaries, a great deal of pressure has thus been placed on both academic developers and academics to prepare themselves, not only for the broader curriculum transformation but also to embrace specific demands such as the decolonisation agenda. Amongst other things, academic developers have been encouraged to focus on the professionalisation of their practice by undertaking higher education qualifications or teaching qualifications, in the hope of building a group of academic developers with strong curriculum theory knowledge who could explore what kinds of knowers they need to be to work collaboratively with colleagues across disciplines. Importantly, there is a strong belief that it is chiefly through longer-term development approaches that the capacity of our academic and academic development staff can be built to enable them to engage in meaningful curriculum design work. We, therefore, argue that this approach will disrupt previously unquestioned curriculum practices in higher education in general, (Quinn, 2012b:28), but also the resistant technikon culture that continues to shape current curriculum design practices in our institution. Our institution has adopted this strategy by developing a Postgraduate Diploma in Higher Education for lecturing staff working at universities of technology and similar contexts. This Diploma focuses on curriculum development, the higher education context, assessment, using technology in teaching and learning, workplace learning, learning facilitation, scholarship of teaching and learning, including quality of teaching and learning. The programme encourages academics to be critically reflexive about their practice by questioning: the relevance of context for teaching and learning; what they teach; how they teach; and why they teach what they teach, using theoretical lenses. It is largely the role of academic developers from our institution to contribute to the professionalisation of university teaching through this Diploma.

Professionalising the practice of academics also entails giving academics access to deep understandings of theories, orientations and values that underpin curriculum, without which, students are likely to be denied "epistemological" (Morrow, 2007) and "ontological access" (Barnett, 1994). This further, enhances the knowledge and understanding of academics in making relevant and responsive knowledge choices within their disciplines. Notwithstanding the progress made in improving the qualifications of most academics, especially in our institution, and improving their status as disciplinary experts and researchers, we realise that significant shortcomings still exist regarding their professionalisation as teachers, and their ability to implement principled curriculum, pedagogical and assessment practices. We also concede that knowledge of the discipline alone is not sufficient to disrupt the thinking of academics or lead to radical engagement with curriculum change. In such cases, the role of academic developers in creating conducive environments is critical. Apart from contributing to the professionalisation of teaching by academics, and as part of our academic development work, we have introduced a variety of activities to assist academics to embrace the decolonisation discourse. We have organised seminars and guest lectures by experts and renowned scholars such as Ndlovu-Gatsheni, Manathunga and others who are doing pioneering work on decolonisation of education and curriculum.

The envisioned role of academic developers in driving curriculum transformation

Given the mounting pressure for academics to work towards transforming and decolonising their institutions, and our own experience of working together with academics in designing curriculum at a university of technology, we envision a changed role for both academic developers and academics. This new role must be underpinned by academic developers' ability and capacity to theorise practices in which a curriculum transformation agenda might be advanced (Quinn, 2012a). Thus, the role of academic developers is pivotal in advancing socially just and transformative higher education which exposes students to epistemic ways to contribute to knowledge in the different disciplines. However, we believe that this role can only be effectively fulfilled when there is a genuine partnership between academic developers, academics, and students on curriculum design practices in higher education. Such a partnership will not be realised unless academic developers are empowered and have strong curriculum theories and analytical tools to help them to work with mainstream academics and students in designing curriculum (Candy, 1996:15). Accordingly, academic developers could become critical change agents to drive curriculum change and the decolonisation agenda by engaging academics in disrupting existing pedagogical practices. They should further influence the evolution of institutional culture and agency where all partners (academic developers, academics and students) have a common understanding of what a transformed decolonised curriculum in different disciplines might be.

A transformed decolonised curriculum at universities of technology should be understood within a particular context that includes regional mandates of these institutions that prepare students for particular careers and occupations. Thus, the curricula should "face both ways" as they are intended to advance applied knowledge of specific disciplines on the one hand, and work closely with industries and professional bodies on the other.

Apart from constraining the curriculum transformation agenda, the technikon history and culture has forced us as academic developers to adopt new roles as agents and advocates of transformation. This role demands skills, knowledge, authority and agility for handling the broad transformation agenda. The larger part of our work with academics entails ensuring that they are well acquainted with their terrain, which includes knowledge of the broad higher education legislative context and specific legislative bodies that professionalise and regulate their disciplines, and that they understand their institutional and disciplinary contexts and the impact these have on curriculum work. Both academic development and academic work must be underpinned by a deep understanding of higher education as an interdisciplinary field of study, as well as a strong research and evidence base rather than common-sense ideologies, ideas, assumptions and beliefs (Stierer, 2008; Maton, 2014). Quinn (2012a) views these attributes as prerequisites for intellectual and strategic leadership for successful academic developers who are expected to be strategic "knowledgeable others" who can negotiate change and guide institutions in managing curriculum reform. Being an academic developer or an academic at a university of technology in an unstable environment that demands transformation and transformative ways of dealing with curriculum is thus complicated. Curriculum development in our institution has been a long drawn-out and arduous journey because of the unique nature and history of the institution explained in preceding sections. Thus the creation of spaces for academics, academic developers and students to disrupt existing practices about curriculum and knowledge has become even more critical.

While the role of academic developers is critical in creating spaces for curriculum design and development in partnerships and further pioneering the course of curriculum transformation, at universities of technology and perhaps at other types of universities, they need to acknowledge existing power differentials between themselves, disciplinary experts and students. Within these partnerships, academics must take ownership of their academic programmes and curriculum design, because they are disciplinary experts, while the academic developers in their support role must ensure that design practices are theoretically grounded in informed curriculum design principles and knowledge choices that privilege students and society at large (Blackmore & Blackwell, 2006). Both academics and academic developers must, therefore, ensure that within the spaces of curriculum debates, all stakeholders are equal. The role of academic developers is further to appraise academics in specific disciplines about their important role as "recontextualisation agents" (Luckett, 2001) and the authority they have to influence the transformation/decolonisation agenda by choosing relevant knowledge and curricula from their fields or disciplines to develop transformed responsive curricula. Academic developers should encourage disciplinary experts to articulate the curriculum orientations and theories that underpin their programmes. They should decode the "official regulative discourses", that is, basic concepts, theories, principles, rules and values of discipline and the "pedagogic regulative discourses" (sound knowledge and curriculum choices, sequencing, ways of transmitting subject knowledge), enacting the curriculum and how learning is assessed (Bernstein, 2000). They should also be encouraged to ensure epistemological and ontological access for students in a post-colonial, post-apartheid university of technology.

Mindful of the importance of the official and pedagogic regulative discourses, academic developers similarly should be able to identify the social power underlying interactions between students and academic staff where, on the one hand, students' attributes are paramount and specialist knowledge is often underplayed; on the other hand, a situation where specialised knowledge that comprise principles and procedures is important (Howard & Maton, 2011). Thus, we argue that academic developers could, after being exposed to curriculum theories, create disruptive spaces in which curriculum transformation in the post-colonial context may be better understood. Part of their critical role is to work closely with academics to make explicit to the students what constitutes legitimate knowledge within different disciplines and how this could be taught, accessed by students and assessed, to ensure that transformative and emancipatory learning does take place (Maton, 2000). McLaren (2002 in Belhari-Leak, 2016:4) argues that "to drive pedagogic transformation, we need to engage in pedagogies that do not merely domesticate and pacify students". Academics, students and academic developers need to question epistemologies and ontologies and the relevance of different pedagogical modes including critical pedagogy, radical pedagogy and generic modes in curriculum transformation in the decolonial period (Vorster & Quinn, 2017:38).

There are, however, challenges which could impede the envisioned role of academic developers in leading curriculum design reforms. Firstly, rarely acknowledged is the reality that most disciplinary experts or teachers in universities are unaware of their role in interrogating curriculum guidelines that might have been proposed by the Department of Higher Education and Training (DHET) and the CHE.

Second, there is a need to resolve the artificially created tension around roles, expertise and domains of academic disciplines, and the domains and expertise of academic developers. In the past, and perhaps today in some universities, academic developers were largely marginalised in these debates partly because of the artificially created tension around expertise within the domain of academic disciplines, as opposed to the domain and expertise of academic developers. Third, there is a need to dispel the myths created by the former technikon culture that the role of academics in universities of technology is to implement curricula prescribed by the DHET and professional bodies or developed by academic developers. Even in the current context, academics at universities of technology have largely been passive, giving the academic developers the sole responsibility to initiate and drive the decolonial agenda. Academic developers should, therefore, exercise agency based on professional judgement from informed positions and make use of various institutional teaching and learning structures as disruptive spaces to challenge existing beliefs about curriculum development. Academic developers in our institution have to challenge common-sense understandings that view curriculum development as the sole preserve of curriculum developers. The resulting belief should be that all academics should consider themselves as curriculum developers, and therefore work together with academic developers and students (in teams) to design curricula appropriate to their disciplines and contexts.

Vorster and Quinn (2017) argue that academic developers can play a significant role in challenging technicist approaches to curriculum development if they can reconceptualise their work with academics and create spaces to contribute to decolonising university cultures and structures. The concern, however, is that theoretical content for most professional qualifications at universities of technology, and perhaps at traditional universities, still relies heavily on knowledge from the global North. The role of academic developers in this is to support academics to develop expertise that will allow them to be responsive not only to the student, the discipline, the professional, the society and the industry but also to the demands for a decolonised curriculum.

We concede that there are no easy ways to ensure that academic developers and academics understand their critical roles in curriculum development, especially in our context. The past two decades have been about investing time and resources in developing academics and academic developers by encouraging them to improve their disciplinary qualifications to postgraduate level; to enrol in postgraduate diplomas in higher education and attend workshops, seminars and conferences focusing on teaching and learning, pedagogy and assessment (Monnapula-Mapesela, 2017). A proposed framework and the role academic developers and academics can play as theorists and how they might contribute to conversations around creating disruptive spaces for academic developers, academics and students to decolonise the curriculum are discussed below.

The envisioned role of academics and academic developers as curriculum theorists

Our position is that not much will be achieved in transforming curriculum in the decolonial context unless academic developers' and academics' practices are, not only informed by their everyday life experiences and practices but more importantly by curriculum design theories.

We argue that currently, deeper engagement with theories of the North and South as well as orientations and values that underpin curriculum are lacking at some institutions, especially at universities of technology. This could be attributed firstly, to the national push towards recurriculating, which has so far focused on repackaging curriculum according to the HEQSF, and secondly, the fact that most institutions and academics have seen compliance with the HEQSF as a technical requirement rather than an opportunity to critically interrogate their curricula using theoretical lenses. What would contribute to genuine curriculum transformation is the ability to go beyond the HEQSF and generic modes by interrogating what it means to ensure that students are enabled both epistemological (Morrow, 2007) and ontological access (Barnett, 1994).

In our institution, we challenge academics to not only see their role exclusively as that of preparing students for employment without questioning underpinning epistemologies. We encourage them, with some success in a small number of cases, to critically question the use of generic frameworks and approaches (outcomes, competence, graduate attributes) to guide their curriculum design and practices, arguing that these alone cannot provide disruptive spaces for curriculum transformation as these are silent about the nature of knowledge and theories underpinning it.

We argue that academic developers who are able to theorise about curriculum can provide a useful framework to create disruptive spaces and, therefore, contribute to meaningful discussions about decolonised curriculum. Without recognising themselves as curriculum theorists able to critically examine their practices and anchor them on curriculum theories, academic developers in partnership with academics or even students, are unlikely to make meaningful contributions to the current debates to transform curriculum in the decolonial context.

We appropriated Michael Young's (2013; 2014) ideas to argue that academic developers and academics should have a deeper understanding of competing curriculum theories from the North and the significance of reclaiming their roles as curriculum theorists if they are to have any chance of creating disruptive spaces for transforming curriculum in the decolonial context. We thus agree with Young that the roles of both curriculum theory and curriculum theorists have reached crises in the discourses of curriculum design specifically in relation to the issue of "access to knowledge that is largely neglected" (Young, 2013:103). Young attributes this "crisis" to the apparent reluctance of curriculum theorists to engage with epistemological issues concerning questions of truth, and the reliability of different forms of knowledge, and how such issues have both philosophical and sociological dimensions. The diverse reasons for this reluctance at a university of technology were highlighted in the preceding sections. However, of utmost importance is Young's argument that "you cannot have a curriculum theory without a theory of knowledge" (2011:197). Unfortunately, the academics we work with do not usually have such a theory. They can name the knowledge they think their students need to acquire, but they do not always know how to justify or critique their knowledge choices. They also do not always know how to design their curricula and teach in ways that ensure epistemological access for all students.

Using Young's (2013) theoretical framework, we argue that the creation of disruptive spaces requires deliberate action by academic developers as curriculum specialists to become critical of existing curriculum practices by recognising the crucial role of curriculum theory, and their roles as curriculum specialists. Thus, the role of academic developers should be to work collaboratively with mainstream academics to analyse knowledge and develop alternatives to existing forms of curriculum. Young (2011:201) sums up this challenge by arguing that

> ... as curriculum theorists we have to become like 'dual specialists'. Our primary specialization is curriculum theory. However, we also need a level of familiarity with the specialist fields we are investigating – whether it is university engineering or early reading. On the whole, this is where curriculum theory falls down and even perhaps why it does not develop: the two forms of specialization, curriculum theory and the particular field under investigation, which are rarely brought together. There is much to do.

As curriculum theorists, academic developers should have specialist knowledge based on curriculum theory that generates analysis and critiques its different forms and proposes better alternatives for curriculum transformation. The reality, in our context and at other institutions, is that those entrusted to design curricula, have seemingly lost their primary focus on what is taught and learned, and how existing theories could contribute to practices in various contexts, including higher education (Priestley, 2011; Lindén, Annala & Coate, 2017).

As we work with our colleagues on developing new academic programmes we have not only witnessed a lack of the use of theories in curriculum development, but also a fear to venture into using both theories from North and South. These have resulted in some new curricula which seem to be underpinned by contradictory theories, ideologies and beliefs. The role of academic developers is, therefore, to encourage robust use of theory to critique and address issues arising from the old and current curricula, including the need to decolonise the curriculum. This position in no way suggests uncritical adoption or abandoning of curriculum theories inherited exclusively from Western canons, but rather that such theories should be deconstructed to reconstruct alternative curriculum theories drawing from the South epistemologies, rich histories and values for curriculum transformation in the post-colonial context.

The underlying assumption is that academic developers and disciplinary experts should not leave decisions about knowledge acquired in universities, to curriculum theorists from the North, or to pragmatic criteria, administrators, politicians and employers without critiquing such decisions (Young, 2014). To some extent, the tendency for many academics to focus exclusively on pragmatic considerations, especially the expectations of employers, is understandable, as universities of technology are still grappling with understanding their mandate as universities. The creation of disruptive spaces to decolonise curriculum and contribute to a socially just higher education is likely to happen when academic developers and academics as theorists in both traditional universities and universities of technology base their decisions about curriculum on sound curriculum theories. This could contribute to enabling students to acquire knowledge that will take them beyond the learning experience within the institution to also lay the foundation for knowledge that will equip them with epistemic competencies for engaging in high-level cognitive activities, theorising, becoming reflexive, generating ideas and applying these in new situations (Luckett, 2001).

The danger which is rarely appreciated is that technicist approaches guiding curriculum currently have in many cases been prescriptive and disempowering to academics and academic developers, as they have not encouraged deep engagement with curriculum theory that could enable academic developers to analyse, critique existing epistemologies, and create disruptive spaces. The ensuing lack of theory has resulted in situations where learning as a negotiated activity and freedom of choice (for both students and teachers) is controlled by tightly defined learning outcomes and their assessment criteria rather than curriculum theories (Lindén et al., 2017; Wheelahan, 2009). This means that academic developers sometimes only focus on outcomes, competences or assessment-driven curriculum instead of theory- driven curricula. This has the potential to inhibit the provision of access to knowledge that would enable creative spaces for a truly transformed curriculum.

Young's research (2014) provides a sound springboard for rethinking the roles of academic developers and academics as they attempt to decolonise curriculum. He argues that those who prescribe models for curricula seldom engage with critical analyses, which might force them to examine their assumptions. In the prescriptive approaches, critical analyses and engagement are normally not encouraged as there are likely to be no disagreements with their prescriptions such as outcomes, objectives, competences, or functional skills. This is the case in our institution. At one point, curriculum development was driven by the executive management of the university. Under their leadership, there was little interrogation of the theoretical underpinnings and assumptions of curricula. Instead, there was an overemphasis on satisfying the needs of business, industry and the immediate needs of communities in the region at the expense of engaging with the specialised theoretical knowledge of specific disciplines.

While the critical and normative roles of curriculum theory are distinguishable, they are not mutually exclusive in developing better curriculum theory and curricula that could make a difference in real life situations. We argue that curriculum partners (academic developers, academics students and others) need to recognise both the critical and normative roles of curriculum theory, as these provide a framework to examine the social impact of generic modes (competency-based and outcome-focused approaches) currently shaping curriculum design discourses at universities of technology. These roles should provide guidelines for curriculum design and practice, with certain norms to justify curriculum decisions without being prescriptive about what is appropriate or not (Young, 2014). Such guidelines would enhance the understanding of connections between theory and practice, along with the mechanisms and the powers behind curriculum decisions by the students, academics and academic developers (Lindén et al., 2017). This approach could form the foundation for discourses on how to counter the effects of coloniality on curriculum.

Academic developers and academics often find themselves isolated and lose whatever authority they have without curriculum guidelines and principles derived from curriculum theory (Young, 2014). As highlighted in the preceding section, a more helpful strategy is that academic developers and academics should be able to theorise a curriculum transformation agenda that exposes students to epistemic activities. The re-imagined curriculum development approach should be grounded on curriculum guidelines, principles and "rules" derived from curriculum theory that privilege epistemic access rather than technicist approaches to and generic modes of curriculum design. The two roles should provide the basis for academics and academic developers to question and critique whether pragmatist, generic modes or even critical pedagogy inform current practices. Similarly, academic developers and academics should have access to the theoretical tools for critiquing existing traditions or curriculum practices (Young, 2014). However, the creation of spaces to interrogate decolonisation of curriculum is unlikely to occur if academics and academic developers avoid interrogating current practices, including generic modes or watered-down theories in partnership with students using normative and critical theories.

Conclusion

We argue that academics and academic developers in higher education have the potential to appreciate their role in curriculum development and to engage in curriculum discourses that challenge existing practices and create disruptive spaces for curriculum development in post-colonial and post-apartheid society. Curriculum development opportunities provided by academic developers in creating disruptive spaces for a decolonised curriculum are ones that prioritise both the critical and normative roles of curriculum theory. This will create spaces for interrogating curriculum assumptions while being grounded on insights into "rules" or norms that guide curriculum design and practices that privilege access to knowledge as opposed to the technicist curriculum theory and generic approaches (outcomes and competence or, assessment). Academics should bring their disciplinary knowledge and expertise, while academic developers introduce academics to theories of knowledge and curriculum to help them design better curricula.

The need for development and empowerment of academic developers cannot be over-emphasised. They must have the knowledge and credibility to work with academics. Many academics at universities of technology come from the old technikon dispensation, and have only recently begun to embrace the idea of developing their agency beyond teaching, to thinking about curriculum development. There is a pressing need for a new academic culture that places academics and students at the centre of the curriculum transformation agenda. Academics need support and development which can be offered to them by academic developers. We hope that our newly developed postgraduate diploma in higher education for lecturing staff working at universities of technology will achieve some of these curriculum design aspirations.

Although we acknowledge transformation milestones achieved by the sector, we believe that academics in universities of technology need to develop an appetite for analysing, reflecting on and critiquing curricula. This would contribute to increasing the pace of curriculum transformation, and decrease the possibilities of curriculum designers falling prey to superficial approaches that continue to hinder student success, condone exclusion of selected races and the covert marginalisation that has become a proxy for apartheid in this context. The role of academic developers is to enable academics to develop the will for theoretically grounded curriculum design practices and to curb the negative implications of using practices that continue to stifle curriculum transformation.

For higher education to achieve meaningful decolonisation of curriculum in the post-colonial and post-apartheid settings, those who develop curriculum need to critically analyse the strengths and weaknesses of curriculum theories and epistemologies from the North and those from the South, to build theories to inform curriculum transformation debates. This entails deconstructing theories and epistemologies from the North and reconstructing them to develop alternative theories of curriculum and epistemology for the Southern contexts.

References

BADAT, S. & SAYED, Y. 2014. Post-1994 South African Education: The Challenge of Social Justice. *The ANNALS of the American Academy of Political and Social Science*, 652(1):127-148. [https://doi.org/10.1177/0002716213511188]

BARNETT, R. 2004. The Purposes of Higher Education and the Changing Face of Academics. *London Review of Education*, 2(1):62-73. [https://doi.org/10.1080/1474846042000177483]

BARNETT, R. 1994. *The Limits of Competence: Knowledge, higher education and society. Society for Research into Higher Education Series.* Buckingham: Open University Press.

BELHARI-LEAK, K. 2016. New Academics, New Higher Education Contexts: A Critical Perspective on Professional Development. *Teaching in Higher Education*, 22(5):485-500. [https://doi.org/10.1080/13562517.2016.1273215]

BERNSTEIN, B. 2000. Pedagogy, symbolic control, identity: Theory, research, critique. *Critical Perspectives Series.* Revised Edition. Lanham, Maryland, US: Rowman and Littlefield Publishers. [https://doi.org/10.1177/136078049600100208]

BLACKMORE, P. & BLACKWELL, R. 2006. Strategic Leadership in Academic Development. *Studies in High Education*, 31(3):373-387. [https://doi.org/10.1080/03075070600680893]

BOUGHEY, C. 2010. *Academic Development for Improved Efficiency in the Higher Education and Training System in South Africa.* Johannesburg: Development Bank of Southern Africa. [https://bit.ly/2kop207]

CANDY, P.C. 1996. Promoting Lifelong Learning: Academic Developers and The University as a Learning Organisation. *International Journal for Academic Development*, 1(1):7-18. [https://doi.org/10.1080/1360144960010102]

CHE (COUNCIL ON HIGHER EDUCATION). 2013. *The Higher Education Qualifications Sub-Framework.* Pretoria: CHE. [https://bit.ly/2m0dfp8]

CHE (COUNCIL ON HIGHER EDUCATION). 2011. *Higher education Qualifications Framework Implementation Handbook.* Pretoria: CHE. [https://bit.ly/2kvpb1R]

DE SOUSA SANTOS, B. 2001. Nuestra America: Reinventing a subaltern paradigm of recognition and redistribution. *Theory, Culture and Society*, 18(2-3):185-217. [https://doi.org/10.1177/02632760122051706]

DU PRE, R. 2010. Universities of Technology in the context of the South African higher education landscape: Universities of Technology – Deepening the Debate. *Kagisano*, 7. Pretoria: CHE. [https://bit.ly/2mmYb4Z]

FATAAR, A. 2018. Decolonising Education in South Africa: Perspectives and Debates. *Educational Research for Social Change*, 7:vi-ix. [https://bit.ly/2mrEtFs]

HELETA, S. 2016. Decolonisation of Higher Education: Dismantling Epistemic Violence and Eurocentrism in South Africa. *Transformation in Higher Education*, 1(1):1-8. [https://doi.org/10.1016/j.linged.2018.11.001]

HOWARD, S. & MATON R. 2011. Theorising knowledge practices: a missing piece of the educational technology puzzle. *Research in Learning Technology*, 19(3):191-206. [https://doi.org/10.1080/21567069.2011.624170]

Knowledge Hub. 2015. What is unique about universities of technology, and what are the benefits of studying at these institutions? *Bridge: Linking Innovators in Education*. [https://bit.ly/2miLhoF]

Lindén, J, Annala, J. & Coate, K. 2017. The Role of Curriculum Theory in Contemporary Higher Education Research and Practice. In: J. Huisman & M. Tight (eds). *Theory and Method in Higher Education Research*, 3:137-154. [https://doi.org/10.1108/S2056-375220170000003008]

Luckett, K. 2001. Responding to equity and development imperatives: Conceptualizing astructurally and epistemically diverse undergraduate curriculum in post-apartheid South Africa. *Equity and Excellence in Education*, 34(3):26-35. [https://doi.org/10.1080/1066568010340304]

Maldonado-Torres, N. 2007. On Coloniality of Being: Contributions to the Development of a Concept. *Cultural Studies*, 21(2-3):243. [https://doi.org/10.1080/09502380601162548]

Manathunga, C. 2018. Decolonising the curriculum: Southern interrogations of time, place and knowledge. *SOTL in the South*, 2(1), 95-111. [https://bit.ly/2kOY0iC]

Maton, K. 2014. *Knowledge and knowers towards a realist sociology of education*. London: Routledge. [https://doi.org/10.4324/9780203885734]

Mbembe, A. 2016. Decolonising the University: New Directions. *Arts and Humanities in Higher Education*, 15(1):29-45. [https://doi.org/10.1177/1474022215618513]

Mbembe, A. 2015. Decolonising Knowledge and the Question of the Archive. [https://bit.ly/2lRCNF1]

Monnapula-Mapesela, M. 2017. Developing as an Academic Leader in a University of Technology in South Africa: Dealing with Enabling and Constraining Teaching and Learning Environments. *Critical Studies in Teaching and Learning*, 5(2):69-85. [https://bit.ly/2lXE9hy]

Morrow, W. 2007. *Learning to Teach in South Africa*. Cape Town: HSRC Press.

Muller, J. 2009. Forms of knowledge and curriculum coherence. *Journal of Education and Work*, 23(3):205226. [https://doi.org/10.1080/13639080902957905]

Ndlovu-Gatsheni, S. 2013. Why Decoloniality in the 21st Century? *The Thinker*, 48(10):5-9. [https://bit.ly/2kvpxWf]

Ntshoe, I.M. 2012. Reframing Curriculum and Pedagogical Discourses in Universities of Technology. *South Africa Journal of Higher Education*, 26(2):198-213. [https://doi.org/10.20853/26-2-158]

Ntshoe, I.M. 2003. The political economy of access and equitable allocation of resources to higher education. *International Journal of Educational Development*, 23(4):381-398.[https://doi.org/10.1016/S0738-0593(02)00070-6]

Priestley, M. 2011. Whatever Happened to Curriculum Theory? Critical Theory and Curriculum Change. *Pedagogy, Culture and Society*, 19(2):221-237. [https://doi.org/10.1080/14681366.2011.582258]

Quinn, L. 2012a. Introduction. In: L. Quinn (ed). *Re-imagining academic staff development: Spaces for disruption*. Stellenbosch: African Sun Media, 1-13. [https://doi.org/10.18820/9781920338879]

Quinn, L. 2012b. Enabling and Constraining Conditions for Academic Staff Development. In: L. Quinn (ed). *Re-imagining academic staff development: Spaces for disruption*. Stellenbosch: African Sun Media, 36-50. [https://doi.org/10.18820/9781920338879

Ramoupi, N.L.L. 2014. African Research and Scholarship: 20 years of lost opportunities to transform higher education in South Africa. *Ufahamu: A Journal of African Studies*, 38(1):269-286. [https://bit.ly/2lZMW2s]

RSA (Republic of South Africa). 1997. *Higher Education Act 101 of 1997*. Pretoria: Government Printing Works.

RSA DoE (Republic of South Africa. Department of Education). 2007. Higher Education Qualifications Framework. *Government Gazette*, Notice 30353(3) of 5 October. Pretoria: Government Printing Works. [https://bit.ly/2kltInj]

Scott, I. 2009. Opening Perspectives on the First Year. In: B. Leibowitz.; A. van der Merwe & A. van Schalkwyk. *Focus on First-Year Success. Perspectives Emerging from South Africa and Beyond*. Stellenbosch: African Sun Media, 17-35.

STENHOUSE, L. 1975. *An Introduction to Curriculum Research and Development.* London: Heinemann.

STIERER, B. 2008. Learning to Write about Teaching: Understanding the Writing Demands of Lecturer Development Programmes in Higher Education. In: R. Murray (ed). *The Scholarship of Teaching and Learning in Higher Education.* New York: Society for Research into Higher Education and Open University Press. 34-45.

TYLER, R.W. 1949. *Basic principles of curriculum and instruction.* Chicago, Illinois: University of Chicago Press.

VORSTER, J. (ED). 2016. *Curriculum in the Context of Transformation: Reframing Traditional Understanding and Practices.* Grahamstown: Rhodes University. [https://bit.ly/2klunVP]

VORSTER, J. & QUINN, L. 2017. The 'Decolonial Turn': What Does it Mean for Academic Staff Development. *Education as Change*, 21(1):31-49. [https://doi.org/10.17159/1947-9417/2017/853]

WHEELAHAN, L. 2009. The problem with CBT (and why Constructivism Makes Things Worse). *Journal of Education and Work*, 22(3):227-242. [https://doi.org/10.1080/13639080902957913]

YOUNG, M. 2011. A Knowledge-Based Approach to the Curriculum for a University of Technology. Revised version of the paper presented to senior staff at the Central University of Technology, Free State in Bloemfontein, 30 May.

YOUNG, M. 2013. Overcoming the crisis in curriculum theory: A knowledge-based approach. *Journal of Curriculum Studies*, 45:101-118. [https://doi.org/10.1080/00220272.2013.764505]

YOUNG, M. 2014. Curriculum Theory: what it is and why it is important. *Cadernos de Pesquisa*, 44(151):190-202. [https://doi.org/10.1590/198053142851]

CHAPTER 13

Constructing curriculum in a time of transformation

A department's experience in South Africa

Theresa Gordon & Gilberte Lincoln

Introduction

In this chapter, we reflect on the post-1994 history of curriculum development in the reframing of post-apartheid higher education. This reflection is narrated from the perspective of two lecturers in the field of urban and regional planning at a university of technology in South Africa. We have for two decades navigated the requirements to develop curricula in response to new curriculum frameworks and parameters prescribed by national and institutional policies and legislation, guidelines provided by professional bodies, and administrative processes involved in ratifying and operationalising the curriculum.

The transformation of higher education in democratic South Africa has resulted in many challenges. The key shift was from privileged access to higher education to opening access to those hitherto excluded. In particular, building transparency and accountability of the higher education sector was foregrounded in policy. However, national higher education frameworks, programme structures, curriculum content and delivery continued to be contested by some higher education role players (RSA DoE, 1997:4-5).

The professional and academic field of urban and regional planning ("Planning") has not been immune to rapid changes and powerful interests. The colonial past and the effects of apartheid are profoundly spatial in scope and have multiple socio-economic and political impacts. The definition and application of Planning under colonial and apartheid rule as a system for control, segregation and regulation have in post-apartheid South Africa shifted to prioritise equitable distribution of resources and services, social engagement and responsiveness to a wider development agenda within the profession and education sector.

The field of urban and regional planning has a strong professional and academic identity (Muller, 2009:214) with clear ideas of its conceptual coherence, substantive knowledge requirements and supporting technological skill sets. The separation between the technical and professional realms has its roots in British constructs of the profession from the 1950s and was perpetuated and racialised pre-1994 in South Africa. In this conceptualisation of the workplace, professionals were considered to be capable of strategic, abstract thinking, and the technicians were required to execute and operationalise policies and plans.

This chapter deals with how we as a department had to navigate the bureaucratic load of national policy shifts in higher education and the reconfiguration of our profession post-1994 for us to make choices about an academic route – and to develop a new curriculum (Muller, 2009:221). Many of the challenges stem from our context within the university of technology sector, situated in the "curricula in-between – curriculum at the boundaries – that face both inwards to disciplines and outwards to the field of practices" (Shay, 2016:772, citing Muller, 2009).

Over the past 30 years, Planning in South Africa has been rooted in activism, with some academics contesting apartheid pedagogic paradigms and engaging in transformation struggles to contribute to building democratic practices in the field. Urban and regional planners work within a diverse range of activities to create new human settlements and improve existing areas. Social justice in which equity, participation, and legal rights are considered, forms part of the normative framework in our field. This includes redress to land, services, spatial justice, efficiency, sustainability and spatial resilience in the natural and built environment (RSA, 2013).

The Department of Town and Regional Planning ("Department") at Durban University of Technology (DUT) is one of the youngest in the Planning education landscape in South Africa. The genesis of the Department was in a former technikon, located in Durban, and born out of the need to train black planners under apartheid conditions. The Department was the only provider of the national and higher diploma in the region. The Department has offered, at various stages, diplomas, a higher diploma, a Bachelor of Technology degree, bachelor's and master's degrees. The Department is currently phasing out its Diploma and Bachelor of Technology programmes and is now offering traditional bachelor's and honours degrees.

The story of our curriculum practices is intertwined with the change across multiple sectors, including education, universities, government, professional bodies and our students. We are two staff members in the Department of Town and Regional Planning with 28 or so years of teaching experience respectively. Both of us have come from activist backgrounds in the fields of development, gender and trade unionism. This has and continues to influence our practices.

The chapter is organised as follows. We first contextualise higher education under apartheid and identify three key influential post-apartheid events in the higher education sector in South Africa. We then outline the history of curriculum intervention and practices of our Department, which is divided into four inter-related periods.

The first key national event post-apartheid was the White Paper on Higher Education Transformation resulting in the Higher Education Act of 1997 (RSA DoE, 1997). The Act proposed profound changes to higher education by providing access to higher education to those formerly denied entry. The Act emphasised, inter alia, the role of technology and the knowledge economy in higher education. The second event was the formulation of the National Plan for Higher Education of 2001 (RSA, 2001) that ushered in the reshaping of the architecture of the higher education system, using the instrument of mergers to diversify the sector. The third event was the implementation of the Higher

Education Qualification Sub-Framework (HEQSF) in 2013 (CHE, 2013). It is a single qualifications framework for higher education aimed at facilitating the development of a single national coordinated higher education system.

The first of the four inter-related periods which impacted on the Department began with the transition to democracy (1984 to 1994). During this time, we saw ourselves as activists needing to subvert the curriculum content prevalent in the Planning discourses of the time. The second period, between 1995 and 2006, deals with the highly contested transformation agenda within the higher education sector, which the Department engaged with at multiple levels. In the third period, between 2006 and 2011, there was confusion and delay while conflict ensued between stakeholders in finalising the HEQSF. The final period, from 2011 to the present, represents a mixed bag of wins and losses in curriculum continuity and outcomes for our academic and professional field and our Department.

Activism and subversion: 1984–1994

The institutionalisation of apartheid through the Extension of University Education Act of 1959 (RSA, 1959) resulted in universities designated for students from particular racial groups. This segregation had far-reaching influences in terms of the language of instruction, staffing, governance, resourcing and types of curriculum offerings (Bozalek & Boughey, 2012; Barnes, Baijnath & Sattar, 2010; McKenna, 2012). At that time, two types of institutions were in place. Technikons were established to deliver technical training, exposure to the workplace and award diplomas similar to British and American vocational training institutions, whereas academic universities offered degree programmes. The ML Sultan Technikon (where we began our careers as Planning lecturers) was considered a "historically black and disadvantaged" institution with inbuilt inequalities such as limited funding and a small range of educational choices and limited research activity.

The Department was established 35 years ago, at the then ML Sultan Technikon in the inner city of Durban. At that time, it was one of two higher education institutions in South Africa that trained a limited number of black planners mainly to service the planning administration needs of the apartheid homeland system.

The technikon system was based on a convener model in which a uniform set of codified programme offerings was on offer through the National Education Department 151 Report (RSA DoE, 1993). All technikon programmes were accredited through the Certification Council for Technikon Education (SERTEC). While the curriculum policy represented a top-down approach with the key purpose of producing technical planners to support government departments and private professional planners, there was a degree of autonomy at individual technikons within the broad parameters of subject guidelines.

From the late 1980s onwards, during the slow dismantling of apartheid, the removal of influx control and growing urbanisation and expansion in informal settlements, the content taught by the staff in the Department reflected activism and subversion of the curriculum. This was in large part due to the agency of the staff in the Department. It represented a shift from top-down bureaucratic and technical procedural planning to include a normative and critical approach which foregrounded informality in the economy and settlement patterns, participatory and action planning methods and acknowledged the political nature of planning. Some of the subject content such as environmental and project management in the Bachelor of Technology programme at universities of technology was ahead of its time as this did not generally form part of the mainstream Planning curricula in South Africa.

Furthermore, the demand for access to higher education from black students resulted in increased numbers of students onto the ML Sultan campus from approximately 4000 students in the early 1990s to approximately 12 000 students by 1995 (Barnes, Baijnath & Sattar, 2010:236). The increased demand for access to our programmes began in the early 1990s and included students from the predominantly lower Living Standards Measure bands, and rural and urban communities from across the country. The majority of these students was the first generation to gain access to higher education. Underpinned by a commitment to social justice, our Department was one of the first Town and Regional Planning departments to increase our student intake. Our student numbers increased from an average of 15 first-year students to 60 in this period. Changes taking place in the restructuring of local government and the anticipated need for increased Planning capacity motivated the increase in numbers as the country moved from four provinces and 11 homelands to nine new provinces, eight metropolitan areas, 44 district municipalities, and 226 local municipalities, all which would need qualified planners (Lincoln, 2016:555).

Setting the scene for transformation, engagement and support: 1995–2006

The official end of apartheid in 1994 and the start of democracy heralded the transformation of the structural architecture of the higher education system with a view to democratising knowledge and opening access to higher education to those formerly denied entry. The Higher Education Act of 1997 (RSA, 1997) established new national structures within the education sector. These structures included the Council on Higher Education (CHE), the South African Qualifications Authority (SAQA), the National Qualifications Framework (NQF), and National Standards Setting Bodies. The purpose of these structures was to assist with the implementation of education policy and quality assurance and promotion in the higher education and training sector. Standards generating bodies (SGBs) across sectors were established with the primary purpose of establishing standards and outcomes for particular academic fields and disciplines. These competencies were couched in the language of outcomes-based education (OBE), drawn from the Australian education system. For many higher education providers, this galvanised entire sectors into extensive consultations about their fields with a wider group, including related professionals and stakeholders, with a focus on exploring the content, skills and competencies needed for curriculum planning.

The professional Planning landscape

The transformation of Planning in South Africa reflects a complex history of the professionals operating in a multifaceted context. This milieu included the regulatory framework of various Statutory Councils,[1] two voluntary professional associations and rapid legislative and regulatory changes impacting on Planning practitioners generally. However, unlike other professions, the Planning fraternity was slow to respond to changes in the education sector and was fragmented between the old guard and the new order. Inertia and disarray characterised the state of the Planning profession before 1994. The Planning regulatory framework was firmly situated within

---

1 Two Acts have governed planning: The Town and Regional Planners Act of 1984 (SACTRP) (in operation until July 2004); the Planning Professions Act, No 36 of 2002 (SACPLAN) (operational from July 2004). Both Acts mandated to regulate the profession through the *registration* of professional and technical planners, the *accreditation* of planning qualifications from higher education institutions and *disciplinary matters* to protect the public from unprofessional planning work. Two voluntary associations are represented on the Council. SACTRP formally engaged with the education sector through its Education Sub-committee, represented by the "traditional" universities. The technikons were invited to this structure as "observers" for the first time in 1995.

apartheid Planning and the role of voluntary associations at the time (Harrison, Todes & Watson, 2007). This fragmented scenario continued into democracy and was evidenced, for example, in the inability on the part of the sector to establish institutional champions for the Planning Standards Generating Body 12 process. Similarly, the deferral in establishing the new statutory South African Council for Planners (SACPLAN) prolonged this delay; an opportunity lost for the Planning sector in higher education to shape their standards.

Planning academics relied on other instruments to address the standards generating gap. In particular, they used what became known as the "Bloemfontein Competencies" developed in 2000 by Planning educators in South Africa (Faling & Todes, 2004). These reflected a broad set of learning outcomes that were largely internationally aligned. This was in contrast to other professions such as engineering and surveying, who were quick off the mark to fulfil their professional responsibilities in generating competencies and standards. Planning exerts a significant influence across the built environment yet is a small profession. Therefore, the demands on Planning's existing capacity since democracy must be seen within the national transformation project where planners were thinly spread. Traditional universities, being ambivalent about the dictates of OBE, exacerbated this.

Institutional imperatives

Within the above context and from the early 1990s, ML Sultan Technikon and the Planning Department underwent sustained and multiple transformation pressures. Our institutional changes included the first merger of a higher education institution in South Africa in 2003, two changes in institutional name from the Durban Institute of Technology to the Durban University of Technology in 2007 (Barnes, Baijnath & Sattar, 2010), and changes in institutional leadership represented by six vice-chancellors. In the face of unprecedented demand for access to higher education from students previously denied such access, our Institution faced yearly student protests calling for affordable and relevant education. The student body was highly politicised and frequently invoked the Freedom Charter and discourses on free education in their demands. We were also mindful of the need to diversify our student body in terms of equitable gender intake and accepting students from rural and urban catchment areas. We were aware of the needs of the many first-generation students that were coming into our programmes.

Department responses

Our Institution, along with the rest of the technikon sector, was the first to engage with the overhaul of qualifications from 1995 to 2006 that introduced a new suite of qualifications spanning vocational and formal education. The impact of changes in the higher education sector through the new policy of OBE (Kraak, 1999), and the change in focus to a university of technology in 2007, also influenced the introduction of a suite of new qualifications. With the establishment of the National Qualifications Framework Act in 2008 (RSA, 2008), a key consideration in offering degrees at technikons was to remove the barriers to entry for technikon graduates into traditional university programmes through the articulation of pathways. In our case, this included the registration of the new National Diploma and replacement of the National Higher Diploma with a Bachelor of Technology degree.

From 1995–2003, two staff members from our Department became part of a team of 30 or so cross-disciplinary specialists on the National Standards Body 12 (Physical Planning and Construction) for the built environment to support the work of the Planning SGB. Between 1994 and 2000, the Department went through an intensive process of restructuring and registering new programmes with the revised NATED Report 151. In parallel, the Department underwent a professional accreditation visit in 1998 from the South African Council of Town and Regional Planners, who made a case for the registration of Bachelor of Technology graduates as full professionals. Two further SERTEC quality assurance events in 2000 and 2001[2] took place. The Committee on Tutorial Matters of the technikon sector established the use of generic guidelines (Genis, 1999). The key purpose of the guidelines was to assist the technikon sector to define their qualifications, nomenclature, and suite of programme offerings, modularisation options, and teaching methodology and assessment practices.

For our Department, this was an intense period of reflecting, rethinking, reworking, restructuring and making changes within the rapidly changing South African and global context of Planning education. Shay (2016:768) refers to "legitimation" and "curricula at the boundaries" in which the needs of both the academy and the professional workplace are considered and through this process curriculum then becomes legitimate. There is no doubt that the

---

2   The SERTEC visits in 2000 and 2001 were respectively to accredit the full programme offering and accredit the Work Integrated Component and student placements.

contestation related to curriculum development which took place during this period placed demands on academics, the profession, and the workplace.

In this time span, the Department's capacity was built through intense engagement with the then Academic Development Unit (ADU). The ingrained and inclusive curriculum development practices of the lecturing staff in the Department were refined through collaboration with the academic support staff from ADU. These collaborations encouraged us to engage in curriculum practices which were part of the Departmental iterative and action-orientated dialogue. The practice of including student voices in curriculum forums, staff-student meetings and industry liaison through Advisory Committees,[3] and a wide range of qualitative student feedback instruments have been invaluable for refining curriculum. These processes sensitised academics to the material conditions facing our students. For example, as a result of these insights, all students were provided with the necessary technical equipment at registration, to lessen financial disadvantages. The Department has been able to sustain this practice and costs are built into the academic fee structure. While providing equipment did not address the myriad of other challenges facing disadvantaged students, it allowed for a more level playing field for students in the teaching and learning spaces.

For the Department, this period was a shift from a "technical" focus to a more generalist Planning curriculum reflecting the current competencies needed by those in the profession. The introduction of the Bachelor of Technology, a one-year degree with a focus on design, environment, management and Geographic Information Systems, following a three-year National Diploma, allowed graduates to register for professional registration for the first time with the newly established South African Council for Planners (RSA, 2002). It opened access to professional registration for a much larger cohort of graduates from the university of technology sector. From 1996 to 2018, the university of technology sector in South Africa has produced a cohort of approximately, 3 000 Planning graduates. This represents a significant increase in qualified Planners for the profession in South Africa.

By the 2000s, our two programmes were well known in the academic sphere and the workplace. Articulation between the universities of technology and the traditional universities was well established as a result of protracted

---

3   Advisory Committees, made up of industry representatives, graduates and current students, were required to be established in all technikon academic departments to advise on curriculum work and changes in work requirements, amongst others, and continues to this day.

negotiations with the Education Advisory Committee of the Council (SACPLAN) and professional bodies. Our BTech graduates were able to enter master's programmes at traditional universities such as the University of KwaZulu-Natal, Pretoria University, the University of Cape Town and the University of the Free State. In addition, there was articulation between the three former technikons (now universities of technology).

At this time, our qualifications appeared to be closely aligned with the needs of South African society. The field of Planning was seen as part of the national development agenda, which was focused on ongoing developmental challenges such as housing backlogs, service delivery and infrastructural needs. The response in the form of local government Planning, the resurgence of strategic spatial Planning and the foregrounding of environmental issues were clearly reflected in our field's Bloemfontein Competencies (RSA, 2006).

The National Plan for Higher Education and the merger

The National Plan for Higher Education (2011) prioritised the establishment of a unified and nationally coordinated education system. The ML Sultan and Natal Technikon were the first higher education institutions to merge in 2002 as part of this plan (CHE, 2016) and was renamed the Durban Institute of Technology (DIT). ML Sultan Technikon was racially integrated from inception, whereas the Natal Technikon, a "white" technikon under the previous dispensation, was racially integrated in the late 1980s. The limits of this chapter preclude analysis of the complex nature of merger processes. In sum, its impact was felt in the life of the new institution for a sustained period. Mergers saw the introduction of more control mechanisms in higher education in the form of new managerialism and increasing neoliberal marketisation and administrative load on academics (Gordon & Lincoln, 2005).

Soon after the merger, the financial deficits of the new institution resulted in the Audit and Integration of Management Systems project in 2003, an austerity measure introduced by management (DIT, 2003). Our Department, because of the size, shape and the financial criteria used, was "put on probation", resulting in a shift in focus away from our core business, and a push to become "entrepreneurial" academics. This required staff to generate income through delivering short courses, to engage with knowledge production through research output, for staff to register for PhDs and a focus on efficiency in the system in terms of student throughput and pass rates. This scattered approach resulted in wasting substantial time and Departmental resources, rather than utilising these more strategically (Gordon & Lincoln, 2005). As mentioned, the merged institution has had six Vice-Chancellors since amalgamation, which contributed to a prolonged period of internal restructuring. Moreover, the Institution's identity, purpose and nomenclature changed over time from Technikon to Institute of Technology and then to University of Technology. These changes resulted in ongoing internal departmental restructuring and realignment.

Qualification alignment

As alluded to earlier, in 2004, higher education institutions were required to ensure that all their qualifications aligned with SAQA requirements. An institutional mechanism to assist this process was a requirement for each department to devise a Departmental Development Plan. The newly established Centre for Higher Education Development at the then DIT supported the departments in devising their Plans. This period signalled a weakened institutional capacity to support curriculum within academic departments largely due to changes in the size and shape of the institution. It was at a time when departments most needed support with recurriculation, but due to the merger restructuring, the Centre for Higher Education Development lost many of their key staff and were left with very little capacity to support departments.

Key changes at this time included the falling away of the technikon convener system and the reregistration of all existing qualifications with SAQA in 2006, in line with the transformation objectives outlined in the White Paper (RSA DoE, 1997) and the size and shape debate lead by the CHE on differentiation and diversity within a seamless national qualification system (Barnes, Baijnath & Sattar, 2010:12). This required making choices between what Muller (2009:221) describes as occupational fields and professional qualifications in our sector that ultimately settled on a professional degree.

Waiting for an implementation plan for the Higher Education Qualifications Sub-Framework: 2006–2011

In 2006, our Department, with the assistance of Centre for Higher Education Development staff, began reviewing our existing academic offerings for registration on the new HEQSF, Gazetted on 6 October 2007 (RSA DoE, 2007). The two existing programmes offered by our Department, namely, the National Diploma: Town and Regional Planning and the BTech: Town and Regional Planning were resubmitted to SAQA for approval. However, there was no implementation plan for the new HEQSF, and all existing qualifications rolled over until the framework was finalised. The result was a waiting game.

Recurriculation and a proposal for a coursework master's

As outlined in the previous section, while curriculum processes focused on restructuring the existing National Diploma and BTech programmes in the early 2000s, by 2011 new programmes were shaped. The review of our current curricula and deliberations on new programmes were informed by discussions with colleagues in similar departments in the university of technology sector in South Africa and also by international literature on Planning education and practice (Friedmann, 2005; Healey, 2006; Rakodi, 1997; RTPI, 2003; Frank, 2006; Diaw, Nnkya & Watson, 2002). From these discussions emerged discourses of sustainability, resilience, informality, applied new technologies, community engagement and large-scale infrastructure projects. The Qualifications Authority, our institution and the Planning profession foregrounded international benchmarking. In our curriculum planning, our Department took the call for international comparability seriously, as discussed below.

In the mid-2000s the Department decided to develop a coursework master's qualification. There were two main reasons for this. Firstly, we were constantly aware of our fragile financial viability, and we believed that one way of offsetting this was to offer a master's degree programme. Secondly, we needed postgraduate students to generate and support research in the Department to develop our future tutors and young academics (DUT, 2008). A substantial amount of time was spent on curriculating this proposed qualification. An international expert was flown in to run a week-long workshop, and the Centre for Higher Education Development ran internal curriculum workshops. However, the delay in the revision of the HEQSF placed the approval of our proposed master's degree on indefinite hold. This intensive curriculation process was ultimately abandoned because it became increasingly clear that it would be very difficult to garner support and access the resources to support a coursework master's degree. By 2015, the Department opted to offer an "off-the-shelf" generic research-based master's qualification.

As previously indicated, the SGB for Planning required by SAQA was established in 2006 but did not get off the ground. There was not enough sustained interest from academia and voluntary professional bodies, for example, the South African Planning Institute did not have the human resources available. Therefore, the status of the SGB for the field of Town and Planning was never finalised. As a result, the competencies for the profession, which should have been generated by the SGB, and which needed to be in place to guide any new programme development or ongoing reflection on existing curricula, was in limbo until 2014 when SACPLAN published a set of competencies. This was by no means an ideal situation in which the Council played the role of both player and referee: standards setting and quality assurer.

Opportunities for international conversations: International benchmarking and African networks

In this section two international opportunities for bench-marking and networking will be briefly looked at in terms of the implications for our curricula, namely, the UK's Royal Town Planning Institute visit in 2007 and the activities of the Association of African Planning Schools from 2008 onwards.

We invited the Royal Town Planning Institute to benchmark our programmes. The Royal Town Planning Institute visited the Department in 2007 and produced a belated benchmarking report (RTPI, 2009) that proved to be inconsequential. The Department was commended for its good practices and high standards, but the Royal Town Planning Institute's set of learning outcomes were not explicitly applied to our programmes to provide a basis for direct comparison with similar programmes in the UK or elsewhere. At the end of this process, we had not gained any additional insight into curriculum practices internationally.

In the second instance, the Department engaged with the activities of the Association of African Planning Schools to gain insight into what was happening in Planning schools on our continent. The expressed purpose of the Association of African Planning Schools was "improving the quality and visibility of Planning pedagogy, research and practice in Africa, and promoting Planning education advocating ethical, sustainable, multicultural, gender-sensitive, and participatory Planning practice" (AAPS, 2012:1). The Association of African Planning Schools ran three well attended Revitalising Planning Education conferences in the period of 2008 to 2012 (Watson & Odendaal, 2013:100). The aim of the 2010 conference was "to agree on the methodological as well as substantive elements of curricula reform in Planning education in Africa" (AAPS, 2009:2-3).

These conferences and various workshops organised by the Association of African Planning Schools were critical in raising a continental African academic identity and a network in the field of Planning education. We attended two of the three conferences. These events also foregrounded the Department's "outsider" university of technology identity at that time as offering only undergraduate programmes. Interestingly, there were no academic curriculum developers present at the conferences; the implicit assumption being that academics could develop programme articulation, curricula structures, teaching and learning modalities, assessment approaches based on their experience as academic programme directors, heads of departments, lecturers and researchers. Notable too was the absence of student participation.

The second conference in 2010 was structured around five themes that were considered underrepresented in Planning curricula: informality, the natural environment and global warming, spatial Planning and infrastructure, access to land by the poor and actor collaboration. These themes were already integrated as significant components of our programmes (DUT, 2011a:17-22). The conference themes encouraged the Department to reflect on the conceptual logic of how and where in our programmes these themes were taught. The focus on informality and decolonising curricula, couched in transformation discourse, clarified our Department's view as to how privilege is structured and justified (Shay, 2016:768).

External and internal quality assurance events

SACPLAN's[4] first visit as a newly constituted statutory accrediting body to our Department took place in 2009. At this point, the programmes offered by the DUT had been accredited eleven years ago, in 1998, by the then South African Council for Town and Regional Planners (SACTRP) when the institution was still a technikon (DUT DTRP, 2008). This time lapse was by no means ideal; the national education landscape and the institution itself was very different eleven years on. SACTRP, which had to deal with shifts in its own internal reconfiguration, was in some disarray in the early 2000s. However, it was kept informed of changes through interim reports produced by the Education and Training Committee, a sub-committee of the old and new Councils. The accreditation outcome, which covered five years from 2004 to 2008, was recorded as "meets the criteria for full accreditation" after a two-year delay in producing the final report.

Furthermore, the DUT internal Departmental evaluation, that runs on a four-yearly cycle, preceded the professional accreditation, that aims to run on a five-year cycle. The internal self-evaluation was a rigorous two-day process run by the DUT's Centre for Quality Promotion and Assurance with a panel consisting

---

4 According to the Higher Education Act and the Higher Education Quality Committee, and the Planning Profession Act of 2002, Section 8(4)(b) and (c), it is the responsibility of SACPLAN to accredit professional planning programmes.

of another department's Head of Department as well as representatives from industry, local government and students. This mechanism is designed as an instrument to support departments' self-evaluation processes and the development of improvement plans.

The external SACPLAN accreditation visit and the internal Centre for Quality Promotion and Assurance-driven self-assessment events were useful for the Department as self-reflective exercises. Although these assessment events were necessary in terms of being accountable, they were ultimately compliance focused. The anticipated injection of criticality and the opening up of discussions on knowledge production and on what it means to be a Planner and an academic in the field of Planning did not take place.

Curriculum development support: A departmental perspective

As previously stated, the Department engaged with the post-1994 changes in the educational landscape through sustained academic conversations with the then Academic Development Unit, usually in the format of workshops and meetings. The new Centre for Higher Education Development continued to engage directly with departments. From 2002 to 2007, the Department engaged with a curriculum developer regularly. It took the form of structured working sessions tackling the SAQA requirements and implications, the ongoing content shifts within the existing programmes and the development of a master's qualification.

The aftermath of the merger and the delay in finalising the HEQSF influenced the Department's curriculum activities in the 2006–2011 phase. It is evident from the internal and external evaluations and benchmarking events from this period, that the Departmental curriculum-related activities were underpinned by the work done earlier in the decade. This took the form of intense engagement with the SAQA processes, the authors' engagement with National Standards Body 12 and the support of an assigned Centre for Higher Education Development curriculum developer.

The fine-grained work done by DUT curriculum developers from 1999–2007 pre- and post-merger is evident in our Departmental records, which show detailed archives of meetings, discussions and workshops tailor-made to our curriculum concerns. Unfortunately, this academic development support petered out completely towards the end of the decade due to stretched capacity across the Institution. From here onwards, academic curriculum developers played an ancillary role rather than providing meaningful department-specific support. Curriculum support was provided via the faculties with senior management and a faculty curriculum officer who was focused on completing checklists, complying with set management systems and filling in proformas. As McKenna (2012:7) cautions, "there is the potential for an institutional culture to become immersed in a 'culture of performativity' (Shore, 2010:25) and for staff development practitioners to be seen as complicit in this, leading to a culture of compliance over critique." Although we were uncomfortable with a culture of performativity, we felt compelled to comply with institutional and national requirements. Despite this, in small ways, we attempted to disrupt the prevailing rule-bound approach to curriculum development and the academic project as a whole through maintaining a student focused approach in institutional curriculum forums.

Despite the difficulties described above, in our opinion, the programme evaluations and curriculum assessment initiatives, the work on the abandoned coursework master's degree, and the international-benchmarking exercise laid the foundation for the Department's capacity and contributed to the "big" recurriculation process that began in 2010.

Curriculating for a new programme

During this period, we developed our new programmes, the Bachelor of the Built Environment: Urban and Regional Planning programme and the Bachelor of the Built Environment (Honours): Urban and Regional Planning programme in line with the new HEQSF (CHE, 2013).

In preparation for this, our Department conducted an intensive two-day curriculum development workshop in 2011. This workshop was conceptualised and run by the academics in the Department. We invited an external academic in the Planning field and an internal academic development specialist to attend the workshop. We engaged with our Institution's programme design policies and directives, the desired graduate attributes, as well as the draft core competencies developed by SACPLAN. We researched core curriculum in international case studies and conducted a survey drawn from our Work-Integrated Learning employers on the desired knowledge and skills required from graduates in the workplace. Similarly, the national discourse on curricula reform, and growing demands on higher education practitioners to include vocational, problem-solving and applied knowledge fed into our curriculum discussions (Shay & Peseta, 2016).

This workshop formed the platform for what was to follow until the registration of the Bachelor of the Built Environment: Urban and Regional Planning programme in 2016. The tasks involved were: the arduous development of the proposed programme structure in line with the Institution's directives; multiple iterations of proformas, checking that the naming of programmes complied with the HEQSF work (CHE, 2013); checking of Higher Education Management Information System categories; assigning credit values and much more. These onerous technical and administrative requirements sapped energy and took some of the focus away from the "real" curriculum work of reflecting on knowledge construction, our students' understanding of the academic project and our pedagogy.

Present struggles – a mixed bag of wins and losses: 2011–2019

From 2011, the DUT began a process of developing an Institution-wide revised strategic plan in response to the impending changes to the existing HEQSF, the possible implications of the changes for programmes offered, and the fundamental challenges facing the university as it changed from a Technikon to a University of Technology. Key focus areas finally adopted in the 2015–2019 Strategic Plan included student-centredness and student engagement, and a major Curriculum Renewal Project for the suites of programme offerings across Faculties (DUT, 2015). The key purpose of the renewal project was that "DUT's curriculum and pedagogy must be intentionally designed to prepare our graduates for employment, critical citizenship and effectively engage with knowledge generation in an increasingly globalised world" (DUT, 2011b). The Curriculum Renewal Project was considered a defining project for the DUT in which critical engagement with the new curricula, the inclusion of general education modules in the liberal arts tradition, theoretical and conceptual learning and the more effective use of technology in teaching and learning, were introduced.

The "general education" component introduced the liberal arts curriculum into the traditional domain of career-orientated technical education. The intention was to develop engaged students who can operate beyond silos, recognising the complexity of contemporary society. The outcome of this model included both compulsory and elective department-specific offerings for all DUT students, in areas spanning the environment and sustainability, globalisation, sociology, academic literacy, language electives, amongst others. Given the nature of Planning as a discipline that is epistemologically underpinned by the social sciences, with social justice and inclusive practices foregrounded, this was an opportunity to enrich our new programmes.

The HEQSF (CHE, 2013), finally promulgated in 2013, had a profound impact on the programme offerings at universities of technology, in particular, the scrapping of the Bachelor of Technology from the framework (CHE, 2013). The previous system allowed for routes of articulation for students across institutional types. The new HEQSF (CHE, 2013) limited "hopping across" academic ladders and represented a closing down of opportunities for students from our programmes. Furthermore, the impact of the new framework on the professional registration of graduates with SACPLAN was unclear. Our graduates raised their concerns with us in workshops held by SACPLAN. Our Department made a submission to SACPLAN urging them to resolve the uncertainty created by the HEQSF (CHE, 2013) for the professional status of BTech graduates from universities of technology. To date, these concerns have not been addressed. This contributed to our Department's fundamental change in programme offerings from diploma and technical degree offerings to bachelor's degrees which we anticipated would create the best academic and professional access for our students.

SACPLAN: Professional accreditation for 2009–2013 and guidelines for competencies and standards for Curricula Development 2014

The SACPLAN accreditation visit took place in 2014. At this point, the DUT had already submitted its Programme Qualification Mix[5] to the Department of Higher Education and Training and the Department had already developed the set of module descriptors for the future Bachelor of the Built Environment: Urban and Regional Planning. In effect, this accreditation was looking back on programmes that would no longer be on offer by the next SACPLAN accreditation visit scheduled for 2020. As a result, this round of accreditation was fundamentally compliance driven.

SACPLAN's newly minted Planning Competencies (SACPLAN, 2014) was released after our accreditation visit and therefore not included as criteria. These competencies required retrofitting into the above-mentioned set of module descriptors for the future Bachelor of the Built Environment

---

5   A Programme and Qualification Mix is a list with relevant details of all qualifications submitted by all universities in South Africa which are to be approved by the Minister of Higher Education and Training.

(Hons): Urban and Regional Planning programme, in addition to the required DUT graduate attributes, creating another administrative burden for the Department. Contestation took place around the HEQSF (CHE, 2013) levels and the hierarchy of qualifications as these related to the requirements for professional registration in the field of Planning. As discussed previously, bridging the gap left by the Bachelor of Technology qualification has not yet been articulated by the Department of Higher Education and Training nor SACPLAN. Given that the Bachelor of Technology was previously a pathway to master's programmes, this silence left it up to universities of technology to find a solution very quickly in the face of questions and concerns from our graduates and our field in general. The Bachelor of the Built Environment (Honours): Urban and Regional Planning programme will be the progression to our master's programme, but articulation with other master's programmes has not been finalised.

The initial intensive curriculation processes in 2011–2012 were largely a Departmentally driven project with little theoretical or content-related input from the academic support sector. The period from 2012 to the submission of the new bachelor's degree to the Department of Higher Education and Training in 2015 was an ongoing process of managerialist compliance; with directives from the weekly re-curriculation meetings, to the Centre for Quality Promotion and Assurance, to online submissions to the CHE and SAQA.

2019 Curriculum activities

At the time of writing, our Department had completed a successful mid-term review of the roll-out of the first half of the Bachelor of the Built Environment (Honours): Urban and Regional Planning programme. We are concurrently reviewing our module descriptors as we roll these out for the first time. Reflective curriculum practices continue even though the intensive re-curriculation project has been completed.

Currently, our Department is bursting at the seams with 230 students across three programmes. This increase in numbers is as a result of the demand created by the phasing out of the Bachelor of Technology programme and the ever-increasing pressure to take in more students to improve the financial viability of the Department. The phasing in of the new Bachelor of the Built Environment (Honours): Urban and Regional Planning programme and the phasing out of the old National Diploma has created a slew of administrative tasks needing to be undertaken. This is on top of the requirement for staff to undertake research and complete higher degrees. The impact of this at a

Departmental level has been the increasing administrative load imposed by the managerialist agenda of "surveillance and evaluation, bureaucracy and administration" (McKenna, 2012:8).

Conclusion

In reflecting on the curriculum practices of the Department, it is evident that the alignment of our curricula to the national development transformation objectives in a democratic context has been arduous. The field of Planning, by its very nature, is implicated in issues of transformation and social justice. Students who register for our courses generally see the field as potentially transforming and life-changing and as a relevant profession that can make an impact on society. This context has shaped our academic practice in the following ways: to increase access to higher education, to generate programme and curriculum content that is relevant, and a push to develop a more inclusive profession.

The continuity of our Department's engagement with curriculum development is partly a result of relatively stable staff in the Department over the last 30 years. The institutional memory of our staff is a significant factor in the social production of curriculum development. The knowledge and curriculum practices gleaned over a substantial time frame forms a basis for transfer and co-production of the curriculum with new staff. Continuity, memory, transfer and co-production: these constitute significant components of the Department's resilient curriculum practices. Sound student relations have furthermore contributed to positive inputs and responsive curricula.

Some curriculum development initiatives were disheartening exercises in futility. The abandonment of our coursework master's qualification was due to a lack of institutional resources and the delays and contestations in the national higher education field at the time. The academics and practitioners in the field of Planning were unable to consolidate the SGB formation, and as a result, were unable to own the process. The dropping of the Department's draft unit standards once the HEQSF decided to move away from unit standards was yet another waste of our resources.

The international interactions with the Royal Town Planning Institute and Association of African Planning Schools were useful as they fed into our curriculum activities but did not have a significant impact in terms of innovative practices or content. The external SACPLAN accreditation visits and the internal Centre for Quality Assurance-driven self-assessment events were useful for the Department as self-reflective exercises but not the injection of innovative ideas and criticality that we were hoping for. In short, these were in the main compliance-focused events.

The fine-grained work undertaken by DUT curriculum developers from 1999 to 2007 – pre- and post-merger – should be celebrated. Academic curriculum developers are currently cast in the role of administrators rather than "doers" within the confines of an aggressively managerialist higher education paradigm (CHE, 2016). At present, the Department's intention to continue with its action-research based approach to curriculum development seems to be a quixotic project in the face of fewer resources, more students, an escalation of compliance-based administrative work and a loss of focus on the academic project. From our perspective, we want to engage with academic curriculum developers as we navigate the rollout of our new programmes within the rapidly shifting national and global challenges of the 4th industrial revolution, Artificial Intelligence, new technologies and knowledge areas and applications. In our view, these new challenges will continue to disrupt curriculum practices and require sustained conversations on how we conceptualise choices as academics, academic developers and universities. To engage with these challenges, we require disruptive spaces that allow us to interrogate our roles in the academic project.

References

AAPS (ASSOCIATION OF AFRICAN PLANNING SCHOOLS). 2012. Constitution of the Association of African Planning Schools. [https://bit.ly/2lVbYzL]

AAPS (ASSOCIATION OF AFRICAN PLANNING SCHOOLS). 2009. Concept Note for Discussion: Preparation for Association of African Planning Schools, 2nd Conference on Revitalising Planning Education, 2010. Draft 2.

ASMAL, K, HADLAND, A. & LEVY, M. 2011. *Kader Asmal: Politics in my blood: A Memoir*. Johannesburg: Jacana Media.

BARNES, T.; BAIJNATH, N. & SATTAR, K. 2010. *The restructuring of South African higher education: Rocky roads from policy formulation to institutional mergers, 2001-2005*. Pretoria: University of South Africa Press.

BOZALEK, V. & BOUGHEY, C. 2012. (Mis)framing Higher Education in South Africa *Social Policy and Administration*, 46:688-703. [https://doi.org/10.1111/j.1467-9515.2012.00863.x]

BAWA, A.C. 2014. Towards Relevance, Responsiveness and Resilience. *Strategic Plan 2015-2019, Durban University of Technology*. [https://bit.ly/2lR9BOh]

CHE (COUNCIL ON HIGHER EDUCATION). 2016. *South African higher education reviewed: two decades of democracy*. Pretoria: CHE. [https://bit.ly/2klWpk1]

CHE (COUNCIL ON HIGHER EDUCATION). 2013. *The Higher Education Qualifications Sub-Framework*. Pretoria: CHE. [https://bit.ly/2mePCcr]

CHE (COUNCIL FOR HIGHER EDUCATION). 2011. *Higher Education Qualification Framework Implementation Handbook*. Pretoria: CHE. [https://bit.ly/2kECKfy]

Diaw, K.; Nnkya, T. & Watson, V. 2002. Planning education in sub-Saharan Africa: Responding to the demands of a changing context. *Planning Practice and Research*, 17:337-348. [https://doi.org/10.1080/026974502200005689]

Du Toit, A. 2007. Autonomy as a Social Compact. *CHE Higher Education, Institutional Autonomy and Academic Freedom (HEIAAF)*, 4 (February 2007). Pretoria: CHE. [https://bit.ly/2mePIRl]

DIT (Durban Institute of Technology). 2003. Vice-Chancellor Communique, 18 August.

DUT (Durban University of Technology). 2011a. Department of Town and Regional Planning: Student Handbook.

DUT (Durban University of Technology). 2011b. Note on Curriculum Renewal at DUT: Curriculum Task Team.

DUT (Durban University of Technology). 2008. Motivation to the Department of Education to offer a Master's Programme: M.Technology: Planning Infrastructure and Environment. Unsubmitted Document.

DUT DTRP (Durban University of Technology. Department of Town and Regional Planning). 2008. Accreditation Report for the South African Council of Planners (Sacplan) 2004-2008. Unpublished Report.

Faling, W. & Todes, A. 2004. Employer perceptions of planning education in South Africa. *Town and Regional Planning*, 47:31-43. [https://bit.ly/2kRqs3p]

Frank, A.I. 2006. Three decades of thought on planning education. *Journal of Planning Literature*, 21:15-67. [https://doi.org/10.1177/0885412206288904]

Friedmann, J. 2005. Globalization and the emerging culture of planning. *Progress in Planning*, 64:183234.[https://doi.org/10.1016/j.progress.2005.05.001]

Genis, E. 1999. Technikon Qualifications in the National Qualifications Framework: Guideline for the preparation of Technikon Qualifications for registration. Committee of Technikon Principles.

Gordon, T. & Lincoln, G. 2005. Financial Modelling: When good education practice is not enough. Lessons Learned. Paper at SAADA Conference, Durban University of Technology, Durban, 27-30 November.

Harrison, P.; Todes, A. & Watson, V. 2007. *Planning and transformation: Learning from the post-apartheid experience*. London: Routledge.

Healey, P. 2006. Relational complexity and the imaginative power of strategic spatial planning. *European Planning Studies*, 14:525-546. [https://doi.org/10.1080/09654310500421196]

Kraak, A. 1999. Competing education and training policy discourses: A 'systemic' versus 'unit standards' framework. In: J.D. Jansen & P. Christie. *Changing Curriculum. Studies on Outcomes-based Education in South Africa*. Kenwyn: Juta, 21-58.

Lange, L. 2017. 20 Years of higher education curriculum policy in South Africa. *Journal of Education*, 31-57. [https://doi.org/10.17159/10.17159/2520-9868/i68a01]

Lincoln, G. 2016. Regional Planning in South Africa: An unfulfilled mandate from 1994? In: S. Ledwon & G. Perry (eds). Cities we have vs Cities we need. 52 International Society of City and Regional Planners Conference. Durban, South Africa: ISOCARP. [https://bit.ly/2kEDrWc]

McKenna, S. 2012. Interrogating the Academic Project. In: L. Quinn (ed). *Re-imagining Academic Staff Development: Spaces for Disruption*. Stellenbosch: African Sun Media.

Muller, J. 2009. Forms of knowledge and curriculum coherence. *Journal of Education and Work*, 22: 205226. [https://doi.org/10.1080/13639080902957905]

Quinn, L. 2012. *Re-imagining academic staff development: Spaces for disruption*. Stellenbosch: African Sun Media. [https://doi.org/10.18820/9781920338879]

Rakodi, C. 1997. The urban challenge in Africa: Growth and management of its large cities. Tokyo: United Nations University Press.

RSA (Republic of South Africa). 2013. *Spatial Planning and Land Use Management Act 16 of 2013*. Pretoria: Government Printing Works.

RSA (Republic of South Africa). 2008. *National Qualifications Framework Act 67 of 2008*. Pretoria: Government Printing Works.

RSA (Republic of South Africa). 2002. *Planning Profession Act 36 of 2002*. Cape Town: Government Printing Works, 1-40.

RSA (Republic of South Africa). 2001. National Plan for Higher Education. *Government Gazette*, 429(22138), 3-91.

RSA (Republic of South Africa). 1997. *Higher Education Act 101 of 1997*. Pretoria: Government Printing Works.

RSA (Republic of South Africa). 1959. *Extension of University Education Act 45 of 1959*. Pretoria: Government Printing Works.

RSA DoE (Republic of South Africa. Department of Education). 2007. Higher Education Qualifications Framework of October 2007. *Government Gazette*, 30353, 5 October.

RSA DoE (Republic of South Africa. Department of Education). 1997. Education White Paper 3: A programme for the transformation of Higher Education. *Government Gazette*, 386(18207), Notice 1196, 24 July.

RSA DoE (Republic of South Africa. Department of Education). 1993. Formal Technikon Instructional Programmes – Report 151, 1 April 1993. Degree Programmes. Pretoria: DoE.

RTPI (Royal Town Planning Institute). 2009. Royal Town Planning Institute benchmarking visit to the Durban University of Technology. Confidential Report.

RTPI (Royal Town Planning Institute). 2003. Education Commission Final Report.

Sacplan (South African Council for Planners). 2014. Guidelines for Competencies and Standards for Curricula Development. Midrand: Sacplan. [https://bit.ly/2m6p0Kx]

Shay, S. 2016. Curricula at the boundaries. *Higher education*, 71:767-779. [https://doi.org/10.1007/s10734-015-9917-3]

Shay, S. & Peseta, T. 2016. A socially just curriculum reform agenda. *Teaching in Higher Education*, 21:361-366. [https://doi.org/10.1080/13562517.2016.1159057]

Shore, C. 2010. Beyond the multiversity: Neoliberalism and the rise of the schizophrenic university. *Social Anthropology*, 18:15-29. [https://doi.org/10.1111/j.1469-8676.2009.00094.x]

Todes, A.; Harrison, P. & Watson, V. 2003. The changing nature of the job market for planning in South Africa: implications for planning educators. *Town and Regional Planning*, 46:21-32.[https://bit.ly/2m6AXjm]

Watson, V. & Odendaal, N. 2013. Changing planning education in Africa: The role of the Association of African Planning Schools. *Journal of Planning Education and Research*, 33:96107.[https://doi.org/10.1177/0739456X12452308]

CHAPTER 14

Defending the diploma

Academic developers as curriculum collaborators in technical contexts

Christine Winberg

A crisis in vocational higher education

Under apartheid, the South African higher education system comprised two basic types of higher education institutions: universities and technikons; the latter provided diploma-level higher education, usually although not always, in technical fields. Universities and technikons were segregated, and different institutions were designated for different racial groups. The Higher Education Act (RSA, 1997) changed the landscape of South African higher education by merging historically white and historically black institutions. It also attempted to address the "fragmentation, inequality and inefficiency that are the legacy of the past" and "create a learning society which releases the creative and intellectual energies of all our people towards meeting the goals of reconstruction and development". The Act also changed the nomenclature of higher education institutions to "universities", "comprehensive universities", and "universities of technology" to encourage diversity in the higher education system (Cloete, 2010). South African universities of technology were thus created by decree, in a way that was similar to the creation of the post-1992 universities in the UK. That is, they were not expected to meet any particular criteria to be awarded the title "university of technology", unlike, for example, in Ireland where the polytechnics and institutes of technology were expected to meet certain criteria before they were acknowledged as fully-fledged universities (for example, Elwood & Rainnie, 2012). The South African higher education system is hierarchical with research-intensive universities occupying the highest level, the comprehensive universities focusing on mass higher education, and the universities of technology offering technology-based qualifications.

The specific mission of the universities of technology was to drive the technological aspects of South Africa's ambitious reconstruction and development plan. Hence in 1995, immediately following the first democratic elections in South Africa, the Technikons Act (RSA, 1993) was repealed, and Technikons were permitted to offer degrees – which they did, often without clear criteria for the award of undergraduate or postgraduate degrees (Cloete, 2010). The role and position of South African universities of technology within the National Plan for South African higher education is a topic of debate (RSA, 2001; Coleman, 2016). The six South African universities of technology are still under construction, trying to identify their institutional "distinctiveness", including the types of undergraduate and postgraduate qualifications they will offer. It is a sector in which there is considerable internal diversity, as is common in higher education systems under development (Clark, 2004; Morphew & Huisman, 2002), with some universities of technology showing progress in the establishment of research centres, industry and science-council partnerships and the successful graduation of master's and doctoral students. In other words, the universities of technology are still learning about what they can be and should be.

Despite their aspirations, most of the programmes offered by South African universities of technology are diploma-level qualifications that prepare students for direct entry into labour markets, supported by practice-oriented curricula, internships, and other forms of work-integrated learning. Diploma programmes educate technicians and technologists whose skills are important for developing economies (Banks & Chikasanda, 2015). Although most programmes are designed for specific professions and are accredited by professional bodies, many researchers and educators agree that there is a need to improve students' transition into the world of work (Baldry, 2016). In the past, university of technology graduates, on average, secured employment within 3-6 months of graduation (Van Broekhuizen, 2016), but this trend has reversed, and many diplomates currently struggle to find appropriate employment in the fields for which they are qualified. While many factors affect the employment of graduates, the mismatch between the skills that graduates develop in their university studies and those that employers require from graduates in the 21st century has been highlighted as a contributing factor (Pauw, Oosthuizen & Van Der Westhuizen, 2008). Kraak (2015) argues that this skills mismatch has exacerbated South Africa's skills shortages and adversely affected the employment prospects of diplomates more than other higher education cohorts. The skills mismatch contributing to growing student unemployment has been identified as "academic drift":

> We're not sure who we are ... as a sector we are hard on ourselves ... we are below par ... and I ascribe it to academic drift. ... Despite the fact that universities of technology are supposed to be closer to commerce and industry and have more opportunities ... We train technicians and technologists, not engineers, and not artisans. We need to ... admit that what the former technikons did was not so bad. The [Higher Education] Act says that technikons are now universities, but these definitions are lacking depth and are outdated.
> (Professor Lourens van Staden, Chairperson of the South African Technology Network, quoted in Dell, 2016)

It is the concerns raised about "academic drift" in universities of technology that this study addresses, focusing on how faculty-based academics and academic developers might collaborate in the development of appropriate curricula for diploma-level qualifications in technical fields. Technical programmes demand the regular review and updating of curricula because of the rapid changes in technical environments (Banks & Chikasanda, 2015). The role of academic developers in reviewing and developing technical curricula is a contested one and made even more complex when technical qualifications are undervalued by the institutions offering them.

All diploma programmes were declared invalid by the South African Council on Higher Education (CHE) in 2008, and the expectation was that new diploma-level programmes would replace these diploma programmes by 2016. While curriculum development in the context of specialised technical diplomas was understood to be a matter for faculty experts, the CHE programme accreditation process had requirements that created opportunities for faculty and academic development collaboration. There was very little guidance for this national recurriculation exercise, the single paragraph below being the only CHE statement on the purpose of diploma programmes (although it provided technical specifications for diplomas):

> [A diploma] primarily has a vocational orientation, which includes professional, vocational, or industry specific knowledge that provides a sound understanding of general theoretical principles as well as a combination of general and specific procedures and their application. The purpose of the Diploma is to develop graduates who can demonstrate focused knowledge and skills in a particular field. Typically they will have gained experience in applying such knowledge and skills in a workplace context. (CHE, 2013:8)

These few requirements left diploma programmes open to a wide range of interpretations – with many of the academics involved in the curriculum renewal project understanding the adverb "typically" to imply that workplace experience, whether in the form of clinical practice, industry experience, fieldwork, or the many other forms of practice found in diploma programmes was optional.

Academic developers in technical fields

Academic development has a long history within technical and science disciplines. According to Barrow and Grant, the first academic developers were "well-qualified academics from 'respectable' disciplines" (2012:469) with the perceived authority to participate in and advise on technical programmes. Several higher education institutions, particularly those with strong engineering (Olsson & Roxå, 2012) or health science programmes (Haider, Khalid, Leto, Verhovsek, Rochwerg, Manolakos & Patel, 2016), have continued the tradition of embedding disciplinary-based academic developers in technical departments. It has been a more recent trend, linked to rapidly increasing numbers of students in higher education, to locate teaching and learning centres and academic developers outside of faculties. These independent centres generally grew out of "central services such as registry, human resources, or library and information services" (Gosling, 2009), or out of student counselling centres (Walsh, 2017). Currently, more academic developers are located outside of faculties than within them (Henderson, Beach & Finkelstein, 2011), and because they provide professional development across a diversity of fields and disciplines, they tend to offer generic pedagogical training. The lack of a science or technical specialism amongst many academic developers has limited their roles as curriculum developers in technical programmes as "potentially 'inappropriate to ... science disciplines'" (Trowler & Cooper, 2002:17).

However, the idea that curriculum work in technical curricula is the sole domain of technical lecturers is changing. Firstly, curriculum development has become a specialised field in which academic developers are increasingly gaining expertise (Hobson, Knuiman, Haaxman & Foster, 2018). Secondly, technical fields themselves are incorporating more diverse content areas, and including concepts that are "philosophical, sociological, anthropological and psychological" (Placklé, Könings, Jacquet, Libotton, Van Merriënboer & Engels, 2017); often these concepts are more familiar to academic developers than technical experts. Thirdly, there is a need for the curriculum development team to become more interdisciplinary as the technical curriculum "no longer adheres to the boundaries of a single discipline and has become tightly integrated, often relying on interaction of multiple disciplines" (Lozano & Lozano, 2014:138). Curriculum development is increasingly influenced by socio-political contexts, the exclusion or low representation of black and non-traditional students in technical fields (Killpack & Melón, 2016), and the "decolonial turn" in science teaching (Le Grange, 2016). The growing awareness of the need for technical programmes to serve a broader educational purpose has created a space for academic developers in curriculum development, and for curriculum development as an interdisciplinary project (Henderson, Beach & Finkelstein, 2011), if not a "transdisciplinary" one (Sharunova, Butt, Kresta, Carey, Wyard-Scott, Adeeb, Blessing & Qureshi, 2017).

Theoretically framing collaboration between technical lecturers and academic developers

Legitimation Code Theory (LCT) (Maton, 2014) is a sociological framework that seeks to identify the knowledge structures underpinning practices and the specialist dispositions of the people who engage in them. LCT thus provides a way of theorising the knowledge bases of technical education, as well as an understanding of the social dispositions of those who engage in technical education. LCT "Specialization" dimension explains that there are epistemic relations to knowledge and social relations to knowledge-based practices. Maton argues that for every knowledge claim there is the existence of both an epistemic relation to the knowledge underpinning a particular practice, and a social relation to the dispositions of the knower engaging in the practice (Maton, 2014). LCT Specialization dimension was used by the curriculum researchers to theoretically frame collaboration between lecturers in technical fields and academic developers in curriculum work. Specialization reveals the complexity of different forms of knowledge and the different kinds of subjects and identities that arise from different knowledge practices. Specialization thus "helps to overcome knowledge-blindness without succumbing to knower-blindness" (Maton, 2014:202). The positions taken by practitioners in this study, who differed in their disciplinary knowledge and their orientations to curriculum development, can be represented on the Specialization plane (see Figure 14.1).

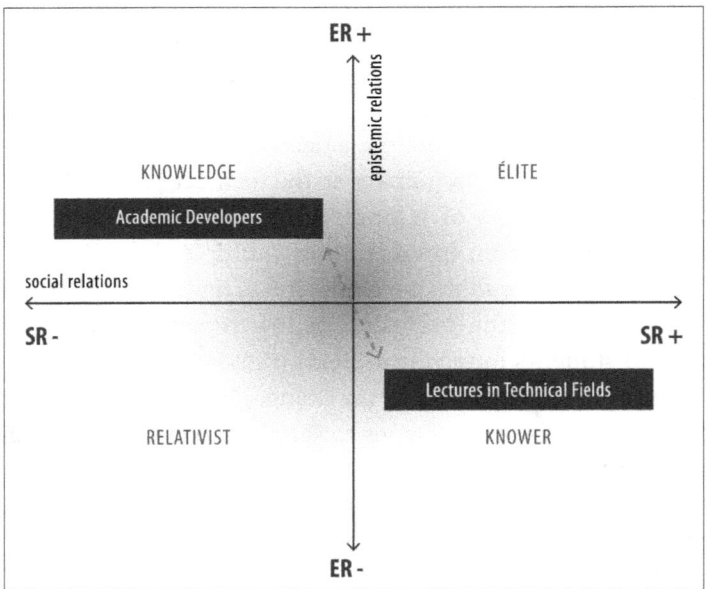

FIGURE 14.1 The Specialization Plane
[After Maton, 2014:29]

The vertical axis represents epistemic relations, in this case, it represents curriculum development practices that are strongly governed by scientific and technical knowledge. The horizontal axis represents social relations, in this case, curriculum development practice that is aligned to the teaching and learning relationship. Academic developers are thus placed in the "knower" quadrant because their orientation is more about pedagogy, about how students acquire knowledge (Matthews, Lodge & Bosanquet, 2015). Academic developers value the educational process, emphasising students' positive higher education experiences, internal motivation and intellectual growth. This is very different from the technical lecturers, who are more practically oriented, and for whom education is focused on the more pragmatic requirements of workplaces. They are thus placed in the "knowledge" quadrant. Technical qualifications can be found in different fields – engineering, applied sciences, accountancy and auditing, information technology, health sciences – each with its particular orientations to curriculum development and its pedagogical traditions – thus technical lecturers would be scattered across the continua. Most would, however, be characterised by stronger epistemic relations and weaker social relations, that is, stronger relations to technical knowledge and weaker relations to the facilitation of student learning. The academic developers, while aware of the importance of scientific and practical knowledge in technical qualifications, would tend to emphasise social relations, that is, the teaching and learning practices through which students acquire this knowledge.

The opposite locations of the technical lecturers and the academic developers on the Specialization plane mean that curricular collaboration is likely to be difficult, particularly when different aspects of the programme compete for curricular "space". In terms of the theoretical framework, what would be required for productive collaboration, is for academic developers to strengthen epistemic relations to technical programmes by developing a deeper understanding of the technical and practical knowledge base of the diploma, and for the technical lecturers to strengthen social relations, by developing a deeper understanding of the teaching and learning relationship (represented by the arrow in Figure 14.1). Developing an understanding of, and appreciation for, one another's different areas of work and expertise, would make interdisciplinary collaboration feasible (Englund, 2018). In interdisciplinary scholarship, this is called "interactional expertise" (Collins & Evans, 2015); that is, when each collaborator has a sufficient understanding of the others' disciplines or fields, collaboration becomes productive. An additional enabler of interdisciplinary work is the presence of a "boundary object" (Star & Griesemer, 1989), that is, an area of common ground or common concern for all participants in the curriculum project. The common ground might be to achieve "technical compliance" with the Council on Higher Education's curriculum requirements, as has often been the case in university of technology approaches to quality assurance (McKenna & Quinn, 2012); or common ground might, more productively, be found around improving students' experiences on diploma programmes. Galison (1997) explains that complex terminologies and concepts across disciplines make interdisciplinary collaboration difficult; thus, successful collaboration requires a "reduced common language" for communicating across research communities. Academic developers would need to "translate" educational terminology into terms and concepts that would be easier for technical lecturers to understand, thus enabling them to strengthen social relations in curriculum development practices. Finally, Nowotny, Scott and Gibbons (2001) recommend "transaction spaces" – safe spaces for collaboration, particularly at the start of an interdisciplinary project. Concepts from interdisciplinary scholarship, namely "interactional expertise" (Collins & Evans, 2015), "boundary objects" (Star & Griesemer, 1989), "inter-languages" (Galison, 1997) and "transaction spaces" (Nowotny, Scott

& Gibbons, 2001), are drawn on to show, in practical ways, how academic developers might strengthen epistemic relations, and how technical lecturers might strengthen social relations in productive interdisciplinary collaboration towards shared curricular understanding and practice.

A research design for studying curricular collaboration in technical programmes

In much academic development research, there are intersections between research and practice, researchers and practitioners. This was the case in this study. The description of the research methods below explains the different strands of curriculum development work, curricular research, and their inter-relationships.

The curriculum development project

The context of this study was a university of technology that was undergoing a large-scale curriculum renewal project. Curriculum development teams were established, comprising academic developers, the departmental academics who would teach on the new programmes, and academics from "service" departments, that offered Mathematics and Physics. One of the key focus areas of the curriculum project involved ways to include more basic sciences in diploma-level programmes to enable articulation between the diplomas and Bachelor of Science degree programmes that the university was beginning to offer. The inclusion of these more academic subjects was understood by the academic developers and the Physics and Mathematics lecturers as introducing what some call "powerful knowledge" (for example, Wheelahan, 2010) into practical diploma curricula. The technical lecturers, however, were concerned that the inclusion of additional mathematics and science subjects would detract from the practical nature of the diploma programme, which was key to developing students' practical competence required in the field of practice.

The curriculum research project

Placing the diploma programmes on a stronger scientific base was something that required evaluation. But it was mainly because the research site had been singled out in several reports (for example, Kraak, 2015) as experiencing rising graduate unemployment across technical fields, largely ascribed to "academic drift", that it was decided to establish a research project alongside the curriculum project to study the impact of introducing more basic sciences into technical diploma programmes.

The research team

The research team comprised a project leader, academic developers working in Engineering, Applied Sciences, and the Health Sciences, as well as faculty-based and service academic staff (that is, Mathematics and Physics lecturers) who had an interest in curriculum research. All research team members were also participants in the curriculum development work on the new diploma-level qualifications, and several members of the research team were undertaking their master's or doctoral studies on the curriculum renewal process.

TABLE 14.1 Sources of data for the study

	Programme	Participant Researchers	Data Source 1	Data Source 2
1	Diploma in Chemical Engineering	Academic Developer 1	CHE Application (completed)	Focus group interview
		Mathematics Lecturer 1		
		Physics Lecturer 1		
		Chemical Engineer 1		
2	Diploma in Civil Engineering	Academic Developer 1	CHE Application (completed)	Focus group interview
		Mathematics Lecturer 2		
		Civil Engineer 1*		
		Civil Engineer 2		
3	Diploma in Mechanical Engineering	Academic Developer 2	CHE Application (work-in-progress)	Individual
		Physics Lecturer 2		Group interview
		Mathematics Lecturer 3		
		Mechanical Engineer 1		Individual
4	Diploma in Electrical Engineering	Academic Developer 2	CHE Application (completed)	Focus group interview
		Mathematics Lecturer 4		
		Physics Lecturer 1		
		Physics Lecturer 2		
		Electrical Engineer 1		
5	Diploma in Radiotherapy	Academic Developer 3	CHE Application (work-in-progress)	Focus group interview
		Radiation Therapist 1**		
		Radiation Therapist 2**		
6	Diploma in Emergency Medical Rescue	Academic Developer 4	CHE Application (work-in-progress)	Focus group interview
		Physics Lecturer 3		
		Paramedic 1		

* Civil Engineer 1 requested to teach the Physics 1 course and became the "Physics Lecturer" for the programme.
** Radiation therapists 1 and 2 taught both the Medical Physics courses and Radiation Therapy subjects.

Data collection

The research team accumulated considerable data over the three years of curriculum renewal. As the curriculum renewal project neared its end, a number of focus group interviews were conducted with participants and researchers in which the CHE curriculum documents-in-progress or recently completed were discussed. The focus groups were programme-based and included the academic developer serving on the curriculum development team, the Physics and Mathematics "service" lecturers who were part of the curriculum development team, and one or two programme lecturers (see Table 14.1). (In one department a focus group proved too difficult to arrange, so individual interviews were conducted instead.) The interviews were artefact-based, that is, they were conducted with the most recent copies of the curriculum documents. The focus groups were asked to identify the selection of topics, activities and assessment tasks, and to explain why they were considered necessary for the diploma programme.

Data analysis

The interviews were recorded, and the recordings were transcribed by a professional transcriber, and initially coded using NVivo qualitative data analysis software. A second analysis ascribed Specialization codes to indicate whether the participants were expressing stronger (ER+) or weaker (ER-) epistemic relations, or whether they were expressing stronger (SR+) or weaker (SR-) epistemic relations. The ways in which the progression changed, that is, whether epistemic relations that tended to be weak due to lack of field knowledge, were becoming stronger (ER-↑), or whether weaker social relations were strengthening (SR-↑). The coding extract in Table 14.2 shows how positions were constantly shifting. The Physics lecturer strengthened social relations (SR-↑) when he talked about the benefits of the logic of Physics for students, the academic developer strengthened epistemic relations (ER-↑) when she proposed a "practical logic" for the technical curriculum.

TABLE 14.2 Examples of data analysis methods

Participant	Transcription	*In vivo* code	Specialization code
Physics Lecturer 1	Time is important to progress logically from one Physics concept to the next ...	"progress logically ... Physics concept"	ER+, SR−
Academic Developer 1	Can you teach just that one Physics concept that you need without teaching the progression ... the ones that build up to it?	"Can you ...?" (Question)	ER−↑, SR+
Physics Lecturer 1	If the students don't understand the logical progression ... then they are just fiddling ... then it's just trial and error ...	"students don't understand ..."	ER+, SR−↑
Chemical Engineer 1	In my experience, engineers, use the logic of problem-solving ... CDIO ... they're not solving Physics problems ... they're solving engineering problems ...	"problem-solving ..."	ER+, SR−
Academic Developer 1	So ... is it always the practical logic that needs to guide the curriculum logic?	"practical logic" (Question)	ER−↑, SR+

Technical lecturers and academic developers collaborating on curricula

The key research findings, clustered into four categories, explain how stronger epistemic relations were achieved by the academic developers through their development of interactional expertise over time, while the technical lecturers strengthened social relations through a focus on the boundary object of student success within, and beyond, the diploma programme. The academic developers' role in translating educational terminology and concepts enabled shared understandings, and their skilled ability to create safe "transaction spaces" were key to the successful collaboration.

From strangers in a strange land to becoming "bilingual"

In an article, titled *Strangers in a Strange Land*, Adendorff (2011) analysed the confusing experiences of faculty-based academics entering the field of higher education studies. Academic developers entering the world of technical education had similar disorienting encounters. Technical education was a foreign world to the academic developers in this case study, most of whom came to academic development from language or educational disciplines. Academic Developer 1 describes her first experience of observing practical teaching in Mechanical Engineering:

> ... it's not like a classroom teaching situation, but it is ... teaching ... or now I see that as teaching ... and even more ... I've come to really appreciate what [the lecturers] are trying to do.
>
> (Academic Developer 1)

Academic Developer 4 similarly explains her observations of clinical teaching in Radiation Therapy:

> There is a lot of actual teaching [in the clinical environment] ... I mean ... it's all about teaching ... I see the teaching ... and I must say ... compared with classroom teaching ... the students love it. (Academic Developer 4)

In both cases, the academic developers, despite their unfamiliarity with teaching in technical and clinical spaces, that is, their weaker epistemic relations to the disciplinary and field knowledge of the diploma programmes, appreciated what the technical lecturers were trying to achieve, and acknowledged that their teaching and learning practices had value, not least to students whose interests were practically-oriented. The interactions between programme lecturers and academic developers over the three years of the curriculum project, even though their life-worlds and teaching and learning practices were relatively far part, meant that collaborators had learned a considerable amount about one another's disciplines and practices.

The academic developers realised that for their educational knowledge to have any impact on curriculum development, it would be important for them to strengthen their epistemic relations to the fields in which they were working. The four academic developers in this case study were undertaking or had recently completed, doctoral studies that were relevant to the curriculum renewal project – they were thus reading the research literature on curriculum development in technical fields, presenting papers in engineering or health education conferences, and writing articles for discipline-based educational journals:

> For me to speak with authority to my colleagues on teaching and learning issues I need to understand their world ... in fact my discipline requires me to do that ... to learn from each other about teaching and learning. (Academic Developer 3)

The long time span of the project enabled the academic developers to develop enough interactional expertise, that is, strengthening of epistemic relations to the technical fields, for productive curriculum collaboration. As one of the academic developers explained:

> I've worked with them so much ... I've learned all the technical terms ... I've been in the classroom and in the clinic ... it's like I've become bilingual. (Academic Developer 4)

The metaphor of becoming "bilingual" exemplifies the nature of the interactional expertise needed for collaborative curriculum work, as well as the importance of communication across disciplinary and field boundaries.

The efforts made by the academic developers did not go unnoticed by the technical lecturers, who were open to ideas from academic developers who were prepared to learn about their worlds, and who appreciated the importance of diploma-level qualifications:

> [The Teaching and Learning Centre] was invaluable ... I mean once I established ties with them ... they have really helped me to carry on with [the diploma curriculum project] and gave motivation ... I'm actually trying to act inside our department trying to motivate others now.
> (Civil Engineer 1)

Finding common ground: Student learning as "boundary object"

The curriculum teams found common cause around student learning, and by placing the student at the centre of the curriculum. As one of the team members explained:

> The lecturer is not the important one ... the classroom belongs to the student. The student should learn through being involved ... but with the expert there to help them.
> (Civil Engineer 1)

Students' voices tend to be absent in curriculum development work (Bovill, Cook-Sather & Felten, 2011). At the time of the curriculum renewal project, the call to "decolonise the curriculum" following student protests (Le Grange, 2016) was not part of mainstream discussions in technical education. The focus was on "epistemological access" (Morrow, 2009), rather than epistemological justice. In the absence of actual student voices in the curriculum project, academic developers' contribution to the curriculum teams was to place epistemological access high on the agenda. This involved the academic lecturers in strengthening social relations to their field. For example, Radiation Therapist 2 explained that additional academic literacy and professional communication courses were included in the new curriculum as a direct result of prior collaboration with an academic developer, which raised her awareness around providing access to content knowledge:

> I had joint classes with [an academic developer] previously on giving [students] a piece of text background to a topic ... and then I go through the scaffolded reading exercise on it ... that whole notion of scaffolding a concept ... I incorporated it into the curriculum.
> (Radiation Therapist 2)

Following discussions with an academic developer, Physics Lecturer 2 changed his Physics curriculum to one that took a more "hands-on" approach to enable students' epistemological access to Physics concepts:

> [Academic Developer 2] showed me how I could have used something physical ... a machine part ... to demonstrate something better ... so I use a different approach now.
> (Physics Lecturer 2)

That an academic developer recommends using a "machine part" shows the extent to which she had strengthened epistemic relations to the field, while the lecturer's willingness to "use a different approach" shows a strengthening of social relations. The curriculum teams expressed similar ideas about how the curricula that they had developed (or were in the process of developing) were trying to support student learning:

> I think this curriculum is an attempt to improve teaching and learning broadly ... trying to create better learning experiences for our students. (Civil Engineer 2)

While teaching and learning practices in classrooms had impacted curriculum design, participants also explained how curriculum work had impacted their classroom practice:

> My involvement in this project has made me reflect quite a bit on the way I teach my own students. (Chemical Engineer 1)

One of the Radiation Therapists, explaining how she normally lacked the time to reflect on her teaching practice, found that she "got quite a degree of satisfaction and development from the curriculum project" (Radiation Therapist 2) and had used her experiences on the curriculum team to change some of her practices. Another participant contrasted curriculum meetings with normal departmental meetings:

> People sort of show and tell when we have our curriculum meeting ... sometimes we'll have something to share with maybe what we've done that we want to use in the new curriculum ... so that is put on the agenda ... so I think that these meetings ... these reflections ... are very different from when we have our [departmental] strategic planning that's very formalised. (Electrical Engineer 1)

The collaboration dispelled the idea that technical lecturers have narrow epistemic relations to training students in the technical knowledge and skills required for practice, and instead showed that they were equally concerned with social relations concerning the quality of students' learning and their adequate preparation for life beyond the university:

> You know in terms of curriculum developmental as a tool ... it's a tool we can use to develop our students ... to make a life for them. My philosophy is ... what I believe as a teacher is ... I must be there to co-ordinate the way they learn ... so that is how I think about the curriculum ... the technical knowledge must be there ... students must find that knowledge ... but I have to coordinate that. (Chemical Engineer 1)

Thus, while the technical lecturers and academic developers had different kinds of expertise which they brought to the curriculum renewal project, it was their commitment to ensuring that their students had positive and productive experiences that prepared them for meaningful work that united them as a team.

Facilitators, experts and brokers

The inclusion of more of the basic sciences in the new diploma programmes was the focal point of many curricular discussions. While no one disputed that the basic sciences underpinned the technical programmes, the issue was how much science was needed, which concepts should be selected, and how these should be sequenced. The technical lecturers struggled to defend the worth of practical training in diploma-level qualifications due to power differentials in the curriculum team. The technical lecturers tended to have technician's qualifications, while the Mathematics and Physics lecturers all had PhDs in their disciplines. The technical lecturers experienced additional marginalisation in the light of their own departments' aspirations to offer professional engineering degrees rather than technician qualifications, and the university's general shift towards valuing research over teaching expertise. As one of the lecturers put it: "... in this department people don't really care too much [about the diploma]" (Civil Engineer 1).

The Mathematics and Physics lecturers tended to feel that a core curriculum in their disciplines was necessary, while the technical lecturers felt that the focus of basic sciences should be on concepts that were relevant to the field of practice. The academic developers tried to understand the positions of both the technical and Mathematics and Physic lecturers, assuming the "broker" role described by Jacobs (2007), by asking basic questions about the issues at stake such as:

> Can you teach just that one Physics concept that you need without teaching the progression ... the ones that build up to it? (Academic Developer 1)

The academic developers tried to clarify issues and find a "transaction space" beyond polarised views of practical and theoretical knowledge to discuss curricular matters. This was no easy task:

> It was quite a tense thing at times ... (Paramedic 1)

Facilitating the work of such a diverse team is key to academic development work. Reflecting on the work of developing a new curriculum, an academic developer described her mediating role:

> It was a collective effort ... you put what needs to be taught for the year up on the board, and everyone would get together, and people will have some discussion

> amongst themselves about when it would be better for students to take a certain course and so on ... and then there'd be a lot of co-operation and communication amongst staff to get a better dispensation for everybody. (Academic Developer 3)

Practical theories for understanding curriculum

Academic developers have always supported new academics' transition to university teaching and learning (Matthews et al., 2014); in the case of technical or vocational programmes this role is particularly important as lecturers often come into academia with work experience, but with limited knowledge of curriculum development, pedagogy and assessment (Placklé et al., 2018). Paramedic 1, a new academic, explained how Academic Developer 3 supported his learning about curriculum:

> I mean things like a curriculum framework ... or the learning outcomes as we called it at the time ... I hadn't been introduced to that until I met [Academic Developer 3] because it wasn't something that we knew about in the field ... and I really appreciated that ... I certainly got supported in developing my curriculum. (Paramedic 1)

Part of the technical lecturers' appreciation of the academic developers' contribution was their theoretical understanding of curriculum, and their ability to "translate" theoretical knowledge into terms that made sense in the context of technical diploma programmes. Matthews and colleagues, in their study of academic developers working in science faculties, showed how academic developers acted as trusted experts, disseminating their educational knowledge within interdisciplinary groups (Matthews et al., 2015:246). The academic developers in this project drew on Shay's (2013) work on curriculum differentiation, to advance the idea that in vocational education the "logic of curriculum derives from practice" (Shay, 2013). The technical lecturers had a tacit understanding of this practical orientation but did not have the educational concepts to support their approach. Academic Developer 2 coined the term "practical logic" as the driver of curricular selection and sequencing in technical curricula. "Practical logic" and its variants such as "the logic of clinical practice" (Academic Developer 4), subsequently became a key principle for technical curriculum design. The term and concept of "practical logic" provided the technical lecturers with a tool to contrast the logic of the scientific disciplines with the logic of the technical practice for which the diploma programme was preparing students.

Working with academic developers helped both the technical and the Mathematics and Science lectures to develop a deeper understanding of the technical curriculum. Technical lecturers developed greater confidence in their insistence on the importance of "practical logic" in the diploma. Paramedic 1 explained:

> ... if you've got a problem, how are you dealing with it? Because if you just sit and say ... oh, we haven't got this or that equipment ... and we sit on our hands ... then what's going to happen? Are you just going to leave the patient? (Paramedic 1)

Participants agreed that the students would need a logical approach to problems encountered in practice, and this had encouraged Physics Lecturer 3 to change the logic of the Physics curriculum to reflect the logic of medical rescue:

> I've redesigned that whole Physics course [for medical rescue] in a way that articulated better with what they were doing, and it was more interesting to the students and more logical in terms of their practice ... so the students could get more value out of the course. (Physics Lecturer 3).

The academic developer in the Electrical Engineering group introduced curriculum mapping tools that enabled the team to compare Mathematics topics with those in Electrical Engineering subjects. They agreed that there were many cases of misalignment, with some topics needed for Electrical Engineering 1, such as setting up measuring systems only offered in Mathematics 2; while topics that were needed for almost all Electrical Engineering 3 applications were offered in Mathematics 1 at too low a level. Mathematics Lecturer 4 found that changing the Mathematics curriculum to align better with the Electrical Engineering subjects resulted in a more active and engaged class:

> Well ... looking at students how they fell asleep in my class ... yes ... I'm trying my utmost to keep them awake in class ... and I see now with my first years when they are interacting around an engineering problem ... while they're actually working on it in my [Mathematics 1] class ... they are more focused. (Mathematics Lecturer 4)

Terms and concepts such as "Mathematical tools" and the "Physics toolbox" became used as a shorthand amongst the teams to address issues of alignment between the basic sciences and the technical subjects.

Conclusion: Specialization reconsidered

The research team of lecturers and academic developers set out to understand the difference between "academic drift" and an appropriate knowledge base in technical diplomas, focusing on the role of Mathematics and Physics in technical curricula, and trying to understand how the basic sciences related to the field of practice and practical knowledge. The study has implications for academic developers working in technical and vocational fields. The first implication is the need for academic developers to attain "interactional expertise" (Collins & Evans, 2015), that is, to develop enough knowledge about the field in which they were working to enable meaningful collaboration. In this study, the willingness of the academic developers to learn about the technical fields created the basis for a range of collaborative practices. Academic developers, particularly those who work in curriculum, have powerful theoretical tools to bring to a collaborative curriculum project (Hobson et al., 2018), but theories are not useful if the academics who teach on technical programmes do not understand them. Thus the second implication for academic developers is the need to adapt their tools and terminologies for technical contexts, or to find equivalents that technical lecturers might be more familiar with. While technical lecturers are likely to have a tacit understanding of what they want to achieve in curriculum design, academic developers can provide access to the concepts and terms that make these ideas explicit, and the team can then develop a shared terminology for curriculum development in technical programmes. The practical help that academic developers offer concerning student engagement, lesson planning, and so on, needs similar adaptation to technical environments. Thirdly, academic developers in technical fields need to find out about pedagogies in these fields, usually through the discipline-specific educational literature and through attending discipline-specific educational conferences. Keeping up to date with key developments in technical education provides academic developers with the legitimacy and know-how needed to work with technical colleagues and advise on educational matters. Fourthly, academic developers need the interpersonal skills to negotiate curricula with lecturers, many of whom have a technical-rational worldview, and very little understanding of, or respect for, education as a discipline. Academic developers (at least in this case study) found themselves playing a mediating role between departmental colleagues, some of whom were undervalued in the team because they chose a teaching role rather than a research one.

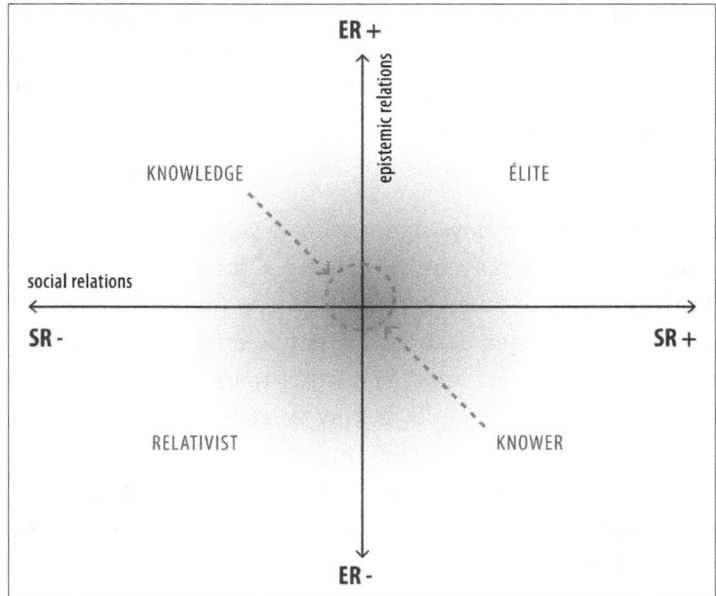

FIGURE 14.2 Strengthening and weakening epistemic and social relations to enable collaborative work in technical contexts

The dashed arrows in Figure 14.2 represent the journeys on the Specialization plane that technical lecturers and academic developers need to take if they are going to engage in a productive collaboration around curriculum. The arrows are dashed to represent temporary journeys away from their disciplinary bases to engage in the new "transaction space" of curriculum development. The academic developers need to strengthen epistemic relations to technical curricula by finding out more about the fields and practices of the technical areas in which they are working. Translating educational knowledge for technical lecturers involves weakening social relations to curricula to a level that is appropriate for the technical field and lecturers. The technical lecturers need to lower epistemic relations and strengthen social relation in order to access the specialised curriculum knowledge of the academic developers. The strengthening and weakening of epistemic relations and social relations occur through curricular conversations, rather than formal training. These informal methods of learning have been shown to be powerful in collaborative work (Englund, 2018). By drawing on both technical field knowledge, which in LCT terms, has stronger epistemic relations and weaker social relations, and curricular knowledge, which has weaker epistemic relations and stronger social relations, collaborators shift towards the "elite" quadrant, a space of optimal strength of epistemic relations and social relations that avoids polarised positions and supports productive collaboration. Shifting towards the "elite" quadrant, represented by the circle, is equivalent to the "transaction space" (Nowotny, Scott & Gibbons, 2001) needed for productive interdisciplinary work.

Academics and academic developers who develop and research technical curricula have a role to play in developing a principled understanding of technical programmes because without a strong understanding of technical diplomas there is a danger that the most powerful knowledge base of the university of technology sector will be further marginalised and undermined. Academic developers have a role to play in supporting the transformative possibilities of students engaged in technical higher education by understanding the curricular forms that enable engaged learning towards competent practice in technical fields. Diploma-level qualifications represent expanded life opportunities and possibilities of meaningful work for school leavers who did not achieve a bachelor's degree entrance pass. This is, therefore, an opportune time to reconceptualise the diploma as a qualification and the role that flows and transitions between diploma-level education and work practices could play in strengthening diploma curricula, student learning, and innovative teaching. Reclaiming practical knowledge and defending the diploma is a necessary step in re-building the university of technology sector.

References

ADENDORFF, H. 2011. Strangers in a strange land – on becoming scholars of teaching. *London Review of Education*, 9(3):305-315. [https://doi.org/10.1080/14748460.2011.616323]

BALDRY, K. 2016. Graduate unemployment in South Africa: social inequality reproduced. *Journal of Education and Work*, 29(7):788-812. [https://doi.org/10.1080/13639080.2015.1066928]

BANKS, F. & CHIKASANDA, V.K.M. 2015. Technology Education and Developing Countries. In: J.P. Williams, A. Jones and C. Buntting (eds). *The Future of Technology Education. Contemporary Issues in Technology Education*. Singapore: Springer, 217-238. [https://doi.org/10.1007/978-981-287-170-1]

BARROW, M. & GRANT, B. 2012. The 'Truth' of Academic Development: How did it get to be about 'Teaching and Learning'? *Higher Education Research and Development*, 31(4):465-477. [https://doi.org/10.1080/07294360.2011.602393]

BOVILL, C.; COOK-SATHER, A. & FELTEN, P. 2011. Students as co-creators of teaching approaches, course design, and curricula: implications for academic developers. *International Journal for Academic Development*, 16(2):133-145. [https://doi.org/10.1080/1360144X.2011.568690]

CHE (COUNCIL ON HIGHER EDUCATION) 2013. *Higher Education Qualifications Sub-Framework*. Pretoria: CHE. [https://bit.ly/2kqPFBA]

CLARK, B. 2004. *Sustaining change in universities: continuities in case studies and concepts*. Maidenhead: Open University Press. [https://doi.org/10.1353/rhe.2005.0043]

CLOETE, N. 2010. Higher Education Differentiation: the good, the bad and the incomprehensible. Paper presented at Stakeholder Summit on Higher Education Transformation, Cape Peninsula University of Technology, Franschhoek, 22-23 April. [https://bit.ly/2m0mDc9]

COLEMAN, L. 2016. Asserting academic legitimacy: the influence of the University of Technology sectoral agendas on curriculum decision-making. *Teaching in Higher Education*, 21(4):381-397. [https://doi.org/10.1080/13562517.2016.1155548]

COLLINS, H. & EVANS, R. 2015. Expertise Revisited, Part I – Interactional Expertise. *Studies in History and Philosophy of Science Part A*, 54:113-123. [https://doi.org/10.1016/j.shpsa.2015.07.004]

DELL, S. 2016. Rebranding 'second class' universities of technology, 18 November 2016. *University World News Global Edition*, 437. [https://bit.ly/2fIibHf]

ELWOOD, L. & RAINNIE, A. 2012. Strategic Planning in Ireland's Institutes of Technology. *Higher Education Policy*, 25(1): 107-129. [https://doi.org/10.1057/hep.2011.25]

ENGLUND, C. 2018. Exploring interdisciplinary academic development: The Change Laboratory as an approach to team-based practice. *Higher Education Research and Development*, 37(4):698714. [https://doi.org/10.1080/07294360.2018.1441809]

GALISON, P. 1997. *Image and Logic: A Material Culture of Microphysics*. Chicago: University of Chicago Press. [https://doi.org/10.1063/1.882027]

GOSLING, D. 2009. Educational Development in the UK: A Complex and Contradictory Reality. *International Journal for Academic Development*, 14(1):5-18. [https://doi.org/10.1080/13601440802659122]

HAIDER, S.; KHALID, Z.; LETO, D.; VERHOVSEK, M.; ROCHWERG, B.; MANOLAKOS, J.J. & PATEL, A. 2016. A Blueprint for Global Health Curriculum Development: The McMaster Internal Medicine Residency Program Experience. *Canadian Journal of General Internal Medicine*, 7(3):86-88. [https://doi.org/10.22374/cjgim.v7i3.134]

HENDERSON, C.; BEACH, A. & FINKELSTEIN, N. 2011. Facilitating Change in Undergraduate STEM Instructional Practices: An Analytic Review of the Literature. *Journal of Research in Science Teaching*, 48(8):952984. [https://doi.org/10.1002/tea.20439]

HENDERSON, C.; YERUSHALMI, E.; KUO, V.H.; HELLER, K. & HELLER, P. 2007. Physics faculty beliefs and values about the teaching and learning of problem-solving. II. Procedures for measurement and analysis. *Physical Review Special Topics: Physics Education Research*, 3(2):020110. [https://doi.org/10.1103/PhysRevSTPER.3.020110]

HOBSON, J.; KNUIMAN, S.; HAAXMAN, A. & FOSTER, J. 2018. Building a Successful Partnership between Professional Staff and Academics to Improve Student Employability. In: C. Bossu and N. Brown (eds). *Professional and Support Staff in Higher Education. University Development and Administration*. Singapore: Springer, 313-326. [https://doi.org/10.1007/978-981-10-6858-4_26]

INGERMAN, Å.; BERGE, M. & BOOTH, S. 2009. Physics group work in a phenomenographic perspective – learning dynamics as the experience of variation and relevance. *European Journal of Engineering Education*, 34(4):349-358. [https://doi.org/10.1080/03043790902989382]

JACOBS, C. 2007. Towards a critical understanding of the teaching of discipline-specific academic literacies: Making the tacit explicit. *Journal of Education*, 41(1):59-81. [https://bit.ly/2m0EWxS]

KAISERFELD, T. 2013. Why new hybrid organisations are formed: Historical perspectives on epistemic and academic drift. *Minerva*, 51(2):171-194. [https://doi.org/10.1007/s11024-013-9226-x]

KILLPACK, T.L. & MELÓN, L.C. 2016. Toward inclusive STEM classrooms: What personal role do faculty play? *Life Sciences Education*, 15(3):1-9. [https://doi.org/10.1187/cbe.16-01-0020]

KRAAK, A. 2015. The value of graduate destination survey data in understanding graduate unemployment: a focus on the universities of technology. *South African Journal of Labour Relations*, 39(1):93-113.

Le Grange, L. 2016. Decolonising the university curriculum. *South African Journal of Higher Education*, 30(2):1-12. [https://doi.org/10.20853/30-2-709]

Lomask, M.; Crismond, D. & Hacker, M. 2018. Using Teaching Portfolios to Revise Curriculum and Explore Instructional Practices of Technology and Engineering Education Teachers. *Journal of Technology Education*, 29(2):54-72. [https://doi.org/10.21061/jte.v29i2.a.4]

Lozano, F.J. & Lozano, R. 2014. Developing the curriculum for a new Bachelor's degree in Engineering for Sustainable Development. *Journal of Cleaner Production*, 64(2014):136-146. [https://doi.org/10.1016/j.jclepro.2013.08.022]

Matthews, K.E.; Crampton, A.; Hill, M.; Johnson, E.D.; Sharma, M.D. & Varsavsky, C. 2015. Social network perspectives reveal strength of academic developers as weak ties. *International Journal for Academic Development*, 20(3):238-251. [https://doi.org/10.1080/1360144X.2015.1065495]

Matthews, K.E.; Lodge, J.M. & Bosanquet, A. 2014. Early career academic perceptions, attitudes and professional development activities: questioning the teaching and research gap to further academic development. *International Journal for Academic Development*, 19(2):112-124. [https://doi.org/10.1080/1360144X.2012.724421]

Maton, K. 2014. *Knowledge and Knowers: Towards a Realist Sociology of Education*. Abingdon: Routledge. [https://doi.org/10.4324/9780203885734]

McKenna, S. & Quinn, L. 2012. Lost in translation: transformation in the first round of institutional audits. *South African Journal of Higher Education*, 26(5):1033-1044. [https://doi.org/10.20853/26-5-202]

Morphew, C.C. & Huisman, J. 2002. Using Institutional Theory to Reframe Research on Academic Drift. *Higher Education in Europe*, 27(4):491-506. [https://doi.org/10.1080/0379772022000071977]

Morrow, W. 2009. *Bounds of Democracy: Epistemological Access and Higher Education*. Cape Town: HSRC Press. [https://bit.ly/2m6Xmgw]

Nowotny, H.; Scott, P. & Gibbons, M. 2001. *Re-Thinking Science: Knowledge and the Public in an Age of Uncertainty*. Cambridge: Polity Press.

Olsson, T. & Roxå, T. 2012. A Model Promoting Conceptual Change in Higher education – An Integrated Approach. Research and Development. *Higher Education: Connections in Higher Education*, 35:213-223. [https://bit.ly/2ktLhlc]

Pauw, K.; Oosthuizen, M. & Van Der Westhuizen, C. 2008. Graduate unemployment in the face of skills shortages: a labour market paradox. *South African Journal of Economics*, 76(1):45-57. [https://doi.org/10.1111/j.1813-6982.2008.00152.x]

Placklé, I.; Könings, K.D.; Jacquet, W.; Libotton, A.; Van Merriënboer, J.J.G. & Engels, N. 2018. Students embracing change towards more powerful learning environments in vocational education. *Educational Studies*, 44(1):26-44. [https://doi.org/10.1080/03055698.2017.1331840]

RSA (Republic of South Africa). 1993. *Technikons Act 125 of 1993*. Pretoria: Government Printing Works.

RSA (Republic of South Africa). 1997. *Higher Education Act 101 of 1997*. Pretoria: Government Printing Works.

RSA (Republic of South Africa). 2001. National Plan for Higher Education. *Government Gazette*, 429(22138), 3-91.

Sharunova, A.; Butt, M.; Kresta, S.; Carey, J.; Wyard-Scott, L.; Adeeb, S.; Blessing, L. & Qureshi, A.J. 2017. Cognition and transdisciplinary design: An educational framework for undergraduate engineering design curriculum development. *Engineering Education*, 16:1-8. [https://doi.org/10.24908/pceea.v0i0.10353]

Shay, S. 2013. Conceptualising curriculum differentiation in higher education: a sociology of knowledge point of view. *British Journal of Sociology of Education*, 34(4):563-582. [https://doi.org/10.1080/01425692.2012.722285]

Star, S.L. & Griesemer, J.R. 1989. Institutional Ecology, 'translations' and Boundary Objects. *Social Studies of Science*, 19:387-420. [https://doi.org/10.1177/030631289019003001]

TROWLER, P. & COOPER, A. 2002. Teaching and learning regimes: Implicit theories and recurrent practices in the enhancement of teaching and learning through educational development programmes. *Higher Education Research & Development*, 21(3): 221-240. [https://doi.org/10.1080/0729436022000020742]

VAN BROEKHUIZEN, H. 2016. Graduate unemployment and higher education institutions in South Africa. *Stellenbosch Economic Working Papers Series*, WP08/2016, 16 August. [https://bit.ly/2kWy9W1]

WALSH, R. 2017. A Case Study of Pedagogy of Mathematics Support Tutors without a Background in Mathematics Education. International Journal of Mathematical Education in Science and Technology, 48(1):67-82. [https://doi.org/10.1080/0020739X.2016.1220028]

WHEELAHAN, L. 2010. *Why Knowledge Matters in Curriculum: A Social Realist Argument*. Abingdon: Routledge.

CHAPTER 15

Disrupting academic reading

Unrolling the scroll for academic staff

Sandra Abegglen, Tom Burns,
Dave Middlebrook & Sandra Sinfield

Introduction

The room is abuzz. Three teams pore over different, difficult and challenging academic articles on the theory and practice of Higher Education. Each text, not a traditional A4 offprint, but an unfurled paper scroll – a series of A3 pages sellotaped side by side to form a continuous run of pages; expansive, panoramic, wide-open to the senses and to comprehension. The scrolls are draped over tables, blue-tacked to the walls, and spread-out on the floor. The participants are working on them intently: highlighting and annotating, marking text and graphics with boxes, circles, lines, arrows, symbols, and crosshatching certain parts of the text and homing in on others. Their thinking is recorded in a riot of colours – from muted pastels to bright, vibrant bolds, from markers to highlighters to plain graphite pencils – and accompanied by a mounting hubbub of focused and engaged conversation, as we examine details, facts marshalled, and arguments formed. We hear the excitement of discovery, voices of scepticism and occasional bursts of laughter. This is the serious and playful business of academic reading on our Facilitating Student Learning module. (Sandra and Tom)

We work in what in the United Kingdom (UK) is called a Widening Participation university, one that recruits "non-traditional" students, those that are the first in their families to enter higher education, that are mature, and that usually have family and work commitments. Our students are often framed as "deficit" and in need of "fixing". They are described as "Mickey Mouse students for whom a Mickey Mouse degree is quite appropriate" (Brockes, 2003:n.p.); where "deficit" and "fixing" tend to mean socialising them as quickly as possible into the middle-class mores and practices of the university; encouraging them to silence their troublesome voices and disguise their troublesome selves as swiftly as possible (Tett, 2000).

As educationists and academic developers who work with discipline staff to develop their ability to teach our students, our disruptive apprehension is that while our students may arrive with lower academic capital than other students, they have lived rich lives. They have energy, motivation and commitment – and they are desperate to find their voices in this powerful (academic) domain: they want to have their "say". At the same time, they are aware of the reductive lens through which they are viewed; they realise that they must be colonised to survive (Freire, 1970) – or resist and fail. We want our students to resist and succeed at university; to find their academic voices without losing themselves in the process.

A key arena for this successful resistance is the tricky curriculum domain of academic reading. Typically undertaken in isolation, our students find this reading not only overwhelming, but also disempowering and silencing. Our unconventional response is to enlist to our cause the ancient bookscroll: the bound book unbound. This is the story of using the scroll, text unrolled to its fullest extent and engaged with dialogically, with academic staff. Focusing on curriculum innovation and emancipatory practice, we argue that scrolls can change the way our staff teach – and this has the potential to change how our students experience university and university life.

Context

In our academic development unit, the Centre for Professional and Educational Development, we offer certificated and non-certificated staff development opportunities. The certificated offerings include a Postgraduate Certificate (PGCert), a Postgraduate Diploma (PGDip), and a Master's in Learning and Teaching in Higher Education (MALTHE). In *Facilitating Student Learning*, one of the modules offered for all three course iterations, we cover creative and emancipatory practice to help our diverse staff help our equally diverse students (LMU, 2017) to be successful. In short, our task in this module is to support our staff to develop curricula that enable our students to enter their epistemic communities with the approach, outlook, strategies and practices that allow them to study successfully and powerfully. In the *Facilitating Student Learning* module, we encourage staff to re-imagine their curricula in emancipatory ways – and this includes developing more inclusive approaches to academic literacy and academic reading.

We have come to understand just how deeply questions of access are interwoven with conceptions of academic literacy, and how the particular culture of academic literacy in UK higher education and elsewhere serves as an incapacitating maze; a bewildering set of challenges and dead ends rather than, as social justice policy would have it, a system of pathways to success. Ours is a literate culture, and we access and practice our literacy in very particular and, arguably, very narrow ways, especially at university. This has implications for our non-traditional students; implications as to who will succeed and who will not; and who will have full agency to participate in academic life, and who will be marginalised and shamed. Ultimately there are also implications as to who will live a life buoyed by a successful, satisfying degree and career beyond university, or potentially leave our institution mired in debt and struggle. For what is apparent is that those with greater academic and more mainstream cultural capital (Bourdieu, 1984) than that possessed by our students do tend to do better in higher education. That is, those from more traditional middle-class homes tend to have more knowledge of and practice within academia. These students arrive in higher education with greater self-efficacy (Bandura, 1982), which allows them to act more confidently in academic spaces and to be more readily validated in the university classroom. These students tend not to be crushed by the occasional negative experience or temporary academic setback. Learning and achievement for these traditional higher education students are not "win-lose" situations. With knowledge of academic literacies and a sense of academic self-efficacy, they will find their way around an academic system into which they have been initiated from birth.

Our experience of working with non-traditional students allows us to challenge the assumptions underlying the classist and cultural "othering" (see, for example, Miller, 2008) they suffer within educational domains. Our students have multiple experiences that they bring with them to our University. We have had students who have worked on nuclear submarines and taught overseas in kindergartens and the slums of Brazil. Our students may have been nurses or policemen, they may have worked on building sites or on shop floors. While they may not yet be experienced in academic practice, academic reading and writing, they have other strengths that higher education could, but typically does not, recognise. Thus, placed as "academic outsiders" (Sinfield, Burns & Holley, 2004), our non-traditional students experience the power imbalance of higher education, and find themselves excluded and sidelined by the power imbalance inherent in academic reading (see, for example, Hoskins, 2008).

We argue that academic reading at university, while an essential part of the university curriculum, and essential for academic success, is a socio-political activity, with widening participation students particularly excluded by the middle-class habitus and discourse of higher education. To challenge this dynamic, we work with academic staff urging them to develop more inclusive curricula especially by changing the way they engage with and support their students through the alienating practice of "reading for learning".

Scrolls and book rolls as curriculum disruption

Working as educationists and academic developers in a university where the majority of students is mature and have care and/or work responsibilities, our overarching task is to help our staff support these students, enabling them to develop a self-efficacy and resilience to university study similar to those middle-class students already groomed for success. We do this by imagining the curriculum differently. We work with our undergraduate students in creative and empowering ways (Abegglen, Burns & Sinfield, 2017; Abegglen, Burns & Sinfield, 2016a; Abegglen, Burns & Sinfield, 2016b). We are not trying to "fix" their supposed deficits with injections of "skills" or plugging them into remedial packages designed to "bring them up to speed" (Burns, Sinfield & Holley, 2009), but allowing them to explore and question academic practice and discourse and by building their self-confidence so that they can understand and navigate academia and make it their own. It is this emancipatory practice that we have developed with non-traditional undergraduate students that we take back into our academic development practice with staff – disrupting their taken-for-granted, potentially negative, apprehensions of our students, revealing how they might develop more empowering and emancipatory curricula, and moving them into more inclusive praxes.

In common with students everywhere, our undergraduates "read for their degree", and we realised that academic reading is a key arena for their successful negotiation between the need for "academic objectivity" and their own subjective and lived experience: reading is political practice enacted.

Typically undertaken in isolation and painful silence, our students tend to find reading for higher education study disempowering, an arena in which they are positioned as "deficient", and for which they are often criticised and shamed. At the same time as we "wrestled" with the exclusionary nature of academic reading, a surprising question took hold of our imaginations: could the book itself be part of the problem? Could the bound codex format, arguably, the foundational user-interface object across two thousand years of literacy, be an as-yet unrecognised source of difficulty for our students? Could the fragmented presentation of text – and content – the endless process of turning pages, paper or digital, be driving or at least increasing the isolation and disempowerment that our students experience when they read for their studies?

One of our co-authors, Dave Middlebrook, has experimented with unrolled paper scrolls in education (see Middlebrook, 2015). His work provided a means of testing our hypothesis. Like many of our students, Dave has learning differences and had a great deal of difficulty in school. He speaks openly and convincingly about not being comfortable with books, of feeling "locked out"; of not being able to skim, scan or pre-read in any meaningful sense; of not being able to carry information or main ideas across page turns; of information lost or jumbled or, quite simply, missed altogether; of the substantial cognitive load imposed by the book's fragmentation; of the impossibility of carrying on a conversation about content scattered across so many pages; of the breakdown of shared thinking when the simple act of turning pages places the page-turner in control and the other person in the role of powerless observer; and of confusion and exhaustion winning out over the desire to complete a reading task (Middlebrook, 2016a).

He speaks, in contrast, of what happens for him when books are unrolled as scrolls – when vast swaths of text become immediately accessible to the senses and can be visually, tactilely and kinaesthetically comprehended; when skimming and scanning are easily and rapidly done; when random access is intuitive and immediate; when there is no need to carry information or main ideas across page turns; when the physical act of moving back and forth across the scroll's wide-open span provides a tangible sense of connection, immersion, and journey; when readers can step back to *farstand* (see below) and move in close to *understand*; when all participants in a conversation are on equal footing, and conversations are sustained, detailed and deep.

Dave's work (Middlebrook, 2015, 1994a, 1994b) prompted us to experiment with scrolls in our classrooms – to unroll our undergraduate students' books, and then stand back and watch as they engaged dialogically at the whole-text level, as they initiated sustained discussions with their peers, and, as evidenced by ongoing bouts of laughter, had great fun while learning.

Outsider staff: The textscroll and the more inclusive curriculum

> In the Ancient World, the margins surrounding the columns on a scroll were sometimes decorated with illustrations of vines and flowers. The word for each column of text was pagina – the Latin word for a garden trellis. The symbolism was clear: each column of text was a doorway to the garden of knowledge. Today, many of our undergraduate students struggle to find a way into the garden of knowledge. A significant percentage of them never make it: they drop out or give up. This raises fundamental questions: Why are undergraduates, especially non-traditional students, experiencing the doorway to the garden of knowledge as closed? Rather than continually demonising students who won't or can't read, could we open the door if we presented text as scrolls rather than a set of pages infolded and bound together? (Dave)

As our students are culturally diverse, our academics also come from diverse backgrounds and cultures; from different higher education systems across the globe and from different industries. When entering higher education and teaching for the first time, they can feel just as disempowered as their students (Harrington, Sinfield & Burns, 2016). Moreover, because of their varied backgrounds, they also come with a range of different philosophical approaches to teaching and learning. This can add to their insecurity – making them feel like "outsiders" pitched against "traditional" academics. They wonder: How can I make sure that my students can function critically and effectively – and hopefully gain power and voice, self-respect and self-efficacy – in an environment that is familiar to neither of us? Our role in the all our courses in general, and the *Facilitating Student Learning* module in particular, is to help these staff members experience differing learning, teaching and assessment practices so that they feel more empowered themselves -- and thus are able to empower their students. Most recently, in our *Facilitating Student Learning* module, this has included the use of scrolls to help staff see reading, and the teaching of reading, differently.

A scroll can be made by printing off or photocopying a chapter or article, on one side of the paper only and preferably enlarged to A3-size, for there is something intrinsically friendlier and more accessible about the enlarged text. The pages are then sellotaped together side by side to produce a scroll.

Disrupting academic reading

Scrolls do quite a few things for teaching and learning that modern books, bound or digital, cannot. The scroll's expansive, panoramic display is wide-open to the senses, to exploration and discussion. With unrolled books spread out in front of us, often extending twenty metres or more, the structure and flow of ideas is instantly visible. Random access, the ability to move anywhere in the text, is excellent: rapid, easy, and fully contextualised. The scroll's unfurled display invites all readers, staff and students, to get up and move about, to walk back and forth across the span, to feel how their bodies scale to the text, to move in close to understand the details (*understandan*), and to move back to *farstand* the larger context.

The word *understand* has deep historical roots. Its close relatives – *firststanding*, *forstanding* and *farstanding* – have faded from use, while *understand* still survives. The message from these words is fundamentally physical and spatial, acknowledging that where you stand shapes your perspective. No current words or idioms communicate the idea as effectively and elegantly. *Farstanding* along with the easily inferred *nearstanding* (not historical but it fits the pattern) are useful for building new awareness of how we think about reading and how we think about thinking. Scrolls invite academics and students to gather, share and discuss within the "bookspace"; which is a powerful space in which to be, in which to learn how to navigate and understand academia, and in which to become, in the fullest sense, a reader, a thinker, an academic.

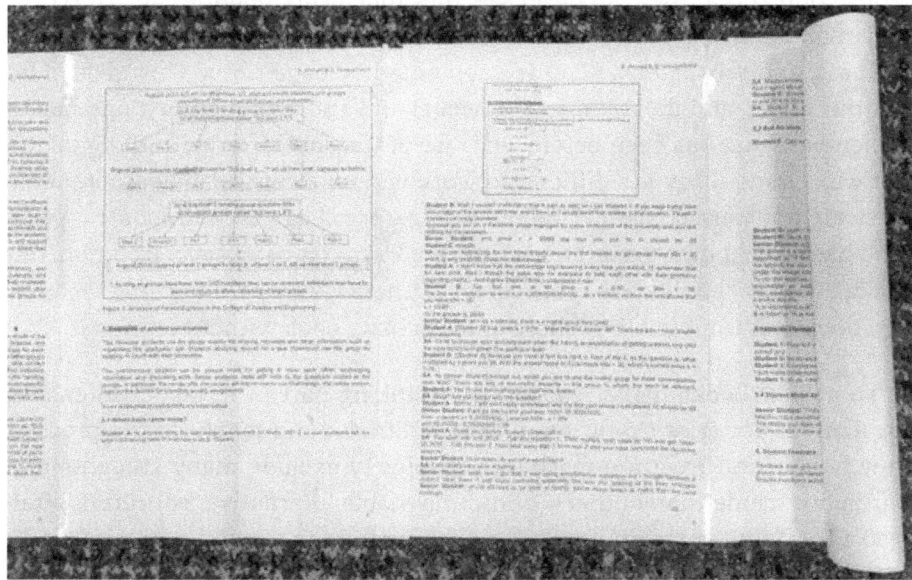

IMAGE 15.1 Scroll

These beneficial attributes stem from a simple fact: scrolls are literally explicit, which is to say, that once unrolled or unfolded (*ex+plicare*), the content that they hold is spread-out; laid bare in front of our eyes and thus wide open to understanding (Whitney, 1895). *Explicit* and *implicit* are ancient words. Each perfectly describes a common book form: explicit for the unrolled scroll and implicit for the bound codex. Notably, both were formed on the same root: *plicare*, which means *fold* or *roll*. The rather substantial difference in meaning between these two words hangs entirely on their respective prefixes: the *ex-* tells us about the energetic opening-up of the scroll's expansive, panoramic, comprehensible display; the *im-*, in contrast, perfectly describes the complicated, confusing, and concealing process of infolding (*im+plicare*) used to make the signatures of a book. This is a process that hides and effectively entangles the book's content deep within the folds, with the unintended result that the implicit book is, by comparison to the explicit scroll, complicated and difficult *to know*.

Our modern bound books, and their digital cousins as well, for they are modelled after the bound book, are the polar opposite of explicit: they are implicit, which is to say that they are infolded (*im+plicare*), such that the content is hidden from view and difficult to access. They are never opened more than a crack to the reader; two facing pages is all that one can ever see at any one time. To compensate for the implicit construction, readers must page back and forth repeatedly to gain some, usually flawed, sense of the larger context that they can never see; they must work relentlessly to discover and make sense of content that is scattered across many pages: words, pictures, and typography, all of it fragmented by page turns. This takes a lot of time, effort, and most important, visual and auditory memory; one has to remember what has been before. Because of this, books, print and digital are not welcoming. They are difficult to work with and difficult to comprehend. They are not learner friendly. Where a single scroll can accommodate a party (and has been known to start a few), the book's message is one of isolation: "Sit down", it says, "I only have room for you." There is no space to come together in a book; it is impossible to share and discuss a book without leaving it.

In short, our books make reading, the thinking part of it, labour-intensive; for many it becomes overly complicated, difficult and lonely. In the process, they hobble and frustrate teachers, completely exclude many students and partially exclude many others. Without a viable alternative, educators often resort to a "sink or swim" mentality: "I'm not here to teach you how to read"; and students often give way to despair: "I can't do it." Hence the challenge:

how do we help staff to teach students from diverse backgrounds, with often unhappy learning experiences and diverse learning approaches, how to understand and navigate academic reading – and hence how to navigate an essential part of the academic curriculum?

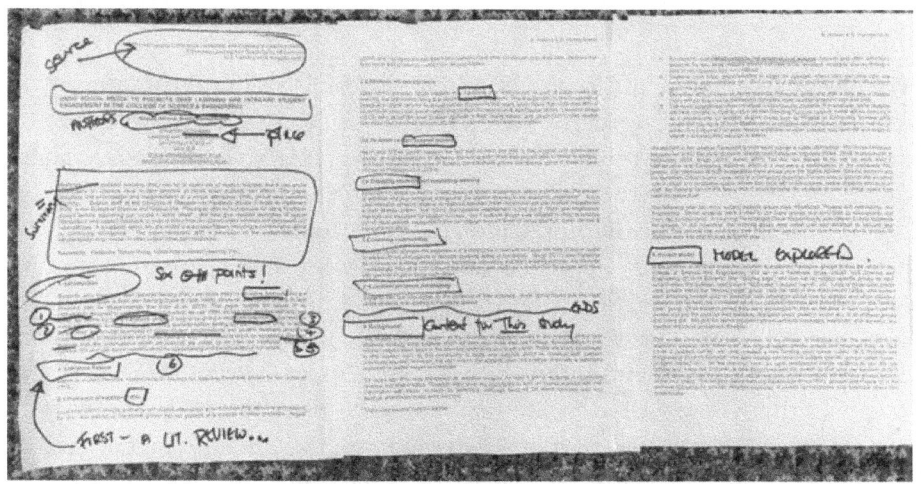

Image 15.2 Annotated scroll

As educationists and academic developers, we used textscrolls to teach staff how to teach reading more proactively and successfully so that they make reading part of the more inclusive and empowering curricula so necessary for the successful participation of those students typically excluded from or unwelcome in higher education. Scrolls present text in a different format. This creates opportunities. And one of the things scrolls do particularly well is meet people where they are, rather than where the university wants them to be. Scrolls allow staff and students to access the content. Unlike the bound codex, scrolls are inviting and welcoming to a wide range of readers; accommodating a variety of skill levels, learning approaches and cultural backgrounds. They support and encourage conversation in ways that book-forms cannot; they are much more learner-friendly and much easier to comprehend. To be clear: they do not "dumb down" book content; rather, they present the same challenging content in a different form: unbound. It is a simple change: from pages bound to pages unrolled; but it has far-reaching consequences.

Unrolling the text: How we used scrolls in facilitating student learning

> One of the most powerful things I ever learned to do was to photocopy chapters – and write all over them while I was reading. I felt in charge – I took control of my reading. Everything changed when I did that. (Student, cited in Burns & Sinfield, 2016:57)

We have experienced the power of annotating our printout or photocopy of an article or chapter, so when Dave interviewed a 6th Grade teacher in the US about literally ripping up textbooks to produce textscrolls that cover walls, floors and whole classrooms, so that students could walk around and see the writing and interact with it (Middlebrook, 2016b), we were intrigued. This seemed like emancipatory practice indeed. And we love this, the transgressive nature of it, the tearing apart and joining up and making use of texts. We have seen the scroll break down undergraduate fear of academic reading as students gain control and influence over the text in front of them. The text mapping that we practised in the *Facilitating Student Learning* module with our staff participants was part of a dynamic, creative and critical curriculum designed to break down staff fear of teaching, and their fear of teaching academic reading. We wanted to "de-school" (Illich, 1970) our staff, disrupting their taken-for-granted assumptions of academic practice and of our students; and to achieve this we enacted with them exactly the way that we used scrolls with our undergraduate students.

For our staff participants we produced three key texts as scrolls, one per group, and gave our staff learners coloured felt tips, and a set of questions and prompts to seed their active engagement with their text. We chose each text for its relevance to the staff and their participation in our module: Norman Jackson (2005), *Making Higher Education a more Creative Place*; David Thornburg (2007), *Campfires in Cyberspace: Primordial Metaphors for Learning in the 21st Century*; and Lee Campbell (2018), *The "Performance" of Peer Observation: Practice, Pedagogy and Power Relations*. Hence, they had a reason to engage with whichever text was allocated to them. To initiate engagement, we asked participants to notice what was going on in the text as a physical, constructed thing. We asked them to identify structure: intro and outro; headings and paragraphs; images, charts and diagrams: the way the text appeared on the paper itself. This meant, unrolling the text and moving about, walking back and forth along its length, stepping close for details and stepping back for the big picture: the literal, physical embodiment of understanding and its ancient sibling, far standing. Immediately choices had to be made: "Do we spread this across the tables, stick it to the wall, settle on the floor and cluster around it? Where do we begin? What do we do with the text?" Participants were forced to interact peer to peer and self to scroll, propelled into a hands-on relationship with the text. There was discussion and engagement with each other and the text, a key feature of collaborative learning (Vygotsky, 1978); underscoring of the importance of "being with" (Nancy, 2000) and revealing that meaning and knowledge are socially constructed and embodied. Arguably, this form of engagement with the words presented in the textscroll also distantiates and reveals the very constructed nature of a text (any text) and contributes to making all learners, staff and students, conscious of their learning.

The *Facilitating Student Learning* module is delivered in a more relaxed and reflective manner than is perhaps expected of a postgraduate qualification for teaching in higher education. Even so, there was slight panic when we outlined the task and even more so when we asked participants to get up and start moving, to read. When academics are students, they also ask: "Am I doing it right?", looking for reassurance. However, in the textscroll session, our participants were instead disrupted; in answer to their implicit: "Isn't reading static and solitary?", we said: "No – get up – move – interact." Despite this, for most, this challenge became a joy as moving, talking, thinking and acting became one: a learning process was underway. This is where the scrolls revealed their strength: they engaged. They allowed exploration in a space in which it was safe to take risks; one with a focus on *process* and not outcomes.

We deepened the scroll session by explaining how we use textscrolls with undergraduate students, of how we also celebrate and reveal reading as a form of slow academia (Berg & Seeber, 2016). We argued that scrolls enable us to slow things down; they make room for exploring and thinking more deeply. We revealed to the staff participants that when working with undergraduate students, once they have engaged with a textscroll in just the way that the staff themselves had done, we may feed in a small assignment question to push the interaction further. Once the undergraduates have this new focus, an actual assignment question, we have seen them move from noticing the structures of a text, to seeking information in the text – and to answer a real question. This gives working with scrolls a different sense of urgency and purpose, modelling academic inquiry as research, as looking for, not knowing the answers in advance, not trying to give the teacher the right answers (Holt, 1981). This is not teaching reading as a decontextualised skill or set of skills to master, but it is modelling academia as collegiate and dialogic practice, active learning in a non-threatening mode.

What the lecturer did: Curriculum and pedagogical innovation

We have found that many of our staff participants immediately make use of the textscroll in their practice to develop more inclusive and empowering curriculum experiences for their students. We share here two examples from our most recent teaching.

The first one is from a lecturer working with non-traditional students from BSc Health and Social Care (levels 5 and 6 – years two and three). This lecturer reported back from her practice:

> I have used scrolls with my students either to discuss and/or critique a sampler assignment or to go through a piece of literature/article during the sessions. Though it's a pre-requisite for them to come prepared with the readings beforehand some of them tend [not to have] so instead of letting them go or to make them read individually, it's better to involve them with this technique.

She was particularly happy with how the textscroll helped her change the dynamic in the classroom and encouraged the students to read – and to read more successfully. She said that the student feedback was mostly positive, because:

- it helps them to engage well with the literature and with each other;
- it was less time consuming and more interesting as compared to having an individual read at home; and
- it helps them understand better.

This shows that when our staff participant used scrolls with her students, they allowed for more meaningful and positive interaction with academic texts. Scrolls invite the novice student in and give meaning to the dialogic process that is inherent in academic reading and academia. While slowing the reading process down, the overall process of understanding is accelerated, opening up new ways of engaging with content and with other people. It is a way of illustrating (for teaching and learning) and managing (for actual practice) the process of moving from pre-reading to comprehension and synthesis: helping readers to think across different texts and topics to develop intertextual and synoptic understanding; bringing all together and seeing things under the same general aspect. It is a practice that can develop engaged, analytical and critical students who are prepared for the challenges of the twenty-first century and who have successful and joyful university experiences.

There may be concern that this reading technique disadvantages those students who feel threatened by engaging with texts publicly and students with specific learning difficulties, especially those with dyslexia or dyspraxia, who need longer to comprehend texts. Thus, we share a second example of using textscrolls with final year (level 6) Design students. At our University, this cohort typically has a larger proportion of students with dyslexia or dyspraxia than other courses (for reasons yet to be explored). The lecturer in question gave her Design students the task of illustrating texts produced by Literature students. Thus, the Design students had to read and make meaning of complex texts from an alien discipline – and to make those texts their own. They had to re-genre (English, 2011) those meanings via illustrations and translate them into their knowledge and practice: they had to engage in deep learning (Atherton, 2005). It appears that using textscrolls made this process more successful than in previous years. The Design lecturer describes the work undertaken as follows:

> In my last practical teaching session ... I tried out the text-mapping exercise we were introduced to in Workshop 3 ... It fitted well with my current studio project, where we are collaborating with staff and students from English Literature and Creative Writing, to design, illustrate and publish an anthology of creative and critical writing. The project pairs students from both English Literature *and* Creative Writing and Visual Communications. In this early stage of the project, my students have just been assigned a piece of creative or critical writing by the English Literature and Creative Writing students. As some graphic design and illustration students are not necessarily used to digesting and working with long and sometimes complex literary texts, I thought the scrolls would be a great key for them to unlock an understanding of their texts, especially as it helps give a visual dimension to the text – and my students are visual thinkers ...

> I made a scroll for each student of their assigned text. The students felt quite excited about receiving their texts in this unusual physical format. I asked them to fully unfurl their scrolls and find space to look at and interact with it, using highlighters and pens to mark out sections, highlight keywords and phrases and activate some meaning from the text, treating it as a visual entity in a spatial dimension (not that I used those very words!). I encouraged them not to make a detailed reading of the text but to scan it and get to the end, not worrying about 'getting it' all but simply achieving a 'sense' of it. My hope was that this would feel like an accessible way into the text for the students. They eagerly tucked in and spent 20 minutes working with their scrolls ...

> The students then divided into groups of three and each spent a couple of minutes talking to each other about their texts – describing the 'who, what, where, when', the themes, characters and ideas in the text, its structure (e.g., poetic form, essay) and what they wanted to find out next about their text.

> I think it was useful for the students, there was a good energy in the room. The exercise was a fun and enjoyable way to break down a long-ish text, and at least one student who started the session feeling very unsure and nervous about working with a text (on William Blake – an inspiring but potentially intimidating subject) went away more confident. I will certainly use the technique again.

This member of staff related the success of this approach in particular to the dialogic (Bakhtin, 1981) and social (Lave & Wenger, 1991) nature of textscrolls as well as the emancipatory approach to teaching and learning (Holt, 1970) that they enable:

> The exercise used a dialogic approach to classroom practice, helping to form a community of practice and bolster students' confidence in their ability to tackle the project in a way that would gain them a successful outcome (encouraging resilience and self-efficacy).

This taps into the Holtian idea that the learning process should not set students up for failure as in the traditional classroom. But rather, we can teach in ways that encourage students to question what they are looking at and being asked to do, rather than to answer the question (or respond to the brief) in a way that pleases the teacher (or the system).

This is something we have also experienced when using textscrolls with both our staff learners and widening participation students. Textscrolls create powerful learning spaces that make content not only visible, but also accessible: creating powerful curriculum spaces in which learners can become, in the fullest sense, readers, thinkers and academics.

Conclusion: Re-imagining reading towards a more inclusive curriculum

There are undergraduate students who "work out" academic reading, who relish that invitation to sit down for a solitary read. However, the majority of our students struggle with it. We argue that especially for non-traditional students, scrolls are an opportunity to experience positively the process of inspecting, analysing, and understanding written texts, of reading intertextually and mastering what the American philosopher Mortimer Adler termed "syntopical reading" (Adler & Van Doren, 1940/1972). That is to say, scrolls can be the bridge to the highest levels of academic reading practice, of reading analytically across texts and topics and of synthesising from them new comprehensions and new questions. Without scrolls, many students, especially non-traditional students, will stop engaging with academic books and articles. With scrolls, students of all ages and backgrounds can very quickly learn to engage in academic, university-level, reading because they make written words, and content, accessible. By doing so, scrolls "unflatten" (Sousanis, 2015) the academic playing field. They enable learners with different backgrounds and knowledges to participate. So, in its own simple, low-tech way, the ancient unrolled book turns out to be a great leveller – by facilitating reading success.

As Educationists and Academic Developers, we work with staff from diverse cultures and multiple contexts. Often feeling like academic "outsiders" themselves, staff are aware that they have "outsider" students who in the eyes of the world, and even in their own eyes, appear to lack the key skills of criticality, creativity, research and problem-solving necessary for higher education. It can become all too easy for our staff to see their undergraduate students as the sum of all their lacks, rather than as active learners bravely embracing the risks inherent in higher education study. Part of our task in our academic development unit and our *Facilitating Student Learning* module is to challenge the overarching education narrative which tasks us to "fix" these students. Our undergraduates are skilled in many ways, and these skills can be harnessed. It is our responsibility in our work with academic staff to help them see possibilities and opportunities and to open up their curricula to create more positive university experiences for their students.

Traditional students historically have taken advantage of higher education and used it as a springboard for personal and career development. However, our students' profiles – mature, first in the family to enter higher education, lone carers, low-income families and very diverse cultural backgrounds – mean that instead they may become overwhelmed, defeated by the alienating and exclusionary practices of higher education and by particular approaches to academic literacy. The need then for us is to work with staff to change curriculum and pedagogy design so that they create a higher education experience that is fit for all students; one that values them as the people they are and the academics they are becoming. In the *Facilitating Student Learning* module, we argue that we need to foster the creative praxes necessary to produce empowering curricula and pedagogy that develop self-actualising and resilient (Kukhareva, 2015) students.

On our PGCert, PGDip and MALTHE courses, and especially in the *Facilitating Student Learning* module, we have harnessed the transgressive power of scrolls not least because our non-traditional students feel particularly excluded and positioned as excluded, especially by academic reading (Hoskins, 2008).

When we used textscrolls with our staff, our intention was that they would experience the revelatory and empowering nature of the scroll and make it part of their teaching practice. For some of our staff it appears that the experience of working with textscrolls has been immediately practice-changing: they have implemented textscroll sessions with their students so that they, perhaps for the first time, experienced texts in positive ways. At the very least, the staff experienced for themselves the power of authentic and emancipatory reading strategies. They were in a position to see reading not as a decontextualised set of skills to be taught to deficit students: they now had the choice to make academic reading more successful and inclusionary and successful for those who typically experience reading as problematic and alienating.

With our staff participants, we also had joy; joy as they wrestled with their coloured felt tips and found new ways into the reading of complex academic texts. This joy was subsequently experienced by and with their undergraduate students when they too realised that they could successfully manage and navigate several feet of text.

We recommend readers to take this case study as a starting point to experiment with scrolls and with re-imagining a more powerful, inclusive and emancipatory curriculum. Scrolls help us expand thinking, help us engage with text through our senses, help us to share our thinking and, most importantly, help us to love (the work of) reading. The scroll can be a door opener to the garden of knowledge, and to closer collaboration between teacher and learner. This expands the horizons and the breadth and depth of the university experience for all – staff and students.

References

ABEGGLEN, S.; BURNS, T. & SINFIELD, S. 2017. 'Really free!': Strategic interventions to foster students' academic writing skills. *Journal of Educational Innovation, Partnership and Change*, 3(1):251-255. [https://doi.org/10.21100/jeipc.v3i1.589]

ABEGGLEN, S.; BURNS, T. & SINFIELD, S. 2016a. Hacking assignment practice: Finding creativity and power in the fissures and cracks of learning and teaching. *Journal of Learning Development in Higher Education*, 10. [https://bit.ly/2kMJ1pz]

ABEGGLEN, S.; BURNS, T. & SINFIELD, S. 2016b. The power of freedom: Setting up a multimodal exhibition with undergraduate students to foster their learning and help them to achieve. *Journal of Peer Learning*, 9:1-9. [https://bit.ly/2kWX9MQ]

ADLER, J. & VAN DOREN, C. 1940/1972. *How to read a book: The art of getting a liberal education*. New York: Simon and Schuster.

ATHERTON, J.S. 2005. Learning and teaching: Deep and surface learning. *At-a-glance*, Southern Cross University. [https://bit.ly/2m8cmL2]

BAKHTIN, M. 1981. *The dialogic imagination: Four essays*. Austin: University of Texas Press.

BANDURA, A. 1982. Self-efficacy mechanism in human agency. *American Psychologist*, 37(2):122-147. [https://doi.org/10.1037/0003-066X.37.2.122]

BERG, M. & SEEBER, B. 2016. *The slow professor: Challenging the culture of speed in the academy.* Toronto: University of Toronto Press. [https://doi.org/10.3138/9781442663091]

BOURDIEU, P. 1984. *Distinction: A social critique of the judgement of taste.* London: Routledge.

BROCKES, E. 2003. Taking the mick. *The Guardian*, 15 January. [https://bit.ly/2kucsMR]

BURNS, T. & SINFIELD, S. 2016. *Essential study skills: The complete guide to success at university.* London: Sage.

BURNS, T.; SINFIELD, S. & HOLLEY, D. 2009. A journey into silence: Students, stakeholders and the impact of a strategic governmental policy document in the UK. *Social Responsibility Journal*, 5(4):566-574. [https://doi.org/10.1108/17471110910995401]

CAMPBELL, L. 2018. The 'performance' of peer observation: Practice, pedagogy and power relations. *Academia*. [https://bit.ly/2mtkOF8]

ENGLISH, F. 2011. *Student writing and genre: Reconfiguring academic knowledge.* London: Continuum.

FREIRE, P. 1970. *Pedagogy of the oppressed.* New York: Continuum.

HARRINGTON, K.; SINFIELD, S. & BURNS, T. 2016. Student engagement. In: H. Pokorny & D. Warren (eds). *Enhancing teaching practice in higher education.* London: Sage, 106-124.

HOLT, J. 1981. *Teach your own: A hopeful path for education.* New York: Delacorte Press.

HOLT, J. 1970. *What do I do Monday?* New York: Dutton.

HOSKINS, K. 2008. Academic reading: Online literature review and blog. [https://bit.ly/2mtkdmP]

ILLICH, I. 1970. *De-schooling society.* New York: Harper and Row.

JACKSON, N. (2005). Making higher education a more creative place. *Journal for the Enhancement of Learning and Teaching*, 2(1):14-25. [https://bit.ly/2m0h7Xl]

KUKHAREVA, M. 2015. Resilience. *TEDx Talks*, 12 January. [https://bit.ly/2mn4qFZ]

LAVE, J. & WENGER, E. 1991. *Situated learning: Legitimate peripheral participation.* Cambridge: Cambridge University Press. [https://doi.org/10.1017/CBO9780511815355]

LMU (LONDON METROPOLITAN UNIVERSITY). 2017. Our key statistics: Important information about the University. [https://bit.ly/2m6f8Rm]

MIDDLEBROOK, R.D. 2016a. About the project's founder. *The Textmapping Project.* [https://bit.ly/2kYYcvA]

MIDDLEBROOK, R.D. 2016b. An interview with Kimberly Burke DeRose, 1/26/16. *The Textmapping Project: Data Points: A series of interviews with educators about scrolls and textmapping.* [https://bit.ly/2moH4zL]

MIDDLEBROOK, R.D. 2015. Why use scrolls? *The Textmapping Project.* [https://bit.ly/2m3zOcF]

MIDDLEBROOK, R.D. 1994a. Using scrolls. *The Textmapping Project.* [https://bit.ly/2m74iKA]

MIDDLEBROOK, R.D. 1994b. The benefits of scrolls and text mapping. *The Textmapping Project.* [https://bit.ly/2m74p8Y]

MILLER, J. 2008. Otherness. *The Sage encyclopaedia of qualitative research methods.* London: Sage, 588-591.

NANCY, J.L. 2000. *Being singular plural.* Stanford: Stanford University Press.

SINFIELD, S.; BURNS, T. & HOLLEY, D. 2004. Outsiders looking in or insiders looking out? Widening participation in a post-1992 university. In: J. Satterthwaite, E. Atkinson & W. Martin (eds). *The disciplining of education: new languages of power and resistance.* Stoke-on-Trent: Trentham Books, 137-152. [https://bit.ly/2kWetl5]

SOUSANIS, N. 2015. *Unflattening.* Cambridge, MA: Harvard University Press.

TETT, L. 2000. I'm working class and proud of it – gendered experiences of non-traditional participants in higher education. *Gender and Education*, 1(2):183-194. [https://doi.org/10.1080/09540250050009993]

THORNBURG, D. 2007. *Campfires in Cyberspace: Primordial metaphors for learning in the 21st century.* [https://bit.ly/1Huwv05]

VYGOTSKY, L. 1978. Interaction between learning and development. In: M. Gauvain & M. Cole (eds). *Readings on the development of children*. New York: Scientific American Books, 34-40.

WHITNEY, W.D. (EDS). 1895. *The century dictionary: An encyclopedic lexicon of the English language*. New York: The Century Company. [https://bit.ly/2m46GyT]

CHAPTER 16

Advancing democratic values in higher education through open curriculum co-creation

Towards an epistemology of uncertainty

Asanda Ngoasheng, Xena Cupido, Oluwaseun Oyekola, Daniela Gachago, Ashton Mpofu & Yolisa Mbekela

Introduction

Critical pedagogues such as Freire (2005), Giroux (1983, 1997), Apple (2013), McLaren (2009) and hooks (1994) see education as a political project – a means to empower and conscientise oppressed groups of people. Education is regarded as a political project, but with the caveat that it is only transformative if all actors involved (lecturers, students, management, community practitioners and employers) use their agency in collaboration within and beyond institutional structures.

In our experience, university structures are not enabling for student voices and participation in curriculum development processes. Students are usually recipients of knowledge and on the periphery of knowledge creation and research. These were also the sentiments expressed in the 2015–2017 student protests in South Africa – #RhodesMustFall (RMF) and #FeesMustFall (FMF) – that called for decolonising the academy and its curricula. The Fallist movement challenged exclusionary practices, the hegemony of higher education institutions and the untransformed structures and cultures that continue to marginalise and alienate students from the process of knowledge creation.

We believe that the responsibility for creating spaces of disruption in curriculum development does not only lie with academics and academic staff developers. Rather curriculum development should be distributed between developers, academics, community practitioners, employers, students and other stakeholders. Informed by this belief, we embarked on a project aimed at bringing multiple voices into the curriculum development process.

In this chapter, we reflect on the resultant curriculum co-creation process in which stakeholders not usually consulted or involved in the curriculum development process such as students, employer representatives, community workers and advisory committees were engaged. Although we were not clear on the process to undertake initially, we were open to imagining and exploring new possibilities. We share our experience of developing relationships in this collaborative process and the emerging guidelines for equitable participation in curriculum development, decision making and implementation.

Our aim for this project was to develop guidelines for deconstructing power dynamics that would open spaces for multiple stakeholders and academic staff to co-create in curriculum development and research. The following questions guided us:

1. How do we make the invisible, visible – power structures, hegemonies, dominant narratives, exclusive language, positionality?

2. What are the most effective strategies for co-creating a curriculum around diverse perspectives?

In this chapter, we provide a historical perspective on curriculum development in South Africa and particularly at universities of technology.[1] We then describe

---

1 Universities of technology focus on technology innovation and transfer and offer technological career-directed educational programmes. They engage with industry to produce innovative problem-solving research. Many of the programmes offered include work-integrated learning

our journey in developing an approach to co-creation that could be used in developing a curriculum and other co-creation projects. Over a year, we worked together and co-created workshops, conference presentations, academic abstracts, book chapters and a journal article. It resulted in a process that tested how a partnership across different role-players in academia can work. We also explored new ways of thinking and developed guidelines for co-creation, provided at the end of this chapter.

Historical perspectives on curriculum development in South Africa

During apartheid, higher education, like all other aspects of South African life, operated within a complex system of racial division. There were different universities for different language groups and different races. As cited in Boughey (2010), in 1983, the University Amendment Act (Act 83 of 1983), known as the "Quota act", was passed to allow a restricted number of black students to access previously "whites-only" universities. In 1994, democracy came with conversations about widening access to higher education for South Africans of all races. In 1997, the Higher Education Act (RSA, 1997) was introduced to transform the higher education landscape. A series of university mergers followed this Act that was an attempt to widen access and fill in the people and resource gaps between historically white and black institutions (CHE, 2007). Three new types of institutions emerged from this process – traditional universities, universities of technology and comprehensive universities[2] (Breier & Herman, 2017:353). Beyond reducing the number of available institutions and implementing a wider distribution of resources, the mergers were also meant to help historically disadvantaged institutions develop the academic scholarship previously denied them before and during apartheid (Du Pre, 2010).

The foundations of universities of technology are firmly rooted in the former technikon system, that was meant to prepare graduates for the world of work (Du Pre, 2010). We only conducted applied research with strong industry links, so graduates understood the industries they were being trained to enter. Technikons were also established to advance the growth of technology within higher education. Individual Technikons were not involved in designing

---

    that requires students to complete a structured programme while working in an organisation (Knowledge Hub, 2015)

2   Traditional universities offer theoretically oriented university degrees; universities of technology offer vocational oriented diplomas and degrees; and comprehensive universities offer a combination of both types of qualification.

curricula – this was the responsibility of various statutory bodies and lecturers were expected to implement existing curricula.

The Cape Peninsula University of Technology (CPUT), the location of the project, is one of the largest tertiary institutions in South Africa with campuses in five different locations. Although it is a "young" institution, it has a long history. It was established in January 2005 as a result of a merger of different institutions to transform them from a former whites-only and a coloureds-only institution into one multiracial institution. The historical context outlined above continues to influence and shape current teaching and learning practices at CPUT. The postapartheid higher education system is characterised as having "obvious structural changes, some form of agential change, yet very little to no change at the level of culture" (Monnapula-Mapesela, 2017:70) and CPUT is no different. The RMF and FMF student movements highlighted this lack of change in culture and challenged institutions to interrogate the nature of the knowledge taught to students as well as the dominant discourses that continue to advance privilege. The decolonisation of the curriculum was, according to activist students, meant to lead to closer introspection on curriculum development and its processes and the lecturer – student relationship. Student activists were calling for the inclusion of students as partners in curriculum development.

The idea of students as partners, change agents, producers, and co-creators of their learning, has since become a necessary consideration for higher education institutions globally and in South Africa. It is a marked change from traditional curriculum development process in which students are on the periphery, with clearly defined roles for academics as decision makers and students as recipients of predetermined knowledge without voice and agency (see, for example, Bovill, Cook-Sather, Felten, Millard & Moore-Cherry, 2015). Involving students in curriculum development as partners in the co-creation process is considered to be a "counter-narrative that challenges traditional and neoliberal views, creating spaces for relational narratives" (Matthews et al., 2019:281) in curriculum development.

Towards an epistemology of uncertainty: Establishing a new curriculum development pathway

According to Leibowitz, Bozalek, Carolissen, Nicholls, Rohleder and Swartz (2010:129) "for students to learn to live in an age of uncertainty or unsafety, it is also true that the lecturers themselves have to be prepared to learn, and to venture into hidden areas of self and unfamiliar theoretical study".

The dominant teacher-centred approach at our institution (and arguably in many higher education institutions) limits, participatory and critical approaches to learning. Decisions regarding what to include in the curriculum and the textbooks selected at South African universities generally celebrate Western ideas and neglect African epistemologies. The need to involve students in the knowledge creation process is difficult but necessary. Our experiences of teaching in South Africa (particularly in universities of technology) have taught us that students tend to become anxious when required to source information from multiple sources as they are used to textbook-based learning. A sense of anxiety and uncertainty engulfs them and stands in the way of full participation in the creation and implementation of new and continually changing curricula. Previous experiences have also shown that even when lecturers have intentions to create transformative teaching and learning spaces where students are invited to co-create their learning experiences, students do not automatically accept this.

Ironically, one of the challenges we face as lecturers attempting to decolonise the curriculum is student resistance to new approaches to curriculum development. While activist students who took part in the FMF and RMF movements are vocal about curriculum transformation, many students still resist new forms of teaching and learning. One of the key reasons behind students' resistance is the pedagogy used in most South African basic education institutions that encourages and rewards what Freire terms the banking education model – where knowledge is transmitted from the teacher to the student through a predetermined and set curriculum (Saleh, 2013). Primary and secondary school education is still defined by a prevalence of transmission-based pedagogies and the dominance of oral discourse, with teachers employing behaviourist practices such as chorusing oral drill sequences or whole-class reading of fragmented sentences or texts from the board (Hoadley, 2012). In our experience, much learning in higher education, but more specifically in universities of technology, continues to rely on similar methodologies. The context above makes a case for why it's necessary to develop student and lecturer capacity before co-creation of the curriculum can take place. Bevis and Watson (2000:8) suggest that, in this model of curriculum development, students and teachers can participate as "collegial participants". However, for this to be successful teachers and students must be provided with the necessary guidance to become comfortable with engaging in the creation of a dynamic and critical curriculum across power differentials.

Becoming colleagues through common experiences

Davis and Steyn (2012) suggest that when working with participatory, liberating pedagogies, addressing positionality allows identification of dominant positions and pedagogical assumptions that may influence the process. Our project team consisted of differently positioned individuals in terms of race (black, coloured, white) and nationality (South African, Nigerian and Austrian). The team was also inter-disciplinary with members from journalism, engineering, and academic staff development. For us, the journey to becoming a team was not an easy one and is an ongoing process. There have been critical moments on this journey, that we reflect on here to offer a glimpse into different team members' thoughts and feelings on the journey.

Our reflections, some written straight after meetings, some written for this chapter, are examples of how we individually and collectively experienced the process of co-creating the curriculum. We reflect on our various meetings and encounters, and workshops facilitated, decisions we took and the challenge of collaboratively writing given our diverse positionality, disciplinary backgrounds and academic practices. These writings not only allow insight into the process, but they also position us and our subjectivities. The way we write says a lot about who we are and where we are coming from (in terms of gender, age, race, discipline and academic seniority).

Positionality also plays a role in how we engage with each other and who we are becoming in this process of co-creation across difference. It also has an impact on how we see the world and how the world engages with us. We have woven our reflections from our different positionalities and used literature and theory to analyse and explain what was revealed to us in the process of co-creation. For this reason, we adopted an auto-ethnographic approach in this project. Through this qualitative approach, we were able to delve into our own lives and link it to other peoples' lives and experiences, connecting the autobiographical and the personal to the cultural, social, and political. We draw from Ellis and Bochner (2000:739) who state that "an autobiographical genre of writing [that] displays multiple layers of consciousness, connecting the personal to the cultural".

Our key positionalities are[3]:

- Lecturer A: (Black) African, female
- Lecturer B: (Black) African, male

---

3   Racial categories used, see Kornegay, 2005.

- Academic Staff Developer A: White, female
- Academic Staff Developer B: (Black) Coloured, female
- Student A: (Black) African, male
- Student B: (Black) African, male

Act One: Setting the scene

At the beginning of this project four of the authors of this paper, the two academic staff developers and two faculty academics, met a couple of times to start planning and setting up space for this project. Most of our time in these meetings was taken up by trying to get to grips with what co-creation, and "doing things differently" would mean, as the reflections below show.

In these reflections, we explored our roles within the institution as well as the structures and systems that hold all of this together. To help us to do this, we used social realist Margaret Archer's (1995) concepts of structure, culture and agency. Archer's work on structure and culture helped in our sense-making of the multilayered and complex interactions within higher education and how the transformation of social structures can take place (Vorster & Quinn, 2017). The structural domain within the university typically consists of the various "roles, organisations, institutions and systems" (Archer, 1995:1). Archer (1995) defines culture as propositions and constructs, ideologies and theories, beliefs and values that exist independently of whether people are aware of them, believe in them or agree with them. Exploring the cultural system within the university necessitates an interrogation of the dominant discourses that convey the ideas, beliefs, theories and values. Agency, derived from human reflexivity, is a process of internal deliberation in which concerns, commitments and knowledgeability play a role (Winberg, 2017). This becomes evident in our reflections. Our initial approaches were fairly teacher-centred, and we assumed our roles and responsibilities as academics and teachers. Later, we started questioning the power structures and our roles in perpetuating them by regularly reflecting on how we engage with each other in this process.

Decolonising pedagogies call for disrupting colonial power by first acknowledging its structures and the impact of these structures on practices and processes (Iseke-Barnes, 2008). It soon became clear to us that we had to look earnestly at our identities and inter-disciplinary toolkits and how they affected each of us and our thinking. We got stuck in being participants in a study that had an administrative responsibility at an institutional level to appoint a "project leader" to run the project and report on it while creating a space of equality and research partnership with students. Our intention was for students and staff to share power in curriculum decision-making. However, as Cook-Sather (2014) recognise, there are challenges inherent in this approach because of the structural constraints when organising a course, such as lecturers being subject discipline experts and the need for lecturers to comply with quality assurance responsibilities of the institution.

We interspersed the following sections with a selection of our reflections, written at various points in the process whenever critical moments arose and as we were trying to make sense of how processes were unfolding.

> **Lecturer A:** I am excited and nervous when I am informed that I have received the grant for the curriculum co-creation project. Excited about my first experience of research leadership. Nervous that I have to lead a co-creation and collaboration project. A scary prospect, as I have to think about what that means in practical terms. This will be my opportunity to get the answers I have been looking for. I want to know all the possible factors leading to a lack of student capacity in the curriculum co-creation process. Are students aware of it? How do they think about it?

> **Academic Developer A:** I am excited about the project; I want to know how do we include more stakeholders, where are their voices? We are missing students. I fear giving up control, where will this project lead us?

> **Academic Developer B:** The struggle for me is being open to [listening] – actively and carefully to others instead of constantly placing my prior experience and knowledge at the forefront. Challenging the status quo, common terminology and the meaning we have made of it constantly contaminates my thinking and possibly influences the direction I take.

Our reflections highlight the struggles related to structure, culture and agency that we had to grapple with from the beginning. Universities operate in hierarchical ways, and we internalised this hierarchical approach as seen in the statement "*lead a co-creation and collaboration project*" that assumes individual leadership in what should be a participatory process. Letting go of familiar structures challenged us from the beginning as seen in one of the reflections "*I fear giving up control*" and "*the struggle is being open to listen[ing], actively and carefully*". While we were aware that the project would change us, we were not aware of the depth of the change that would take place as will be demonstrated by later reflections. We link the personal and the political to move away from an individual therapeutic approach that allows us to not see behaviours and practices as pathologies but as deeply embedded in the structures and cultures we are dealing with.

We recognised that the project was calling for a new way of developing curriculum, and we, therefore, began thinking about how to liberate the project and ourselves from the thinking in ways we were accustomed to, so that as lecturers and students we could all become more equal, active participants in this educational project (Freire, 2005). We wondered how we would manage to create the space required for this, given our previous experiences with students and curriculum. Our experiences had shown higher education as structured in a way that fosters hierarchies between staff and students.

We went back to our initial inspiration, Freire (2005) and decided to focus on using dialogic pedagogies to disrupt the prevailing structures that marginalise some and maintain the privilege of others. We were going to allow ourselves to undergo the experiment we wanted to report on by working alongside students as colleagues. We began by inviting students to participate in the project and realised that we would have to create a participatory approach that allowed students to enter and stay as equals in the process.

Act Two: Engaging students as partners in research

Two postgraduate engineering students joined the team. We had put out a call to students from different faculties to join us but ended up with engineering students because these were the students who responded and we felt it would be an interesting dynamic to test out a co-creation project that had an engineering lecturer and engineering students who had to work as equal partners. When we decided to invite students into the project, we were not sure how we would move our relationship from student-lecturer to colleagues and research partners.

Our first meeting started as a research subject interview with most of the attention focused on introducing the project and explaining the research – that immediately set up hierarchies of those who were "in the know" and those who "were not". We asked students to share their experiences of being in higher education, and it became clear that this method would not work in building a research partnership and deconstructing the power differentials and hierarchy in the room. We had to find a new method that would create equality and relatability amongst all of us. Our previous work with facilitating race dialogues and workshops helped us come up with an equalising ice-breaker activity.

We were all part of higher education, and even though we were in different positions, what we had in common was that we had all gone through the higher education system as students. The ice-breaker activity required all present to write down five words that described their experiences of postmatric education – as an undergraduate student, a postgraduate student and a lecturer or teaching assistant. This seemed to work and helped to change the power dynamics in the room. As we shared our experiences of education, we began to embrace the diversity, and the similarities in the room and an equal relationship began to emerge organically. What we envisaged as a short ice-breaker developed into two hours of rich sharing of experiences, discovering commonalities but also differences in our experiences that spanned two continents, three disciplines and differently positioned institutions.

We experienced significant shifts in our thinking. We began seeking ways to challenge the binaries of student versus lecturer. It was through the identification and collective discussion of our various roles that we realised commonalities. The dialogic nature of the process contributed to reconfiguring pre-established power relations. We found that through this open space and engagement, sharing, talking and reflecting, a new setting for curriculum co-creation emerged. Organically, a "relocation" of knowledge exchange developed that challenged and disrupted conventional forms of "situated knowledge" (Westman & Bergmark, 2018). We, as academics were satisfied with the first academic-student meeting, but it was up to the students to decide if we could enter a research partnership and the next phase. We were anxious to find out what the students thought of the whole process and how they experienced it.

> **Student A:** We felt most welcomed in that first meeting, and we freely participated. The objectives of the project were explained, and we openly shared our experiences as we had thought it was more of a one-off interview. Everyone was asked to give reflections of their days as students (undergraduate and postgraduate). It was interesting to note the difference in cultures, societies and systems in different institutions. Everyone was able to at least point at the flaws in their institutes that needed decolonisation and viable solutions.

> **Student B:** The idea to be research partners with people of different backgrounds brought me a challenge of shifting from what I know and move to a space of the unknown. I tried to figure out what could be relevant to the project from my engineering background.

Through the ice-breaker discussions, we seemed to have opened an educational space for co-creation. The student reflections indicate a shift in the power hierarchy to a more open and participatory process as stated: "*We felt most welcomed in that first meeting.*" The second statement, "*The idea to be research partners with people of different backgrounds*", led to the opportunity for lecturers and students to develop their collective agency and the potential to participate as active subjects (Saleh, 2013). This allowed us to work together more equitably by engaging in dialogue with collective reflections in face-to-face meetings. We realised what Freire (2005) meant by dialogue as a co-operative activity involving respect for each other. This was reflected in the following statement: "... *we spoke about our experiences as students and lecturers ... and we were sharing deeply within a few minutes*". While we developed a space of mutual respect and commonality, we needed to remain mindful of the critique levelled at attempts to liberate the curriculum. One of the main critiques of Freire's ideas is that ultimately, the teacher/student relationship is not questioned enough (Ellsworth, 1989). In our case, it might be argued that the fact that the students involved in the project were at a postgraduate level may have influenced the shift in thinking, minimising the typical power relations that exist between a lecturer and an undergraduate student. This would also support Bevis and Watson's (2000) argument that co-creation might be easier with mature students.

Act Three: Embracing discomfort

Critical realism and decolonial pedagogy accompanied us as the theory we could use in building a framework and methodology for the complex process we were engaged in. We knew the only way to facilitate the co-creation of a curriculum in an unequal space, with unequal relationships, was to engage in dialogue. We had to deconstruct the power structures of institutions and colonisation to understand, disrupt and destroy them. The process for this was not always clear, and all of us were on an uncertain journey of discovery.

> **Lecturer B:** It's been a fluid process from the beginning, but there is still a central theme that keeps bringing us back to the core. Is it co-designing that's the central theme? Or the fact that we are challenging the norm? If challenging the norm and search for an innovative way of learning is the central theme, then we might need to challenge the terminology or pedagogy of co-designing ... This process is challenging our individuality.

Working as equitable partners in this project revealed the levels of discomfort that lecturers experienced in a co-created process of curriculum development. The principles of partnership, namely respect, reciprocity and shared responsibility, became an important guide for us to work as "true partners" (Lubicz-Nawrocka, 2017; Cook-Sather, 2014). The internal resistance that we were going through was reflected in our writing, an unconscious unwillingness of letting go as reflected in the phrase, "*this process is challenging our individuality*".

We had to have courageous conversations as suggested by Vorster and Quinn (2017), about what constitutes knowledge and the implications this holds for epistemological access. More importantly, we needed to recognise the necessity of the kind of discomfort we were experiencing. While we were thinking and challenging ourselves, two calls for papers were brought to our attention. One was a call for a Community Engagement and Social Innovation Conference in Grahamstown, and the other was the call for the development of this chapter. We worked on and sent in an abstract for the book chapter and a workshop abstract for the Grahamstown conference. These tasks seemed straightforward and easy to accomplish for the academics, but we would later find out that it was not the same for all group members. The academic writing process held hidden lessons for our project team.

> **Student A:** I spent about ten minutes reading through the one-page book chapter abstract twice to assimilate its contents. I was well acquainted with the information detailing the background, aim and the identified objectives of the project. However, I was not an education student and therefore felt challenged by the need to read up on the theory on curriculum development for higher education. Additionally, I felt a need to understand the research methodology that we were following, as it was based on Margaret Archer's theory. Although these theories were far from my discipline, I felt that reading and understanding them would improve my contribution [to] the group.

It came as a surprise to the rest of the team that the student participants were not as comfortable with the abstract and writing exercise as the academics were. The students' engineering backgrounds meant that they were not familiar with education theories and felt alienated by the process compared to academics who regularly reflect on teaching and learning even if they are not education theory experts. Only our ongoing attempts at self-reflection and the students' courageous self-awareness allowed us to deepen our understanding of the power dynamics at play. We were struggling to work from a place of equality and epistemic power. As lecturers, we needed to learn to be more open to other perspectives.

> **Lecturer B:** From the second meeting onward, we seem to diverge every now and then, but a common goal kept bringing us back. This could be attributed to looking through the lens of the students. Teachers needed to 'step down' from their 'lofty heights' into the world of the learners.

> **Academic Developer B:** I try to be aware of my own identity and power. Navigating this new space is difficult. Are we capable of free thought? Are we able to allow what needs to emerge, [to] emerge fluently, and are we able to be fluid about this process? These are the questions on my mind. It is scary …

We recognised that the power differential within our context of working together as lecturers and students would constantly emerge, but we needed to move beyond this to achieve our goal. Fricker (2013:1327) suggests using Margaret Gilbert's "joint commitment" model. This model reminded us to reflect on intentionality, purpose, actions, beliefs and political obligation. Despite our differences, our openness to the process and willingness to participate honestly provided us with resilience and a joint commitment to achieving our goals.

Act Four: Disenchanted or disempowered

It was time to make travel arrangements and source funding for a workshop, and we encountered yet another obstacle – how to get our student research partners from Cape Town to Grahamstown (the conference venue). Institutionally, student funding for conferences is available only for thesis-related conferences and via supervisors. Staff members were able to secure funding for travel while students were not able to.

> **Student B:** The constraint of not participating in the workshop at Grahamstown due to funding issues came to me unexpectedly, as I reflected on the invitation to participate in [the] space of equal research partners. The challenge of power hierarchy remained an unresolved puzzle, and it made me question the level to which my contribution would be to the entire project if such limitations would exist onwards.

Funding the trip for all project members was not the only challenge we faced in the wake of our first "public" appearance as the project team. In our preparatory meetings, our diverse ways of seeing and being clashed violently, exposing more differences in our process of co-creation as the following reflection shows.

> **Lecturer A:** It transpired in workshop planning conversations that our understanding of what the project was about was not the same. I was frustrated by the back and forth about what exactly we were doing. Why were we constantly in conflict about which methodology to follow to get to the next step?

> **Academic Developer B:** The conflict in the group has become an unnecessary distraction. It is taking up too much time and space. People are holding onto ideas and positions without listening to each other, which results in frustration. At some point, I am feeling like an outsider looking in – we are singing from the same song sheet, but some of us are slightly off-key.

We decided to use a World Café methodology for the workshop to facilitate large group dialogue. This decision was largely influenced by the work of Manning (2013:76) who emphasises the need to find new ways of igniting "thought that is experienced rather than known". The intention with the World Café was to create such encounters between individuals, across difference, pedagogies, materials, space and time (Springgay, 2014). We used dialogical processes and structured activities such as check-ins and the World Café, based on democratic, "liberating" principles to challenge power dynamics. In talking through the methodology, we were also able to see why we were constantly in conflict. We were working across difference and learning to be comfortable in being challenged while struggling with having our foundational philosophies and approaches to research questioned.

> **Academic Developer A:** After a rocky start, with us not being able to agree on even the smallest bits, we managed to facilitate a difficult process, with participants responding amazingly, allowing us a glimpse into how powerful these methodologies can be but also the importance of a diverse facilitation team (once we got over ourselves).

> **Lecturer B:** The workshop in Grahamstown served as our proof of concept trial. It was scary to kick-start the workshop, but it was amazing to see buy-in from very diverse participants. There were vulnerability, honesty and revelations made. In some instances, it felt as if we provided a voice to what many people have been grappling with no voice or platform, to discuss the issues.

Final Act: Building the first guidelines for co-creation

One of the key elements for a democratic and participatory approach to curriculum co-creation is the development of guidelines for engaging across difference and power hierarchies (Westman & Bergmark, 2018). Finding ways of engaging through a co-created curriculum and research project, despite the challenges, called for rethinking the status quo of clearly defined structures; roles and spaces within higher education as described by Archer (1995). Universities globally have been structured by these roles with academic domains for staff as decision makers, students without voice (Bovill et al., 2015) and with limited community engagement in curriculum development. Increasingly, new forms of engagement have gained interest, where students are considered as partners, change agents, producers, and co-creators of their learning. (Bovill et al., 2015; Carey, 2013; Dunne, Zandstra, Brown & Nurser, 2011). Throughout this project, some principles for co-creation across differences emerged:

1. *Develop an epistemology of uncertainty* by starting with an open methodology: principles are – whoever comes are the right people, whatever happens is the only thing that could have happened, whenever it starts is the time, whenever the conversation happens it is the right moment when it is over (see Stadler, n.d.). Use the methodology and be prepared to look for new approaches once the chosen ones do not work.

2. *Identify all stakeholders in your process and make sure a cross-section of stakeholders is present.* In our case, we were an interdisciplinary, multi-gender, multiracial, multicultural and multinational team.

3. *Recognise and affirm the presence of difference and diversity.* Diversity does not automatically lead to increased representation of diverse voices, opinions, philosophies and methodologies. There needs to be an intention to cultivate difference through recognition of and challenging each other's thinking.

4. *Use dialogical pedagogies to cultivate mutual respect.* Seek methods that build equality; they must be democratic structures and activities, for example, dialogic pedagogies (Freire, 2005) that actively seek to rupture prevailing structures that marginalise some and maintain the privilege of others. Turn hierarchy and structure upside down – those who usually do not lead must lead, marginalised voices must be given prominence.

5. *Build trust and allow for deep vulnerability across different members.* Affect is a very important part of this learning process. It is only in sharing collective experiences, roles, identities and struggles that a sense of connection and belonging can emerge.

6. *Recognise that different people will play different roles in the team at different times.* Some people may take the role of active participant while others may take the role of observer, and this will change at different times of the process. The emotional labour will also not be equal for all in the team all the time. Remain mindful of embracing the principles of partnership: respect, reciprocity and shared responsibility.

7. *Identify missing skills and capabilities and seek external help to fill them.* This is difficult and ground-breaking work. It is important to seek help and external resources if necessary and allow the necessary time for this learning to unfold. This work expands beyond processes and projects and might affect participants beyond institutional spaces. This is a personal and communal journey of transformation so self-care and knowing (while pushing) one's boundaries become as important as caring for others. Expand the dialogue beyond the core group, and beyond the institution, so more voices can contribute.

8. *Intentionality and a shared vision are at the core of the co-creation process.* Focus on relationships and see human beings as interdependent, vulnerable and temporal beings. True partnership and co-creation can only take place when all project participants use their agency to collaborate within and outside their institutions.

9. *The group represents a microcosm of society, and all society's structures of inequality will be replicated each time you gather.* Each team member must be responsible for accepting and giving "call-outs" on blind spots, reflecting and doing better next time. Sometimes backchannel conversations outside the group are helpful to unpack difficult processes in the project. However, all conflicts that arise should be openly discussed in the group.

Conclusion

In this chapter, that is part theoretical and part reflective, we shared our experience of co-creation, the challenges experienced, and the lessons learned. We first described the context by providing historical perspectives on curriculum development in South Africa and particularly at universities of technology. Then we reflected on critical moments in our co-creation journey and finally suggested a list of guidelines for co-creation across difference.

We were working to build a new methodology while having different approaches to research, and our different approaches were clashing and forcing us to re-examine them. Through the process of dialogue and co-creation, we discovered the need to learn from and support a diversity of ideas and thoughts (Cook-Sather & Li, 2013), experiences and knowledge. By engaging in this manner, a pedagogical practice emerged in which all project participants could collectively develop a sense of confidence and capacity (Cook-Sather & Agu, 2013). At the start of the journey, the diversity within our team confronted us. As we progressed, we learned that diversity was the key to the success of the team, but we could not plan that its conflict, differences and commonalities would change along the journey.

Mann (2001:130) in Allin (2014), reflecting on challenges often inherent in collaborative projects reminds us of the context of power, knowledge nexus within universities "noting that within this context, social relations are hierarchically organised according to presumed levels of expertise".

Although we knew the structure and hierarchy of the university, going into the project, it was only through the experience of working together that we were reminded of the stark inequalities. We had to acknowledge that our experiences, knowledge, skills and expertise influenced our various contributions. What became very clear was that power hierarchies are hard to break and who speaks is influenced by hierarchy and experience. We often wondered what kept us going, what made us come back and we concluded that it was a shared goal, even if that goal was not always clearly defined. Co-creating in these new spaces is deeply unsettling and discomforting, challenging us to rethink who we are and what we base this authority on, but can also lead to new and exciting learning opportunities. It needs courage sharing this space - taking responsibility with and for each other, helped us through. In the end, it is the relationships that keep us going, becoming with each other, the mutual vulnerability and interdependence that allowed us to form bonds that saw us through the moments of crisis.

Engaging across racial, gender and class difference in South Africa, is challenging and requires "a set of cognitive, affective, and behavioural skills and characteristics that support effective and appropriate interaction" (Bennett, 2008:97). In moments of crisis (such as exemplified in the decision of who was going to Grahamstown and when we wrote the abstract) open and continuous dialogue and engagement helped us to work through the challenges. Often these moments of conflict were the greatest learning opportunities that brought about the realisation that team members have different roles at different moments. Team members relatively quickly found their roles and positions, more or less comforting, some claiming more active roles, others acting as observers. However, it is important to note that these roles are fluid, always changing, and can and should be challenged. We also need to note, that engaging some stakeholders is easier than others so while we tried to move out of the institutional context, we struggled to engage the community outside higher education and industry in the same way as we did with actors within academic institutions. Our chapter breaks the conventional separation between theory and practice, and curriculum co-development should do the same. It should blend critique and creativity in new ways each time it is run. It can do this by inviting students and lecturers to theorise practical work and doing creative projects that are an extension and articulation of theoretical debates.

Our experience also taught us that, while there are some common guidelines or processes that one can and will follow, to operate in hierarchical, traditional institutions is constraining, but what we learned is that these institutions can be challenged from within. Resistance is possible from the bottom up, and alternative practices, processes and spaces can be created that help navigate these unequal terrains, especially if academics, academic developers, students and other actors collaborate to co-create curriculum (Westman & Bergmark, 2018).

Acknowledgement

We want to thank the WISH Group and in particular the Decolonising Teaching and Learning Practices subgroup, that seeded the first ideas around co-creating curricula. Orson Nava for asking important questions around co-creation of curricula, that stopped us in our tracks, but also allowed us a more meaningful way forward. The British Council and the CPUT RIFTAL fund for supporting us in our journey.

References

ADESINA, J. 2017. Mahmood Mamdani: Meeting the Challenge of Decolonisation. *Thabo Mbeki Foundation: Dedicated to Africa's Renaissance*, 24 May. [https://bit.ly/2mqwrfQ]

ALLIN, L. 2014. Collaboration between Staff and Students in the Scholarship of Teaching and Learning: The Potential and the Problems. *Teaching and Learning Inquiry: The ISSOTL Journal*, 2(1):95-102. [https://doi.org/10.2979/teachlearninqu.2.1.95]

APPLE, M.W. 2013. *Can education change society?* New York: Routledge.

ARCHER, M. 2007. *Making Our Way through the World: Human Reflexivity and Social Mobility*. Cambridge: Cambridge University Press. [https://doi.org/10.1017/CBO9780511618932]

ARCHER, M. 1995. *Realist Social Theory: The morphogenetic approach*. Cambridge: Cambridge University Press. [https://doi.org/10.1017/CBO9780511557675]

BADAT, S. 2010. *The challenges of transformation in higher education and training institutions in South Africa*. Johannesburg: Development Bank of Southern Africa.

BENNETT, J.M. 2008. Transformative Training: Designing Programs for Culture Learning. In: M.A. Moodian (ed). *Contemporary Leadership and Intercultural Competence: Understanding and Utilizing Cultural Diversity to Build Successful Organizations*. Thousand Oaks, California: Sage, 95-110. [https://doi.org/10.4135/9781452274942.n8]

BEVIS, E.O. & WATSON, J. 2000. *Toward a caring curriculum: A new pedagogy for nursing*. Sudbury, MA: Jones and Bartlett.

BOUGHEY, C. 2010. *Academic development for improved efficiency in the higher education and training system in South Africa*. Johannesburg: Development Bank of Southern Africa.

BOVILL, C.; COOK-SATHER, A.; FELTEN, P.; MILLARD, L. & MOORE-CHERRY, N. 2015. Addressing potential challenges in co-creating learning and teaching: Overcoming resistance, navigating institutional norms and ensuring inclusivity in student-staff partnerships. *Higher Education* May. [http://dx.doi.org/10.1007/s10734-015-9896-4]

BREIER, M. & HERMAN, C. 2017. The PhD conundrum in South African academia. *Higher Education Quarterly*, 71(4):352-368. [https://doi.org/10.1111/hequ.12134]

CAREY, P. 2013. Student as co-producer in a marketised higher education system: a case study of students' experience of participation in curriculum design. *Innovations in Education and Teaching International*, 50(3):250-260. [https://doi.org/10.1080/14703297.2013.796714]

CHE (COUNCIL ON HIGHER EDUCATION). 2016. *South African higher education reviewed: two decades of democracy*. Pretoria: CHE. [https://bit.ly/2klWpk1]

COOK-SATHER, A. 2014. Student-faculty partnership in explorations of pedagogical practice: a threshold concept in academic development. *International Journal for Academic Development*, 19(3):186-198. [https://doi.org/10.1080/1360144X.2013.805694]

COOK-SATHER, A. & AGU, P. 2013. Students consultants of colour and faculty members working together toward culturally sustaining pedagogy. In: J.E. Groccia & L. Cruz (eds). *To Improve the Academy: Resources for Faculty, Instructional, and Organizational Development*. San Francisco: Jossey-Bass, 271-285. [https://doi.org/10.1002/j.2334-4822.2013.tb00710.x]

COOK-SATHER, A. & LI, H. 2013. Lessons from international students on campus living and classroom learning. Paper presented at 38th Annual Professional and Organizational Development Network in Higher Education Conference, Pittsburgh, Pennsylvania, 6-10 November.

DAVIS, D. & STEYN, M. 2012. Teaching social justice: Reframing some common pedagogical assumptions. *Perspectives in Education*, 30:29-38. [https://bit.ly/2m5QIqY]

DUNNE, E.; ZANDSTRA, R.; BROWN, T. & NURSER, T. 2011. *Students as change agents: new ways of engaging with learning and teaching in higher education*. Bristol: University of Exeter (Escalate Higher Education Academy Subject Centre for Education). [https://bit.ly/2l4vDgv]

DU PRE, R. 2010. Universities of technology in the context of the South African higher education landscape. Universities of Technology – Deepening the Debate. *Kagisano*, 7 (February). Pretoria: CHE. [https://bit.ly/2mmYb4Z]

ELLIS, C. & BOCHNER, A. 2000. Autoethnography, personal narrative, reflexivity: Researcher as subject. In: N.K. Denzin & Y.S. Lincoln (eds). *Handbook of Qualitative Research*. 2nd Edition. London: Sage, 733-768.

ELLSWORTH, E. 1989. Why doesn't this feel empowering? Working through the repressive myths of critical pedagogy. *Harvard educational review*, 59(3):297-325. [https://doi.org/10.17763/haer.59.3.058342114k266250]

FREIRE, P. 2005. P*edagogy of the oppressed*. New York: Continuum.

FRICKER, M. 2013. Epistemic Justice as a condition of political freedom? *Synthese*, 190(7):1317-1332. [https://doi.org/10.1007/s11229-012-0227-3]

GARRAWAY, J. & WINBERG, C. 2018. Fictive scripting: Reimagining futures of universities of technology. Paper presented at 9th Contemporary Higher Education: Close Up Research For Times of Change Conference, Newlands, Cape Town, 15-16 November. [https://bit.ly/2mxMvwy]

GIROUX, H.A. 1997. *Pedagogy and the Politics of Hope: Theory, Culture and Schooling*. Boulder, Colorado and Oxford: Westview Press.

GIROUX, H.A. 1983. *Theory and resistance in education. A pedagogy for the opposition*. London: Heinemann.

HOADLEY, U. 2012. What do we know about teaching and learning in South African primary schools? *Education as Change*, 16(2):187-202. [https://doi.org/10.1080/16823206.2012.745725]

HOOKS, B. 1994. *Teaching to Transgress – Education as the Practice to Freedom*. New York and London: Routledge.

ISEKE-BARNES, J.M. 2008. Pedagogies for Decolonising. *Canadian Journal of Native Education*, 31(1):123-148. [https://bit.ly/2l4oooP]

KNOWLEDGE HUB. 2015. What is unique about universities of technology, and what are the benefits of studying at these institutions? Bridge: Linking Innovators in Education. [https://bit.ly/2miLhoF]

KORNEGAY, F. 2005. *Race and Ethnic Relations Barometer: A Narrative Analysis of Findings*. Johannesburg: The Centre for Policy Studies, May. [https://bit.ly/2l3tqBM]

LEIBOWITZ, B.; BOZALEK, V.; CAROLISSEN, R.; NICHOLLS, L.; ROHLEDER, P. & SWARTZ, L. 2010. Bringing the social into pedagogy: unsafe learning in an uncertain world, *Teaching in Higher Education*, 15(2):123-133. [https://doi.org/10.1080/13562511003619953]

LUBICZ-NAWROCKA, T. 2017. Co-creation of the curriculum: challenging the status quo to embed partnership. *Journal of Educational Innovation, Partnership and Change*, 3(2). [https://doi.org/10.15173/ijsap.v2i1.3207]

Mann, S.J. 2008. *Study, power and the university*. Maidenhead: Open University Press (Society for Research into Higher Education).

Mann, S.J. 2001. Alternative perspectives on the student experience: Alienation and engagement. *Studies in Higher Education*, 26(1):7-19. [https://doi.org/10.1080/03075070020030689]

Manning, E. 2013. *Always more than one: Individuation's dance*. London: Duke University Press. [https://doi.org/10.1215/9780822395829]

Matthews, K.E, Cook-Sather, A.; Acai, A.; Dvorakova, S.L.; Felten, P.; Marquis, E. & Mercer-Mapstone, L. 2019. Toward theories of partnership praxis: an analysis of interpretive framing in literature on students as partners in teaching and learning. *Higher Education Research and Development*, 38(2):280-293. [https://doi.org/10.1080/07294360.2018.1530199]

McLaren, P. 2009. Critical Pedagogy: A Look at the Major Concepts. In: A. Darder, M.P. Baltodano & R.D. Torres (eds). *The Critical Pedagogy Reader*. New York: Routledge.

Monnapula-Mapesela, M. 2017. Developing as an academic leader in a university of technology in South Africa: Dealing with enabling and constraining teaching and learning environments. *Critical Studies in Teaching and Learning*, 5(2):69-85. [https://bit.ly/2ky81k9]

RSA (Republic of South Africa). 1997. *Higher Education Act 101 of 1997*. Pretoria: Government Printing Works.

Saleh, S.E. 2013. Paolo Freire's philosophy on contemporary education. *University Bulletin*, 15(1):91-111. [https://bit.ly/2m4lDnI]

Springgay, S. 2014. 'Approximate-Rigorous-Abstractions': Propositions of Activation for Posthumanist Research. In: N. Snaza & J. Weaver (eds). *Posthumanism and educational research*. New York: Routledge, 90-102.

Stadler, A. n.d. Doing an Open Space: A Two Page Primer. OpenSpaceWorld.org. [https://bit.ly/2dxNwLI]

Tarling, I. & Ng'ambi, D. 2016. Teachers pedagogical change framework: A diagnostic tool for changing teachers' uses of emerging technologies. *British Journal of Educational Technology*, 47(3):554-572. [https://doi.org/10.1111/bjet.12454]

Volbrecht, T. & Boughey, C. 2004. Curriculum responsiveness from the margins? A reappraisal of academic development in South Africa. In: H. Griesel (ed). *Curriculum responsiveness: Case studies in Higher Education*. Pretoria: South African Universities Vice-Chancellors Association, 57-80.

Vorster, J. & Quinn, L. 2017. 'The decolonial Turn': What does it mean for academic staff development. *Education as Change*, 21(1):31-49. [https://doi.org/10.17159/1947-9417/2017/853]

Westman, S. & Bergmark, U. 2018. Re-considering the onto-epistemology of student engagement in higher education. *Educational Philosophy and Theory*, 23 March. [https://bit.ly/2mrx2xR]

Winberg, C. 2017. 'Extreme teaching': Exercising Agency in difficult contexts. In: B. Leibowitz, V. Bozalek & P. Kahn (eds). *Theorising learning to teach*. Routledge: London.

CHAPTER 17

"I just felt like I was trying to swim through molasses"

Curriculum renewal at a research-intensive university

Cecilia Jacobs

Introduction

In this chapter, I explore the process of curriculum renewal at a research-intensive university, Stellenbosch University (South Africa), from the perspective of programme coordinators. Curriculum renewal has been a strategic priority of the University with the Deputy Vice-Chancellor Learning and Teaching driving an institution-wide curriculum renewal project. The participants in this project are made up of the Deputy Deans Teaching and Learning in the faculties, along with selected programme leaders per faculty, as well as managers from the Division for Learning and Teaching Enhancement, such as the director of the Centre for Teaching and Learning. Although the academic development advisors from the Centre for Teaching and Learning did not form part of the curriculum renewal project team, they were drawn into faculty-based curriculum renewal processes when invited to do so by the academics.

For some academic development advisors this involvement was quite technical, for example assisting with the writing of programme and module outcomes, while for others the involvement was at a much more fundamental level, for example providing theoretical frameworks for curriculum renewal and advising on matters such as overall programme coherence and the role of disciplinary knowledge. The faculties themselves determined the level of involvement of academic developers in their curriculum renewal practices. My involvement in the research component of the institutional curriculum renewal project was as an academic developer and one of a team of researchers. Data from research on this project revealed resistance to and lack of ownership of the process of curriculum renewal. Follow-up research arising from this project (Young & Jacobs, 2017), found that programme coordinators play a pivotal role in the practice of curriculum renewal and that partnerships between academic developers and programme coordinators could provide the kinds of spaces for the disruption and re-imagining of curricula. In this chapter, I take these research findings further by analysing the views of programme coordinators at Stellenbosch University, regarding their role and the role of collaborating academic developers in the practice of curriculum renewal.

Background

Curriculum renewal, as previously mentioned, is a strategic priority of the University and is driven through an institution-wide curriculum renewal project. At the start of this project focus group sessions were conducted with groups of academics who were centrally involved in curriculum renewal, from all of the ten faculties at the University. This data revealed resistance to and lack of "ownership" of the process of curriculum renewal. Participants in these focus group sessions reported that curriculum renewal was often "the job of one person", the programme coordinator, who was often "at the mercy of individual academics" who resisted the process. Many of the academics in these focus group sessions regarded their researcher identity as primary, and they saw curriculum renewal as a low-level responsibility. One programme coordinator described the process of curriculum renewal as "trying to swim through molasses".

Earlier research arising from this project (Van der Merwe, Schoonwinkel & Hubball, 2017:13) identified one of the barriers to successful programme renewal as a narrow focus, "on module level, with a lack of communication between departments and individual module chairs because of the perceived complexity of holistic programme renewal". This same study identified one of the enablers of successful programme renewal as "a dedicated driver who takes ownership of the process ... assisted by a team of dedicated experts, including academics and professional academic support staff focused on curriculum development, assessment strategies, appropriate modes of delivery, policies, etc." Follow-up research (Young & Jacobs, 2017) revealed that when academic developers work in partnerships with academics in curriculum renewal spaces, differing conceptions arise in such collaborations about the role of academic developers in the practice of programme renewal. This has implications for collaborative programme renewal practices. It appears that programme coordinators play a crucial role in the practice of curriculum renewal, and partnerships between academic developers and programme coordinators could provide the kinds of spaces for the disruption and re-imagining of curricula needed at the University.

Theoretical framing

This chapter draws on the broad field known as the Sociology of Education. One of the scholars in this field, Young (2014:11), claims that curriculum theorists have to be "dual specialists", with a primary specialisation in curriculum theory but also a "level of familiarity" with the specialist fields or disciplines being investigated. He asserts that "curriculum theory falls down" because "the two forms of specialisation, curriculum theory and the particular field under investigation, are rarely brought together". The same could be said of the practice of curriculum renewal, which ideally should be informed by two knowledge bases – disciplinary knowledge, as well as knowledge of curriculum design and renewal. In line with Young's thinking about curriculum theory, and from my own experience as an academic developer, I would argue that the practice of curriculum renewal is seldom informed by both of these knowledge bases. Bernstein (1999) makes a distinction between two forms of knowledge, every day and specialist knowledge. The type of knowledge informing the practice of curriculum renewal is a form of specialist knowledge, which is governed by rules which regulate how this knowledge is accessed, transmitted and evaluated. According to Bernstein (1990), specialist knowledge traverses three fields: "production", "recontextualization" and "reproduction".

The field of "production" is where knowledge is produced, and the production of new knowledge generally takes place in the university or private research organisations. This knowledge is disseminated in research papers, books, patents, artefacts, and so on. The field of "recontextualization" is where knowledge is repackaged as programmes, courses, modules and subjects and this recontextualisation of knowledge, in higher education, is usually undertaken by programme committees, module teams, individual academics. It is also sometimes influenced by the national Department of Higher Education and Training, professional bodies and industry. This knowledge is usually disseminated in curriculum documents, such as study guides and syllabi, as well as textbooks and course readers. The field of "reproduction" is where knowledge is taught and assessed. The reproduction of knowledge, in higher education, usually takes place in lecture halls, tutorials, exam venues, and more often now in virtual spaces in the online arena. This knowledge is disseminated through traditional lecturing, teaching and learning activities, and the assessment of what has been taught and learned. These three fields are hierarchically related. The recontextualisation of knowledge cannot take place without the original production of knowledge, and the reproduction of knowledge cannot take place without the recontextualisation of knowledge. Knowledge changes each time it moves from one field to another, and there is a forward and backward movement of knowledge across these three fields. Most academics, to some degree, are involved in all of these three fields.

Curriculum development and the practice of curriculum renewal lie between the fields of knowledge production and reproduction, in the field of recontextualiation. Disciplinary knowledge produced from research, the field of production, is appropriated through a process of "selection" and "sequencing". Specialist expert knowledge is "selected" from the field of production and repackaged, in the field of recontextualisation, into university disciplines and fields of study through textbooks and also into accredited programmes of study made up of subjects and modules. Within and across the subjects and modules making up a programme, this repackaged knowledge is "sequenced" in particular ways to make it accessible to those outside the specialist domains and to facilitate teaching and learning, for example in textbook chapters and content topics in a syllabus. This repackaged knowledge is also "paced" across semester and year-long modules, with different allocations of time to different sections of the programme of study. These programmes are then taught and assessed, in the field of reproduction, as subjects and modules, after a further process of selection and sequencing by lecturers, and the knowledge is pedagogised (Singh, 2002).

There is a struggle in the field of recontextualisation for control about what knowledge gets selected, by whom, and how this knowledge is transformed into pedagogic forms. I am arguing that these struggles need to be informed by both disciplinary knowledge and knowledge of curriculum. To make decisions about what goes into a curriculum, in what order and how much time is allocated to the different sections of the curriculum, curriculum designers in programme committees and module teams need to focus on the broader purposes of their curriculum, or what Johan Muller (2009) calls its "epistemic destiny". My contention is that such meta-level discussions, about the broad purposes of curricula and their overall coherence, are often lost in the detail of what content knowledge should be included or excluded in particular modules making up a programme.

Muller (2009) offers two ways of thinking about curricula more broadly to understand the internal coherence of a curriculum: the qualities of "conceptual coherence" and "contextual coherence". "Conceptual coherence" refers to curricula which are more vertical in nature, where there is a hierarchy of abstraction, and where the sequence of the abstract knowledge matters. Such curricula emphasise learning from principles and produce knowledge from theory. "Contextual coherence" refers to curricula which are more horizontal in nature, where the connections between abstract knowledge are more segmental, and where sequence is less important in knowledge-building. Such curricula emphasise learning by doing and produce knowledge through action. Muller states that all curricula have elements of both qualities, but differ in the emphasis. Some curricula are more conceptual (for example, the formative degrees), while other curricula more contextual (for example, the professional degrees).

While Muller offers us binaries to think with (conceptual/contextual; theory/practice; principles/procedures; head/hand), Barnett, Parry and Coate (2001) offer a third domain to be considered in modern curricula – "being" (or "self", as they term it), which they link to identity. They also state that different disciplines place different emphases on these three domains and they play out with different emphases in the curricula of these disciplines. They argue, however, that all curricula need to have all three domains in them. These domains are referred to in different ways in the literature (Knowledge/Attitudes/Skills; Head/Heart/Hands; Know/Be/Do), but there is general agreement that "Knowledge/Head/Know" refers to the disciplinary/content knowledge that students need to master in modules and programmes; "Skills/Hands/Do" refers to the practical application of that knowledge and what students need to do with that knowledge, while "Attitudes/Values/Heart/Be" refers to the attributes to be developed in students to become the kind of graduates envisaged by the modules and programmes they study.

Earlier, I made the point that the practice of curriculum renewal should be informed by both disciplinary knowledge, as well as knowledge of curriculum design and renewal. This, I would argue, is essential for developing holistic, responsive curricula that take account of all three domains – Knowledge, Attitudes and Skills. At Stellenbosch University, where this study is located, previous research (Van der Merwe et al., 2017) has shown that the researcher identity is primary amongst academics, curriculum renewal is seen as a low-level responsibility, and there is resistance to and lack of "ownership" of the process of curriculum renewal. Programme coordinators appear to play a pivotal role in the practice of curriculum renewal, which is reported as having a narrow disciplinary focus. I believe that this narrow focus is informed by a disciplinary knowledge base, and that the practice of curriculum renewal could be better served by also drawing on the knowledge base informing curriculum theory. This study set out to further interrogate this contention by exploring the process of curriculum renewal from the perspective of programme coordinators.

Methodology

The data presented in this chapter arises from ten focus group sessions with members of faculty programme committees in each of the ten faculties at the University, as well as three follow-up interviews with individual programme coordinators. The ten focus group sessions were the first iteration of data gathering, while the follow-up interviews arose from a second round of data gathering, in which three programme coordinators were purposively selected (Cohen & Manion, 1994) based on the data from the ten focus group sessions. The focus group sessions explored the enablers and constraints to successful programme renewal, while the three follow-up interviews explored more deeply the role of the programme coordinator in the practice of programme renewal. The data from the focus group sessions and interviews comprised transcripts of recordings of the discussions, as well as researcher notes. The data from the ten focus group discussions were analysed to better understand the enabling and constraining factors underpinning the practice of programme renewal for programme coordinators. This analysis was used as a stimulus for the follow-up interviews. These data were analysed using open coding (Braun & Clarke, 2006) initially, after which the coding framework was refined using systematic thematic analysis in an attempt to reveal the complexity underpinning the practice of curriculum renewal from the perspective of programme coordinators. I deliberately chose this "grounded analysis" approach to allow for categories to emerge from the data with "minimal a priori expectation" (Freeman, 1996:372), rather than apply existing theoretical frameworks from the literature to the data.

Findings

A range of enabling and constraining factors were found to underpin the practice of programme renewal for programme coordinators. One of the overarching constraining factors raised by a number of academics across faculties was the resistance to and lack of "ownership" of the process of curriculum renewal. One of the reasons given for this was that they saw curriculum renewal as a low-level responsibility. One focus group participant stated:

> The researcher identity is primary. Lecturers like to stay in their bubbles. Teaching and learning and curriculum renewal [are] seen as a sixth level responsibility. Lecturers see it as someone else's business. There is no ownership.

Another participant in this focus group session endorsed this view:

> What X said is very true. Most people tend to see this sort of thing as sort of a fifth or sixth level of responsibility ... I mean teaching is somewhere down at the bottom of their priorities, and this (curriculum renewal) is even lower.

These were the four subthemes that emerged most often across the ten focus group sessions. These will be explained in more detail below:

- Curriculum renewal as the work of the programme coordinator;
- The lack of cohesion in the practice of curriculum renewal;
- The different knowledge bases informing the process of curriculum renewal; and
- The need for collaboration across the process of curriculum renewal.

Curriculum renewal as the work of the programme coordinator

Several programme coordinators across the focus group sessions spoke of their role in the practice of curriculum renewal and how curriculum renewal was often seen as the work of the programme coordinator. One programme coordinator described the process as "trying to swim through molasses". She went on the explain what she meant by this:

> ... it's a mental attitude because it involves paperwork they have to prepare. I can't prepare a Form B for somebody else's module. I don't know what's going on in it. I can't do the handbook entries for somebody else's module ... they really have to do their own

stuff and I think ... they don't like administration and they're researchers and they want to crack on with their science. They're not actually interested in getting involved in all this stuff, and NQF levels, and education and things, and paperwork and Form A's and institutional processes and meetings and committees. So I think the molasses is kind of a mixture between wanting to get on with your own work and being nice and safe and contained within your bubble and maintain the status quo and also not wanting to take on more stuff than you've already got, I mean we're all struggling for time, to try and keep our hats on all the various frogs that are jumping around, and actually, I feel sorry for them as well because I can see the despair come into their eyes when you ask them to do something. The problem is that currently they still see it as your problem. They see it as something that you drive.

This shifting of the responsibility for curriculum renewal to the programme coordinator was ascribed to the status of the curriculum renewal, as illustrated by this participant: "What do you expect from something that is a side issue? Curriculum renewal is always something of a knee-jerk reaction" (translated from Afrikaans).

Programme coordinators expressed the need for disciplinary specialists to take ownership of the renewal of their curricula, and for curriculum renewal to become a strategic focus for academics. They acknowledged that there was a need for a strong overall driver at programme level, but that each subject specialist needed to drive the process further.

The lack of cohesion in the practice of curriculum renewal

Participants expressed this theme in a number of ways across the focus group sessions. In one focus group session, the participants remarked on the lack of cohesion across departments teaching on the same programme, stating that many academics "do not know which modules fit where or who does what. They teach their classes, and within departments, there is good cohesion, but not across departments" (translated from Afrikaans). This faculty group also spoke to the need to see the "big picture" and for a philosophy of continuous curriculum renewal rather than seeing curriculum renewal as an endpoint. Another faculty focus group raised the importance of holistic understandings of programmes, and also about how programmes were built up from the modular level to the programme level. Yet another faculty group stated that:

> ... programme renewal in my context is limited, as it often lacks a comprehensive vision of situating higher education adequately in a twenty-first-century context, it does not effectively foreground and prioritise national priorities and issues, it takes place mainly on a micro-level (modular or department level) based on availability and

interest areas of individual faculty and as framed and formalised through the strategic business plans of departments.

This kind of bottom-up approach appears to happen in fragmented ways in individual modules, but curriculum renewal at programme level, which requires a more coordinated effort including a range of role-players, seldom happens, resulting in programmes of study which do not have overall conceptual coherence (Muller, 2009) and many knowledge gaps and overlaps.

The different knowledge bases informing the process of curriculum renewal

This theme emerged across a number of faculty focus group sessions. One faculty referred to successful programme renewal as being "much more than simply a renewal of content" but that it should also "critically consider how the curriculum is contextualised" and "actively engage in the reform of teaching and learning pedagogies and practices". Another faculty member referred to the narrow focus of curriculum renewal and how this process was primarily informed by a disciplinary knowledge base:

> In terms of colleagues, they obviously had the subject knowledge ... I think the technical knowledge is very important because that is what industry buys from us and it is clear when you put together a programme delivering certain knowledge and skills that we need to – you can't let a student leave a programme without that base, so the knowledge comes first.

However, most faculties agreed that the practice of curriculum renewal could be better served by also drawing on the knowledge base informing curriculum theory. This was expressed in several ways. One faculty expressed it in the following way: "For programme renewal one also needs knowledgeable people – experts in the art of curriculum development, assessment strategies and appropriate modes of delivery", while another faculty stated: "We are all academics, specialists in our various fields but I am not sure how many people are specifically specialised in programme design and renewal." These findings appear to support my earlier assertion that the practice of curriculum renewal is seldom informed by both knowledge bases. Findings from yet another faculty focus group session referred to the disciplinary specialists who felt that they lacked the necessary conceptual frameworks to do programme renewal and that in the absence of such frameworks, academics tended to revert to compliance behaviour. Another faculty member, from a faculty which offered professional programmes, felt that it was unrealistic to expect of disciplinary specialists to have both disciplinary knowledge, as well as knowledge of curriculum. This was expressed in the following way:

> ... and then we are not educationalists. If you check, none of us has a qualification in education. I think we expect too much of people who are educated in their professions to now go into didactics and to read about all these things and to pull out the magic thing. We have not been taught to do this. And then still to make a contribution to your profession? I think this is really a huge expectation, that we must actually be a professional educationalist, as well as a professional whatever [translated from Afrikaans].

There was agreement across all faculties that the practice of curriculum renewal ought to be informed by both disciplinary knowledge, as well as knowledge of curriculum, to develop holistic, responsive curricula. Most faculties felt that the best way to achieve this would be through a process of collaboration between experts in these respective fields.

The need for collaboration across the process of curriculum renewal

There were differences of opinion across faculties about how best to achieve the intersection of these two knowledge bases – disciplinary knowledge and knowledge of curriculum. Some argued for "training in the area of programme design and renewal" because "we are not necessarily pedagogical experts", while others argued that it was simplistic to think that disciplinary specialists could be "trained" into a knowledge base. One programme coordinator recounted his experience of attending and completing a short course on curriculum renewal, along with another colleague:

> We were very keen ... we were going to do this short course ... we came back from the course, but we had nothing that we could put into our back pockets and bring back, and this was actually an indication of how unqualified we actually were to do this kind of thing [translated from Afrikaans].

The other colleague who also attended the short course expressed a similar view:

> Even if you consider yourself to be a good teacher at university level, we haven't been trained in education. We trained as a biologist or whatever, so I'm a specialist in X, I haven't got any serious expertise in understanding the philosophy of teaching, and it's very difficult for us then because even if you think you're a good teacher to actually know how to properly do the recurriculation and that is predominantly why we had so much trouble at that short course, because we didn't have that background to any of that, and a lot of the terminology that was used there went over our heads.

Later in the focus group interview, a different programme coordinator spoke to how difficult it was to get her "head around" the knowledge base informing curriculum renewal. She describes the field as "woolly":

> I'm looking for a recipe ... but it's not like that ... I spent hours trying to get my head around this whole thing, how do you try and incorporate this into our departmental thing [referring to programme renewal] because I had nothing to hang it on to, within my skills base.

This first round of data seemed to underscore a point made earlier in the chapter, that it might be unrealistic to expect of disciplinary specialists to have both disciplinary knowledge and knowledge of curriculum. It appears that knowledge of curriculum cannot be "trained" or taught in a short course. Such specialist knowledge is built over time in the same way that other disciplinary knowledge is built. One of the respondents, who had attended the short course, referred to the time it took him to make sense of what he had learned in the short course: "It took two years ... for me to understand what happened there."

The analysis of the first round of data seemed to suggest that the best way to achieve holistic programme renewal was through a process of collaboration between experts in the disciplinary field, as well as experts in the field of curriculum design and renewal. This assertion was explored more deeply in the second round of data gathering and analysis.

In the interviews, each of the three programme coordinators explored their respective roles and also the issue of ownership of the process of curriculum renewal. One of the programme coordinators reported that she had "never wanted to be like the one person that has to carry this weight of doing the programme renewal. It was their programme, and people were happy that the process was being coordinated by me, but it was their process, not mine".

This respondent, in describing her role as a programme coordinator, distinguished between two roles that she played – coordinating the spread of content and technical knowledge of the modules making up the programme, and also coordinating a more social process of building trust and working together as a collective towards the goal of programme renewal. Another programme coordinator saw his role as that of a mediator and a translator "bringing back messages, translating it, mediating it, but then also hopefully empowering colleagues". He described "the messages" as the philosophy underpinning programme renewal, and mentioned examples such as "critical citizenship, graduate attributes and decolonisation". He also referred to a more social role, which he described as "just an ear" to listen to and reflect on what colleagues want to do with curriculum renewal, as also "some motivation", particularly for younger colleagues who need a more experienced colleague to turn to.

The programme coordinators who were interviewed agreed that this was a process that needed to be undertaken by the academics themselves, and could not be outsourced, for example, to consultants. The programme coordinators saw their role as being a "vehicle" for ensuring the overall coherence (Muller, 2009) of the practice of curriculum renewal:

> They don't have a clear picture and understanding of where does that module fit into the programme and sometimes a particular module fits into more than one programme and that understanding of translating how does this module contribute to the eventual student attributes ... so even young lecturers or lesser experienced lecturers that do a credible job with the module have limited knowledge and ability as to how does that module translate into the bigger programme objectives.

Another programme coordinator explained that each lecturer would "battle for our own credits" and that it was the job of the programme coordinator to resolve matters such as: how many credits go into each year of the programme, and where to cut credits in particular modules. She saw her role as bringing "the bigger picture" and mediating the "give and take" of the process of programme renewal, which she described as "working through what all the different voices are telling us ... and then we had to work through how we're going to get there. Ja, we had some give and take situations. This is not ticking the boxes ... so we realised there is no easy fix for this. It had to come from a process". This process is referred to in the literature as the struggle for control of the field of "recontextualization" (Bernstein, 1999).

While the programme coordinators understood their overarching role as seeing the bigger picture, they also alluded to a different role for the leaders of the individual modules making up a particular programme:

> So the technical knowledge – there the module coordinators strongly guided us to, you know, if we place it in this module then that dovetails very nicely with this and students following that module have these sequence of modules that goes with it.

As alluded to earlier, this is referred to in the literature as the processes of selection and sequencing (Bernstein, 1999), where the disciplinary knowledge is selected from the field of production and repackaged, in the field of "recontextualization", into programmes of study made up of modules, which are sequenced in particular ways to make them accessible to students. Programme coordinators appeared to be ensuring that selection and sequencing decisions were based on both the disciplinary knowledge that was needed to "produce the student", and the "bigger picture" drivers, such as "critical citizenship, graduate attributes and decolonisation".

The finding from the faculty focus group sessions, that the practice of curriculum renewal ought to be informed by both disciplinary knowledge as well as knowledge of curriculum, was confirmed in the interviews. One of the programme coordinators expressed it in the following way:

> I think we didn't have the in-house knowledge and know-how and probably practice in how to go about this task in a sound educational way, one could almost say. Certain terms like: 'What is a teaching outcome?' or 'How does the outcome need to be aligned to the assessment?' Those things are maybe just concepts floating around.

The programme coordinators expressed the need for "somebody from outside", because they did not feel that this was part of their role: "This is not my specialist field, my field of expertise." When questioned about what they brought to the process of curriculum renewal, they were quite clear that it was disciplinary knowledge that they brought: "I know X [referring to the discipline], I've got that knowledge and I've got the technical knowledge, I understand the industry out there and what they need of my students." They also described the knowledge that the module leaders brought to the process of curriculum renewal, as disciplinary knowledge:

> The average lecturer in a faculty, to him programme renewal is content-orientated, if not driven ... the starting point is too often the content. I think we're too much content-orientated and our understanding of what the purpose of the curriculum is, is not sufficiently translated in terms of the outcomes and how to achieve that, but more on a sort of minimum, minimalistic requirements of a curriculum that is still based on content.

When questioned about the curriculum knowledge that was needed and who would bring that to the process of curriculum renewal, the programme coordinators were also very clear, signalling the role of the academic developer:

> X [the academic developer] provided me with that know-how and the support. It took that unknown factor away [of] 'I don't know where to start'. But advising me whenever I got stuck, I felt that was the role of X, and also facilitating whenever I felt that the group now needed instruction, like what a good Form B is like or to write outcomes. I don't know how to do it. I'm a [names discipline]. I could rely on her to provide me with that subject knowledge and also facilitate the process to the different groups ... X is an Education specialist. They've done many before ... I also didn't have the authority.

One programme coordinator referred to the bringing together of these two knowledge bases as "reciprocal", while another described it as: "Whenever I got a bit out of my depth, or I needed support of how to go about the process, X was there. But what I did, X couldn't do and vice versa. So to me, that was very clear." All three of them endorsed the view arising from the ten faculty focus group sessions that there was a need for collaboration between disciplinary specialists and academic developers across the process of curriculum renewal. This reciprocal relationship was further explored in the interviews. One programme coordinator referred to her role as a coordination role and the role of the academic developer as a facilitation role. She described the difference in the following way:

> I would put the programme together. I would represent my programme at our Faculty Programme Committee. I would coordinate any changes in the yearbook. I could communicate between my programme members, people teaching in the module, module coordinators. We looked at all the changes that we proposed, see that the credits work out right, that there are no class clashes. I could coordinate it, and in some ways, I put it together. So my role, I felt, was coordinating it between the colleagues and then in terms of colleagues, they obviously had the subject knowledge so they knew that you [could] not do X [the programme] without X [a subject] in the first year. I ensured that the programme answers to what is needed to train a [names the programme] person and also to make sure that the industry is happy with that person. So in terms of the technical knowledge, I think the staff were well equipped of putting a programme together. So for me, that was a coordinating role, but I really relied on the facilitation of X.

The facilitation role of the academic developer was described as providing the "knowledge of" and "instruction on how to" do programme renewal. When this role was further explored, the programme coordinator offered the following:

> She sent some reading material, because, ja, scientists want to know, OK? And she never overloaded us ... you don't want ten PDFs attached to an e-mail. So she digested some of the stuff for us. Every meeting we had a presentation relevant to where we were but having her there. It's like, whenever, I think of the things that I don't know how to do, I just keep on procrastinating. If I know what to do, even if it's stuff that's going to take a long time, I actually start with it, but if I don't know how to open up this box, and what's in the box, then it's ... you can't believe that you've procrastinated so long on this. But I feel that X helped opening up that box for us by ... not only providing the knowledge but making it accessible by saying, 'Guys, you can actually do it, see you're halfway there, you've already done this'.

Another programme coordinator referred to the knowledge base informing curriculum theory as residing in people, like academic developers, but also in the kinds of spaces that academic development units provide and the body of literature on curriculum theory:

> It's people, so there [are] people, for example, when I sit around a table, and I listen to a person ... so attending some of your workshops or extending some of the initiatives time and again brought me into contact with people referring to literature in whatever way and then, I thought, OK well that might be interesting to read that article on curriculum renewal. So I gained a lot of very interesting information through people and their references and cross-referencing and a body of literature ... So with the help of the computer and the ... whole world-wide web and Google it's so easy to get access to that, but somebody's got to make you aware of there's this source ...

This programme coordinator described the interaction in academic development spaces as helping people to think anew, and helping them "to think in alternative ways from what they are busy doing". He identified the Academic Development Unit as a networking space, linking the faculty to broader campus processes because faculties were "kind of removed from the rest of campus" and "very much living in a little bubble here, not realising what's going on on the rest of campus". He also saw the Academic Development Unit as assisting him in "reaching the bigger discourses on teaching and learning, and that always helps me to know I'm part of something bigger than just this one faculty". Later in the interview, he described the Academic Development Unit as a space that provided "continuity":

> Whenever I go there, I feel I'm going to a place where there [are] people that continuously think and reflect on teaching and learning, and, therefore, I see it as a place of people with expertise. But I also see it as a place where there's coordination of what's happening on the whole of campus. So I'm not just approaching to get some info to bring back ... it is a kind of a hub for networking and bringing people together.

It appears that when academic developers work collaboratively with academics in curriculum renewal spaces, the conversations around curriculum renewal are qualitatively different. As one programme coordinator reflected: "It's a lot of concepts ... it's a kind of a sharing of knowledge ... it's always in a certain sense for me more a theoretical exercise. That's also why I like it because it opens up new ways of thinking and reflecting and continuously I learn new concepts there." He goes on to refer to the Academic Development Unit as a "place of energising" him to do the curriculum renewal work he has to do as a programme coordinator in the faculty.

Conclusion

It appears that the curriculum conversations that take place outside of faculties are qualitatively different to the curriculum conversations that take place within faculties. When programme coordinators have curriculum conversations within their disciplinary groups, because they share a common knowledge base, they may then be able to move quite quickly to talking about the application of this disciplinary knowledge base to the practice of curriculum renewal. Their curriculum conversations then remain caught up in the micro-level issues of curriculum renewal. However, when programme coordinators talk to people outside of their faculties, such as academic developers, there are different knowledge bases that are interacting with each other. It is possible that those conversations, and the ways in which they take place in such cross-disciplinary spaces, tend to be more theoretical initially because there isn't a shared knowledge base and therefore the application to practice takes a little longer. This allows for dialogue on the macro-level issues of curriculum renewal. This conjecture seems to be borne out by the views of the programme coordinators who see the curriculum workshops that are run by academic developers as opportunities to "share these kinds of theories that we are not normally using ... OK, well here they hear concepts that normally we're not discussing in faculties". Another programme coordinator described these curriculum conversations as developing "a value system and a philosophy" which ought to be driven by "teaching experts" who needed to be "the in-house translators, facilitators and demonstrators of that philosophy". This would imply a particular kind of collaborative relationship between disciplinary specialists and academic developers in the practice of curriculum renewal. Academic developers would be "translators" of the discourses of curriculum theory; "facilitators" of philosophical conversations around the macro issues driving curriculum transformation, and "demonstrators" of how the lessons from curriculum theory can be put into practice in the process of curriculum renewal.

Luckett and Shay (2017:10) argue that curriculum renewal can be one means of challenging and dismantling injustices towards the goal of equity of access and outcomes. They challenge academics to interrogate assumptions informing the norms of their curricula and suggest that all academic staff rethink their curricula and pedagogic practices through "dialogues in safe, participatory processes". The data presented in this chapter suggest that collaborative curriculum conversations amongst disciplinary specialists, programme coordinators and academic developers provide the spaces for such safe dialogues and participatory processes. However, for these spaces to generate productive conversations, academic developers themselves need to be able to create and hold the more critical theorised spaces and resist narrower instrumental views of the curriculum renewal process. This has implications for the field of academic development in South Africa, where academic developers who are new to the field would need to be inducted (Quinn & Vorster, 2014) or mentored into theories informing the practice of curriculum design and renewal so that they are able to act as "translators" of the discourses of curriculum theory. In addition to this, creating disruptive, creative and participatory processes requires skilled facilitation, and academic developers who are new to the field would benefit from mentoring in this area as well. Finally, it is incumbent on research-intensive universities to recognise the specialised nature of academic development work and provide the platforms for collaborative curriculum conversations that can shift the resistance to and lack of "ownership" of the process of curriculum renewal.

References

Barnett, R.; Parry, G. & Coate, K. 2001. Conceptualising Curriculum Change. *Teaching in Higher Education*, 6(4):435-449. [https://doi.org/10.1080/13562510120078009]

Bernstein, B. 1999. Vertical and Horizontal Discourse: an essay. *British Journal of Sociology of Education*, 20(2):157-173. [https://doi.org/10.1080/01425699995380]

Bernstein, B. 1990. *The structuring of pedagogic discourse*. London: Routledge.

Braun, V. & Clarke, V. 2006. Using thematic analysis in psychology. *Qualitative Research in Psychology*, 3(2):77-101. [https://doi.org/10.1191/1478088706qp063oa]

Cohen, L. & Manion, L. 1994. *Research Methods in Education*. 4th Edition. London: Routledge.

Freeman, D. 1996. The 'Unstudied Problem': Research on Teacher Learning in Language Teaching. In: D. Freeman & J.C. Richards (eds). *Teacher Learning in Language Teaching*. Cambridge: Cambridge University Press.

Luckett, K. & Shay, S. 2017. Reframing the curriculum: a transformative approach. *Critical Studies in Education*. [https://doi.org/10.1080/17508487.2017.1356341]

Muller, J. 2009. Forms of knowledge and curriculum coherence. *Journal of Education and Work*, 22(3):205-226. [https://doi.org/10.1080/13639080902957905]

Quinn, L. & Vorster, J. 2014. Isn't it time to start thinking about 'developing' academic developers in a more systematic way? *International Journal for Academic Development*, 19(3):255-258. [https://doi.org/10.1080/1360144X.2013.879719]

Singh, P. 2002. Pedagogising Knowledge: Bernstein's Theory of the Pedagogic Device. *British Journal of Sociology of Education*, 23(4):571-582. [https://doi.org/10.1080/0142569022000038422]

Van der Merwe, A.; Schoonwinkel, A. & Hubball, H. 2017. The Scholarship of Educational Leadership in a South African Research-intensive University Context: Strategic Approaches to Undergraduate and Graduate Degree Programme Renewal. In: O.M. Alegre de la Rosa (ed). *International Perspectives: Research on University Teaching and Faculty Development*. New York: Nova Science Publishers.

Young, M. 2014. Curriculum Theory: What it is and why it is important. *Cadernos de Pesquisa*, 44(151):191-201. [https://doi.org/10.1590/198053142851]

Young, G. & Jacobs, C. 2017. Legitimacy and educational development units' participation in programme renewal. Paper presented at the Legitimation Code Theory Conference, Sydney University, 3-7 July.

CHAPTER 18

Academic development insights into decolonising the Engineering curriculum

Karin Wolff

Introduction

South Africa's National Development Plan (NPC, 2011) highlights the urgency of producing well-equipped Science, Technology, Engineering and Mathematics (STEM) graduates for a dynamic and complex 21st century, particularly with respect to addressing national (and global) Sustainable Development Goals in our emerging economy. Recruitment, retention and graduation rates across STEM (Science, Technology, Engineering and Mathematics) areas remain critical challenges in the South African context. Globally, massification in higher education has seen increasing numbers of school leavers gaining physical access to tertiary education systems, but in South Africa only an average of 50 per cent of students ever complete a qualification (CHE, 2015). There have been a number of significant attempts to improve undergraduate retention and success rates. A key initiative is additional funding for foundational support or what are termed extended curriculum programmes. These are programmes allocated an additional, subsidised year of study to the formal qualification period. Other initiatives include mentorship programmes, first-year experience support and a range of academic development initiatives to assist students. Academic staff, on the other hand, have only recently begun to receive funded support such as the Teaching Development Grant to assist them in facing the challenge of increasingly underprepared school leavers (Quinn, 2012). The Teaching Development Grant funding has enabled academics to undertake short courses, receive educational support and training in various forms at different institutions, and embark on project-based initiatives to improve teaching practices. Academic development practitioners run many of these initiatives. For STEM academics in South Africa, teaching challenges in large, diverse classes are compounded by increasing calls for "decolonising the curriculum" – a curriculum consisting primarily of what is regarded as an integrative accumulation of high-level propositions that are broadly shared (Muller, 2009). The decolonisation view suggests that these propositions (or concepts) are deemed forms of Eurocentric capital designed to "enculturate students into taking on a Western scientific way of knowing, replete with its canonical knowledge, techniques, and values" (Aikenhead, 2006:387). The challenge for STEM academics attempting to enable South African students to access "broadly shared" concepts in meaningful ways in the African context may well be that of differentiating between forms of knowledge and ways of knowing. Maton (2014) cautions that reducing knowledge to knowing confuses epistemology with learning. Morrow points out that "knowledge itself is an outcome of a kind of discussion called inquiry" (2009:10) and that "learning how to be a participant in communities of inquiry is at the heart of what we understand by education" (2009:11).

Sociologists of education have been justifiably preoccupied with what it means to participate in a "community of inquiry". Morrow (2009) talks about not confusing physical access with "epistemological access", which is really about learning the "grammar of inquiry" of a field – how meaning is made in different disciplines and communities of practice. Using Barnett's (2000) epistemological, ontological and praxis curriculum dimensions as a framework, "learning the grammar of inquiry of a field" suggests learning to participate in the knowledge "goods" (Morrow, 2009) by way of a curriculum which embraces "the domains of being, knowing and action" (Barnett, 2000:263).

This chapter focuses on an academic development initiative designed to enable Engineering educators to become participants in a community of enquiry so that they can improve student success. The guiding question for the chapter is: *How can educators be encouraged to examine the relationship between the epistemological (knowledge), ontological (self-identity) and praxis (action) dimensions in Engineering education?* Engineering educators generally have particular specialisations within STEM, but the Engineering profession is a synergy between Science, Technology and Mathematics in service of meeting society's needs. These different disciplinary fields and contexts demonstrate significantly different "grammars of inquiry" and, therefore, different ways of *knowing, being* and *doing*. Seeing these differences and examining their interrelationships represents a first step in developing a more informed perspective on what "Engineering education" entails. The sociologist, Basil Bernstein (2000), presented a case for differentiating between different knowledge structures based on how they emerged in the field of production and how these structures underpin power relations in society. This has implications for a just pedagogy. Bernstein's contribution to characterising different disciplinary organising principles has subsequently been operationalised by Legitimation Code Theory (LCT) instruments for the empirical analysis of "knowledge practices" (Maton, 2014).

Using the LCT Specialisation concept of *epistemic relations* and formative feedback data drawn from a staff development programme in Engineering education, this chapter introduces the *epistemic plane* as a tool for the analysis of knowledge practices. The *epistemic plane* differentiates between the *what* and *how* of a phenomenon and is graphically represented as a Cartesian plane with four quadrants called *insights*. These insights – *purist, doctrinal, situational* and *no/knower* – enable one to appreciate how different disciplines and contexts require different "ways of thinking, being and doing". The chapter presents examples of Engineering staff (in academic development sessions conducted by the author/researcher) using the *epistemic plane* to look at their curriculum and pedagogy in different STEM knowledge areas within Engineering education. This initiative served to (1) enable staff to question assumptions around the use of ostensibly standardised terminology; and (2) inform their understanding of who exactly their students are.

The chapter hopes to demonstrate how the use of theoretically-informed research instruments can enable academics to enrich their understanding of knowledge practices in complex socio-technical contexts. It is this understanding that could mark a necessary first step towards decolonising the Engineering curriculum.

Academic development in Engineering and the decolonisation debate

A recent critical review of the literature on academic or professional development initiatives for STEM educators (Winberg, Adendorff, Bozalek, Conana, Pallitt, Wolff, Olsson & Roxå, 2018) reveals a predominantly generic approach to curriculum and pedagogy with little attention to the nature of individual STEM disciplines and the relationship between them. The review concludes that "the literature shows how little we know about teaching STEM concepts" (2018:11) and supports the point made by Muller that "the issue is pedagogical rather than epistemic – the problem lies with the practices of teaching and learning rather than with the logic of the knowledge" (2014:260). STEM academics are often assumed to understand their field which can unproblematically be translated into the classroom (Felder, Woods, Stice & Rugarcia, 2000). However, persistently low STEM enrolment, retention and graduation rates (UNESCO, 2010; CHE, 2015) suggest otherwise, and not only have implications for meeting those Sustainable Development Goals requiring STEM expertise but have also led to concerted efforts to support STEM educators.

Engineering is an ideal STEM field in which to interrogate academic development strategies that address the curricular and pedagogic implications of educating for 21st-century "supercomplexity" (Barnett, 2000). As in the case of the health sciences, in Engineering we find forms of knowledge and practices that straddle the traditional pure disciplines and increasingly complex, sociotechnical forms of 21st-century practice. Much of the criticism from employers of Engineering (and health sciences) graduates revolves around their inability to apply theory (Griesel & Parker, 2009), demonstrate the necessary technical skills (Manpower Group, 2015) and exercise the necessary "soft skills" such as collaboration, communication and leadership (Beaton, 2017). This feedback suggests that the *ontological* and *praxis* dimensions of the curriculum (Barnett, 2000) are being sacrificed in favour of the traditionally dominant *epistemological* dimension. A number of academic development initiatives over the past decade in South Africa have explicitly begun to address these three dimensions, highlighting the higher education mandate to enable "knowledge, skills and citizenship" attributes (DHET, 2013).

The call for educational reform is predominantly driven by the social sciences (Leibowitz, 2017) with a stronger focus on ontological questions. STEM knowledge forms, on the other hand, are intricately linked to the investigation, understanding and relatively consensual representation of physical phenomena over centuries of scientifically-driven progress which has produced a cumulative body of "powerful knowledge" (Wheelahan, 2007). One view is that this knowledge represents an enchanted vision of the benefits of modernity derived from centuries of predominantly Western, Eurocentric, "White, bourgeois, male" representations, and which has resulted in the subjugation of societies, the perpetuation of colonial violence and a deficit approach to victims of colonisation (De Oliveira, Stein, Ahenakew & Hunt, 2015). The dilemma for STEM educators facing the challenge to decolonise the curriculum is that the body of knowledge that constitutes their fields is regarded as relatively "fixed". The question of access to the epistemological (Morrow, 2009) has shifted much of the focus to curricular and pedagogic initiatives to enable understanding of concepts and their representation as accepted by STEM fields. Engineering, on the other hand, although today regarded as based on the so-called hard sciences (natural and mathematical), is, in fact, closer to the original medieval mechanical arts – which were not part of the medieval university system (Muller, 2009). Engineering is applied in the nature-society-technology nexus (UNESCO, 2010) – which suggests a more complex set of relations between forms of knowledge (epistemology) and practices (praxis) in significantly different potential social contexts (ontology).

Social realism postulates a view of "knowledge practices as both emergent from and irreducible to their contexts of production" (Maton, 2014:11). The epistemological access focus of STEM educators has shifted in recent years to enabling understanding of the "emergent" – an understanding of the principles and procedures generated by the field of knowledge production. The decolonisation question raises the uncomfortable relationship between what has emerged (what is known) and the context of production (how it came to be known). Leibowitz criticises the social realist tendency to foreground what is known, arguing that "it does not encourage multiplicity, including a welcoming of new epistemologies" (Leibowitz, 2017:100). Legitimation Code Theory (Maton, 2014) offers an approach to knowledge practices which enables a relational, explanatory, pluralistic and multidimensional view:

> ... the organising principles of knowledge shape the spatial and temporal reach, modes of engagement, and forms of development of social fields. They are key to social inclusion and social justice ... (Maton, 2014:13)

This chapter explores the introduction of LCT instruments into the Engineering education space in academic development sessions. The intention is to demonstrate how Engineering educators (teaching each of the STEM subject areas) are enabled to "see" and engage with a multidimensional view of curriculum, its forms of knowledge in their contexts and how this view can potentially contribute to the first steps towards decolonising the Engineering curriculum.

Academic development research context and methodology

This study is located within the broader context of an Existing Engineering Education Staff Capacity Enhancement Project, titled "Enhancing Engineering academics' pedagogical competencies for Engineering-in-Context". The Engineering-in-Context (EiC) project is funded by the South African Department of Higher Education and Training, the Newton Fund and the Royal Academy of Engineers. The purpose of the grant is the enhancement of Engineering educators' pedagogical capacity in diverse institutional contexts to contribute to positive undergraduate students' experiences and employability outcomes. The grant is shared across four institutions (one UK-based university and three South African universities) and includes several research and training activities led by a team of collaborating academic development practitioners. As a postdoctoral Engineering education scholar at the time of the EiC project, I collaborated as an academic development practitioner at two of the South African Universities, identified as HEI-1 and HEI-2.

I had worked at both institutions in an academic development capacity at various stages, so was familiar with the Engineering faculties and institutional contexts. In my academic development capacity, I supported staff (including the EiC participants) in the development, implementation and research of formal subprojects funded by their respective educational research and/or innovation centres. These projects range from technology-enhanced learning activities to industrial site visits and are embedded within larger institutional programme renewal initiatives. The EiC project offered an ideal framework within which to build a broader "community of enquiry" amongst Engineering educators with varying degrees of experience in both teaching and educational research.

As part of the EiC project, my academic development sessions include mentorship, workshops and practice-sharing opportunities between staff in departments and across the two participating institutions. These sessions included the integration of approaches and findings of my doctoral- and postdoctoral industry case studies on Engineering problem-solving. This research provided EiC participants with a glimpse of the complexity of the Engineering work for which they are preparing their students, as well as the tools through which to understand that complexity. This chapter draws on illustrative data from the industry case studies, the related theoretical and methodological approaches (Wolff, 2015), and data from focus group interviews with EiC participants, workshop feedback surveys and researcher observation notes. One of the key outputs for EiC participants is the development of a teaching portfolio. These reflective portfolios provide additional insights into the participant initiatives. A summary of the data sources and types is presented in Table 18.1. Methodologically, the data offer a rich and qualitative source of perspectives on the participants' views of their disciplines, profession, roles and challenges.

TABLE 18.1   Engineering-in-Context (EiC) research data

Data Sources and Types			
Researcher	EiC	HEI-1	HEI-2
• Engineering problem-solving case studies *(Publications)* • Observation notes *(Researcher journal)*	• Focus group interviews *(Independent transcriptions)* • Reflective teaching portfolios *(Online websites)* • Workshop feedback surveys *(Electronic texts)*	• Process Engineering Curriculum redesign project *(Curriculum and assignment documents; Student feedback surveys; Focus group interviews)* • Chemical Engineering site visit project *(Facilitator interview transcriptions; Student feedback surveys)*	• Technology gap project *(Focus group interview transcriptions; Online surveys)* • Industrial Engineering curriculum redesign project *(Curriculum documentation; Departmental discussion notes)* • Engineering mathematics project *(Assignment documents; Student feedback texts; Assessment documents)*

Theoretical framework in context

Curriculum structures

If we are to put forward an argument for seeing curricula as entailing epistemological, praxis and ontological dimensions (Barnett, 2000), which have to be brought into relationship with each other in service of not only successful, but also socially just education, then different curriculum structures are likely to have different sets of relationships and implications for educational processes. Bernstein (1975) differentiates between collection type curricula – where high-status contents stand in closed relation to each other – and integrated type curricula, in which "the various contents are subordinate to some idea which reduces their isolation from each other" (1975:80). The former sees a long initiation into the discipline by way of a didactic "educational relationship [that] tends to be hierarchical and ritualised" (1975:82) and in which the student is socialised "into knowledge frames which discourage connections with everyday realities" (1975:99). This is evident in STEM curricula which foreground chemistry, physics or biology, for example. The integrated curriculum, on the other hand, is dependent on a *relational idea* with a focus on general principles and a self-regulatory pedagogy which emphasises "ways of knowing" rather than "states of knowledge" (1975:102). Learning, here, is achieved through a deep understanding of different disciplinary types and their inter-relation with each other to form general, overarching principles. In theory, the Engineering curriculum could be said to be a more integrated curriculum structure, combining elements of physics, mathematics and technology in service of an overarching *relational idea*: solving a particular problem for society. As a result of my familiarity with the Engineering faculties in both HEI-1 and HEI-2, I was aware that their programmes demonstrate an initial collection code curriculum structure, with subject areas like Chemistry, Physics and Mathematics often taught by non-departmental staff. Both HEI-1 and HEI-2 curricula transition into a disciplinary integrated structure in the second half of the Engineering qualifications, in that the subject areas combine the disciplinary bases. However, even these integrated subject areas tend to remain siloed in their pedagogy.

In his earlier work, Bernstein (1971) refers to elaborated and restricted "codes" as descriptors for the range of resources people can draw on to make meaning in specific contexts. These resources are further developed in relation to how people make meaning in everyday contexts using their available "repertoires", which are sets "of strategies [...] and their analogic potential for contextual transfer" (Bernstein, 1996:158). A "reservoir" represents the total sets of repertoires in a particular community. Although Bernstein used these definitions in relation to everyday discourse, I believe the distinction can be extended to formal educational knowledge as captured in his differentiation between collection and integrated type curricula. He argues that the less isolated a community is, the greater the opportunity for the "circulation of strategies, of procedures and their exchange" (1996:158). Using these concepts, one might say that an inward-looking curriculum and pedagogy focused only on a particular discipline may give rise to a relatively restricted orientation to meaning, despite the fact that there exist multiple forms of abstractions representing particular phenomena in that discipline. This may set up a relatively restricted "repertoire" of strategies on which a student may draw. One such example would be the textbook-bound focus on mass and energy balances in thermodynamics where little reference is made to real-world examples or comparable processes in different Engineering areas. In contrast,

I would suggest that an elaborated orientation to meaning is facilitated when the principles and procedures of a particular disciplinary phenomenon are enriched by drawing on different repertoires, and hence potentially add to a collective reservoir of strategies for a community as a whole. A good example is an explicit connection between Mechanical and Electrical Engineering principles, where concepts such as "force" are linked to those of electrical current (Bailey-McEwan, 2009).

Elaborated orientations to meaning for the 21st century

> The world is now highly complex and incredibly interdependent. Particular events or problems will often have multiple interlocking structural causes ... (Mingers, 2014:26)

The argument in this chapter is that there is a unique contextual relationship in each configuration (system) of forms of knowledge, ways of knowing and kinds of *knowers* in knowledge-practice environments, whether these be educational, industrial or social. Optimal teaching and learning require a part-whole understanding of all the system components, which together constitute a "structure of interrelated parts [and structural] powers or tendencies" (Mingers, 2014:54). Each of the subsystem elements (such as the different disciplines and contexts) represents a kind of knowledge-practice code – in other words, a way of thinking and doing in a particular contextual moment in relation to particular forms of knowledge. Transformative learning (for staff, students and practitioners alike) is enabled through recognising and realising (Bernstein, 2000) these codes. Being able to consciously shift from one kind of code to another, as in the case of complex Engineering problem solving (Wolff, 2018c), can contribute significantly to developing an elaborated orientation to meaning. Similarly, I believe that one of the key academic development roles is to enable academics to recognise, realise and shift between knowledge practice codes.

Bernstein (2000) may be said to have captured an early form of "code shifting" in his term "recontextualization" – the process by which knowledge generated in the field of production makes its way into curricula, pedagogy and practice based on the selection of "what counts" by particular stakeholders (*whom*) at particular times (*when*) and places (*where*) for particular purposes (*why*). Hence, we see in a diploma qualification, for example, the labour market and employers requiring a clear focus on practice as opposed to theory. These curricular decisions reflect particular "orientations to meaning" in particular contexts. I suggest that the word "context" here is key: a lecturer may focus so intently on the abstract representation of a particular phenomenon that the student's understanding may be restricted to only one form. By the same token, a lecturer using a fixed practical example for application of a particular abstract concept (ostensibly to enable theory-practice integration) may equally be demonstrating a restricted orientation to meaning, which can lead to an understanding that is trapped in one specific context. Wheelahan (2007) argues that such context-dependent learning is restrictive and denies students the opportunity to access "powerful knowledge".

Encoding and decoding codes: Legitimation Code Theory (LCT)

Learning that entails connecting the *what*, *why* and *how* is at the heart of "epistemological access" (Morrow, 2009). I suggest that the addition of *by whom* and *for whom* in the context of *where* and *when* contributes to a systems' view of the part-whole relations in a curriculum for supercomplexity (Barnett, 2000), thus connecting the ontological (*who*) to the epistemological (*why* and *what*) and praxis (*how*) dimensions of the curriculum. In LCT terms, this connection is suggested by the term "cumulative learning" (Maton, 2013). LCT offers multiple conceptual and analytical tools to interrogate, understand and articulate what knowledge practices look like in the contexts of *knowers* and fields. For the purpose of this chapter, the primary tool is that of the LCT Specialization dimension's *epistemic plane*.[1] Captured as a Cartesian representation (Figure 18.1) of the relationship between a phenomenon (*what*) and its approaches (*how*), the *epistemic plane* enables a more nuanced interpretation of different kinds of STEM knowledges, as well as literally making space for *knowers* (*who*). The two axes represent continua between strongly or weakly bounded phenomena and approaches, and thus present four ways of "seeing" a knowledge practice, or four *insight* codes. Using examples from the current study, the codes could be described as follows.

---

[1] Note that in this section analytical terms are italicised throughout to avoid common-sense interpretations.

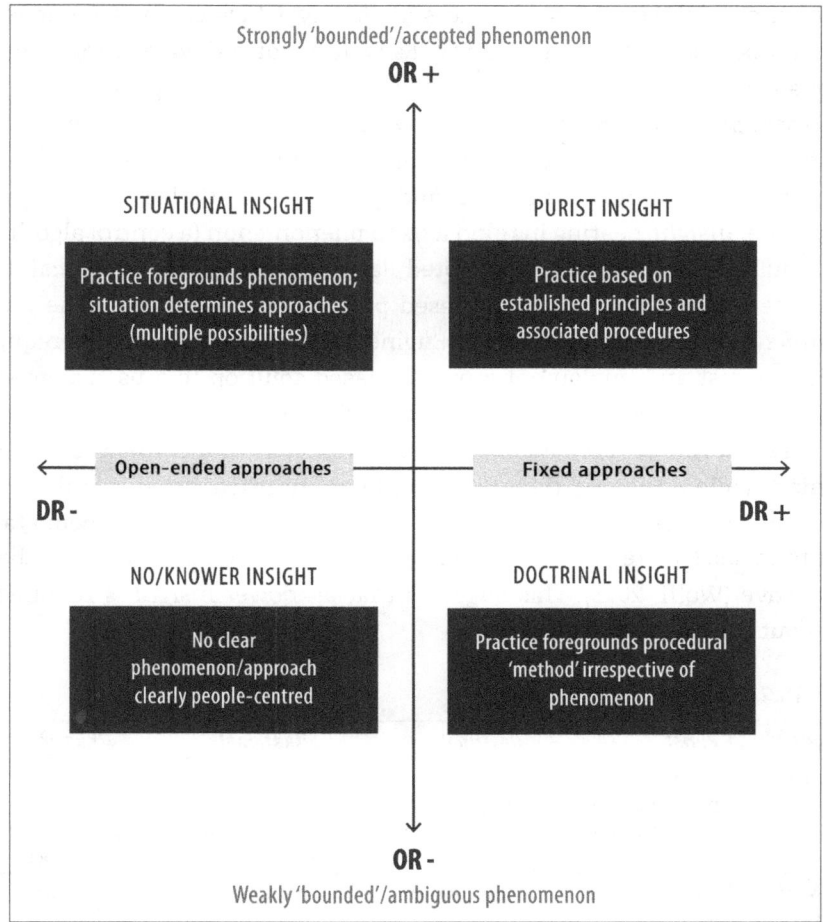

FIGURE 18.1 Annotated *epistemic plane*
(Maton, 2014:177)

The examples given in Table 18.2 represent what I have called "disciplinary home base" *insights*. Thermodynamics is concerned with the laws of energy and heat exchange captured in numerous uncontested formulae. The field is not ambiguous about the related phenomena, nor its approaches. A predominantly *purist insight* is thus required to grasp and translate the laws of thermodynamics. Mathematics, on the other hand, can be applied to any phenomenon, and hence we see a predominantly *doctrinal* approach to manipulating figures and numbers within established equation forms, such as the standard differential equations used to relate physical properties and change over time. A *situational insight* is necessary for any phenomenon requiring the application of technology or software.

An example is the teaching of process modelling, which can be accomplished with numerous software platforms. Each form of software (programming language) is significantly different and has to be learned independently. One of the research participants had previously experimented with a colleague from a different institution, where they trialled teaching the same course using different programming languages and platforms. Both lecturers required *situational insight*, bearing in mind a fixed phenomenon (a control algorithm) and multiple approaches (a scripted language versus a Graphical User Interface assisted block-diagram based programming language). The fourth example comes from Mechatronics Engineering, where students are required to design, test and implement a project-based solution to a particular – but idealised – real-world problem. They are allocated a group, given a budget and a real-world context, and expected to research that context and bear it in mind while designing their solution. Industry research reveals that real-world projects see the greatest challenges with people: suppliers being tardy, user manuals (written by people) being out of date, and supervisors not being supportive (Wolff, 2015). This suggests that a *knower insight* is required to carry out the project effectively.

TABLE 18.2 *Epistemic plane* insights

Insight	*Purist*	*Doctrinal*	*Situational*	*No/Knower*
Descriptor	Strongly bounded phenomenon with a fixed approach	Fixed approach irrespective of phenomenon	Strongly bounded phenomenon with multiple possible approaches	Unclear phenomenon and approach(es) OR knower focus
STEM context	Physics: Thermodynamics in Chemical Engineering	Mathematics: Calculus in Mechanical Engineering	Programming: Control design in Process Engineering	Design project: Project-based learning in Mechatronics Engineering
Example	"Any system which is free of external influences becomes more disordered with time." Entropy: $\Delta S = Q/T$	A first-order differential equation (ODE) is a mathematical relation that relates an independent variable, an unknown function and the first derivative of unknown function: $F\left(t, y, \frac{dy}{dt}\right) = 0$	Develop a dynamic mathematical model using either Python, Matlab or Excel to describe a chemical process.	Design and implement a PLC-controlled solution for the efficient identification and sorting of plastic waste at XYZ company.

Although presented as disciplinary "home bases", in each example case, access to the phenomenon or approaches can be facilitated by shifting to a different *insight*. Thermodynamics could be introduced through drawing on a student's experience of their coffee cooling (*knower insight*) or the latest volcanic eruption in Sicily (*situational insight*). Similarly, using Newton's Second Law of motion which relates force to mass and acceleration (*purist insight*), one can shift to a *doctrinal insight* by converting this relationship into a mathematical differential equation. However, the most common form of code shifting that has tended to occur in higher education is restricted to the right-hand side of the plane, where *doctrinal* examples of *purist* principles are drilled or practised. This is most evident in typical tutorial problem sheets. Students generally only encounter more open-ended approaches in their final capstone projects, where they are required to draw on *situational insight*. The dominant complaint from industry about graduate inability to solve open-ended problems suggests that our current curriculum and pedagogy are not facilitating the kind of code shifting required for 21st century contexts.

Academic development code-shifting initiatives with Engineering educators

All first sessions with the EiC participants under my care at both HEI-1 and HEI-2 began with an introduction to my research in the industry: Engineering problem-solving processes. One of the reasons for this approach was to circumvent perceptions of power relations between disciplinary experts and external education-based specialists (Jacobs, 2007). In both institutional contexts, my experience has been that Engineering academics find "sociological or educational discourse alienating" (Auret & Wolff, 2018:106) and that their default perception of academic development practitioners is that they are "outsiders". To facilitate a more collaborative, interdisciplinary approach to the collective challenge of improving pedagogy for Engineering contexts, I used my Engineering problem-solving research as a mediating device to both justify my position as an academic development practitioner in their midst, as well as subliminally induct the Engineering academics into the usefulness of the theoretical tools. This approach, in my experience, appears not only to have given me a certain legitimacy in the Engineering education space, but also to introduce Engineering academics to the sociological terminology in an accessible way. I modelled code-shifting strategies by constantly using Engineering terminology and processes as metaphors in the educational context. The industry research, methodology and academic development strategy introduced perspectives which allowed for application to their contexts. This section begins with a brief overview of the relevant industrial research findings and then moves on to examples of the EiC participants' code shifting as facilitated through the academic development sessions.

Engineering problem-solving insights

For my PhD and postdoctoral studies, I researched industrial sites from 2013 to 2017 using the *epistemic plane* to map how Engineering practitioners approach, analyse and solve real-world problems. A key discovery was that different industrial contexts have different orientations to "what counts". In the Research and Development small business sector, I found a stronger focus on *purist* principles and *situational* possibilities – in other words, most of the knowledge practices are focused in the top sections of the *epistemic plane*. In contrast, in large scale manufacturing sectors, employers expect adherence to *doctrinal* procedures to ensure that employees meet their production targets. In the third industrial category – the modular systems sector – a different problem-solving pattern was evident. Here, machine builders or systems integrators design and implement a tailor-made solution (based on the *situational* requirements) which needs to improve the client's *doctrinal* processes. In other words, practitioners providing such a service need to shift diametrically between two different ways of thinking. The most successful participants across the case studies demonstrated iterative code-shifting practices, recognising when and how to consider a particular principle, process, possibility or person. My data found that in 83 per cent of all the case studies (41 in total) the predominant cause of Engineering problems occurs in the *knower* quadrant (Figure 18.2), whether it be operator error or supplier documentation or miscommunication. Furthermore, practitioners' inability to shift from right (fixed approaches) to left (open-ended approaches) emerged as the dominant problem-solving challenge.

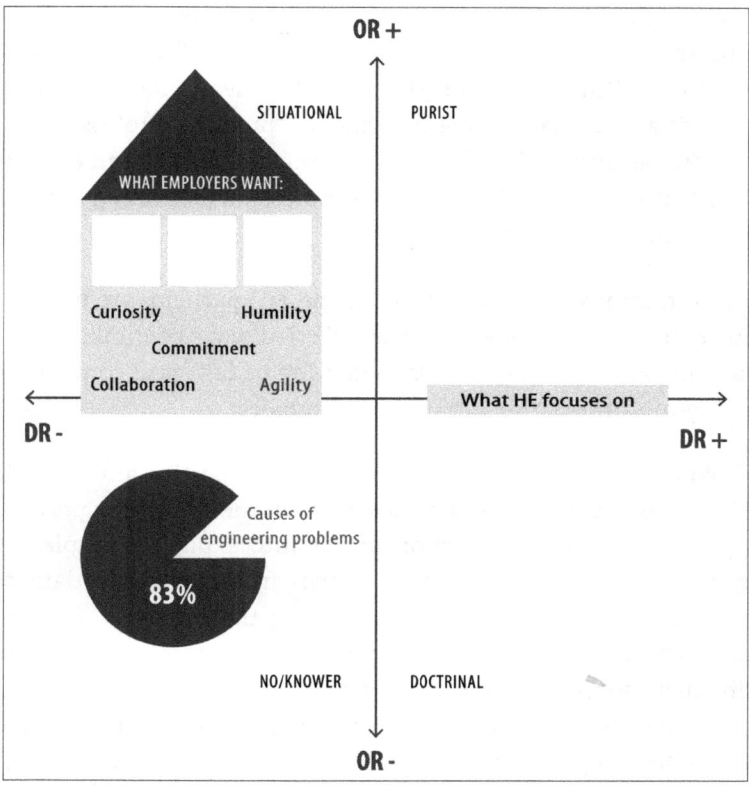

FIGURE 18.2 Engineering problem-solving findings

My work with Engineering educators on a range of curriculum redesign workshops confirmed the industrial research findings that Engineering higher education in South Africa is predominantly focused on the right-hand side of the plane, that is a tendency towards fixed phenomena and approaches. This is confirmed in reviews of curriculum texts at HEI-1, where the primary aim is the development of *purist insights* (Wolff, Dorfling & Akdogan, 2018), and HEI-2, which sees a focus on *doctrinal insights* (Wolff, 2018b). When set in relation to the employer surveys on required graduate abilities, there is evidence of distinct code clashes. In an interview with over 100 Forbes company CEOs, the top "skills" in addition to the traditional "soft skills" of leadership, teamwork and communication are listed as curiosity, agility, collaboration and humility (Beaton, 2017). At first glance, these attributes reside on the left-hand side of the *epistemic plane*, further illustrating the disjuncture between what it is that higher education does and what it is that the labour market wants. However, industrial research suggests that all four *insight* quadrants are necessary, given that each represents a different kind of code or way of thinking. The successful problem solvers recognised when and how to be analytical or methodical or open to possibilities, and they exhibit iterative code-shifting behaviour (Wolff, 2018a). Given that the specifications for Engineering qualifications are designed to "produce" professionals for the labour market at three different levels, the mismatch between education (on the right-hand side of the plane) and the profession (expecting left-hand side capabilities) must be addressed.

Using these findings, my objective with the EiC participants was to enable academic staff to collectively "see" the different ways of thinking (or *insight* codes) and engage with useful tools to develop pedagogical competencies for Engineering-in-Context, the aim of the EiC project.

The following first subsection draws on written participant reflections on the nature of their subject areas as described in their teaching portfolios and feedback forms. The second section moves into explicit examples of code-shifting strategies in their pedagogy drawn from the same data sources. The participant reflections are analysed using the *epistemic insight* codes, indicated where appropriate alongside the alphanumerical identifiers indicating institution and unique participant number. The section ends with academic staff reflections that explicitly indicate a move towards transforming their curricular and pedagogic approaches.

Orientations to meaning and shifting perceptions

A common comment to emerge from participants at both institutions concerns the lack of collaboration or practice-sharing across subjects in the same qualification, indicating a collection code curricular approach. Furthermore, a fairly standard trajectory is observed in the curriculum across the qualification period: fundamental sciences first, then Engineering science theory, to Engineering science application and design. Although one would expect a transition to an integrated curricular approach as students encounter Engineering application and design, the predominant orientation to subject "content" irrespective of its disciplinary nature or location in the qualification period appears to have been governed by *insights* entirely located on the right-hand side of the *epistemic plane* (Figure 18.1). The following three examples support this:

> My subject [Material Science – second year] ... [has] a [high] ratio of theory and concepts to method and calculations. Students are often overwhelmed with the amount of 'facts' that they are faced with and a thick textbook that they have to 'learn'.
>
> *(Purist* – HEI-1-5)

> My third-year Chemical Engineering module, concerned with the properties and design of particles and particle-based process units, is very difficult or impossible to capture in a single, phenomenologically based mathematical equation. [Most of this] knowledge is encapsulated in [the] heuristic, parametrised equations derived from statistical model fitting to observed data, without a clear physical interpretation.
>
> (*Purist/Doctrinal* – HEI-1-4)

> My main concern [in Facilities Management second year] is that students need to be rigorous, systematic. They must learn to apply the methods.   (*Doctrinal* – HEI-2-4)

The perception of all subject content being predominantly underpinned by *purist/doctrinal insights* is further evidenced in curriculum mapping exercises using the *epistemic plane*. One of the HEI-1 EiC participants with whom I had been working before the project had been introduced to several LCT tools. His initial interest was in trying to understand the impact of industrial site visits on final year Chemical Engineering students. Using the *epistemic plane* to map all third- and fourth-year subjects, he found only two project subjects located on the left-hand side in the *situational quadrant* (Wolff et al., 2018). His subsequent analysis of the student site visit feedback as part of the EiC project demonstrated a significant code shift for the students, into both the *situational* and *knower insight* quadrants:

> I never realised how mineral processing plants are involved with surrounding communities ... hearing the challenges faced by many operators showed there is much opportunity for improvement both technologically and socially.
>
> (Final year HEI-1 student)

The original purpose of the site visits had been to consolidate student understanding of the theoretical concepts and to aid them in carrying out their final year capstone projects. Student feedback, however, focused predominantly on what Engineering educators regard as "soft skills". This EiC participant found the *epistemic plane* a useful explanatory device to examine the disjuncture between the curriculum, industry expectations and student perceptions.

A similar curriculum mapping exercise at HEI-2 led to the discovery that most of the focus was on drilling and practising *doctrinal* procedures (whether Mathematics or Engineering Technology) as staff were confronted with students "who struggle with basic mathematics and computer skills" (HEI-2-3). This observation of the dominant praxis dimension of the curriculum led to a lengthy and engaged discussion on what exactly the epistemological principles were underpinning their particular qualification. The entire department embarked on an exercise to identify necessary codes and code-shifting strategies to enable the development of a more holistic graduate (Wolff, 2018b). Interestingly, collectively the department decided that an overarching principle in their Engineering field is that of "*Ubuntu*" – a shared humanity (Mbembe, 2011) – indicating the recognition of the ontological dimension of their curriculum.

The experience of being inducted into different ways of "seeing" their disciplines in context, as well as being participants in the EiC project, led to overwhelmingly positive post-workshop feedback on the importance of collaboration across subject areas, departments, faculties, institutions and industries. All the participants began to engage in explicit code-shifting pedagogies, as detailed in the following section.

Code-shifting pedagogy

For most of the participants, addressing challenges in the teaching, learning and assessment space had begun with a review of the curriculum as a result of the national mandate to redesign curricula to meet the requirements of the Higher Education Qualifications Sub-Framework (CHE, 2013). The understanding that more effective learning could be achieved by enabling students to shift from one way of thinking to another, iteratively or cyclically, manifested in different approaches to teaching:

> I have changed the way I use my pre-allocated lecture periods [by introducing a] hands-on lecture ... in an electronic venue, where all students have access to a computer ... [and can] grapple with existing case simulations and are encouraged to ... get a feel for the effect of different parameters on their system.
>
> (*Situational/Doctrinal* – HEI-1-4)

This HEI-1 participant found it essential to create a "playground" for students, where they could experiment and observe different approaches to different cases, demonstrating the diametrical shift between the *doctrinal* rules of one approach and the *situational* possibilities of different approaches and parameters. Her colleague, similarly, refers to a shift to creating "a space where students learn through actively engaging with the concepts" (HEI-1-7), referring to his novel use of different coloured Lego blocks to teach Thermodynamics, thus indicating a shift from the *purist* to *situational* quadrants.

A further shift is demonstrated by the first lecturer when she interrupted her introductory lecture on Process Control Theory to allow students to muse about "practical applications for process control, such as designing an automatic control system for a household greywater system" (HEI-1-4) during one of the most severe droughts in the region, where all households were concerned about water-saving practices. This pedagogic shift from *purist* to *situational insight* naturally led to the *knower* quadrant with different students sharing their different experiences of the water crisis. Here we see the explicit inclusion of ontological elements in the curriculum, as well as a code shift to more open-ended approaches to phenomena extended beyond the textbook.

At HEI-2, "it is common for between eight and twelve first languages to be present in one classroom" (Barris, 2019:62). Here, an EiC participant described her approach to encouraging students to discuss concepts in their home languages in groups because then "the students express themselves more freely and that helps them understand the subject matter better" (HEI-2-2). A colleague from a different department tasked with teaching second-year mathematics to mechanical Engineering students described how she had explicitly introduced code shifting across the entire *epistemic plane*, by issuing group tasks such as:

> In your group, use the following differential equation to identify a particular structure on campus carrying a point load of X gallons of material with X density. (HEI-2-5)

This task sees the explicit movement from *doctrinal* mathematics to *purist* principles related to density to physically identify a real structure (*situational*) by groups of different kinds of *knowers*. This lecturer commented that student approaches to the task had surprised her. She received feedback such as:

> I found it fascinating how one simple equation can represent a real structure with a real and significant purpose. (HEI-2-5 student)

This student's feedback suggests that lecturers may take for granted that students understand the significance of what they are studying, particularly in the mathematical sciences.

Towards decolonising the curriculum

The most significant code shift for the project participants is that into the *knower insight* quadrant (Figure 18.3). One HEI-2 participant declared: "I now see students as partners in the sharing of knowledge and that they have a lot to contribute to the overall teaching and learning experience" (HEI-2-1). Making space for students is one thing, but explicitly acknowledging our South African students and context as sources of invaluable forms of knowledge, and knowing is the key to decolonising the curriculum:

> In my lectures, I have started using terms and examples that students relate with. For example, using a traditional welding procedure of repairing pots at home when introducing the Welding topic. (HEI-2-2)

> I am trying to provide an environment where students can identify with what I am saying using current events and localised examples. I also try to create an environment where students are free to share their ideas without a feeling that they will provide a 'wrong answer'. (HEI-2-1)

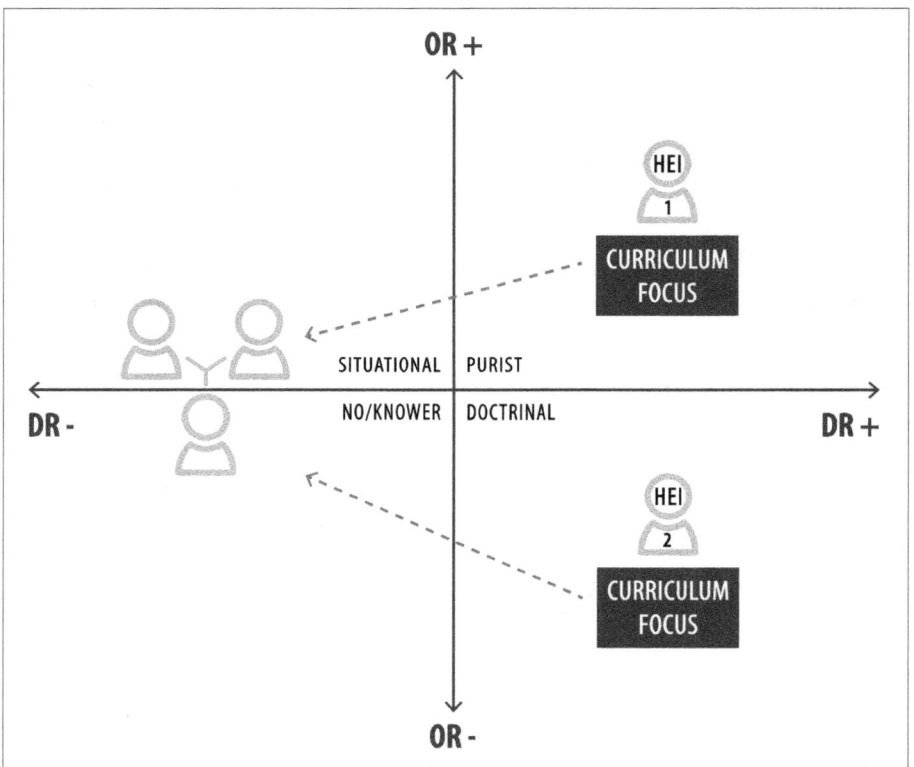

FIGURE 18.3 EiC participant code shifting

Acknowledging how context affects different students' grasp of fundamental chemistry principles to tackle estimation questions represented a major learning curve for a group of participants at HEI-1. Initially, the group was concerned about student inabilities to estimate, for example, how many ping-pong balls could fit into an Olympic-size swimming pool (Tadie, Pott, Goosen, Van Wyk & Wolff, 2018). When the question arose during an EiC session of how many of their students had ever seen an Olympic-sized swimming pool or even knew what a ping-pong ball was, the educators were challenged to interrogate their ontological assumptions. Afforded the opportunity to be part of a "community of enquiry" in the EiC context, their discussion led to the collective revision of course material and increased awareness of how students can be enabled to "visualise" concepts:

> The role of the knower or the background of the student also becomes strongly relevant and determines the context of the visualisation processes ... [The] phase change from 100 [degree Celsius] to 0 [degree Celsius] [can be] taught with reference to everyday examples ... Students might draw parallels with a pot or kettle boiling, water freezing in a fridge, summer (experiences of hot climate), winter (experiences of very cold climates). (HEI-1-2)

However, accessing knowledge epistemologically and ontologically through contextualised examples and students' own anecdotal experiences needs to be carefully facilitated:

> Another aspect of my teaching philosophy is to tailor-make explanations based on what a particular student knows and understands ... to make knowledge accessible to a diversity of student learning approaches and preparedness. Students are different, and finding the right 'in', the right analogy and level of detail to illuminate a concept is [important]. (HEI-1-4)

Conclusion

The desire to transform curriculum and pedagogy to contribute to a socially just educational experience begins with "seeing". Using the LCT concept of the *epistemic plane* as an accessible tool to interrogate ways of thinking underpinning knowledge practices, academic staff members involved in an international collaborative project at two South African institutions were enabled – as a community of enquiry – to embark on code-shifting strategies to more effectively include the ontological and praxis dimensions of the curriculum. The participant experiences, as described in this chapter, bear testimony to the value of academic developers collaborating with academics and introducing theoretically informed instruments to enable critical reflection and dialogue. Two examples of participant feedback highlight two particular benefits. The first example sees an educator mediating his understanding by drawing parallels between his discipline and the sociological tools to which he had been introduced:

> In some respects, it is because of the similarities between my own discipline and the LCT [Legitimation Code Theory] framework that I've found it so powerful – it's a strong and predictive analytical tool. (HEI-1-6)

The second example demonstrates the value of a sociological lens in enabling new insights:

> I now see that the content of the subjects that I teach can be greatly enhanced by applying the principles based on the Epistemic plane. It has also made me realise how the Engineering discipline as a whole has clear shortcomings when it comes to developing a well-rounded student who is ready for employment. (HEI-2-3)

In response to research findings and industry surveys on the inability of graduates to operate effectively enough on the left-hand side of the plane, all the participants developed strategies to introduce open-ended or alternative approaches to particular phenomena. Without consciously having engaged in the decolonisation debate, it is evident that the academic development initiatives led to participants' explicitly taking a more proactive stance towards understanding their students in their particular contexts. The shift towards more inclusive pedagogies – drawing on students' experiences and perspectives on scientific phenomena – makes for a welcome step towards decolonising the Engineering curriculum. Finally, the introduction of a different set of lenses through which to examine "ways of thinking, being and doing", subconsciously shifted the participants into the left-hand side of the *epistemic plane* and saw their adoption of strategies to enable precisely the same code shifting necessary for developing the elaborated orientation to meaning so necessary for an inclusive and just higher education system.

References

AIKENHEAD, G.S. 2006. Towards decolonizing the pan-Canadian science framework. *Canadian Journal of Math, Science and Technology Education*, 6(4):387-399. [https://doi.org/10.1080/14926150609556712]

AURET, L. & WOLFF, K. 2018. A control system framework for reflective practice. *Institute of Electrical and Electronic Engineers*, 106-114. [https://doi.org/10.1109/EDUCON.2018.8363215]

BAILEY-MCEWAN, M. 2009. *Difficulties of Mechanical Engineering students in developing integrated knowledge for the cross-discipline of Mechatronics: A conceptual investigation.* Johannesburg: University of the Witwatersrand. [https://bit.ly/2lANtrF]

BARNETT, R. 2000. Supercomplexity and curriculum. *Studies in Higher Education*, 25(3). [https://doi.org/10.1080/713696156]

BARRIS, K. 2019. Using the low ground to get high: The pedagogic value of teaching plagiarism. *Current Writing: Text and Reception in Southern Africa*, 62-70. [https://doi.org/10.1080/1013929X.2018.1547021]

BEATON, C. 2017. Top employers say millennials need these 4 skills in 2017. *Forbes*. [https://bit.ly/2l0ZhDf]

BERNSTEIN, B. 2000. *Pedagogy, symbolic control and identity: Theory, research, critique.* Revised Edition. London: Rowman and Littlefield.

BERNSTEIN, B. 1996. *Pedagogy, symbolic control and identity: Theory, research, critique.* London: Taylor and Francis.

BERNSTEIN, B. 1977. *Class, codes and control, III: Towards a theory of educational transmissions.* London: Routledge.

Bernstein, B. 1975. *Class, codes and control.* London: Routledge. [https://doi.org/10.4324/9780203011430]

Bernstein, B. 1971. *Class, codes and control: Theoretical studies towards a sociology of language.* London: Routledge. [https://doi.org/10.4324/9780203011430]

CHE (Council on Higher Education). 2015. *Vital stats public higher education 2013.* Pretoria: CHE. [https://bit.ly/2kEgHFL]

CHE (Council on Higher Education). 2013. *The Higher Education Qualifications Sub-Framework.* Pretoria: CHE. [https://bit.ly/2mePCcr]

De Oliveira, A.; Stein, S.; Ahenakew, C. & Hunt, D. 2015. Mapping interpretations of decolonization in the context of higher education. *Decolonisation: Indigeneity, Education and Society,* 4(1). [https://bit.ly/2KeUENd]

DHET (Department of Higher Education and Training). 2013. White Paper for post-school education and training, 20 November. Pretoria: DHET. [https://bit.ly/2lBkOTe]

Felder, R.; Woods, D.; Stice, J. & Rugarcia, A. 2000. The Future of Engineering Education II. Teaching Methods That Work. *Chemical Engineering Education,* 34(1):26-39. [https://bit.ly/2nahkI5]

Geyser, H. 2018. Decolonising the games curriculum: Interventions in an introductory game design course. *Open Library of Humanities,* 4(1). [https://doi.org/10.16995/olh.217]

Griesel, H. & Parker, B. 2009. *Graduate Attributes: A baseline study on South African graduates from the perspective on employers.* Higher Education South Africa and South African Qualifications Authority. [https://bit.ly/2l1FJyJ]

Jacobs, C. 2007. Towards a critical understanding of the teaching of discipline-specific academic literacies: making the tacit explicit. *Journal of Education,* 41:59-81. [https://bit.ly/2m0EWxS]

Leibowitz, B. 2017. Cognitive justice and the Higher Education curriculum. *Journal of Education,* 68:93-111. [https://bit.ly/2mz8V0k]

Louw, T. & Wolff, K. 2018. Experimenting with engagement: an intervention to promote active reflection during laboratory practicals. *Institute of Electrical and Electronic Engineers,* 736-743. [https://doi.org/10.1109/EDUCON.2018.8363303]

Manpower Group. 2015. *Talent Shortage Survey.* USA: The Manpower Group. [https://bit.ly/2IzYhNg]

Maton, K. 2014. *Knowledge and Knowers: Towards a realist sociology of education.* New York: Routledge. [https://doi.org/10.4324/9780203885734]

Maton, K. 2013. Making semantic waves: A key to cumulative knowledge-building. *Linguistics and Education,* 24:8-22. [https://doi.org/10.1016/j.linged.2012.11.005]

Maton, K.; Hood, S. & Shay, S. 2015. *Knowledge-building: Educational studies in legitimation code theory.* London: Routledge. [https://doi.org/10.4324/9780203885734]

Mbembe, A. 2011. Democracy as a community of life. *The Humanist Imperative in South Africa,* 4:187-192. [https://bit.ly/2l1GUy9]

Mingers, J. 2014. *Systems thinking, critical realism and philosophy.* London: Routledge. [https://doi.org/10.4324/9781315774503]

Morrow, W. 2009. *Bounds of democracy: epistemological access in higher education.* Cape Town: HSRC Press.

Muller, J. 2014. Every picture tells a story: Epistemological access and knowledge. *Education as Change,* 18(2):255-269. [https://doi.org/10.1080/16823206.2014.932256]

Muller, J. 2009. Forms of knowledge and curriculum coherence. *Journal of Education and Work,* 22(3):205-226. [https://doi.org/10.1080/13639080902957905]

NPC (National Planning Commission), 2019. *National Development Plan Vision 2030.* Johannesburg: NPC. [https://www.nationalplanningcommission.org.za/National_Development_Plan]

Quinn, L. (ed). 2012. *Re-imagining academic staff development: Spaces for disruption.* Stellenbosch: African Sun Media. [https://doi.org/10.18820/9781920338879]

TADIE, M.; POTT, R.; GOOSEN, N.; VAN WYK, P. & WOLFF, K. 2018. Expanding 1st-year problem-solving skills through unit conversions and estimations. *Institute of Electrical and Electronic Engineers*, 1041-1049. [https://doi.org/10.1109/EDUCON.2018.8363344]

UNESCO, 2010. *Engineering: issues, challenges and opportunities for development*. Paris: Unesco Publishing. [https://unesdoc.unesco.org/ark:/48223/pf0000189753]

WHEELAHAN, L. 2007. How competency-based training locks the working class out of powerful knowledge: a modified Bernsteinian analysis. *British Journal of Sociology of Education*, 28(5):637-651. [https://doi.org/10.1080/01425690701505540]

WINBERG, C.; ADENDORFF, H.; BOZALEK, V.; CONANA, H.; PALLITT, N.; WOLFF, K.; OLSSON, T. & ROXÅ, T. 2018. Learning to teach the STEM disciplines in higher education. *Teaching in Higher Education*. [https://doi.org/10.1080/13562517.2018.1517735]

WOLFF, K. 2018a. A language for the analysis of disciplinary boundary crossing: insights from engineering problem-solving practice. *Teaching in Higher Education*, 23(1):104-119. [https://doi.org/10.1080/13562517.2017.1359155]

WOLFF, K. 2018b. Closing the loop in engineering educator development: Using theoretical and empirical research to inform curriculum and teaching. *Institute of Electrical and Electronic Engineers*, 77-85. [https://doi.org/10.1109/EDUCON.2018.8363211]

WOLFF, K. 2018c. Theory and practice in the 21st-century engineering workplace. In: S. Allais & Y. Shalem (eds). *Knowledge Curriculum and preparation for Work*. London: Sense Publishers. [https://doi.org/10.1163/9789004365407_011]

WOLFF, K. 2015. *Negotiating disciplinary boundaries in engineering problem-solving practice*. Cape Town: University of Cape Town.

WOLFF, K.; DORFLING, C. & AKDOGAN, G. 2018. Shifting disciplinary perspectives and perceptions of chemical engineering work in the 21st century. *Education for Chemical Engineers*, 24:43-51. [https://doi.org/10.1016/j.ece.2018.06.005]

CHAPTER 19

Creating spaces for the emergence of new realities in science curriculum thinking

Ann Cameron & Kershree Padayachee

Introduction

"This is science, for goodness' sake, there is nothing to 'decolonise'!" The frustration inherent in this outburst, which came from one of the science lecturers during a curriculum development course called *Learning and Teaching in Science*, captures a common reaction by science lecturers at the University of the Witwatersrand (Wits) in the wake of the #FeesMustFall student protests of 2015 and 2016 in South Africa. A trust in science, and the power of science and the scientific method to explain the way the world works has meant that for many science lecturers the call for decolonisation of the curriculum appears to belong to debates outside of the interests and concerns of the science that they teach and practice.

Not all lecturers respond as angrily or defensively as the one described above. Some express a sense of relief at being able to talk about the difficulties they had experienced in becoming scientists. Others are willing to consider science as only one of a number of different ways of knowing and understanding the natural world, and are willing to listen and think about how they could use what they learn during the course to reduce the sense of alienation felt by many students. During the course, lecturers are introduced to selected theories and conceptual underpinnings of learning and teaching in science, and these are then linked to their own experiences as both learners and as teachers. The lecturers are encouraged to think critically about their role in the epistemological and ontological development of their students; to reflect on current teaching and learning realities; and to re-imagine curricula that are more responsive to the needs of students, society and current and future global issues.

This chapter offers the outcome of a conversation regarding science lecturers' reactions and responses to the course. This conversation has taken place over a period of time, between Ann, who is an academic developer in the Faculty of Science, and Kershree, who is a science education lecturer in the Faculty of Humanities. We both hold qualifications in the Biological Sciences and Education, and while located in different Faculties, have both worked in academic staff development for many years. Over the past few years we have been grappling with challenges related to curriculum decolonisation and how to meaningfully engage science lecturers in discussions that could deepen their understanding of the role they play in this regard. The lecturers who attend the course are not usually familiar with the philosophical underpinnings of education. Our work with these academics has served to encourage and support them in becoming increasingly reflective in relation to their teaching role. In this chapter, we consider the nature of the internal shifts experienced by these lecturers during the course, and on our role as academic developers in this transformative process.

The student protests of 2015 and 2016 were found to be important in driving a significant shift in lecturers' responses to the course. Issues that previously had largely been seen to lie outside their role as teachers suddenly required attention. Challenges related to concepts such as epistemological access (Morrow, 2007) and the decolonisation of the curriculum, for example, could no longer be approached on a "take it or leave it" basis. Before the protests, lecturers tended to approach teaching development courses and workshops wanting "tips and tools" for enhancing their teaching, with little time or thought given to understanding education as a principled discipline. However, as Ramsden (1992) puts it:

> There is a prevailing impression that the busy lecturer has no time to acquire an understanding of the subject of education. 'Don't give me theory, just give me something that works' is a plea that there is every temptation to answer. This plea is part of a certain way of looking at teaching, and it is approximately the reverse of the truth about how to improve it. No university chemist or historian would apply it to their own discipline. No physician or architect would apply it to their own practice. No progress in any subject, including education, can be made without the reflective application of knowledge to the right problems. (Ramsden, 1992: Preface)

Therefore, despite lecturers' expectations of receiving a set of tools in the course, education theory was included in the course from its inception, to encourage reflection that could lead to enhanced practice.

We recognised that the rapid shifts in the wider higher education landscape, triggered by the student protests, meant that lecturers would need to engage with these shifts in ways that could be potentially uncomfortable and disconcerting. This realisation highlighted the need for us, as academic developers, to reflect on and conceptualise the transformative process that lecturers were undergoing, both as individuals, and in relation to their roles as teachers, as they were introduced to what was, for many, a new discourse. Our ongoing discussions led us to Otto Scharmer's framework for personal and organisation transformation, called Theory U (2009). Theory U is a development framework that can be used to deal with difficult institutional challenges in a way that is conscious, intentional and strategic. During the *Teaching and Learning in Science* course, assumptions about knowledge, values and power were often surfaced through examining the nature and purpose of curriculum. For participants who had not previously questioned the canons of science, the course presented a space for both discomfort and development. Thus while the course had not been developed explicitly around this Theory U framework (detailed later), we realised that it provided a useful analytical tool to understand how the course served to stimulate a change in thinking. We also realised that it offered a more intentional way for us to think about our growing understanding of what it means to decolonise the science curriculum and how we could provide opportunities for lecturers to rethink their approaches to teaching and learning. We are very aware that being able to assess the success or value of the academic development initiatives that we offer is notoriously difficult. However, comments made by lecturers in the feedback provided on the course, gave us an indication of progression through at least some of the stages of Theory U.

Background to the *Learning and Teaching in Science* course

The course is offered as part of the Science Faculty probation programme and, as such, it is our main opportunity to engage with groups of novice lecturers. Before the protests, the course had served as a basic introduction to educational philosophy and theory. Its main purpose, in the postapartheid landscape, was to raise awareness of challenges related to the teaching and learning of science and the recognition in South Africa of Indigenous Knowledge Systems. The course had originally been designed to challenge a particular philosophy of science held by some science lecturers, that is, scientific positivism, which is the belief that the only authentic knowledge is that which can be scientifically or logically proven. However, in light of rapid changes in student diversity over the years, where the number of students holding their own epistemological belief systems was growing, such views of science were inadvertently creating learning barriers for an increasing number of students.

Once challenges related to epistemological access had been brought to the fore through the protests, our university responded to the call for decolonisation by asking academics to make conscious shifts in praxis to enable improved access to the forms of knowledge required by students within their disciplines. There was, at least initially, no deep engagement by science lecturers about what knowledge students were to be given access to, or how, and many continued to believe that the universalist nature of their fields of science protected them from having to engage with questions of epistemology. The *Learning and Teaching in Science* course was thus experienced by many lecturers as a first-time exposure to the philosophy of education and to discussions around the role they played in the epistemological and ontological development of their students. Their reactions ranged from enthusiastic interest in what it might mean to decolonise their disciplines, to those who continued to express resistance and reluctance. Some lecturers regarded decolonisation as simply a matter of introducing more local examples in their teaching: "I already have South African and African examples, but I will try to find more." For these lecturers, decolonisation was easy and they were willing, where possible, to find examples that were relevant to the real-world experiences of their students. Other lecturers suggested that shifts in the teaching and learning of science had already been addressed from the early days of South Africa's democracy, in response to the increasing diversity of the study body, and that revisiting this issue was a waste of time. In general, however, there was acknowledgement amongst most academics in the sciences that something did need to shift. What this shift potentially entailed is where the uncertainty and discomfort lay.

The Council on Higher Education's monitoring brief on decolonising the curriculum (CHE, 2017:5) explains that decolonisation, in the context of students' feelings of alienation, requires "deliberate attention to surfacing and inducting students into specific forms of meaning-making, with a move away from thinking of curriculum as something received, but rather as a co-constructed set of understandings". The problem for many lecturers was how to do this without compromising the full spectrum of the principled, "universally true" knowledge of their disciplines. While science has been defined in many ways, most definitions embed the notion of science as the systematic study of the structure and behaviour of the physical and natural world through observation and experiment. Essentially it is a quest for understanding the physical and natural world, based on evidence that is so strong as to leave little or no doubt about its validity. There is a general acceptance amongst scientists and science lecturers that one can only become a "knower" within the discipline through deep and critical engagement with the principled knowledge of that discipline, guided by those who have achieved mastery and who have developed a particular trained disciplinary gaze (Maton, 2014). Students enter first year with untrained, social gazes and are gradually socialised into adopting the "legitimate cultivated gaze" (Maton, 2014:136) through immersion in the knowledge of the discipline. There is an expectation in this process of becoming a legitimate knower in a particular discipline of science, that students will "hone their self-identities and belief systems and forge allegiances to the culture of academic science" (Aikenhead, 2010:111). Consequently, science lecturers tend to maintain firm control over what they believe constitutes legitimate knowledge in their courses. In designing and enacting their curricula, they prioritise the legitimacy of disciplinary knowledge over other forms of knowledge that students may possess. This is where the idea of decolonisation of the curriculum is deeply challenging because, as noted by Vorster and Quinn (2017:12), "the decolonising discourse creates a constraining contradiction for lecturers whose identities are strongly tied to the traditional canon of their disciplines". For science lecturers, their own identity would have been forged through the process of disciplinary acculturation that they would have undergone in their training, and this is what they want to pass on to their students.

However, the process of disciplinary acculturation can be challenging, particularly for students of indigenous cultural heritage in countries previously colonised by European powers. This is because university curricula used in such countries have almost exclusively promoted a Eurocentric view of the world. Research studies in the 1990s (see, for example, Aikenhead & Jegede, 1999;

Cobern, 1996; Jegede, 1997; and Ogunniyi, 1996) led to a theorising of why science was found to be difficult by many students. By taking into account that different cultures understand and explain nature in different ways and that science represents only one of multiple human ways of understanding the world, ideas such as "collateral learning" (Jegede, 1995) and "cultural border crossing" (Aikenhead, 1997) were used to pave the way for research that considered the effects of Indigenous Knowledge Systems on the teaching and learning of science. Evidence from research in previously colonised countries, including Canada (Aikenhead, 1996) and South Africa (Manzini, 2000), has demonstrated that worldview beliefs can have a significant impact on the uptake of science in school and university classrooms. While some students manage to navigate the "cognitive borders" between their belief systems and that of science, others find it difficult or impossible in relation to their own belief systems, because to them it presents a contradictory or unacceptable view of the world (see, for example, Dzama & Osborne, 1999).

Such theories quickly found traction in South Africa after the demise of apartheid, where they were later complemented by Morrow's (2007) concept of "epistemological access". This notion alerted educators to the reality that many students remain excluded from meaning-making, because the specific ways of knowing, thinking and understanding that are linked to the norms, codes, principles and practices of academic disciplines, including science, are often not made explicit to students by the lecturers. Also noteworthy is that it is not just students who experience the epistemic challenges that are associated with differences in culture. As the staff demography has changed over the past two decades, increasing numbers of academic staff members have related their own experiences, during the *Learning and Teaching in Science* course, of issues and challenges related to their "border crossing" into science.

Changing beliefs about science knowledge and science education

In South Africa, democracy brought with it a rethinking of the education system, which included the requirement to acknowledge the existence of multiple worldviews linked to its cultural diversity and heritage. However, this requirement, aimed at the whole education system, was taken up slowly and in a limited way in science education at secondary school level (Gundry & Cameron, 2008). In higher education, where there is far more autonomy with regard to the curriculum, it was largely ignored. However, after the student protests, lecturers were challenged to address what we call "epistemological complacency". There has been growing awareness that decolonisation is not simply about the inclusion of more African knowledge or African examples in the curriculum (Mbembe, 2015), but that it entails a far more complex and nuanced approach to make it meaningful. However, the view has persisted that curriculum is predominantly about the content that is "delivered" to students (Fraser & Bosanquet, 2006). The idea of the curriculum as a negotiated process in which graduate identity is developed, as a Chemist or Geologist, for example, is often lost in the urgency of getting through content in the time that is available. Our role, through our work with lecturers, is therefore to try to raise awareness and create the conditions that can lead to viewing curriculum differently.

The *Learning and Teaching in Science* course was developed in a context of fiscal constraints associated with changing subsidy regulations, which made it critical for lecturers to develop their teaching expertise to improve learning in order to improve the throughput rates. The course was made compulsory for all new academic staff in the Science Faculty, with longer serving members of staff invited to attend. It offered a space for lecturers to become aware of their teaching and learning "blind spots" (Scharmer, 2009) and to become familiar with scholarly literature on teaching in the sciences. It thus presented lecturers with an opportunity to explore new ways in which they might approach their teaching.

Theory U as a tool for analysis

We realised that the design and intention of the course to expose science lecturers to what could, at least for some, be new ways of understanding their role as teachers, resonated with Scharmer's "Theory U" (Scharmer, 2009). Figure 19.1 illustrates the reflective journey described by Theory U that individuals or/and groups may experience during the process of organisational and/or personal transformation and change. Starting on the left side of the U, participants begin with a consideration of the important issues, for example, curriculum decolonisation. They are encouraged to think about how they feel about these issues. Participants are then invited to suspend judgement and listen to other perspectives. As they engage in various discussions and activities, they are requested to listen deeply and attentively, to pay attention to their own biases and assumptions, and to note how they are responding, not just cognitively but also at a deeper more emotional level, to what might be emerging. Scharmer calls this stage "sensing" or "leaning into feeling", which can profoundly influence the response to what is being learned. At this point, a lecturer (in this case) may experience a sense of "push back" and hold firm to old ways of thinking and being, resulting in comments such as "It's science for goodness' sake! There's nothing to 'decolonise'!" However, for others, this stage signals a shift to the bottom of the U, namely "presencing".

Presencing, which is a portmanteau of "presence" and "sensing" (Scharmer, 2009), involves the development or emergence of connection with what is in oneself at the level of the heart, with the possibility that this awareness, or consciousness, or attention, will lead to an intention, which can be transformative in everyday work. Presencing is characterised by quiet reflection on what has been learned, what might need to be let go of, and what might need further exploration. This stage of self-reflection and introspection then leads to the shift up the right side of the U, where participants commit to making changes, however small, in a stage called "crystallising". They then begin to consider new possibilities, which Scharmer calls "prototyping". The final stage is "realising", where actions are taken to create new ways of thinking and acting.

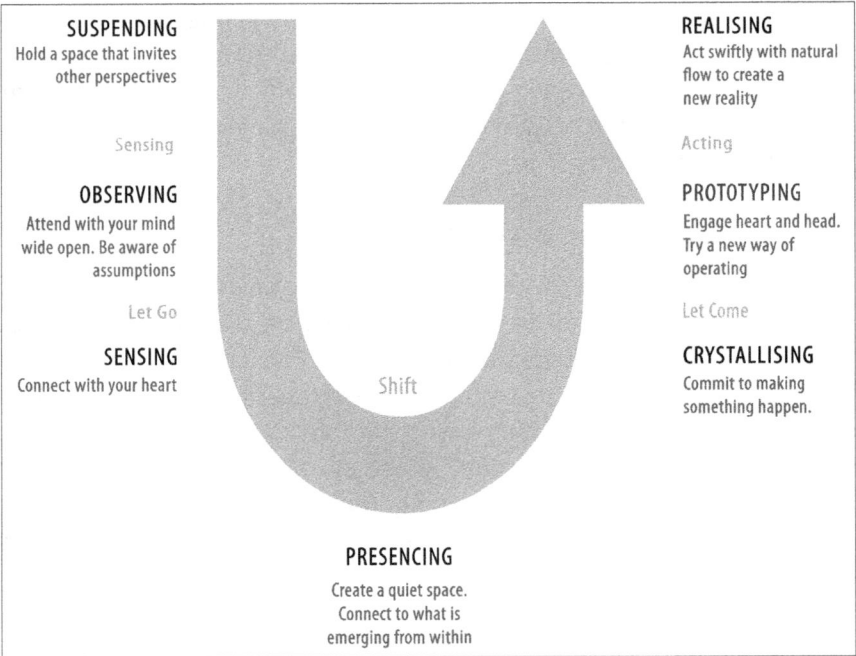

Figure 19.1 Theory U, a model for transformative change (Scharmer, 2009)

While Theory U has been applied by us as a post-facto analytical tool rather than as a methodological framework for the course, evidence of movement through the U could be found in comments in the feedback on the course. Various comments signalled possibilities for change in course participants' understandings and their approaches to teaching and learning. We realised that the course does indeed take participants on a journey through the stages of the U described above.

How the course facilitates transformative shifts

The course is designed to encourage lecturers to explore their own beliefs and understanding of teaching. This reflection begins by remembering their own experiences as students and listening to the experiences shared by others. Lecturers are then invited to see their students as individuals who share the same hopes, dreams and fears that they might have had as students. They are also encouraged to acknowledge different hopes, dreams and fears linked to students' backgrounds. Lecturers' exploration of their own experiences of university is an important starting point, resulting in awareness that the difficulties they struggled with are no different from those being experienced by their students.

The initial reflection on the student experience is followed by reflection on the role of the university lecturer. Unless academics are designated to purely research posts, they are employed as "lecturers" when appointed, which many understand as being about transmitting powerful discipline-based knowledge and the skills of science to students. To be a "science lecturer" is to be deeply connected with beliefs in objectivity, rationality and logic. Emotion and feeling are traditionally deliberately removed to strengthen the validity and reliability of claims. Some lecturers believe that their role is simply to prepare and deliver course materials, set assessment tasks and grade student papers. They believe that what the students do with what they are taught is "up to the students". However, while the title "lecturer" persists, the focus of university policies and the demand for improved throughput rates has provoked a shift, first from lecturing to teaching, and then from teaching to learning.

In the course, participants are also invited to think about their past teachers and how these people might have shaped their notions of "good" teaching. They are asked to identify the best teacher they ever had and write down all the qualities that contributed to why they regarded this person as their best teacher. They are then asked to speak about what it was that made this person so special, and the shared experiences are used to compile a list of attributes of a "good" teacher. The lecturers are then invited to think about learning and how they themselves learn. The intention of these reflections is for them to think about their conceptions of teaching and learning and to share these with their peers, before they are introduced to theories and concepts from the higher education studies literature.

Some of the participants find aspects of the course uncomfortably challenging in relation to how they have viewed their role as a lecturer. For some, discomfort emerges as they hear colleagues speak about the pain of their experiences as students in a "foreign and uncaring" environment. For others, discomfort comes from exposure to policy documents such as the Wits Lecturer Contract of Commitment (Wits, 2005), which states that lecturers have a "moral responsibility to teach their students well". Here they also learn that the "learning needs and diverse backgrounds of students should be taken into account in all teaching"; that students are "entitled to respectful, caring and attentive conduct"; and that "students should be known by name by at least some of the staff in the schools in which they study". These imperatives provoke questions such as: What does it mean to teach well? What does it mean to care for your students? How should diversity be taken into account? How can you possibly know the names of 400 students in your course? However, the mandates in the code of conduct for teaching staff and in policies that position Wits as a "student-centred university" can be used to connect the lecturers with their own experiences of having been a student and of having been taught well or poorly. Some feel relieved that they are encouraged to focus on teaching and to care about their students. The pressure in a research-intensive university to be research productive has meant that some lecturers are advised to spend their time on research in preference to developing or re-shaping curriculum materials or making time for their students. After the course, they feel more confident in being able to point out that according to the Wits Lecturer Contract of Commitment, they were under a "moral obligation to teach well" and that time spent with students or on curriculum development is not wasted. For many of the lecturers, learning about these policies was the most significant aspect of the course as it gave them the freedom to choose to spend time on their teaching:

> The course gave me hope that there is more to teaching than the transference of facts.
> (2017 J3)[1]

> I liked the new information about teaching and learning. Honestly, we think that we know how to teach, but there are many things that we learned from this course.
> (2018 J8)

---

1   This refers to the year the participant attended the course and the number of the feedback form.

> I have learned about the important role we play as teachers and that having a vested interest in the personalities of your students can make a big difference to your success as a lecturer.
> (2018 M1)

Theories such as worldview theory (Cobern, 1996) and socio-cultural constructivism (Cobb, 1994; Packer & Goicoechea, 2009) are used in the course to stimulate discussions on epistemology and encourage lecturers to understand that students may come to their courses with different worldviews, and that these need to be respected:

> The course emphasised the importance of being aware of and more sensitive to the fact that my students' worldview can differ from mine.
> (2017 J2)

> The course brought to my attention what curriculum decolonisation really means. It also helped me to understand that as a scientist I cannot be blind to the issues affecting the university community, i.e. transformation and decolonisation.
> (2018 J5)

> Day 3 on integrating alternative worldview in my teaching was most valuable for me. I like the phrase 'decolonisation and transformation'. These are concepts that have shaken science out of its 'privileged' position as 'THE' truth or the only knowledge. Human beings are at the centre of everything 'science' and that needs to be acknowledged.
> (2018 M3)

In Theory U, as discussed earlier, the issue of "presencing" and emergence at the bottom of the U is marked by a growing awareness and inner attention that leads to a sense of possibility for the future. According to Scharmer (2009), this stage involves three movements: a horizontal movement, where there is listening and connecting to things outside of the self; a vertical movement, where there is a connecting with deeper inner intention, that is, a connection between attention and intention; and a third movement, which is connecting with the "now", where the first two movements lead to "emergence" where new possibilities arise. We found many comments in the evaluations that supported the notion of emergence:

> The course is a mind opener, unveiling the various philosophies around higher education and the 'hot' issues around transformation and access, including epistemic violence and Eurocentrism. After this course I feel very prepared to embark on this wonderful journey as an agent of change.
> (2018 J2)

> The way I view students is definitely going to be influenced by this course. And I will now approach my job with a holistic view of educational philosophies and the various issues around epistemic access and the ontological development of my students.
> (2018 J2)

> The course provides valuable insight into teaching and learning. It makes one aware of various other interpretations of materials and situations. I am now open to a wider range of ideas and understanding of concepts. There are many views on the same situation. I've learned to be more sympathetic and empathetic with regard to my students. (2018 M4)

We also found evidence of participants having experienced the "crystallising" stage, where the person involved in the process of change commits to taking action:

> I will try to get a better sense of the character/background of my students during the breaks. I will also try to encourage my students to express their views on how they are coping. I will look at how my learning outcomes align with my forms of assessment and try to find ways of re-enforcing knowledge through multiple forms of assessment, flipped learning and having students reflect on their own understanding. (2018 M1)

> [I will] definitely include formative assessment in my classes. Work harder to create a sense of community in my classes. Encourage students to help and interact with each other. (2017 J2)

The final stage of the U, "realising", involves the emergence into the engagement of head and heart, where a new way of operating is put into practice, leading to a new reality. In the context of teaching and learning, the enactment of the changes in practice that lecturers commit themselves to during the course, could only become visible to us through follow-up, for example if we were invited to undertake a peer review. However, in the context of our reflection on the course, the application of Theory U as a lens through which to analyse and understand the opportunity for change afforded by the course has shown how it can be used intentionally, in the future, as a methodological framework for facilitating change.

Student learning, and how this is being enabled by lecturers, is now central to the notion of Wits as a "student-centred" university (Wits Vision, 2022). It is here that the fundamental focus of our work as academic developers lies. Our role is to create opportunities for reflection through workshops or courses that introduce lecturers to teaching and learning policies, to educational philosophy, and to theory that underpins new approaches to science higher education. The *Learning and Teaching in Science* course is an attempt to facilitate a shift in lecturers' understanding of teaching and help them to see, with new eyes, their students, their role as a science lecturer, alternative possibilities for teaching and learning, and perhaps even a broadening of what counts as legitimate knowledge. The focus of science lecturers is their area of specialisation, which is underpinned by particular rules and logics. This is where their interest (and academic identity) lies and what they spend their time on. To connect them to the idea that teaching and learning are relational, and to have them commit to being more sensitive to student needs, is a first step towards more deeply considering what it might mean to decolonise the curriculum. In some cases we are not successful, and lecturers remain unconvinced that the issues raised apply to their disciplines or their teaching. For example, one lecturer said: "The third day on teaching and learning in a context of diversity was not so useful. Some aspects were interesting, but no things that are directly transferable to my own subject" (2018 J6). We are therefore aware that not all lecturers experience transformative shifts as a result of attending the course, and that some who claim to be committed to change might revert to their old habits and ways once back in the classroom.

Conclusion

Knight (2018:2) points out that there is as yet no widespread agreement on the definitions of terms such as decolonisation and Africanisation, nor what they mean in educational practice. Unpacking and understanding these terms will form part of an ongoing and evolving discussion in higher education in South Africa and globally. For us, the *Learning and Teaching in Science* course creates a space in which such dialogue can occur, and where lecturers have the opportunity and time to reflect on their own experiences, share them, and listen to the experiences of their peers. The diversity of the groups, in terms of nationality, culture, gender and race, is important for enabling the shifts in perspective that emerge over the three days that the lecturers spend together on the course. Each participant, an expert in their discipline, offers experiences and beliefs that are authentic to them. These may challenge the unvoiced assumptions that may have been made regarding the epistemology and ontology of others in the group, but because the groups are small, and because their science qualifications give them a common platform, the lecturers are respectful of each other and willing to listen to each other.

Our role as academic developers is not to provide answers to the question of decolonisation of science. Like most participants, our understanding of decolonisation is influenced by who we are as individuals, by our personal and professional experiences, as well as by our beliefs about the nature and impact of colonisation in South Africa. Consequently, our understanding may not necessarily resonate with all participants, and is, in fact, constantly evolving too. However, we see it as our role to raise awareness of the complexities of decolonisation by creating a space for reflection and introspection, where lecturers are supported and encouraged to "pay attention to the heart" as well as the mind when thinking about their teaching spaces. We believe, too, that it is important for us to develop an understanding of the emotional and cognitive shifts that lecturers may experience during the course to better support and facilitate change.

References

AIKENHEAD, G.S. 2010. Academic science, Cultural intransigence and Devious Educo-Politics. *Cultural Studies of Science Education*, 5(3):613-619. [https://doi.org/10.1007/s11422-010-9265-7]

AIKENHEAD, G.S. & JEGEDE, O.J. 1999. Cross-Cultural Science Education: A Cognitive Explanation of a Cultural Phenomenon. *Journal of Research in Science Teaching*, 36(3):269-287. [https://bit.ly/2l8iYt1]

AIKENHEAD, G.S. 1997. Towards a First Nations Cross-Cultural Science and Technology Curriculum. *Science Education*, 81:217-238. [https://bit.ly/2lJ1X8R]

AIKENHEAD, G.S. 1996. Science Education: Border Crossing into the Subculture of Science. *Studies in Science Education*, 27:1-52. [https://doi.org/10.1080/03057269608560077]

CHE (COUNCIL ON HIGHER EDUCATION). 2017. Decolonising the Curriculum: Stimulating debate. *Briefly Speaking*, 3 (November). [https://bit.ly/2mJHzEF]

CHE (COUNCIL ON HIGHER EDUCATION). 2014. *Framework for Institutional Quality Enhancement in the Second Period of Quality Assurance*. Pretoria: CHE.

COBB, P. 1994. Where is the Mind? Constructivist and Sociocultural Perspectives on Mathematical Development. *Educational Researcher*, 23(7):13-20. [https://doi.org/10.2307/1176934]

COBERN, W.M. 1996. Worldview Theory and Conceptual Change in Science Education. *Science Education*, 80(5):579-610. [https://bit.ly/2mIC5dm]

DZAMA, E.N.N. & OSBORNE, J.F. 1999. Poor Performance in Science among African Students: An Alternative Explanation to the African Worldview Thesis. *Journal of Research in Science Teaching*, 36(3):387-405. [https://bit.ly/2lGobby]

FRASER, S.P. & BOSANQUET, A.M. 2006. The curriculum? That's just a unit outline, isn't it? *Studies in Higher Education*, 31(3):269-284. [https://doi.org/10.1080/03075070600680521]

GUNDRY, D. & CAMERON, A. 2008. The Conceptual Complexity of IKS in the Physical Sciences Curriculum. In: M.V. Polaki, T. Mokuku & T. Nyabanyaba (eds). Paper presented at 16th Annual Southern African Association for Research in Mathematics, Science and Technology Education Conference, Maseru, Lesotho.

JEGEDE, O. 1997. School Science and the development of scientific culture: a review of contemporary science education in Africa. *International Journal of Science Education*, 19(1):1-20. [https://doi.org/10.1080/0950069970190101]

JEGEDE, O. 1995. Collateral Learning and the Eco-cultural Paradigm in Science and Mathematics Education in Africa. *Studies in Science Education*, 25:97-137. [https://doi.org/10.1080/03057269508560051]

JEGEDE, O.J. & OKEBUKOLA, P.A.O. 1991. The Effect of Instruction on Socio-Cultural Beliefs Hindering the Learning of Science. *Journal of Research in Science Teaching*, 28(3):275-285. [https://doi.org/10.1002/tea.3660280308]

KNIGHT, J. 2018. Decolonising and transforming the Geography undergraduate curriculum in South Africa. *South African Geographical Journal*, 100(3):271-290. [https://doi.org/10.1080/03736245.2018.1449009]

MANZINI, S. 2000. Learners' attitudes towards the teaching of indigenous African science as part of the school science curriculum. *Journal of the Southern African Association for Research in Mathematics, Science and Technology Education*, 4(1):19-32. [https://doi.org/10.1080/10288457.2000.10756116]

MATON, K. 2014. Knowledge and Knowers by Karl Maton – A review essay. *Journal of Education*, 59:127-145.[https://bit.ly/2nf3Sm9]

MBEMBE, A. 2015. Decolonising Knowledge and the Question of the Archive. Unpublished Paper. [https://bit.ly/2PDdp3T]

MBITI, J. 1969. *African Religions and Philosophy*. Oxford: Heinemann Educational Publishers.

OGUNNIYI, M.B. 1996. Effects of Science and Technology on Traditional Beliefs and Cultures. In: M.B. Ogunniyi, (ed). *Promoting Public Understanding of Science and Technology in Southern Africa*. Cape Town: University of the Western Cape (School of Science and Mathematics Education), 38-48.

PACKER, M.J. & GOICOECHEA, J. 2010. Sociocultural and Constructivist Theories of Learning: Ontology, Not Just Epistemology. *Educational Psychologist*, 35(4):227-241. [https://doi.org/10.1207/S15326985EP3504_02]

VORSTER, J. & QUINN, L. 2017. The 'Decolonial Turn': What does it mean for Academic Staff Development? *Education as Change*, 21(1):31-49. [https://doi.org/10.17159/1947-9417/2017/853]

RAMSDEN, P. 1992. *Learning to Teach in Higher Education*. London: Routledge.

SCHARMER, C.O. 2009. *Theory U: Learning from the future as it emerges*. San Francisco, CA: Berrett-Koehler Publishers.

WITS (UNIVERSITY OF THE WITWATERSRAND). 2005. Senate approved document: Lecturer Contract of Commitment. Amended document S2005/1200A.

WITS VISION 2022 Strategic Framework. 2013. Johannesburg: University of the Witwatersrand (Strategic Planning Division). [https://bit.ly/2l1s2Qa]

YOUNG, M, 2013. Overcoming the crisis in curriculum theory: A knowledge-based approach. *Journal of Curriculum Studies*, 45:101-118. [https://doi.org/10.1080/00220272.2013.764505]

CHAPTER 20

Cognitive justice and the higher education curriculum[1]

Brenda Leibowitz

Abstract

This article is set against the backdrop of calls for the decolonisation of the curriculum in higher education institutions in South Africa. It is an attempt to contribute towards the debate on decolonising the curriculum, with a focus on the tasks of academics and academic developers. The first half of the article outlines several key aspects of current theorising about academic development or teaching and learning in higher education, informed by more general debates about education. These aspects limit the potential to imagine a more inclusive or socially just, decolonised curriculum. The second half

---

[1] First published in *Journal of Education*, Issue 68 (2017) [http://joe.ukzn.ac.za]. Included in this volume as a tribute to Brenda "who has made a fundamental and enduring contribution to our academic understanding of teaching, globally and in our South African context. Her colleagues and students honour Brenda for her astute work in advancing the scholarship of teaching and learning at UJ [the University of Johannesburg] and beyond. She will be fondly remembered for her fine intellect, her calm wisdom, her warmth and her kindness. Above all things, Brenda cared deeply for others." (UJ tribute [https://www.uj.ac.za/newandevents/Pages/A-tribute-to-Prof-Brenda-Leibowitz.aspx].)

of the article proposes cognitive justice as a useful concept to lead thinking about how to change the curriculum. It discusses what cognitive justice is and how this intersects with writing on decolonisation. It outlines some of the gaps in this conceptualisation, which would need more attention if this concept were to be useful to take the process of transforming teaching and learning forward.

Introduction

Calls for decolonising the higher education curriculum, arising out of the student protests in 2015–2016 in South Africa, have unleashed much soul searching as well as creative energy and intellectual excitement. At some universities academics, sometimes along with students and other role-players, have been getting together to explore the implications of the calls for curriculum redesign and to discuss what a decolonised higher education curriculum might look like (see report on a workshop at the University of Johannesburg, Leibowitz and Mayet, 2016, or at Rhodes University by Jagarnath,2015, as examples).

A 'decolonised curriculum' is an all-embracing collective noun that lies between abstract and concrete. It could be concrete in that it could imply a system led by design, but it is also abstract, it implies various more formal and more informal aspects of the experience of a student's university learning and the aspects that influence learning, such as social behaviour or residence life. The notion of a 'decolonised currriculum' is all embracing in that it cannot happen in a piecemeal fashion, where one or two individuals tinker with their module frameworks – rather, it requires all role players to become involved. Two important groups are teaching academics, and academic developers, whose task it is to support academics in the redesign of the curriculum.

This article is written from the point of view of an academic developer who has been working in this field on an off for the past two and a half decades. It draws from the literature on teaching and learning as well as from observations of having worked in this professional sphere – the conversations, policy debates, seminars and colloquia, conferences and scholarly journals that inform work in academic development. By way of example, conferences attended include the local conferences Higher Education of Learning and Teaching Association of Southern Africa (Heltasa), Kenton, the South African Education Research Association (SAERA) and internationally conferences of the American Education Research Association (AERA), the Society for Research in Higher Education (SRHE) and the International Consortium for Education

Developers (ICED). The article focuses on the South African context and debates, but with an understanding that these are informed by, and hopefully inform, international scholarly debates. It should be noted that theorising of teaching and learning in higher education draws from a wide range of literatures, including those on adult education, general schooling, and more recently, on childhood education.

This article makes two interrelated points: first, that the way academics and academic developers have been thinking about curriculum change towards more equitable and accessible education has been held captive by logics that prevent thinking of alternative and transformative approaches, and secondly, that a useful way forward would be the concept of 'cognitive justice', but that this concept would require significant elaboration. 'Logics' has been used in the plural, since higher education and academic development are heterogeneous fields, working off a plurality of philosophical and ethical underpinnings, and of understandings of the word 'curriculum' and of 'teaching and learning'. The problem with a discussion that attempts to characterise a field of study over several decades is that it either covers all tendencies, becoming extensive and possibly laborious and descriptive, or it is necessarily selective and possibly impressionistic. For this reason the discussion that follows in the next section, on the views that limit our thinking, is by admission subjective, focussing on the tendencies that as author, I believe are significant and powerful, rather than those that might even have featured more times, if counted. They are also views of left leaning, progressive thinkers, whom I believe have been influential in setting trends in this country. These are a variety of ways of thinking, and these may feature ontology, epistemology or theory. As a final word on the style of argumentation as well as purpose of the article, this represents the attempts of one academic developer to come to terms with and account for her developing understanding of what it might mean to take forward the transformation of the curriculum, such that it becomes more genuinely inclusive.

Limitations of current thinking about teaching and learning in higher education

One important limitation emanates from the literatures about decolonisation and decoloniality themselves. Calls for the decolonisation of the curriculum in South Africa have been couched in arguments derived from the fields of philosophy, politics, literature and psychology, thus the social sciences broadly, for example with reference to contributions by Franz Fanon, Steve Biko,

Ngugi a Thing'o or Edward Said. There have been a small number of South African scholarly contributions on the subject of decolonising the curriculum which link these broader discussions with educational theory – for example on decolonising the curriculum, Le Grange (2016) or Mbembe (n.d. and 2016), on Africanising the university, Seepe (2004) or on Africanising the curriculum (for example, Msila and Gumbo, 2016). By and large theory on teaching and learning with regard to schooling or higher education, has been produced in the West, and within the discourses and paradigms emanating from the West. Whilst in the field of academic development and teaching and learning much literature, bibliographic or case study research has been produced in the global South, certainly from South Africa, the 'big ideas' on which this literature rests remains Western (see, for example, the theorists cited in Msila and Gumbo, 2016, on the subject of Africanising the curriculum). My own work is also a case in point. There is thus no substantive 'decolonised' or 'decolonial' theory, to guide the transformation of the curriculum.

This is related to a second limitation, namely that educationists in South Africa are informed by our own class positions – mostly middle class and by writers that stem from or write about education from this mainly Western and Cartesian, enlightenment point of view. Being so dominant, this perspective influences all aspects of our thinking, leading many of us to an inability to think outside of the hegemonic form (Kumashiro, 2015). Mbembe (n.d.) describes the western hegemonic tradition as humanist, and that it so pervasive that it becomes difficult to see outside the frame: "This hegemonic notion of knowledge production has generated discursive scientific practices and has set up interpretive frames that make it difficult to think outside of these frames." Some ways of thinking are absolutely fundamental to the way we understand the world. Yet as feminist writer Harraway observes:

> It matters which stories tell stories, which concepts think concepts. Mathematically, visually, and narratively, it matters which figures figure figures, which systems systematize systems. (Harraway, 2016:101)

And it matters, what knowledge systems we use to consider how to generate new or more equitable and fair knowledge systems.

In describing these two limitations there is the danger of the suggestion that the literature on decolonisation and decoloniality are outside of the influence of Western enlightenment thinking, that is, that one can draw a strict line between these as separate epistemologies or ontologies. There is also the danger that the article is advancing a strong standpoint theory, namely that one can only write about something if one originates from a particular social position. Neither of these are intended, but one cannot escape the fact that the Western Cartesian and enlightenment approach is so pervasive, that thinking outside of its parameters is extremely difficult.

A third limitation is the manner in which several important interrelated phenomena are seen as bounded: knowledge as separate from learning and as separate from language; the personal as separate from the social; and curriculum as separate from pedagogy or teaching and learning. The vision of knowledge as separate from learning, or doing, is most clearly expressed by the social realists, whose output has been very influential in South Africa. According to Young (2008:183) social realism "Stresses the externality of knowledge that is separate from the processes of knowing and doing". A separation between the social and the personal, as well as between experience and learning, is captured in the quote from Durkheim, who was very influential in the work of the social realists: "One does not recreate science through one's own personal experience, because [science] is social not individual; one learns it (Durkheim, 1956:48, quoted in Young and Muller, 2010:123). This once again denies the embeddedness and contextuality of coming to know so aptly demonstrated in the work of theorists on practice demonstrated by Heath (1983), Holland, Lachicotte, Cain and Skinner (1998) or Lave (2011). The work of the theorists on practice has been popular amongst some academic developers in South Africa, but not as dominant as that of the social realists.

Linked to the idea of knowledge as relatively bounded and autonomous is the trend amongst the social realists to emphasise the rational, cognitive, and the importance of theoretical propositions:

> it is only when we understand the rules that we can meaningfully and purposefully change the rules. This is why theoretical knowledge must be at the centre of all educational qualifications, including occupational qualifications.
>
> (Wheelahan, 2010:145).

Work on learning and emotion by Zembylas (2015, 2010), taken up in the South African context amongst others, by Leibowitz, Swartz, Bozalek, Carolissen, Nichols and Rohleder (2012), stresses that learning is not only cognitive: it is active and affective, and experiential (Michelson, 2015). The problem with the view that knowledge is most importantly theoretical, is once again that it is viewed as disembodied, and separated from process, context and experience. What would be the means for students who do not share social worlds with the world where such theory is developed, to engage with this knowledge?

How would they come to know it? Social realists do not pronounce how students should be encouraged to learn. They specify that their sphere of concern is the curriculum and the place of knowledge within that. However they do imply that it is possible for all students to be able to access powerful forms of knowledge: "... all students should be provided with equality of access to the most powerful forms of knowledge through the means that most reliably enable that access" (Maton & Moore, 2010:8). The assumption that one can design a curriculum around what knowledge is, and not around how people come to know, is a problem:

> Theorizing the nature of knowledge is thus a key task of the sociology of education, because this provides an understanding of the way it should be structured in curriculum so that there is equitable access to it. (Wheelahan, 2010:17)

The artificial separation of private and social, and of learning from knowledge is not the prerogative of the social realists, and is perhaps so dominant in Western educational writing that it is a common-sense notion. Michelson (2015), for example, demonstrates how prevalent this thinking is amongst some writers on adult education and reflection, most notably Kolb. She uses a cameo of adult student, Mary, to demonstrate that when we think and reflect, our thought is social:

> The concepts we use are part of the received structures within which we experience, reflect, and act. Thus, they are shared tools, not individual ones; even when we are thinking on our own, that thinking is mediated through the sociality of language and the social production of meaning. (Michelson, 2015:91)

The point is that whilst it might be useful to separate out learning from knowledge as concepts, or curriculum and teaching and learning, this separation hinders thinking about how education could be more accessible or inclusive, since it forecloses the thinking about the very sociality Durkheim refers to, with regard to how learning takes place.

A further limitation has been the pre-eminence of a social reproduction theory of education, represented by the stringent critiques of capitalist schooling and higher education, Pierre Bourdieu and Basil Bernstein, amongst others. These critiques might be useful as critiques, but cannot be transposed into values or a vision for a way forward. With regard to Bernstein this body of knowledge explains how the social stratification in society is perpetuated through schooling. Further elaborations of his writing by those who write under the ambit of a 'social realist approach to knowledge' (Wheelahan, 2010; Young, 2008; Maton & Moore, 2010), provide a strong heuristic to analyse curricula and qualification frameworks. This critique is also useful in analysing how apparently liberal and progressive curricula obscure the means through which principally the humanities maintain exclusive. The work of Bourdieu and his deployment of the concepts 'social', and 'cultural' capital, and their role in social reproduction, has allowed for a tendency to see education, or let us say knowledge, as a form of capital, and thus as a commodity. In other words, the metaphor of 'capital' has travelled further than its value as a tool for critique – it operates as a metaphor for what should be done with the curriculum. An example and the way the language of capital has permeated current thinking about the curriculum is this extract on the work of Bourdieu in relation to literacy:

> [Literacy is] a discursive space in which certain resources are produced, attributed value, and circulated in a regulated way, which allows for competition over access and, typically, unequal distribution. (Heller, 2008:50)

Bernstein does not use the term 'capital' but his account of the role of social relations in influencing the acquisition of knowledge and the outcome of education, similarly stresses the manner in which education is part of society's reproductive process, impacting on students' access to status and power:

> Finally, social class relations through distributive regulation, distribute unequally, discursive, material and social resources which in turn create categories of the included and excluded, makes crucial boundaries permeable to some and impermeable to others, and specialises and positions oppositional identities. (Bernstein, 2000:207)

The word 'distributive' is evocative, such that in her outline of the social realist approach to knowledge Wheelahan (2010:9) refers to 'distributional justice' which she admittedly does not equate with status and wealth, but with access to powerful knowledge and the ability to participate in the creation thereof. This notion of powerful knowledge as a form of capital has tacitly as well as overtly informed much intellectual and academic development work undertaken in South Africa over the past two decades. It is one of the possible reasons why so much academic development work has focused on making adaptations to the curriculum so that students from 'disadvantaged' backgrounds can be successful within the current system, rather than on transforming higher education and its content more substantially.

The suggestion that the current way of knowing can or should be 'distributed' is not only practically unfeasible – for all but a handful of extremely promising or driven students – but it also forecloses thinking of alternatives. The emphasis of the value of received wisdom is most prevalent amongst social realists. Moore (2010) describes the richness of knowledges as these have been generated over time:

> Collective representations are the product of an immense cooperation that extends not only in space but also through time; to make them, a multitude of different minds have associated, intermingled, and combined their ideas and feelings; long generations have accumulated their experience and knowledge. A very special intellectuality that is infinitely richer and more complex than that of the individual is distilled in them ...
> (Moore, 2010:152)

The problem with the social realist approach is that it does not encourage multiplicity, including a welcoming of new epistemologies.

The notion that it is the present knowledge that should be more equitably distributed is akin to the phrase, 'epistemological access', which implies that all students, irrespective of social and educational backgrounds, should have access to the present knowledge system. This phrase was coined by Wally Morrow (2007) to distinguish between a student's formal access to a higher education institution and the subsequent access to the knowledge therein. It is a useful distinction, and the phrase has become commonplace in academic development literature, including my own publications. It was Yunus Ballim, however, at a provocative keynote talk at a conference at the Central University of Technology in 2015, that led me to consider that the phrase is 'colonialist', as he argued on that occasion.

The problem with an emphasis on the known and the given is partly that it impedes the consideration of what other societies or groups have to offer, and it impedes knowing what has not yet been said:

> In order to identify what is missing and why, we must rely on a form of knowledge that does not reduce reality to what exists. I mean a form of knowledge that aspires to an expanded conception of realism that incudes suppressed, silenced, or marginalised realities, as well as emergent and imagined experiences.
> (De Sousa Santos, 2014:157)

The social realists have also argued that students should be enabled to think the unthinkable. However the implication is that one requires access to powerful knowledge, in order to do so, and that outside of powerful knowledge, one cannot think the unthinkable. The difference in import here could be one of emphasis, or of application.

In this section various approaches to knowledge and learning that have been influential in academic developers' thinking – certainly if I think of my own academic biography – have been outlined. I have argued that these approaches make it difficult to imagine a new, decolonised or more inclusive approach to higher education. In the next section the concept of 'cognitive justice' is posed as a possible way to think differently about teaching and learning.

Cognitive justice

The concept of 'cognitive justice' is a 'normative principle for the equal treatment of all forms of knowledge' (Van der Velden, n.d.:12). This does not mean that all forms of knowledge are equal, but that the equality of knowers forms the basis of dialogue between knowledges, and that what is required for democracy is a dialogue amongst knowers and their knowledges. This dialogue is necessary because the present context where Western knowledge forms are all-powerful, is problematic in two ways. It is inadequate to solve the problems of social injustice and inequality of our times. It thus requires an ecology of knowledges and the availability of new knowledges (De Sousa Santos, 2014). This hegemony of knowledge forms leads to the destruction of other forms of knowledge and other knowledge practices. According to Visvanathan (2002) other knowledges become museumified, meaning that they become an object of study, lifeless and without voice, rather than equal players. De Sousa Santos (2014) calls this hegemony 'epistemicide', in that not only are the forms of knowledge lost or destroyed, but the practices of which they are a part. This destruction includes the natural ecology of the planet. Cognitive justice requires the bringing into relation of different knowledges, 'the plural availability of knowledges' (Visvanathan, 2016:4, 8).

Cognitive justice allows for the unknown, and the awareness that our knowledge forms have absences (De Sousa Santos, 2014). It requires difference in order for democracy and creativity to flow and it is an awareness that all knowledges can and should be flexible: "Cognitive justice is not a lazy kind of insistence that every kind of knowledge survives as is" (Visvanathan, 2016:5, 8).

The call for cognitive justice is by no means a relativist position on knowledge, though it would perhaps lead to more unpredictability within education. Writers have provided criteria for choosing between epistemologies, or for how to decide which knowledge is most appropriate, and under which conditions. De Sousa Santos stresses the important criteria of purpose or of which questions need answering, or that consideration should be given to how the knowledge was produced (De Sousa Santos, 2014). Visvanathan (2007) provides a list of criteria that is by no means comprehensive, but is illustrative of the criteria one might want to develop further:

1. Each knowledge system if it is to be democratic must realise it is iatrogenic in some context.
2. Each knowledge system must realise that in moments of dominance it may destroy life-giving alternatives available in the other. Each paradigm must sustain the otherness of other knowledge systems.
3. No knowledge system may 'museumify' the other. No knowledge system should be overtly deskilling.
4. Each knowledge system must practice cognitive indifference to itself in some consciously chosen domains.
5. All major technical projects legitimised through dominant knowledge forms must be subject to referendum and recall (Visvanathan, 2007:215).

Cognitive justice and related concepts

Cognitive justice, the 'decolonisation of knowledge' 'decoloniality', indigenous knowledge systems and africanisation of the curriculum can be seen as intersecting terms, depending on how one interprets each term. It is rare that protagonists of decolonisation adopt the view that the 'pure', 'essential', 'African' should obliterate the Western, powerful or hegemonic, and mostly call for a "decentring" – making knowledge other than it is (Le Grange, 2016:6) or a 're-centring' of for example African knowledge (Seepe, 2004). It is not and should not be isolationist (Mbembe, n.d.). There are also significant written contributions cautioning against treating the 'decolonisation' term too lightly, and of allowing 'settlers' to escape the severity of harm they are associated with (Tuck & Yang, 2012).

Another approach to decolonisation relevant to cognitive justice is to select those aspects of a culture or epistemology that advance one's ethical project. Makgoba and Seepe (2004:14) argue that to Africanise requires identifying within African epistemology "that which is emancipatory and liberatory". It is not an assumption that what is African is good and should be adopted, and that what is not African should be rejected. The cautionary point with regard to Africanisation made by Prah (2004), is that one should avoid romanticising the past. He also acknowledges the elitism of the middle classes in much of Africa. Most of these writers are not advocating a focus on one pure knowledge, but rather for the value of some form of multiplicity.

An argument against the maintenance of a hierarchic separation of knowledges is the demonstration of the similarities of knowledge systems, and of how societies can learn from one another. Comaroff and Comaroff (2014), showed in how many ways Europe or the global North can learn valuable lessons about social relations and politics from Africa, with examples from Botswana and South Africa. If we can learn from different knowledge systems, we can also learn from comparing them: "Through knowledge we liberate ourselves; through knowledge we question the limitations of a single culture/nationalistic identity" (Anzaldua, 2015:91). We can also use knowledges to answer questions or plug the gaps created by unitary knowledge systems (De Sousa Santos, 2014). Mbembe (2016:37) also calls for an embracing approach to knowledge: "a process that does not necessarily abandon the notion of universal knowledge for humanity, but which embraces it via a horizontal strategy of openness to dialogue among many epistemic traditions".

The focus on the 'how' or attributes of knowledge makers and knowledge seekers is an important contribution to cognitive justice, as it could have implications for how one might want students to learn (for example, that they are more active participants in the class, that the power relations are attended to). This encourages knowledge makers, users or acquirers from the global South to adopt a confident and agentic stand in relation to knowledge (Ndebele, 2016). It "allows Africans to be subjects of historical experiences rather than objects on the fringes of Europe" Makgoba and Seepe (2004:41,42).

Cognitive justice – remaining questions

Frameworks on cognitive justice have been for the most part frameworks about knowledge rather than theorisation of teaching and learning, though educationists such as Van der Westhuizen (2015) or le Grange have begun to write about this. There remain, therefore, a number of areas where these frameworks require further consideration. These areas are discussed in this section.

The idea that knowledges and knowledge practices are intimately bound up with people's cultures, practices and cosmologies (De Sousa Santos, 2014, Visvanathan, 2016) is important in the light of the limitations to the current logics that were discussed in the first part of this article. Knowledge is seen as part of people's practices, thus contextually situated, rather than as autonomous and objective, or 'outside'. This has important ramifications for learning, as this leacademic developers to an important question: if one is not a participant within knowledge practices where particular knowledge forms were generated, how best does one acquire this knowledge? This question should not be interpreted to imply that a student needed to have been an ancient Egyptian, for example, to be able to learn successfully about the wisdom of ancient Egyptians. Rather, it implies that one needs to be a participant in practices that value the learning of other historically prior cultures, one would require an understanding of the purpose of this learning that is shared by a particular community of practice, as well as a sense of what kind of questions this community would want answered by such study. At present, and since the enlightenment period, it is middle class schooling and Western higher education that has set the terms for how ancient or extant cultures are discussed and learnt about. This is a generalisation, as many religious societies that are not considered mainstream encourage the study of ancient languages in more culturally specific ways, where ancient texts might be venerated rather than as viewed as the source of information in the light of current concerns and questions. However, these are not considered universal or hegemonic or typical of higher education practices.

The idea of knowledge as practice or part of practice rather than as autonomous, gives rise to several challenges, or areas of higher education theorisation that require attention. The first is simply, what theories of teaching and learning can be used as a bridge in order to advance cognitive justice in teaching and learning? Admittedly one cannot hope for learners to experience viscerally and via physical or emotional means, everything they need to come to know. However one important domain of experience, alluded to by practice theorists, is that of shared meanings within practical activity (Schatzki, 2001). An important component of academic practices is the tacit or overt understanding of the purpose of a practice. This point is made clearly in relation to academic practices by Reder (1994) or Clark and Ivaniè (1997). Halliday (1985), the functional linguistic who shared ideas with Bernstein. Halliday (1995) made clear and important links between form, function and context – with regard to language, but the spill over from language to knowledge is evident. Thus if learners lived or worked in social contexts where functions of particular practices were self evident to them, they would indeed come closer to experiencing the knowledge, even the theory or rules they need to acquire. If they do not experience these living conditions, one needs to create learning opportunities in which they can engage in the practices, thus acquire the shared meanings and sense of purpose. A more poignant question would be, given that learning requires engagement with the familiar, with knowledge practices from one's own community of practice, as well as with the unknown, with knowledge practices that are not shared with one's own community, how is this leap from the known to the unknown advanced with students?

An important dimension of cognitive justice is that it must be accompanied by social justice (De Sousa Santos, 2014). Echoing the earlier work of Nancy Fraser (Fraser & Honneth, 2003) that social justice is based on the intertwined dimensions of recognition of value (of social categories such as class, race or gender) and distribution of material resources, De Sousa Santos writes that there can be no recognition without distribution (De Sousa Santos, 2001). This is all very well, but how does one advance cognitive justice in situations where there is social injustice, and can one use ideas pertaining to cognitive justice in order to advance social justice? Young states that "[i]t follows that instead of concentrating solely on ideology critique, a social realist approach to the curriculum seeks to identify the social conditions that might be necessary if objective knowledge is to be acquired" (2008:165). He reminds us that Bernstein once said that 'education cannot compensate for society' (2008:171). Given that education is part of society, it would be a mistake to give up altogether on advancing change in education or in the curriculum. Furthermore, given that the education system in South Africa in the main appears to perpetuate rather than ameliorate social inequality along lines of class and race, as has been pointed out in relation to schooling in general by Badat and Sayed (2014) and in relation to higher education by Bozalek and Boughey (2012) and Cooper (2015), *not* to work towards social or cognitive justice at all implies working to perpetuate social *in*justice. Is working towards cognitive justice feasible, in contexts of social injustice?

Critical pedagogy is one tradition which operates as a resource in order to consider how to work towards social justice via the curriculum. This is not sufficient, however, or as appropriate in the South African context (Jansen, 2009) as critical pedagogy has tended to remain within western academic discourses. It would be equally difficult for students not proficient in traditional academic discourses, of which critical pedagogy is generally a part. More recent writing on indigenous knowledge systems (cf. Le Grange, 2016 on higher education, and Pacini-Ketchabaw and Taylor, 2015, with regard to early childhood education, where disrupting colonial practices have become a significant body of work), on disruptive teaching (cf. Kumashiro, 2015), on feminist pedagogy (cf. Michelson, 2015), and on posthumanist pedagogies (cf. the Snaza and Weaver volume, 2015) that transverse the mind-body dualism have promise in this regard. Although these are relatively new under-explored fields, especially with regard to higher education, where substantial translation of concepts is required.

One of the most tantalising questions, is how to bridge the language of Western 'science' with that of alternative languages providing accounts of teaching and learning. The dominant accounts of teaching and learning are provided through the Cartesian, enlightenment lenses of research and theory building, not taking into account how learn is described in folk, religious and other communities across the world. Selected indigenous African ways of describing learning are provided by Banda (2008) with reference to metaphor and idiom, for example. How are these different accounts translated, bridged or brought into conversation with each other?

Conclusion

This article has pointed to some of the limitations in current thinking about teaching and learning in higher education and academic development, limitations which hinder our thinking about how to respond to current calls for the decolonisation of the curriculum. Some of these limitations are mitigated by an elaborated version of the concept of 'cognitive justice'. This concept however has been intended for the general topic of knowledge, rather than for teaching and learning, and thus requires substantial development and bridging, to be of use in current debates. A helpful concept in this consideration is that of 'practice', and of viewing knowledge as a practice rather than as autonomous text. However, given the call for different knowledges to be brought into dialogue with each other, this dialogue will be most challenging. It will require the participation of a broader group of educationists than those of us working in higher education and academic development, who administer, perhaps colonially *to* students, and it will require the dialogue to be conducted in a broader range of languages, discourses and practices.

References

ANZALDUA, G. 2015. *Light in the dark/ Luz en lo oscuro: Rewriting identity, spirituality, reality*. Edited by A. Keating. Durham: Duke University Press. [https://doi.org/10.1215/9780822375036]

BALLIM, Y. 2015. Reflecting epistemological access and the analytical frameworks guiding institutional responses to student learning in South African Higher Education. Paper presented at the First International Conference on the Scholarship of Teaching and Learning. Central University of Technology, Bloemfontein, South Africa, 1–2 October.

BADAT, S. & SAYED, Y. 2014. Post-1994 South African education: The challenge of social justice. *The ANNALS of the American Academy of Political and Social Science*, 652(March):127-148. [https://doi.org/10.1177/0002716213511188]

Banda, D. 2008. *Education for all and African indigenous knowledge systems: The case of the Chewa people of Zambia.* Köln: Lambert Publishing.

Bernstein, B. 2000. *Pedagogy, symbolic control and identity: Theory, research, critique* (revised edition). Lanham: Rowman and Littlefield.

Bozalek, V. & Boughey, C. 2012. (Mis)framing higher education in South Africa. *Social Policy & Administration,* 46(6):688-703. [https://doi.org/10.1111/j.1467-9515.2012.00863.x]

Clark, R. & Ivaniè, R. 1997. *The politics of writing.* London: Routledge.

Comaroff, J. & Comaroff, J. 2014. *Theory from the South: How Euro-America is evolving toward Africa.* Stellenbosch: African Sun Media. [https://doi.org/10.4324/9781315631639]

Cooper, D. 2015. Social justice and South African university student enrolment data by 'race', 1998–2012: From 'skewed revolution' to 'stalled revolution'. *Higher Education Quarterly,* 69(3):237-262. [https://doi.org/10.1111/hequ.12074]

De Sousa Santos, B. 2014. *Epistemologies of the South: Justice against epistemicide.* Boulder, Colorado: Paradigm Publishers.

De Sousa Santos, B. 2001. Nuestra America: Reinventing a subaltern paradigm of recognition and redistribution. *Theory, Culture and Society,* 18(2-3):185-217. [https://doi.org/10.1177/02632760122051706]

Fraser, N. & Honneth, A. 2003. *Redistribution or recognition? A political-philosophical exchange.* London: Verso.

Halliday, M. 1995. Language and the theory of codes. In: A. Sadovnik (ed). *Knowledge and pedagogy: The sociology of Basil Bernstein.* Norwood: Ablex, 127-143.

Halliday, M. 1985. *An introduction to functional grammar.* London: Arnold.

Harraway, D. 2016. *Staying with the trouble: Making kin in the Chuthulucene.* Durham: Duke University Press. [https://doi.org/10.1215/9780822373780]

Heath, S.B. 1983. *Ways with words: Language, life, and work in communities and classrooms.* Cambridge: Cambridge University Press. [https://doi.org/10.1017/CBO9780511841057]

Heller, M. 2008. Bourdieu and 'literacy education'. In: J. Allbright & A. Luke (eds). *Pierre Bourdieu and literacy education.* New York: Routledge, 84-120.

Holland, D.; Lachicotte, W.; Skinner, D. & Cain, C. 1998. *Identity and agency in cultural worlds.* Cambridge, Mass: Harvard University Press.

Jagarnath, V. 2015. Curriculum conversation 6. [https://bit.ly/2nWpFPS]

Jansen, J. 2009. *Knowledge in the blood: Confronting race and the apartheid past.* Lansdowne, Cape Town: UCT Press.

Kumashiro, K. 2015. *Against common sense: Teaching and learning toward social justice* (3rd ed.). New York: Routledge. [https://doi.org/10.4324/9781315765525]

Lave, J. 2011. *Apprenticeship in critical ethnographic practice.* Chicago: University of Chicago Press. [https://doi.org/10.7208/chicago/9780226470733.001.0001]

Le Grange, L. 2016. Decolonizing the university curriculum. *South African Journal of Higher Education,* 30(2):1-12. [https://doi.org/10.20853/30-2-709]

Leibowitz, B. & Mayet, R. 2016. Decolonising the curriculum: Workshop at the University of Johannesburg. [https://bit.ly/2nP4Up4]

Leibowitz, B.; Swartz, L.; Bozalek, V.; Carolissen, R.; Nichols, L. & Rohleder, P. (Eds). 2012. *Community, self and identity: Educating South African university students for citizenship.* Cape Town: HSRC Press.

Makgoba, W. & Seepe, S. 2004. Knowledge and identity: an African vision of higher education transformation. In: S. Seepe (ed). *Towards an African identity of higher education.* Pretoria: Vista University and Skotaville, 13-58.

Maton, K. & Moore, R. 2010. Introduction: A coalition of minds. In: K. Maton & R. Moore (eds). *Social realism, knowledge and the sociology of education.* London: Continuum, 1-13.

Mbembe, A. 2016. Decolonizing the university: New directions. *Arts and Humanities in Higher Education,* 15(1):29-45. [https://doi.org/10.1177/1474022215618513]

Mbembe, A. n.d. Decolonizing knowledge and the question of the archive. [https://bit.ly/2nfxmQX]

MICHELSON, I. 2015. *Gender, experience, and knowledge in adult learning: Alisoun's daughters*. New York: Routledge. [https://doi.org/10.4324/9781315709291]

MOORE, R. 2010. Knowledge structures and the canon: A preference for judgements. In: K. Maton & R. Moore (eds). *Social realism, knowledge and the sociology of education*. London: Continuum, 131-153.

MORROW, W. 2007. *Bounds of democracy: Learning to teach in South Africa*. Cape Town: HSRC Press.

MSILA, V. & GUMBO, M. (EDS). 2016. *Africanising the curriculum: Indigenous perspectives and theories*. Stellenbosch: African Sun Media. [https://doi.org/10.18820/9780992236083]

NDEBELE, N. 2016. To be or not to be? No longer at ease. *Arts and Humanities in Higher Education*, 15(1):15-28. [https://doi.org/10.1177/1474022215613610]

PACINI-KETCHABAW, V. & TAYLOR, A. (EDS). 2015. *Unsettling the colonial places and spaces of early childhood education*. New York: Routledge. [https://doi.org/10.4324/9781315771342]

PRAH, K. 2004. Africanism and Africanisation: Do they mean the same thing? In: S. Seepe (ed). *Towards an African identity of higher education*. Pretoria: Vista University and Skotaville, 93-108.

REDER, S. 1994. Practice-engagement theory: A socio-cultural approach to literacy across cultures. In: B. Ferdman, R. Weber & A. Ramirez (eds). *Literacy across language and culture*. New York: SUNY Press, 33-74.

SCHATZKI, T. 2001. Introduction. In: T. Schatzki, K. Knorr Cetina & E. von Savigny (eds). *The Practice turn to contemporary theory*. London: Routledge, 10-23.

SEEPE, S. (ED). 2004. *Towards an African identity of higher education*. Pretoria: Vista University and Skotaville.

SNAZA, N. & WEAVER, J. (EDS). 2015. *Posthumanism and educational research*. Routledge: London.

TUCK, E. & YANG, K.W. 2012. Decolonisation is not a metaphor. *Decolonisation: Indigeneity, Education & Society*, 1(1):1-40.

VAN DER VELDEN, M. 2006. A case for cognitive justice. Unpublished paper.

VAN DER WESTHUIZEN, G. 2015. Cognitive justice and the advancement of teaching and learning. Paper presented at the Arusha Conference, Learning together for change, Arusha, Tanzania, April.

VISVANATHAN, S. 2016. The search for cognitive justice. [https://bit.ly/2J09aso]

VISNANATHAN, S. 2007. Between cosmology and system: The heuristics of a dissenting imagination. In: B. de Sousa Santos (ed). *Another knowledge is possible: Beyond Northern epistemologies*. London: Verso, 182-218.

VISVANATHAN, S. 2002. Between pilgrimage and citizenship – The possibilities of self-restraint in science. In: C. Odora Hoppers (ed). *Indigenous knowledge and the integration of knowledge system: Towards a philoshophy of articulation*. Claremont, Cape Town: New Africa Books, 39-52.

WHEELAHAN, L. 2010. *Why knowledge matters in curriculum: A social realist argument*. London: Routledge.

YOUNG, M. 2008. *Bringing knowledge back in: From social constructivism to social realism in the sociology of education*. London: Routledge. [https://doi.org/10.4324/9780203073667]

YOUNG, M. & MULLER, J. 2010. Knowledge and truth in the sociology of education. In: K. Maton & R. Moore (eds). *Social realism, knowledge and the sociology of education: Coalitions of the mind*. London: Continuum, 110-130.

ZEMBYLAS, M. 2015. *Emotion and traumatic conflict: Reclaiming healing in education*. Oxford: Oxford University Press. [https://doi.org/10.1093/acprof:oso/9780199982769.001.0001]

ZEMBYLAS, M. 2010. Teachers' emotional experiences of growing diversity and multiculturalism in schools and the prospects of an ethic of discomfort. *Teachers and Teaching*, 16(6):703-716. [https://doi.org/10.1080/13540602.2010.517687]

Index

A

academic
  developers 1, 2, 5, 6, 9, 13, 15-19, 24, 38, 39, 46, 61, 63, 66-71, 79, 84, 102-104, 107, 108, 113, 116, 118, 120-122, 127, 128, 130, 131, 134, 146, 150-153, 156, 160, 165-167, 173, 174, 181, 190, 193, 194, 198-203, 207-211, 213, 214, 218-223, 225, 226, 229-231, 235, 236, 238-254, 279, 283, 285-302, 308, 310, 315, 342, 346, 347, 357-361, 383, 388, 389, 398, 399, 403-405, 407, 411
  development 1, 18, 19, 25, 26, 29, 42, 57, 62, 67, 77, 79, 80, 83, 84, 91, 102-104, 117, 171-174, 178, 180, 183, 184, 189, 190, 198, 199, 230, 237, 241, 244-246, 273, 274, 285, 286, 290, 293, 297, 308, 310, 321, 345, 346, 359, 361, 363-368, 371, 375, 376, 384, 389, 403-406, 409, 410, 416
  drift 285, 290, 299
  leaders 2, 6, 9, 10, 13, 15, 17, 19
  literacies 19, 127-137, 139-144, 146, 275, 295, 309, 321
  project 5, 6, 13, 16, 274, 275, 279
  reading 131, 307-311, 315, 316, 318, 320-322
  staff development 29, 88, 90, 92, 198, 330, 388
Academic Development Unit (ADU) 267, 273, 359
academics xiii, xiv, 1, 2, 4, 5, 8-19, 24, 26-30, 32, 34-36, 38, 39, 43, 46, 55, 57, 60, 61, 63, 66, 68, 71, 72, 82, 91, 103, 110, 112, 113, 117-122, 158, 162, 172, 173, 175, 184, 196-203, 207-211, 217-223, 225, 226, 228-231, 236-254, 260, 265, 267, 268, 270, 272, 274, 278, 279, 285, 286, 290, 293, 298, 300, 302, 312, 313, 317, 320, 321, 326, 328, 331, 334, 336, 342, 346-348, 350-353, 356, 359, 360, 364-366, 368, 371, 375, 383, 388, 390, 395, 403-405
access xiii, xiv, 3-8, 10, 11, 13, 16-18, 25, 32-34, 36, 49-51, 66, 77, 91, 92, 118, 173, 194, 195, 213, 218, 229, 235, 244, 245, 247, 249, 250, 252-254, 260, 261, 263-265, 267, 270, 272, 276, 278, 295, 300, 301, 309, 311, 313-315, 327, 336, 359, 360, 363, 364, 367, 372, 375, 380, 388, 390, 392, 397, 408-410
  epistemological— xiv, 5, 7, 8, 16, 17, 50, 173, 250, 295, 336, 364, 367, 372, 388, 390, 392, 410
  formal— xiv, 4, 6, 118, 410

activism 179, 260, 262, 263
ADDIE 194, 201-204, 206, 207, 210, 211
affect 2, 38, 42, 108, 133, 144, 153, 178, 179, 182, 187, 285, 339
Africanise 88, 406, 412
agency 29, 30, 33, 37, 38, 43, 70, 91, 103, 111, 117, 119, 173, 176, 199-201, 212, 217-219, 221-223, 226-229, 231, 236, 246, 248, 254, 263, 309, 325, 328, 331, 332, 335, 340
alienation 35, 47, 55, 62, 238, 310, 319, 321, 322, 326, 375
AMOEBA 201, 203, 205, 206
apartheid 3, 4, 6, 8, 23, 25, 32, 51, 90, 98, 143, 235-237, 239, 240, 243, 247, 254, 255, 259-265, 283, 327, 392
art explorations 186
articulation gap 7
assessment 4, 5, 7-10, 13, 14, 34, 35, 36, 42, 43, 56, 57, 60, 65, 87-89, 92-94, 99, 103, 110, 112, 114, 116, 134, 140, 141, 144, 172, 180, 181, 211, 238, 240, 244, 245, 247, 249, 252, 254, 266, 272-274, 278, 292, 298, 312, 347, 348, 353, 357, 369, 380, 389, 395, 398

B

barriers 3, 75, 153, 160, 167, 211, 217-226, 228-231, 266, 347, 390
blackness 28, 32, 37, 74, 101, 185, 186, 330, 331
blended learning 19, 194-196, 198, 199, 203, 206, 208, 213, 214
boundary object 289, 293, 295

C

Canada 18, 88, 108, 110, 149, 153-155, 161, 392
Certification Council for Technikon Education (SERTEC) 263, 266
change agent 198, 200, 245, 328, 338
co-creation 107, 108, 110-113, 116, 119-122, 197, 325-335, 337, 338, 340-342
code shift 371, 375, 376, 379, 381, 382, 384
cognitive justice 403-405, 411-416
collaborative
  curriculum conversations 360, 361
  learning 119, 141, 317
  practices 146, 300
  process 19, 109, 127-129, 141, 301, 326
  programme renewal 347

419

collaborative *(cont.)*
   project 131, 146, 154, 294, 300, 340, 360, 361, 383
   reading 181
   relationship 83, 110, 360
   research 130
coloniality 8, 12, 24, 30-39, 51, 52, 65, 68, 69, 74, 75, 239, 240, 253
competencies 3, 143, 252, 253, 264, 265, 267, 268, 270, 271, 274, 276, 368, 378
comprehensive universities 13, 284, 327
concept creation 182, 190
conceptual coherence 260, 349, 353
contextual coherence 349
convener system 14, 27, 42, 242, 262, 269
critical
   ethnography 219
   literacy 134, 142-145
   pedagogy 72, 248, 253, 415
critically reflective practice 72, 139
cultural capital 25, 309
curriculum
   alignment 172
   change xiii, 27, 61, 66, 68, 88, 130, 237, 239, 245, 405
   co-creation 113, 120, 122, 326, 332, 334, 338
   decolonising— 151, 201, 208, 214, 240
   design 2, 14, 35, 42, 87-89, 92, 94, 95, 98, 102, 107, 108, 110, 111, 113, 118, 119, 121, 122, 127, 140, 198, 210, 236, 240, 242, 244-250, 253, 254, 296, 298, 300, 347, 350, 355, 361
   development 2, 5, 16, 18, 24-26, 29, 89, 107, 110, 113, 120-122, 150-152, 198, 212, 235, 238, 240, 241, 244, 246, 248, 249, 251-254, 259, 267, 273, 274, 278, 279, 285, 287-292, 294, 295, 298, 300, 301, 326-329, 335, 336, 338, 340, 347, 348, 353, 387, 396
   hidden— 111-113, 115, 152, 158, 159, 164
   knowledge 11, 17, 32, 34-36, 88, 90, 99, 244, 301, 357
   planning 4, 9, 264, 270
   practices 9, 13, 14, 17, 19, 24, 29, 32, 84, 129, 236, 237, 240, 241, 244, 250, 253, 261, 267, 271, 277-279
   renewal 1, 18, 19, 90, 113, 116, 120, 286, 290-292, 294-296, 345-348, 350-361
   review 45, 46, 54, 56-63, 113, 117, 119
   socially just— 236, 369, 403
   theory 11, 17, 24, 27, 29, 30, 32, 49, 236, 243, 244, 250-254, 347, 350, 353, 359-361

curriculum *(cont.)*
   transformation 2, 7, 45, 46, 48, 49, 88, 107, 145, 151, 193, 194, 202, 206, 237-241, 243-251, 253-255, 329, 360
Curriculum Change Working Group (CCWG) 66

D

decoding
   interview 152, 157, 158, 160
   the disciplines 17, 151-154, 157, 158, 160, 165
decolonial
   criticism 69
   orientations 185
   scholars 67-69, 74
   theory 11, 17, 24, 26, 27, 29-34, 46, 53, 66, 73
   thought 74
   turn 24, 29, 30, 32, 49, 61, 79, 84, 287
decoloniality 30, 31, 51-53, 67, 68, 71, 79, 83, 84, 405, 406, 412
decolonisation 2, 8, 9, 11, 12, 15, 18, 19, 23-30, 32, 35, 38, 39, 42, 45-57, 59-61, 65-67, 69, 71-73, 76, 78, 82, 88, 90-92, 98, 122, 149-159, 161, 163, 165-167, 193, 194, 196-198, 200, 201, 203, 205, 206, 208-210, 214, 226, 236-241, 244-250, 253-255, 272, 326, 328, 331, 334, 342, 356, 357, 363-368, 381, 384, 387, 388, 390, 391, 393, 397, 399, 400, 403-406, 411, 412, 416
Decolonisation Conversation Series (DCS) 66-68, 70-74, 78, 83, 84
deficit
   concept 80
   discourse of— 79, 80
   model 32, 77, 132, 308, 367
   students 77, 308, 322
de-linking 81
democracy 33, 93, 96-99, 101, 116, 122, 236, 262, 264, 265, 327, 390, 392, 411
democratic values 325
dialogical pedagogies 339
dialogic conversations 68, 84
diffractive reading 181, 182, 190
diploma 18, 172, 244, 254, 261, 266, 267, 269, 270, 276, 277, 283-286, 289-295, 297-299, 302, 308, 371
disciplinary specialists 10, 266, 352-355, 358, 360
discursive gap 88, 93, 94, 98-102

disruption 66, 71, 83, 84, 107, 113, 127-129, 134, 135, 137, 138, 142, 143, 146, 157, 193-195, 200, 201, 206, 211-214, 218, 237, 240, 243, 310, 326, 346, 347
  spaces for— 66, 83, 236, 241, 243, 247-250, 252, 254, 279
disruptive innovation 195

E

educational technology 195, 217-219, 221-224, 226, 228-231
emancipatory
  approach 142, 320, 412
  curriculum 129, 133, 310, 322
  learning 247
  practice 308-310, 316
  reading strategies 322
emergence 83, 180, 387, 394, 397, 398
empowered 144, 245, 312, 322
empowering curriculum 315, 318, 321
engineering education 365, 367, 368, 375
Engineering-in-Context (EiC) project 368, 369, 375, 376, 378-383
epistemic
  becoming 12
  plane 365, 372-374, 376-379, 381, 383, 384
  privilege 29
  relations (ER) 287-290, 292-294, 296, 301, 302, 365
epistemology 9, 31, 34, 37, 156, 159, 173, 176, 189, 255, 325, 328, 339, 364, 367, 390, 397, 399, 405, 412
  of uncertainty 325, 328, 339
  post-colonial— 243
  Western— 237
ethical space 150, 152, 156, 166, 167

F

#FeesMustFall (FMF) 88, 95, 130, 237, 326, 328, 329, 387
feminist
  new materialism 172-178, 180, 181, 184, 187, 189, 190
  pedagogy 172, 415
Fifth Dimension Curriculum Transformation Model (5D-CTM) 194, 206, 207, 209-211, 213, 214
foundation programmes 7

G

globalisation 2, 3, 13, 275

H

Higher Education Qualifications Sub-Framework (HEQSF) 239-242, 249, 262, 269, 270, 273-278, 380
high skills 3, 25
humanities 11, 24, 26, 27, 42, 43, 46, 53, 57, 58, 62, 89, 91, 388, 409

I

ideology 5, 14, 15, 25, 30, 31, 34, 37, 39, 47, 88, 95, 98, 99, 101-103, 133, 151, 152, 158, 240, 246, 251, 331, 415
indigenisation 154, 158
indigenous
  epistemology 150, 156
  knowledge 151, 155, 412, 415
information and communication technologies 4
injustice 4, 33, 37, 143, 144, 237, 360, 411, 415
insights 5, 19, 61, 67, 88, 114, 116, 117, 133, 134, 138, 151, 156, 157, 162, 181, 182, 254, 267, 271, 330, 363, 365, 369, 372-379, 381, 384, 398
institutional culture 23, 26, 66, 236, 246, 274
instructional
  design 193, 194, 196-199, 201-203, 205, 206, 210
  discourse 15, 34, 35, 39
interactional expertise 289, 293, 294, 300
inter-languages 289

K

knowledge
  complicit— 18, 150, 166, 167
  disciplinary— 6, 10-12, 17, 89, 91, 151, 158, 195, 196, 211, 212, 254, 288, 346-350, 353-357, 360, 391
  economy 3, 6, 15, 88, 98, 261
  everyday— 9, 10
  powerful— 10, 11, 15, 18, 290, 302, 367, 372, 409, 410
  practical— 289, 299, 302
  practices 6, 65, 287, 365, 367, 371, 372, 376, 383, 411, 413-415
  specialised— 9, 10, 247
  structures 9, 10, 12, 287, 365
  Western— 11, 90, 91, 152, 155, 197, 411
  workers 3

L

leadership 5, 15, 16, 57, 82, 122, 246, 252, 265, 332, 366, 377
Legitimation Code Theory (LCT) 287, 301, 365, 367, 372, 379, 383

M

managerialism 5, 13, 268
marginalisation xiii, 6, 7, 48, 49, 51, 52, 65, 66, 68, 71-74, 76, 81, 88, 103, 113, 151, 158, 160, 163, 164, 186, 197, 220, 225, 248, 254, 297, 302, 309, 326, 333, 339, 410
marketisation 3, 5, 268
massification 2, 13, 235, 363
misrecognition 12, 25, 36, 37
modernity 31-33, 38, 367

N

National Qualifications Framework (NQF) 6, 239, 264, 266
neoliberal 16, 25, 32, 108, 121, 268, 328
non-traditional
    students 287, 309, 310, 312, 318, 320, 321
    universities 19
normative framework 261

O

Occupational Therapy curriculum 128, 129, 131, 142
online learning 194, 201, 205
ontological
    turn 89
    weight 68
ontology 9, 173, 176, 177, 184, 189, 367, 399, 405
outcomes-based education (OBE) 6, 264-266

P

pacing 10
participatory learning 65, 67, 71
pedagogical
    documentation 187-189
    partnership 113, 115, 118, 122
    practices 66, 109, 110, 139, 165, 185, 245, 340
pedagogic device 17, 24, 33, 35, 88, 89, 92-94, 97, 98, 101, 103, 105, 361
pedagogy 6, 9, 26, 27, 29, 35, 42, 43, 68, 72, 83, 84, 88, 89, 92, 118, 139, 153-156, 158, 172, 175, 177-179, 182, 189, 190, 197, 203, 205, 206, 208, 211, 238, 240, 248, 249, 253, 271, 275, 288, 298, 316, 321, 329, 335, 365, 366, 370, 371, 375, 378, 380, 383, 407, 415
physics 18, 175, 176, 290-293, 295, 297, 299, 370, 374
postapartheid 130, 328, 390
Postgraduate Certificate (PGCert) 308
Postgraduate Diploma (PGDip) 172, 244, 308
posthumanism 172-178, 180, 184, 189
posthumanist pedagogy 415
power dynamics 75, 145, 326, 334, 336, 338
private
    good 15
    transcript 220, 229
professional literacies 128, 129, 135
programme coordinators 345-347, 350-352, 354-360
public
    good 7, 15
    transcript 220, 221, 223, 225, 226, 229-231

R

race 8, 31, 36, 37, 47, 48, 54, 55, 61, 62, 68, 74-76, 89, 238, 240, 254, 327, 330, 333, 399, 415
racialised 6, 37, 39, 260
racism 23, 26, 31, 47, 48, 61, 75, 150, 236
recontextualisation 9, 23, 32, 88, 92, 93, 97, 98, 101, 247, 347-349, 356, 371
reflective
    practice 13, 72, 133, 139
    writing 133, 134, 138, 139
regulative discourse 15, 24, 34-39, 247
resistance 68, 157, 158, 162, 201, 220, 221, 230, 308, 329, 335, 341, 346, 350, 351, 361, 390
#RhodesMustFall (RMF) 24, 26, 28, 32, 47, 48, 77, 237, 326, 328, 329

S

scaffolding 77, 140, 141, 295
Scholarship of Teaching and Learning (SoTL) 151, 154
science education 388, 392
scrolls 307, 308, 310-322
selection 10, 12, 42, 210, 211, 292, 298, 332, 348, 356, 357, 371
sequencing 10, 247, 298, 348, 356, 357
shame 76-78, 104
slow reading 181
social
    justice 6, 7, 10, 13, 26, 32, 43, 92, 104, 121, 129, 145, 238, 261, 263, 276, 278, 309, 367, 415
    realism 367, 407
    relations (SR) 287-290, 292, 293, 295, 296, 301, 302, 340, 409, 413
South African Council for Planners (SACPLAN) 264, 265, 267, 268, 271-274, 276-278

South African Qualifications Authority (SAQA) 264, 269, 270, 273, 277

specialisation 2, 347, 365, 399

Specialization 287-289, 292, 293, 299, 301, 372

Standards Generating Bodies (SGBs) 265, 266, 270, 278

STEM 18, 19, 363-367, 370, 372, 374

student
    protests 7-9, 11, 12, 23, 26-28, 31, 32, 50, 79, 88, 130, 226, 227, 237, 265, 295, 326, 387-389, 392, 404
    voice 108-110, 119, 267, 295, 326

student-centred 396, 398

Students as Learners and Teachers (SaLT) 118

students as partners 108, 109, 117, 120, 328, 333, 381

subaltern studies 243

T

technical qualifications 285, 288, 289

technikons 14, 242-244, 246, 248, 254, 261, 262, 266-269, 272, 284, 327

technology 2, 4, 13, 14, 18, 71, 159, 195, 202, 203, 205, 213, 217-231, 235, 237, 239-250, 252-254, 259-261, 263, 266-268, 270, 271, 275-277, 279, 284, 285, 288-290, 302, 326, 327, 329, 340, 367, 368, 370, 373
    integration 219, 221-223, 228, 231

Theory U 389, 393, 394, 397, 398

traditional universities 13, 19, 240, 241, 244, 248, 252, 265, 266-268, 327

transaction space 289, 293, 297, 301, 302

transformation 2, 7, 8, 24, 25, 32, 45, 46, 48, 49, 55, 56, 59, 66, 67, 71, 80, 88, 107, 113, 129, 133, 145, 151, 152, 156, 163, 165-167, 193-197, 199-202, 206, 207, 209, 211-214, 219, 235-241, 243-251, 253-255, 259-262, 264, 265, 269, 272, 278, 329, 331, 339, 360, 389, 393, 397, 405, 406

transformative pedagogies 128

#TransformWits 48

Truth and Reconciliation Commission (TRC) 149, 154

U

universities of technology 13, 14, 18, 235, 237, 239-250, 252-254, 259, 260, 263, 266-268, 270, 271, 276, 277, 284, 285, 289, 290, 302, 326, 327, 329, 340

W

whiteness 18, 24, 37, 39, 46, 55

widening participation xiii, 18, 308, 310, 320

worldview 18, 30, 34, 42, 43, 55, 84, 111, 143, 150, 156, 159, 237, 300, 392, 397

Notes on contributors

SANDRA ABEGGLEN was formerly Senior Lecturer and Course Leader BA Hons Education Studies at London Metropolitan University, United Kingdom and is currently an independent academic based in Calgary, Canada. [orcid: 0000-0002-1582-9394]

MOHINI BAIJNATH is a Researcher at Neil Butcher and Associates, South Africa. [orcid: 0000-0002-1452-5743]

KASTURI BEHARI-LEAK is a Senior Lecturer in the Centre of Higher Education Development and co-chair of the Curriculum Change Working Group at the University of Cape Town, South Africa. [orcid: 0000-0001-9744-510X]

AMANI BELL is an Honorary Senior Lecturer at the University of Sydney in the Sydney School of Education and Social Work and is the Vice-Chancellors' Fellow for the Innovative Research Universities, Australia. [orcid: 0000-0001-6030-651X]

VIVIENNE BOZALEK is a Senior Professor and Director of Teaching and Learning at the University of the Western Cape, South Africa. [orcid: 0000-0002-3212-1910]

TOM BURNS is Senior Lecturer in Education and Learning Development in the Centre for Professional and Educational Development at London Metropolitan University, United Kingdom. [orcid: 0000-0003-1280-0104]

ANN CAMERON is an Associate Professor and Head of the Science Teaching and Learning Centre in the Science Faculty, University of the Witwatersrand, Johannesburg, South Africa. [orcid: 10000-0002-3589-0854]

SHERRAN CLARENCE is an Honorary Research Associate in the Centre for Postgraduate Studies at Rhodes University. She works primarily in the fields of academic staff and academic writing development in South Africa and Sweden. [orcid: 0000-0003-2777-4420]

ALISON COOK-SATHER is Mary Katharine Woodworth Professor of Education at Bryn Mawr College and Director of the Teaching and Learning Institute at Bryn Mawr and Haverford Colleges, USA. [orcid: 0000-0002-0116-7158]

XENA CUPIDO is a Senior Lecturer at Fundani Centre for Higher Education Development, Cape Peninsula University of Technology, South Africa. [orcid: 0000-0002-7343-2467]

ARONA DISON is Coordinator of the Writing Centre and Teaching and Learning Specialist in the Directorate of Teaching and Learning at the University of the Western Cape, South Africa. [orcid: 0000-0002-0325-4140]

LEE EASTON is an Associate Professor in the Department of English, Languages and Cultures and the Department of General Education at Mount Royal University, Calgary, Canada. [orcid: 0000-0002-4925-9764]

DANIELA GACHAGO is an Associate Professor in the Centre for Innovative Educational Technology, Cape Town, South Africa. [orcid: 0000-0003-0677-9273]

THERESA GORDON is Senior Lecturer in the Department of Town and Regional Planning, Durban University of Technology, South Africa.

LUCIA HESS-APRIL is Senior Lecturer and Teaching and Learning Coordinator in the Department of Occupational Therapy, University of the Western Cape, South Africa. [orcid: 0000-0002-7496-0843]

CECILIA JACOBS is an Associate Professor at the Centre for Health Professions Education, in the Faculty of Medicine and Health Sciences, Stellenbosch University, South Africa. [orcid: 0000-0001-7384-9775]

BRENDA LEIBOWITZ was a leading figure in the field of academic development in South Africa and beyond for more than two decades. Her final and significant contribution to the field was undertaken in her role as Chair in the Scholarship of Teaching and Learning at the University of Johannesburg from 2014 to 2018. [orcid: 0000-0002-9966-8291]

ROBERTA LEXIER is an Associate Professor in the Department of General Education at Mount Royal University in Calgary, Alberta, Canada. [orcid: 0000-0002-1670-9642]

GILBERTE LINCOLN is Associate Director in the Department of Town and Regional Planning, Durban University of Technology, South Africa. [orcid: 0000-0003-2877-2224]

GABRIELLE LINDSTROM is an Assistant Professor in Indigenous Studies with the Department of Humanities at Mount Royal University, Calgary, Canada. [orcid: 0000-0003-2882-6579]

KATHY LUCKETT is the Director of the Humanities Education Development Unit and Associate Professor in the Sociology Department, University of Cape Town, South Africa. [orcid: 0000-0002-3544-4221]

NTSOAKI J MALEBO is Department Head and Senior Lecturer in the Department of Life Science at the Central University of Technology, Free State, South Africa. [orcid: 0000-0003-2017-5759]

KELLY E MATTHEWS is an Associate Professor in the Institute for Teaching and Learning Innovation at the University of Queensland in Brisbane, Australia and she is an Australian Learning and Teaching Fellow. [orcid: 0000-0002-6563-4405]

SALLY MATTHEWS is Head of Department and Associate Professor in the Department of Political and International Studies at Rhodes University, South Africa. [orcid: 0000-0002-7635-3908]

YOLISA MBEKELA is a Candidate MEng Mechanical Engineering and a Teaching Assistant at the Faculty of Engineering, Cape Peninsula University of Technology, South Africa. [orcid: 0000-0001-5814-1496]

DAVE MIDDLEBROOK pioneered the use of scrolls and textmapping in education and is the founder of The Textmapping Project (www.textmapping.org). [orcid: 0000-0002-2223-8541]

'MABOKANG MONNAPULA-MAPESELA is Deputy Vice-Chancellor: Academic and Student Affairs at Rhodes University, Grahamstown, South Africa. Prior to this position, she was Senior Director and Associate Professor in the Centre for Innovation in Learning and Teaching at the Central University of Technology, Free State, South Africa. [orcid: 0000-0002-5342-2800]

SHANNON MORREIRA is Senior Lecturer in the Humanities Education Development Unit, University of Cape Town, South Africa. [orcid: 0000-0001-6591-4565]

ASHTON MPOFU is a chemical engineering PhD candidate working on a Water Research Commission project at the Institute of Biomedical and Microbial Biotechnology at the Cape Peninsula University of Technology, South Africa. [orcid: 0000-0003-4055-2670]

ASANDA NGOASHENG is a Research Associate at the Sussex Centre for Rights and Justice at the University of Sussex, United Kingdom.

ISAAC NTSHOE is a Research Professor and the Head of the SoTL project in the Centre for Innovation in Learning and Teaching at the Central University of Technology in South Africa. [orcid: 0000-0002-2038-1723]

OLUWASEUN OYEKOLA is Associate Professor and Postgraduate Studies Coordination in the Department of Chemical Engineering at Cape Peninsula University of Technology, South Africa. [orcid: 0000-0002-7198-7346]

KERSHREE PADAYACHEE is a Senior Lecturer in the Division of Science Education at the Wits School of Education, University of the Witwatersrand, Johannesburg, South Africa. [orcid: 0000-0001-7015-5962]

LYNN QUINN is an Associate Professor in the Centre for Higher Education Research, Teaching and Learning at Rhodes University, South Africa. [orcid: 0000-0002-2922-1312]

SANDRA SINFIELD is Senior Lecturer in the Centre for Professional and Educational Development at London Metropolitan University, United Kingdom. [orcid: 0000-0003-0484-7623]

DIANNE THURAB-NKHOSI is a Faculty Development Specialist at The University of the West Indies, St Augustine, Trinidad and Tobago. [orcid: 0000-0003-0621-9241]

NOMPILO TSHUMA is a Lecturer in the Centre for Higher Education Research, Teaching and Learning at Rhodes University, South Africa. [orcid: 0000-0002-7842-5426]

KEISHA VALDEZ is a Senior Instructional Developer at Boston College, USA. [orcid: 0000-0003-0241-5966]

JO-ANNE VORSTER is an Associate Professor in and Head of Department of the Centre for Higher Education Research, Teaching and Learning at Rhodes University, South Africa. [orcid: 0000-0002-5257-6832]

CHRISTINE WINBERG is the South African Research Chair for Work-integrated Learning and is Director of the Professional Education Research Institute at the Cape Peninsula University of Technology, South Africa. [orcid: 0000-0001-6234-7358]

KARIN WOLFF is Senior Teaching and Learning Advisor in the Faculty of Engineering, Stellenbosch University, South Africa. [orcid: 0000-0002-6150-8364]

MICHELLE YEO is an Associate Professor at the Academic Development Centre and Academic Director of the Institute for the Scholarship of Teaching and Learning at Mount Royal University, Calgary, Canada. [orcid: 0000-0001-9670-2274]

www.ingramcontent.com/pod-product-compliance
Lightning Source LLC
Chambersburg PA
CBHW081202170426
43197CB00018B/2892